Silver Burdett Ginn Science

DISCOVERY

Silver Burdett Ginn

Parsippany, NJ   Needham, MA

Atlanta, GA   Deerfield, IL   Irving, TX   Upland, CA

Authors

William Badders
Science Resource Teacher
Cleveland Public Schools
Cleveland, OH

Lowell J. Bethel
Professor of Science Education
The University of Texas at Austin
Austin, TX

Victoria Fu
Professor of Child Development
Virginia Polytechnic Institute and
State University
Blacksburg, VA

Donald Peck
Director, Center for Elementary Science
Fairleigh Dickinson University
Madison, NJ

Carolyn Sumners
Director of Astronomy and Physics
Houston Museum of Natural Science
Houston, TX

Catherine Valentino
Senior Vice President for
Curriculum Development
Voyager Expanded Learning
West Kingston, RI

Consulting Author

R. Mike Mullane
Astronaut, retired
Albuquerque, NM

Acknowledgements appear on page H46, which constitutes an extension of this copyright page.

Silver Burdett Ginn
A Division of Simon & Schuster
299 Jefferson Road, P.O. Box 480
Parsippany, NJ 07054-0480

ISBN 0-382-41638-4   ISBN 0-382-33385-3

10 11 12 13 RRD 03 02 01 00 99 98

CONTENTS

UNIT

The Solar System and Beyond

THEME: SCALE

Exploring the Night Sky **B4**

UNIT C
Energy, Work, and Machines

UNIT

The Solid Earth

THEME: CONSTANCY AND CHANGE
GET READY TO INVESTIGATE! E2

UNIT

Movement and Control

THEME: SYSTEMS

SCIENCE Handbook

UNIT A

PLANTS

Theme: Systems

GET READY TO

OBSERVE & QUESTION

How are plants adapted to different environments?

Plants are found growing in nearly every environment on Earth—from sandy deserts to woodland ponds. Explore how different plants are adapted to life under widely differing conditions.

EXPERIMENT & HYPOTHESIZE

What are the stages in the life cycle of a seed plant?

Have you ever followed the life cycle of a plant from the time you plant the seed until the time the plant produces its own seeds? It usually takes several months—or even years—for a plant to pass through its life cycle. But with the amazing Wisconsin Fast Plants™ you can see a plant pass through all the stages of its life cycle in just a few weeks!

INVESTIGATE!

RESEARCH & ANALYZE

As you investigate, find out more from these books.

Why Save the Rain Forest?

• **Why Save the Rain Forest?** by Donald Silver, Illustrated by Patricia J. Wynne (Julian Messner, 1993). From this beautifully illustrated book, find out about the wide range of exotic plants living in the layers of the rain forest.

• **The Blossom on the Bough**, written and illustrated by Anne Ophelia Dowden (Ticknor & Fields, 1994). More than just a pretty picture book, this book is filled with information on how plants survive in a variety of climates.

• **A Pocketful of Goobers: A Story About George Washington Carver**, by Barbara Mitchell (Carolrhoda, 1986). Read the fascinating story of how George Washington Carver, a former enslaved person, discovered more than 300 uses for the common peanut.

WORK TOGETHER & SHARE IDEAS

How can you create an arboretum—an exhibit of trees and shrubs— in your classroom?

Working together, you'll have a chance to set up a mini-arboretum of native plants, display plants you've grown from seed, and create an exhibit of local crops. You'll even learn how to prepare a soil mix so that your local plants will have the best mixture of nutrients to grow in.

1

PLANTS—
INSIDE AND OUT

You probably have a favorite animal. But do you have a favorite plant? Think about the plants you have seen in gardens, flower shops, and other public places. Is there one that you like more than the others? In this chapter, you'll learn that plants are unique and interesting living things.

A Time to Explore

Before Hurricane Andrew hit Florida in 1992, thousands of unusual plants lined the paths of Fairchild Tropical Gardens. These plants had been collected from the tropics. Then ferocious winds blew the plants upside down and inside out.

The toppled plants provided an opportunity for botanist Jack Fischer, an expert on tropical plants. He could examine parts of trees normally hidden from view. He discovered growing buds at the tops of palm trees, and he studied the exposed roots of tropical trees.

As research director for the Gardens, Jack Fischer decided to keep an acre of land in its natural state. People could see the effects of the hurricane, and they could witness the regrowth of plant life.

Coming Up

Jack Fischer, research director of Fairchild Tropical Gardens (*far left*); trees toppled by Hurricane Andrew (*near left*)

WHAT ARE THE PARTS OF A FLOWERING PLANT?

When you look in a full-length mirror, what do you see? Your arms, legs, torso, and head make up several distinct parts of your body. A flowering plant has several distinct parts, too. Each part carries out an essential job needed in the life of the plant.

Activity

Take It Apart

Have you ever met General Sherman? General Sherman is a giant sequoia tree that's over 80 m (262 ft) tall and wide enough for a car to drive through. Yet this huge tree has the same basic parts as a geranium. Examine a plant and get to know its parts.

MATERIALS
- potted plant, such as a geranium
- metric ruler
- newspaper
- plastic knife
- cut flower
- hand lens
- *Science Notebook*

Procedure

1. With other members of your group, **observe** a potted plant. In your *Science Notebook*, list all the plant parts you can see. **Infer** what parts might be hidden from view.

2. **Examine** the leaves. **Describe** and **record** their shape. How does a leaf's width compare to its length? How thick is the leaf? How are the leaves attached? **Record** your observations. **Draw** a leaf.

3. **Observe** the stem. **Record** whether the stem has branches. Is the main stem stiff, or is it flexible? **Record** your observations.

Step 2

4. Carefully hold the pot upside down over a newspaper. Tap the bottom of the pot gently until the plant and soil come out. If the soil is stuck to the pot, use a plastic knife to loosen it. You may remove some of the soil so that you can observe parts that were hidden. **Record** your observations.

5. Does your plant have a flower? If your plant doesn't have a flower, **examine** a cut flower. Use a hand lens to **observe** the structures in the center of the flower. **Record** your observations. **Draw** the flower, showing all of its structures.

Analyze and Conclude

1. What are the main parts of a flowering plant?

2. On the drawing of the leaf and the flower, label any parts that you can identify.

3. In what ways is your plant similar to a tree such as General Sherman? In what ways is it different? On what do you base your conclusions?

4. If you have ever examined other plants, how were these plants different from the plant you observed in the activity? How were they the same?

UNIT PROJECT LINK

Turn your classroom into an arboretum or botanical garden. Research the kinds of soil found in your area. Which plants are adapted to grow in this soil? Find out which materials to add to commercial potting soil to make it like the soil in your area. Work with a group to obtain and mix these materials. Make a poster describing the parts of the soil, their source, and the plants that grow best in the soil. Use your homemade soil to grow native plants in a terrarium.

Step 4

Activity
Putting Down Roots

A tiny radish seed doesn't look like much. But with a little water, its roots really get "absorbed" in their work! Examine radish roots in this activity.

MATERIALS
- blunt scissors
- blotting paper
- shallow dish
- water
- soaked radish seeds
- plastic wrap
- hand lens
- food coloring
- *Science Notebook*

Procedure

1. Cut a sheet of blotting paper to fit inside the bottom of a shallow dish. Sprinkle enough water on the blotting paper so that it is damp but not soggy.

2. Sprinkle four to six soaked radish seeds onto the blotting paper. Cover the dish with plastic wrap and set it in an undisturbed spot that is not in direct sunlight.

3. Examine the radish seeds each day, using a hand lens. Record your observations in your *Science Notebook*. Add water when needed to keep the blotting paper damp.

Step 2

4. On the third or fourth day, add a few drops of food coloring to the damp blotting paper. **Predict** how this will affect the seedling. **Discuss** your predictions with other members of your group.

Step 4

5. After ten minutes, **observe** the seedlings again. **Record** your observations. Wait another ten minutes and then **observe** the seedlings again and **record** your observations.

Analyze and Conclude

1. What changes took place in the seeds from the first day to the fourth day?

2. The threadlike structures extending from the growing root are called root hairs. How did the root hairs change when you added food coloring to the dish?

3. Based on your observations, **infer** the role of a plant's root hairs.

4. Suppose two plants were the same except that one plant had many healthy root hairs and the other had many damaged root hairs. **Predict** which plant would be able to take in water faster. **Compare** your prediction with that of other group members.

INVESTIGATE FURTHER!

EXPERIMENT

Like a radish, the carrot is an edible root. A carrot plant has one main root called a taproot. Carefully cut off the lower tip of a carrot and place the cut end in a cup of colored water. Observe any changes after 15 minutes and again after 30 minutes. Then remove the carrot and make another cut 2 to 3 cm above the cut end. What do you observe? Record your observations. What can you conclude about the function of a carrot?

Roots

Did you know that when you sit under a shady tree on a hot summer day, you are seeing less than half the tree? For all of the tree that you see above ground, there is an equal or even greater part of it below ground—the roots. The **roots** are the underground foundation of a plant. They anchor the plant and absorb water and minerals, which then travel to all other parts of the plant. Some roots, such as those of the carrot and beet, store food. Roots, along with stems, leaves, and flowers, make up the four main parts of a flowering plant. The drawings on these two pages show root types and root parts.

Unless you burrow through soil like an earthworm, you usually don't notice

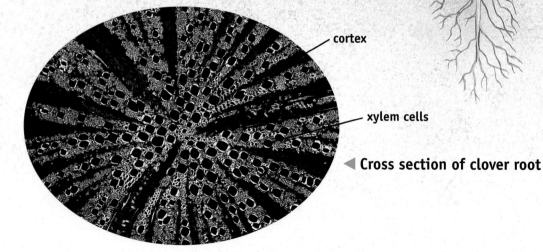

FIBROUS ROOTS Plants such as the grasses have a system of branching roots called fibrous roots. ▶

TAPROOTS Some plants, such as a carrot or dandelion, have one main root, or taproot, that stores food. ▶

cortex

xylem cells

◀ **Cross section of clover root**

roots. But the roots are there, keeping a plant firmly anchored in the soil. Even plants that live in water have roots. Roots of floating water plants hang down from the plant just under the water's surface. Roots of anchored water plants grow in the soil along the shores of streams, rivers, lakes, and oceans. Roots of water plants also keep the plant anchored or store oxygen to help the plants float. ■

epidermis   cortex   phloem xylem

root hair

water
minerals

TRANSPORT IN A ROOT   The red and blue arrows show the paths of water and minerals into a root. *Blue* represents water; *red* represents minerals. ▶

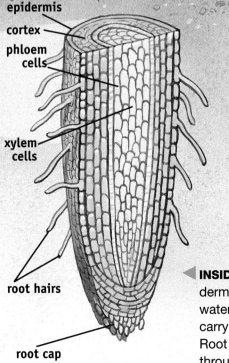

epidermis
cortex
phloem cells
xylem cells
root hairs
root cap

INVESTIGATE FURTHER!

EXPERIMENT

Make your own model of a root. Staple several small strips of paper towel so that they hang down from one large strip. The model should look like a section of root with root hairs coming down from it. Place your root model over a jar half-filled with water. Dip only the lowest edges of the small strips in the water. What happens to the rest of your "root"?

◀ **INSIDE A ROOT**   Epidermis covers the root. Cortex connects the epidermis with the inner core. **Xylem cells** are connecting tubes that carry water and minerals from the soil upward. **Phloem cells** are tubes that carry nutrients from the leaves through the stem and down to the root. Root hairs take in water and minerals. The root cap pushes the root through the soil.

Stems

Have you ever heard the expression "as sturdy as an oak"? Or have you ever heard someone described as "as slender as a reed"? Both comparisons refer to plant stems. The trunk of an oak tree is its stem. The reed is the stem of a grasslike plant. The **stem** is that part of a plant that connects its roots and its leaves. It is the plant's main support above the ground.

The most obvious job of a stem is to hold up a plant's leaves and flowers.

Stems of many flowering plants, such as buttercups, marigolds, beans, and reeds, are green and fairly stiff. They will wilt if they're deprived of water for too long. These kinds of plants die after one growing season. Stems of most larger flowering plants, including roses, oaks, basswoods, and maples, are woody and don't die after one season. A woody plant such as a tree can live for hundreds—sometimes thousands—of years!

CUTAWAY VIEW OF NONWOODY PLANT STEM This stem has thick walls and fibers running through it. The fibers give the stem its strength. This view shows the xylem and phloem cells that make up the transport system of the stem. ▼

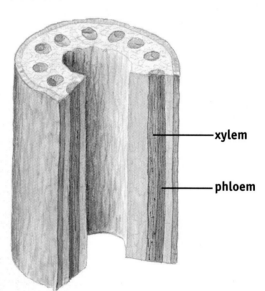

—xylem

—phloem

◀ **A buttercup, a nonwoody plant; at the end of the growing season, this plant dies.**

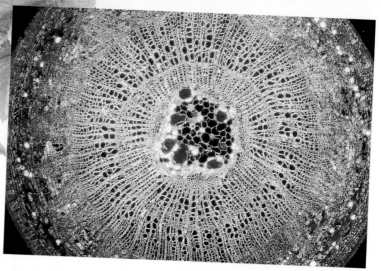

◀ **Basswood, or linden tree; this is a woody plant that can live many years.**

▲ **Young basswood stem as seen through a microscope**

Transport in Stems

Inside stems are tubelike cells that carry water up from the roots and food down from the leaves. One kind of tubelike cells forms a tissue called xylem. Recall that xylem carries water and minerals up from the roots and then through the stems.

Another group of tubelike cells forms a tissue called phloem. Remember that phloem carries sugars produced in the leaves down through the stems to other parts of the plant. Xylem and phloem tubes in the stem connect with xylem and phloem tubes in the root. All the xylem and phloem cells, taken as a group, form the transport system of a plant. ■

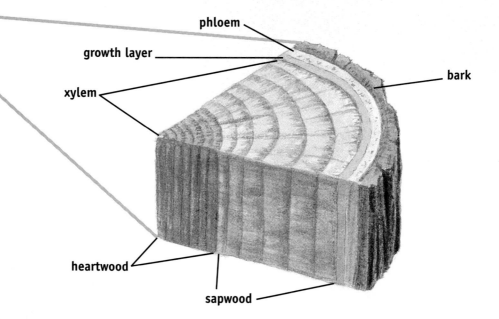

phloem

growth layer

bark

xylem

heartwood

sapwood

▲ **CUTAWAY VIEW OF WOODY PLANT STEM** The trunk, which is actually a woody stem, is formed of many layers of cells. These layers have an outside protective covering called bark. This view shows the transport system of xylem and phloem. Each year the xylem cells form new layers of growth called annual rings.

Leaves

In autumn in some parts of the country, you will find enormous numbers of falling red, yellow, and brown leaves. Why do plants have so many leaves? What do leaves do?

Look at the pictures of leaves on this page. A **leaf**, which is a plant part that grows out of the stem, is the food-making factory of a plant. Many leaves are thinner than a knife blade. In fact, the thin, flat part of a leaf is called a blade. The leaves of broad-leaved plants are shaped so that the greatest amount of leaf can be exposed to the sun. Sunlight is an essential part of the process of photosynthesis, or food-making in plants. The leaves of needle-leaved plants, such as pine and spruce, also carry on photosynthesis.

VEINS Along with the petiole, the veins form the transport system of the leaf. Water enters the leaf through the veins.

BLADE The blade is the broad, flat part of a leaf.

BROAD LEAF Plants such as maple and oak are called broad-leaved trees and have broad, flat leaves. ▶

PETIOLE The petiole is an extension of the xylem and phloem tubes of the stem.

NEEDLE LEAVES Plants such as pine, spruce, and fir have leaves shaped to reduce water loss.

UPPER EPIDERMIS Cell layer that protects the leaf from drying out

PALISADE LAYER Columnlike cells where food making occurs

SPONGY LAYER Loosely-packed cells where food making occurs and where veins are located

VEIN Bundle of cells that contain xylem cells for the transport of water and phloem cells for the transport of sugar and other nutrients

LOWER EPIDERMIS Cell layer that protects the leaf and allows for the exchange of gases

Inside a Leaf

A typical leaf may be very thin, but it's also crammed full of cells, as shown above. If you cut across a leaf, producing a cross section, you'll find several layers of cells. Since the leaf's main function is to manufacture food for the plant, its cells are designed for food making.

Photosynthesis takes place in the two middle layers of cells. The top and bottom layers protect the leaf and keep it from drying out. Another function of the bottom layer is to allow for the exchange of gases needed in food making. A leaf also contains many veins, which allow for the transport of water and manufactured food. ■

▲ The pointy spines of a cactus do not make food. They protect the stem from animal intruders. Cactus spines are modified leaves.

▲ In pea plants some leaves function as tendrils. They twist around objects and support the plant.

Flowers

The most colorful part of a plant is its flower. The **flower** is the reproductive part of a flowering plant. It is inside the flower that seeds are produced. Some plants, such as sunflowers, have big showy flower heads. Other plants, such as grasses, have tiny green flowers that you hardly notice. Flowers come in all shapes and sizes and in a great variety and range of colors. Some plants have tall spikes filled with flowers; others have small flowers with covered hoods. Flowering plants grow wild in nearly all regions of the world, except where the ground is always covered by snow and ice.

Looking Inside a Flower

Many plants have large showy brightly colored flowers that are attractive to insects, birds, and even bats! The flower's beauty is an adaptive feature: It draws animals toward the plant, encouraging them to dip into the flower to draw out the sweet nectar. While the animals remove the nectar, they are

PETALS The often colorful, showy parts of the flower.

PISTIL The **pistil** is the female part of the flower, which is made up of the stigma, style, and ovary.

Snapdragon

FLOWER STALK The flower stalk holds up the flower.

STAMEN The **stamen** is the male part of the flower, which is made up of the anther and filament.

POLLINATING A FLOWER The tiny hummingbird sticks its long tongue into the flower tube to remove nectar. The bird accidentally removes pollen, which is passed on to the next flower. Inside the female part of the flower, the pollen joins with egg cells, and a seed begins to develop. ▶

also accidentally removing pollen. Pollen grains contain the male sex cells. These pollen grains are in turn carried to the next flower, where they are brushed off on the female part of the flower. Without intending to do so, the animals—insects, birds, or bats—pollinate flowers. Pollination sets in motion the process of seed production. A flower can form one to hundreds of seeds. ■

Black-eyed Susan

◀ **VARIETY IN FLOWERS** All these flowers have the same basic parts, even though they look so different.

Ladyslipper

Lily

Plants in Our Lives

Where in the world is your breakfast from? Plants provide many essential parts of your life—from the house you live in to the furniture you sit on; from the foods you eat to the clothes you wear. Even many medicines are made from plants.

Plants on the Move

Where did you eat your breakfast today? Perhaps you sat at a kitchen table made from the wood of pine or oak. While you were eating, in a sense you were really taking a trip around the world. Some of the breakfast foods that you ate come from plants that originally grew in different parts of the world.

Did you eat corn flakes? Corn was first grown in South and Central America. The ears of corn were very small. After each growing season, farmers saved the corn kernels from the largest ears to plant the next year. Over

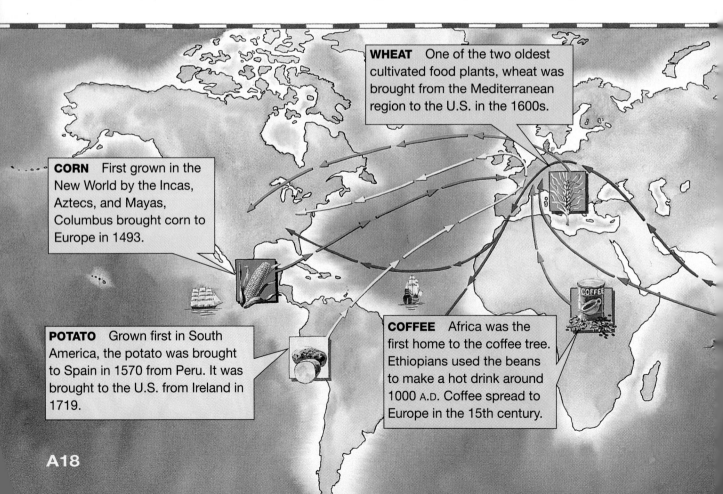

WHEAT One of the two oldest cultivated food plants, wheat was brought from the Mediterranean region to the U.S. in the 1600s.

CORN First grown in the New World by the Incas, Aztecs, and Mayas, Columbus brought corn to Europe in 1493.

POTATO Grown first in South America, the potato was brought to Spain in 1570 from Peru. It was brought to the U.S. from Ireland in 1719.

COFFEE Africa was the first home to the coffee tree. Ethiopians used the beans to make a hot drink around 1000 A.D. Coffee spread to Europe in the 15th century.

hundreds of years, farmers grew larger and larger ears of corn.

Your breakfast might have included a cereal made from rice or a piece of bread made from wheat. Wheat was probably first grown as a food for people about 7000 B.C. in the Near East.

How did crops travel so far around the world? When people traveled or moved to new lands, they took seeds for their crops with them. So over time, crops that were first grown and used by people in one part of the world came to be grown in more distant places.

Food from Plants

Corn, wheat, and rice are examples of seeds that are eaten. These seeds, called grains, are often ground up to make flour. Flour is then used to make bread, tortillas, or pasta.

▲ **Wheat stalks contain grains of wheat that are processed into the flour used to make loaves of bread.**

▲ **Rice plants are harvested from paddies and processed to remove the grains of rice used in cooked rice.**

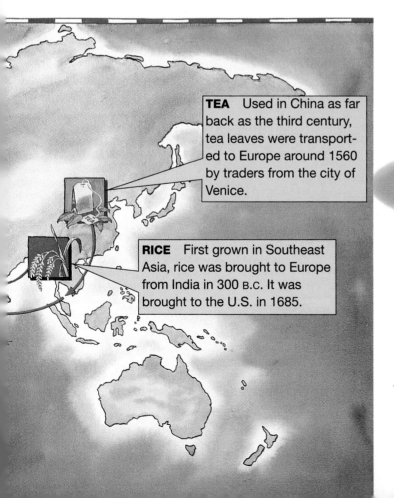

TEA Used in China as far back as the third century, tea leaves were transported to Europe around 1560 by traders from the city of Venice.

RICE First grown in Southeast Asia, rice was brought to Europe from India in 300 B.C. It was brought to the U.S. in 1685.

◄ **Map of worldwide journey of foods over the centuries**

You are probably familiar with many other plant parts that you eat. For example, apples, pears, oranges, and other common fruits develop from the ovary inside a flower. Lettuce, cabbage, and spinach are leaves that you may eat. But did you know that you also eat stems, roots, flowers, and seeds? For example, celery and asparagus are two stems that people often eat. Carrots, radishes, and beets are commonly eaten roots. An artichoke is really the flower of a plant. Flowers from the coral tree, or erythrinas, are a popular food in the southeastern part of Mexico. In Costa Rica, cooks use the flower of the yucca plant in soup.

▲ **SPINACH** Like lettuce and cabbage, spinach is an edible leaf.

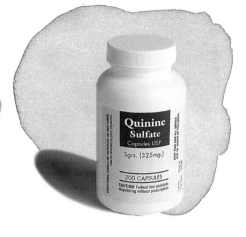

▲ **QUININE** From the bark of the cinchona tree comes quinine, used to treat malaria.

Whenever you eat peas or beans, you are eating the seeds of plants. You may also eat sprouting seeds. You do so whenever you eat bean sprouts or alfalfa sprouts.

The cinnamon you might sprinkle on toast at breakfast comes from the bark of a laurel tree, which grows in Asia.

SCIENCE IN LITERATURE

WHY SAVE THE RAIN FOREST?
by Donald Silver
Illustrated by Patricia J. Wynne
Simon & Schuster, 1993

Now you know that breakfast foods come from all over the world. If you were to look at a world map showing ecosystems, you'd find that most of these plants come from tropical rain forests. There is such a map on pages 44 and 45 of *Why Save the Rain Forest?* by Donald Silver. The book will give you an idea of how much land was covered by rain forests thousands of years ago, when many of these plants were discovered. Then read pages 12 and 13 to learn about the ways the rain forest is a part of your life.

By now, everyone has heard about saving rain forests. But why should they be saved? Read pages 22 and 23 to find out some ways that rain forest plants could save our lives in the future.

▲ **CORN** Like wheat and rice, corn is a grain and a staple of life. It has fed billions of people in vast regions of the world for thousands of years.

▲ **COTTON PLANT** After the cotton plant produces flowers, its seeds are held in a ball of fluffy white fibers. These fibers are separated to make cotton fabric.

Bananas are from a tree first found in Southeast Asia. Grapes and apples were probably first grown and eaten thousands of years ago in the river valleys of the Middle East.

What's your favorite breakfast drink? Orange juice comes from fruit that was first grown in Southeast Asia. Do you drink hot cocoa? The Aztecs of Central America began making something they called *chocolatl* from the seeds of the cocoa plant.

Plants Are Lifesavers

When Europeans came to South America hundreds of years ago, some became ill with malaria. Malaria is a tropical disease that is carried by a certain type of mosquito. The Europeans learned that the native South Americans used the bark of the cinchona tree to cure the fever produced by malaria. The powerful chemical from the tree bark is called quinine (kwī'nīn). Quinine is still used as a treatment for life-threatening malaria.

From a tree that grows in the Pacific Northwest comes a drug that can treat people with some forms of cancer. The drug, called taxol, is from the bark of the Pacific yew tree. Today, quinine and taxol are synthesized, or manufactured, in a laboratory. But they were first discovered in plants. ■

INVESTIGATION 1

1. Imagine that you are a drop of water in the soil below a maple tree. Trace your path as you move into the roots of the tree and up through the plant. Name the structures you pass through.

2. Make a chart of the main parts of a plant and the role of each of these parts.

INVESTIGATION 2

WHAT DO PLANT CELLS LOOK LIKE?

The roots, stems, and leaves that you examined in Investigation 1 are basic parts of all plants. But there is a plant part that is even more basic. In this investigation, you'll investigate plant cells.

Activity

Observing Plant Cells

The part of the onion you eat may grow underground like a root, but it's actually a ball of leaves called a bulb. Onions may not smell very pleasant, but they show the structure of plant cells very well.

MATERIALS
- slice of onion
- tweezers
- microscope slide
- red food coloring
- toothpick
- cover slip
- microscope
- *Science Notebook*

SAFETY
Be careful when handling glass slides.

Procedure

1. Take a section of a quartered onion and snap it in half, as shown. A thin piece of skin should separate from the section. Peel this piece off with the tweezers.

2. Place the onion skin on a microscope slide. Cover it with a few drops of food coloring. Use a toothpick to smooth out the wrinkles. Cover the onion skin with a cover slip.

3. **Observe** the onion skin under a microscope at low power and **draw** in your *Science Notebook* what you see. Repeat your observations under high power.

Step 1

4. The small circle that turned red inside the onion cell is called a **nucleus**. **Label** the nucleus in your drawing.

5. The boundary of the cell is called the **cell wall**. **Label** the cell wall in your drawing.

Analyze and Conclude

1. Like all living things, plants are made of cells. **Describe** the appearance of the cells that you observed.

2. A cell wall is found only in plant cells, not in animal cells. What job do you think the cell wall has?

3. Suppose you looked at a microscope slide taken from a living thing that you had never seen before. How could you tell whether you were looking at a plant cell or an animal cell?

INVESTIGATE FURTHER!

EXPERIMENT

Use a dropper to add two drops of water to a microscope slide. Place a single *Elodea* leaf in the water and cover it with a cover slip. Observe the leaf under a microscope's low power. Then study the leaf under high power and make a sketch of what you see. Describe any structures that you see in the leaf cell that you did not see in the onion cell in the activity. Infer what the functions of such structures are, based on the leaf's role in a plant.

The Plant Cell

When you get up close to a plant—with a microscope, for instance—you can see its cells. The **cell** is the basic unit of all living things. Cells are tiny compartments that are equipped with several basic structures to carry on life activities. The drawing shows the main parts of a plant cell.

CYTOPLASM (sīt'ō plaz əm) The jellylike substance that fills much of the cell; other cell structures are found in the **cytoplasm**.

CHLOROPLASTS (klôr'ə plasts) The structures in which food making occurs; **chloroplasts** contain the pigment chlorophyll.

CELL WALL The **cell wall** is the tough outer covering of a plant cell that gives it a rigid shape; it is made of cellulose.

CELL MEMBRANE A thin layer that surrounds all cells; the **cell membrane** allows water and dissolved materials to pass into and out of the cell.

NUCLEUS (nōō'klē əs) The **nucleus** controls all the cell's activities and is very important in cell reproduction.

VACUOLE (vak'yōō ōl) A **vacuole** is a large storage area filled with fluid that hold various substances, including food.

The Story Tree Rings Tell

The stems and leaves of many small flowering plants die in cold weather. Many trees lose their leaves in cold weather, but their stems, or trunks, remain standing and begin growing again in the spring. If you've ever looked at a cut tree stump, you can see that the trunk has a story to tell. Each spring and summer new growth of xylem and phloem cells occurs in the trunk. Generally the size of the cells varies with the amount of rain. For example, if the spring has been rainy, the xylem cells will be very large. This ring of cells appears light in color.

In the drier summer months, new xylem is also formed, but the cells are smaller and closer together. This ring of cells appears darker in color. So during one growing season layers of transport cells are laid down. The rings that are formed are called annual rings.

ANNUAL RINGS The rings are the result of growth each season. By counting rings scientists can tell the age of a tree.

SAPWOOD Living xylem cells that give the tree support and strength; most of the tree's wood is sapwood.

CAMBIUM The thin growing layer of living cells; it produces phloem cells near the trunk's outer part and xylem cells toward the trunk's center.

OUTER BARK The protective covering of the tree; just like your skin, it protects the tree from disease and from drying out.

HEARTWOOD The innermost part of the tree is made up of old, dried-up layers of xylem. If the heartwood gets rotten, the result is a big hole in the trunk.

Year after year these rings form. So you can tell the age of trees simply by counting the annual rings. The size of the annual rings tells a story about weather conditions that the tree survived. During periods of drought, rings tend to be very narrow. During wet periods, rings tend to be wide.

Several kinds of trees, including cedars from Japan, cypresses from Mexico, and pines from the United States, live for thousands of years. An environment's history can be read in the rings of such trees.

Most trees increase their trunk size by about 2.5 cm (1 in.) each year. But some large trees have interesting ways of growing. The banyan tree, which grows in Asia, appears to have a huge number of trunks. The baobab tree actually stores water in its swollen trunk. In times of drought, the trunk shrinks. ■

The banyan tree develops thick air roots from its branches. They drop to the soil and take root. ▶

◀ The baobab tree stores water in its swollen trunk.

Bamboo trees are the fastest-growing trees on Earth. Their trunks have been known to grow 2.5 cm (1 in.) in an hour! ▶

INVESTIGATION 2

THINK IT WRITE IT

1. Draw a plant cell and then label and explain the role of all the main cell parts.

2. Explain how scientists might learn about changes in climate in a region by reading the annual rings of very old trees.

REFLECT & EVALUATE

WORD POWER

cell
cell membrane
cell wall
chloroplast
cytoplasm
flower
leaf
nucleus

phloem cells
pistil
root
stamen
stem
vacuole
xylem cells

 On Your Own
Write a definition for each term in the list.

 With a Partner
Write each term in the list on one side of an index card and the definition on the other side. Use the cards to quiz your partner.

BUILD YOUR PORTFOLIO

Draw and label the parts of a flowering plant. Briefly describe the function of the stem, flower, vein, root, leaf, xylem, and phloem.

Analyze Information

Study the drawing. Then use the drawing to describe the main parts of the leaf.

Assess Performance

Design and carry out an activity to see how light affects the growth of a plant. Compare your results with those of others. What do the results tell you about how a plant functions?

Problem Solving

1. While walking through an indoor garden, you come upon a huge room where rain forest plants are growing. Some of the plants have leaves more than 1.8 m (6 ft) long. Explain why rain forest plants need such big leaves.

2. You go to a restaurant and one of your friends says she wants to eat a flower, a fruit, a leaf, a stem, and a root. What could she order from the menu to satisfy her wish?

2

PLANT PROCESSES

Plants are Earth's food factories. They spend their days busily making food. When they have made enough food for themselves, they store what's left over, which animals then get to eat. And as if that were not enough, plants even give us much of the oxygen we breathe. Maybe we should call them Earth's superheroes!

The Wild Supermarket

The plants you eat probably come from your local supermarket. But the supermarkets of fields and forests are stocked with good things to eat, too.

- In the southern United States, the wild kudzu is considered a pest. Its monstrous leafy vines can grow a foot a day. They cover trees, houses, and power lines. In Asia, however, kudzu is a valuable food. People eat its leaves, roots, seeds, and its beautiful purple flowers.

- A wild plant called the groundnut helped the Pilgrims survive their first winter in North America. Native Americans showed the hungry settlers how to find and cook the potatolike roots.

- Another plant eaten by Native Americans is the cattail. The bottom third of its stalk tastes much like asparagus.

Read on to find out more about Earth's green superheroes.

cattails

firewee

kudzu

dandelions

◀ A supermarket basket full of Earth's green superheroes

HOW DO PLANTS MAKE THEIR OWN FOOD?

Imagine Earth as a barren wasteland with no plants. Do you think you could survive? Well, think again. Your life depends—either directly or indirectly—on the food that plants produce. In this investigation find out how plants make this food.

Activity

In the Dark

A sugar called glucose is food for plants. To make this food, plants need some basic ingredients and an energy source. In this activity you can experiment to see what might provide this energy source.

Procedure

1. Pour potting soil in two plastic cups so that each cup is two-thirds full.

2. Place three soaked pea seeds in each cup. Cover them with a thin layer of soil.

3. Water each cup until the soil is damp but not soaking wet.

4. Place one cup in a sunny spot or near a bright light. Put the other cup in a dark closet or under a box that will keep out the light. With the members of your group, **predict** which plants will grow better when the seeds sprout. **Observe** the cups daily until the seedlings have developed their first leaves.

Step 1

A30

5. After the first leaves develop, **compare** the heights and colors of the two sets of seedlings. **Record** your observations in your *Science Notebook*.

6. To find out whether food has been made in the leaves, do an iodine test for starch. Your teacher will prepare a leaf from each cup for the test. Place the leaves in a dish. Add several drops of the iodine solution to each leaf and allow the iodine to soak in for 10 minutes. If the leaf turns dark purple, it means that sugar (glucose) has been made in the leaf and has changed into starch. If you cannot tell whether the color has changed, ask your teacher for help.

Step 6

Analyze and Conclude

1. How do the stems of the two groups of plants compare in height and color?

2. Hypothesize the reason for the differences you observed.

3. Which plants are best able to make food?

4. Based on the results of your experiment, what things do you think plants need to make food?

5. What was the variable in this experiment?

INVESTIGATE FURTHER!

RESEARCH

Do plants make the same amount of food in all kinds of light? If you have ever used a prism or seen a rainbow, you know that sunlight is made of many different colors. Design an experiment in which you control the color of light that is received by a plant. Grow the same kinds of plants under different colors of light by placing colored cellophane or plastic wrap between the light source and the plants.

Activity

Making Food . . . and Storing It!

When you come home with groceries, you probably store the food in a cupboard or in the refrigerator. Plants store food, too. In this activity find out some of the places plants store food.

MATERIALS

- goggles
- large piece of paper cut from a bag
- metric ruler
- two small samples of each of the following: corn kernel, potato slice, peanut half, lettuce leaf, radish slice, corn oil, cornstarch
- 2 droppers
- timer
- iodine solution
- paper towels
- *Science Notebook*

SAFETY /////

Wear goggles. Do not eat any food used in this activity.

Procedure

1. Write the name of each of the seven foods you will test on a long piece of paper cut from a bag. Each name should be written 5 cm apart from any other.

2. Rub a piece of food onto the paper beside its name. Use a freshly cut piece of food when testing the solid foods. Use a dropper for the corn oil. Set the paper aside for about 10 minutes so that any wet spots will dry. In your *Science Notebook,* **make a chart** to **record** your observations.

3. Hold the piece of paper bag up to the light and observe each spot. A grease stain means that the food sample contains fat or oil.

4. For each of the foods, do the iodine test for starch (see the previous activity). Place the sample on a paper towel and add a drop of iodine. If the food turns dark purple, the test indicates it contains starch. If the food has so much green color that you cannot detect the results, ask your teacher for a sample from which the chlorophyll has been removed.

Step 2

Analyze and Conclude

1. Which of your samples made a permanent spot on the paper bag? In what form do you think the plants that made the spots store food?

2. Which samples showed a positive iodine test? In what form do those plants store food?

Energy Traps

Imagine that you're walking home from school and you begin to feel hungry. It would be great if you could instantly produce a tasty snack, but you can't. You must either buy a snack or wait until you get home.

Your body can't produce its own food. But plants can produce their own food, using light energy, carbon dioxide, and water. Plants cannot move around to find these things. But they can trap light energy and gather the substances they need to make their own food.

Plants trap energy in the cells in their leaves, which contain hundreds of little disks called chloroplasts (klôr′ə plasts). **Chloroplasts** are tiny cell structures containing a green pigment called chlorophyll. This pigment collects light energy from the Sun. Chlorophyll works much like a solar panel, absorbing light energy, which is then stored as food energy.

Chlorophyll uses the Sun's light energy to change two substances—carbon dioxide and water—into food. Carbon dioxide is a gas found in air. It enters the plant through tiny holes usually found on the underside of the leaves. Water enters the plant through the roots. Recall that con-ducting tissue carries water from the roots to the stems and then to the leaves.

The food produced by a plant is called **glucose** (glōo′kōs), a form of sugar. The process of using light energy to combine carbon dioxide and water to produce glucose is called **photosynthesis** (fōt ō sin′the sis). *Photo-* means "light" and *synthesis* means "joining together." In photosynthesis, light joins carbon dioxide and water together.

Chloroplasts (*inset*) are tiny green disklike cell parts that trap energy during photosynthesis.

A33

PHOTOSYNTHESIS

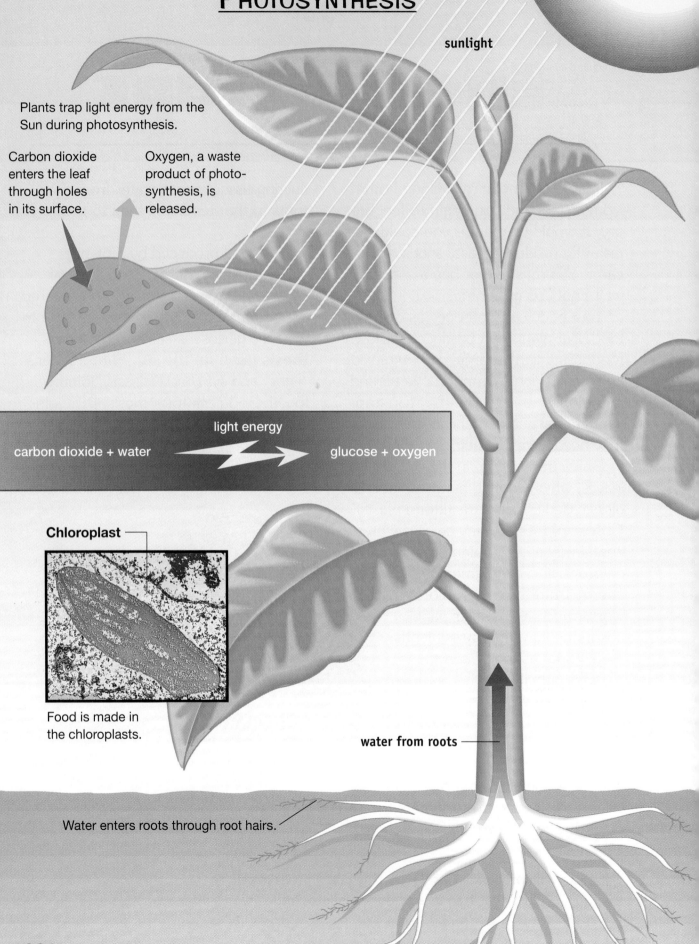

Sun

sunlight

Plants trap light energy from the Sun during photosynthesis.

Carbon dioxide enters the leaf through holes in its surface.

Oxygen, a waste product of photosynthesis, is released.

light energy

carbon dioxide + water ⟶ glucose + oxygen

Chloroplast

Food is made in the chloroplasts.

water from roots

Water enters roots through root hairs.

▲ Radishes store starch in the roots.

In addition to glucose, photosynthesis produces a "waste" product that humans and other animals need to survive: oxygen. This oxygen and any leftover water leave the plant through the same tiny holes through which the carbon dioxide enters.

Plants cannot produce food all the time. Because photosynthesis requires sunlight, the process of trapping sunlight can't take place at night or on very cloudy days. Although carbon dioxide is almost always available, water may be scarce at times. So plants must produce

Lettuce stores starch in its leaves. ▼

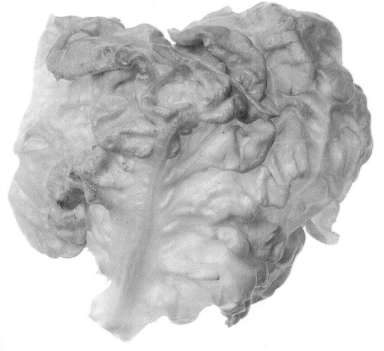

food when light energy, carbon dioxide, and water are all available. Then plants can store the food—generally in the leaves but sometimes in the roots, stems, or other plant parts.

Most plants store extra glucose in the form of **starch**, a chemical that is a chain of sugar molecules. In the activity "Making Food . . . and Storing It!" you found that plants store starch. This starch might be stored in the plant leaves (lettuce), in leafstalks (celery), in roots (carrots), or in underground stems (white potatoes).

▲ Celery stores starch in its leafstalks.

Plants use the energy in glucose to grow, to produce seeds, and, in fact, to carry out all their life functions. They use the energy from glucose in much the same way that we use the energy from the foods we eat. Both plant cells and animal cells use oxygen to release the energy found in food. This process is called **cell respiration** (res pə rā'shən). You'll learn more about this process later in the chapter. ■

A35

Producers and the
Web of Life

The hawk preys on the robin.

The robin preys on the caterpillar.

All living things are linked together in relationships called food chains. A **food chain** is a series of steps showing the transfer of energy among living things. This energy begins with the Sun and is then transferred from living thing to living thing as each thing is eaten.

Plants are the first link in many food chains. They provide both the energy and the minerals needed by the animals that are higher up on the food chain.

As you know, most plants don't feed on any other organisms. (There are a few plants, such as a Venus's flytrap, that actually "eat" insects.) Plants produce their own food, and so they are called **producers**. But plants aren't Earth's only producers. In an ocean food chain, important producers are the plantlike organisms called phytoplankton. Phytoplankton consists of great numbers of floating microscopic organisms. Other producers in the ocean include the large mats of floating seaweed, many of which are kinds of algae.

Living things that obtain energy by eating other living things are called **consumers**. Consumers eat either producers or other consumers. There are several levels of consumer. Consumers that eat only producers are called first-order consumers. In the ocean food

Earthworms feed on the dead hawk. Nutrients from the dead bird pass into the soil, and some are later taken up by roots.

The caterpillar feeds on leaves.

chain shown, the sea urchin is a first-order consumer.

Consumers that eat first-order consumers are called second-order consumers. In the ocean food chain shown, the herring gull is a second-order consumer. It is a consumer that eats a first-order consumer, the sea urchin.

All food chains include **decomposers** (dē kəm pōz′erz), or nature's recyclers. Decomposers, which include worms, some insects, fungi, and bacteria, break down the bodies of dead organisms. By doing this, the decomposers recycle the nutrients that are part of the dead body. In the ocean food chain shown here, fungi and bacteria are among the decomposers. They are decomposing the body of the dead herring gull that has washed up on the shore.

Web of Life

A picture of a food chain can help you to understand how producers and consumers are related. But the true picture is much more complex. Most consumers do not feed on only one other species. Most consumers have varied diets, just as we do. Such diets help consumers survive if one food source, such as one species of plant or animal, becomes scarce or disappears.

The complex feeding relationships among living things are best shown in a food web. A **food web** shows the feed-

An ocean food chain ▶

FUNGI AND BACTERIA decomposers

HERRING GULL second-order consumer

SEA URCHIN first-order consumer

SEAWEED producer

ing relationships and energy transfer among producers, consumers, and decomposers. In other words, a food web shows which organisms feed on which other organisms.

A food web is made up of overlapping food chains. The drawing on page A39 shows a food web of organisms that live in a forest and a nearby stream. Both the bear and the fish are consumers. Which other organisms are consumers? The cattails are producers. Look for other producers. Notice the circle of organisms near the dead mouse. What role do they play in the food web? Imagine that all the fish died of a poison dumped into the stream. How might these deaths affect the insect population in the stream? All the organisms in this food web depend on each other in some way.

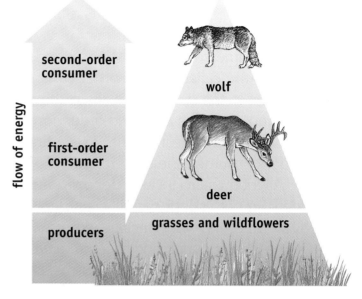

In the energy pyramid above, the producers, such as grasses, have trapped energy from the Sun. When a first-order consumer, such as a deer, eats the grass, it uses some of the energy stored in the grasses. Then when a second-order consumer, such as a wolf, eats the deer, it obtains some of the energy stored in the deer for its life processes.

SCIENCE IN LITERATURE

WHY SAVE THE RAIN FOREST?
by Donald Silver
Illustrated by Patricia J. Wynne
Julian Messner, 1993

Snakes. Slugs. Cockroaches. Bats. They're all part of the complicated web of life called the tropical rain forest. The plants of the rain forest form the framework of that web. On pages 14–19 of *Why Save the Rain Forest?* by Donald Silver, you'll find out how trees, shrubs, and creeping vines form the layers of the rain forest environment. You'll also find out about the creatures that live in each layer.

After reading pages 14–19, try to draw some food chains or a food web for each layer of the rain forest. Then place yourself in the food web. If you're not sure how you fit in, read the rest of *Why Save the Rain Forest?*

▲ **This food web is composed of producers, consumers, and decomposers.**

Flow of energy from producers to consumers is shown by the energy pyramid on page A38. Producers use some of the energy they capture but store only part of it. Thus, consumers have only part of the "captured" energy available to them. So there are fewer consumers than producers in an ecosystem. ■

───── **INVESTIGATION 1** ─────

THINK IT WRITE IT

1. Describe the process of photosynthesis. Include the substances used, the substances produced, and where the process occurs.

2. On a large sheet of paper, draw a food web, using organisms that live where you do. Be sure to identify the producers, consumers, and decomposers in your food web.

HOW DO PLANTS HELP RECYCLE MATTER?

More than a billion years ago, there was little oxygen in the atmosphere. Very slowly, as photosynthetic organisms appeared, the amount of oxygen increased. After hundreds of millions of years, the air contained just as much oxygen as it does today. Without plants, oxygen and other materials would stop recycling in the environment.

Activity

All That Gas

The oxygen you breathe comes from producers. In this activity look for evidence that plants release oxygen.

Procedure

1. Carefully cut a piece of *Elodea* so that it is slightly shorter than the length of a test tube. Using twist ties, loosely attach the *Elodea* cutting to a pencil.

Step 1

MATERIALS

- goggles
- scissors
- *Elodea* cutting
- twist ties
- pencil
- large test tube
- prepared water
- test-tube rack
- timer
- *Science Notebook*

SAFETY

Wear goggles during this activity. Be careful when using scissors.

2. Place the pencil with the *Elodea* in a test tube so that the cut end of the plant is at the open end of the tube.

3. Add prepared water to the test tube so that the *Elodea* cutting is almost completely covered. Place the test tube in the test-tube rack near a bright light or in sunlight.

4. With other members of your group, **predict** what will happen in the test tube. **Record** your predictions in your *Science Notebook*.

5. Without moving the plant, **observe** the *Elodea* after five minutes and again after ten minutes. **Record** your observations. **Hypothesize** about what is happening.

Analyze and Conclude

1. In light, leaves of the *Elodea* make food for the plant. During this process, a gas—oxygen—is also produced. A plant uses some of this gas to carry on life activities and gives off the rest of the gas. What evidence did you find that *Elodea* was giving off a gas?

2. **Infer** the part of the plant from which the oxygen was released and entered the water.

3. How might the activity have been affected if the *Elodea* had been placed in darkness? Explain your answer.

INVESTIGATE FURTHER!

EXPERIMENT

Does *Elodea* give off oxygen at the same rate all the time? With your group, estimate and record the number of gas bubbles per minute your *Elodea* cutting produces. Then observe what happens to the rate of bubble production when you vary the amount of light reaching the plant. Estimate the rate of gas production in strong light, in dim light, and in no light.

Activity
Mystery Drops

You've observed how water enters a plant through its roots and then moves upward through tubes. What makes water move up plant stems? Is it pumped up? In this activity you'll explore this question.

MATERIALS
- goggles
- aluminum foil
- scissors
- 6 plastic cups
- sharp pencil
- 2 leaves with petioles
- petroleum jelly
- water
- plastic tape
- *Science Notebook*

SAFETY

Wear goggles during this activity. Be careful when using scissors and other sharp objects.

Procedure

1. Use scissors to cut out three circles of aluminum foil. Make sure the circles are larger than the diameter of the top of a plastic cup. Use a pencil to carefully poke a hole in the center of each piece of foil without tearing it.

2. At the same time, have your partner completely cover both sides of one of the two leaves with petroleum jelly.

3. Put the petiole of the leaf covered with jelly through the hole in one of the pieces of foil. Dab petroleum jelly around the hole to fill in and seal up the space between the foil and the petiole.

4. Put the petiole of the uncovered leaf through the hole of another aluminum foil circle in the same way. Add petroleum jelly to seal up the space around the hole.

5. Add water to three plastic cups until they are nearly full. Place the petiole of the covered leaf into the first cup so that the petiole is in the water. Smooth the foil over the sides of the cup and place another cup on top, as shown. To the second cup, add the uncovered leaf in the same way. Place the remaining foil circle over the third cup, seal it with petroleum jelly, and cover it with the second cup without adding a leaf. Use several strips of plastic tape to attach each top cup to each bottom cup.

Steps 3–6

WHITE PETROLEUM JELLY
(White Petrolatum)
(U.S.P.)
NET WT. 1 Ounce (28.35 g)

6. Put the three setups in good light. With the other members of your group, **predict** which of the cups will show the greatest amount of change. **Record** your predictions. Check the setups for two days and **record** your observations in your *Science Notebook*.

Analyze and Conclude

1. What changes did you **observe** over the two days? How did your prediction **compare** with what actually happened?

2. **Hypothesize** how the "mystery drops" got on the foil.

3. What you observed was a plant process called transpiration. During transpiration, water vapor leaves a plant through very tiny openings in its leaves. In which of your setups did the greatest amount of transpiration take place? Where did no transpiration take place? Why?

4. How did the water levels of the cups compare?

5. Why did you set up a cup with no leaf at all in it?

EXPERIMENT

Does water come from the top surface, bottom surface, or both surfaces of a leaf? Find out where transpiration occurs. Design your own experiment using the same materials used in "Mystery Drops."

Plants and the Oxygen Cycle

Photosynthetic organisms, which are Earth's producers, are at the base of most food webs. Plants make up a large portion of those producers. Without plants, there would be no animal life on Earth because animals would have nothing to eat. Plants also give off oxygen, a gas that makes up about 21 percent of the air. Humans and other animals need oxygen to survive. Body cells must have oxygen to release energy from food—energy needed for growth and other life processes.

During photosynthesis, plants com-bine water and carbon dioxide. A chemical reaction occurs that produces glucose. Oxygen is a byproduct, or waste material, of this chemical reaction.

When Earth was young, huge mats of blue-green bacteria floated on the oceans. At that time there was little or no oxygen in the atmosphere. Scientists estimate that for about 2 billion years there were few other organisms on Earth besides these bacteria. Over time, as the bacteria carried on photosynthesis, oxygen began to collect in the air. When oxygen reached a certain level, animal life began to develop.

GAS EXCHANGE IN PHOTOSYNTHESIS

Carbon dioxide enters the leaf through tiny openings and is used in photosynthesis.

sunlight

sunlight

water

oxygen

carbon dioxide

glucose

Oxygen exits the leaf through tiny openings and is used by living things to release energy stored in glucose.

Over time, some bacteria evolved into other producers that also carried on photosynthesis. Today the huge numbers of phytoplankton floating at the ocean's surface produce about 70 percent of the oxygen that humans and other animals breathe. The remaining 30 percent of the oxygen we breathe is produced by plants living on land. Photosynthesis carried out by producers in water and on land keeps the oxygen level at about 21 percent of Earth's atmosphere—just right for breathing.

Plants, animals, and most other living things must have oxygen to release the energy contained in food. The process of releasing energy in a usable form is called **cell respiration**. You've probably heard that *respiration* means "breathing." Cell respiration is the use of oxygen to break down glucose. The waste products of cell respiration are water and carbon dioxide.

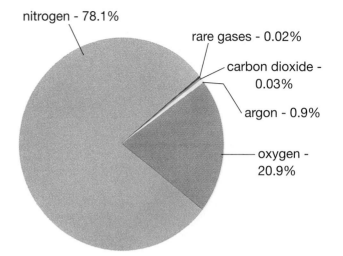

▲ **Percentage of gases in the air by volume**

Plants and other producers, then, keep oxygen cycling through the environment. Oxygen is released as a waste product of photosynthesis. Both producers and consumers use the oxygen to obtain energy from glucose during cell respiration. The carbon dioxide released as a waste product is used during photosynthesis. And the cycle starts again! ■

Photosynthesis produces oxygen that is used in respiration. ▼

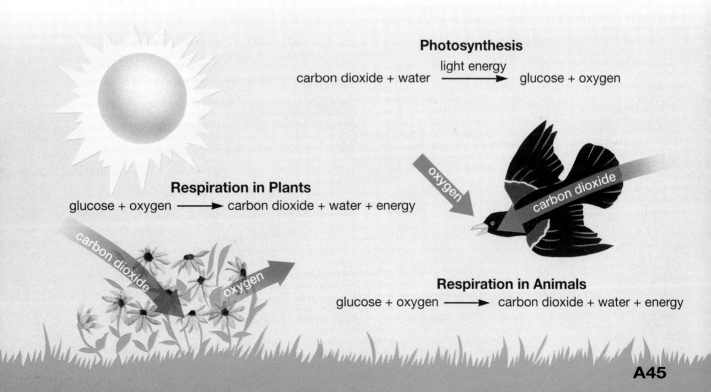

Transpiration

▲ **Stained and magnified stomata**

When it's hot, your body controls its temperature by sweating. Human skin has pores, which are tiny openings that can release water. When the water on your skin evaporates, you feel cooler.

Plant Pores

Plants also have pores, called **stomata** (stō ma′tə). (One pore is called a stoma.) But stomata don't control a plant's temperature. Instead, they control the amount of water in a plant's tissues by releasing water vapor into the surrounding air.

An oak leaf may have as many as 100,000 stomata in an area the size of your thumbnail. Yet stomata take up only 1 percent of a leaf's surface. Most are on the bottom surface of leaves, but some plants have stomata on both leaf surfaces. The cells surrounding a stoma look like tiny pairs of balloons that open and close to control the amount

of water vapor that exits the leaf. Oxygen and carbon dioxide also pass into and out of stomata during photosynthesis and respiration.

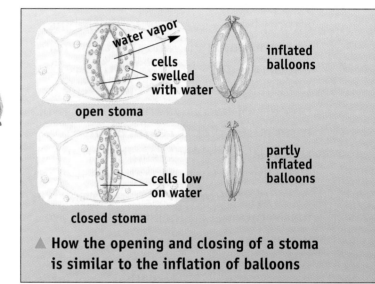

▲ **How the opening and closing of a stoma is similar to the inflation of balloons**

Water Release

The process in which plants release water through stomata is called **transpiration** (tran spə rā′shən). This release of water is part of the water cycle. Most of the water absorbed by a plant's roots is released in this way. A field of corn can absorb about 5 million L (1.3 million gal) of water during a season and can transpire about 4.5 million L (1.17 million gal) of this into the air.

A plant's transpiration rate varies. On humid days, stomata open to release excess water. During windy days, transpiration may slow or even stop.

Pumping Action

Although water is almost continually being released by leaves, it is also being replaced. Water taken in by the roots travels up the xylem cells, passes through the stem, and enters the leaves through the petiole. What keeps the water flowing?

To understand how water moves in a plant, think about a drinking straw. When you suck juice out of the top of a

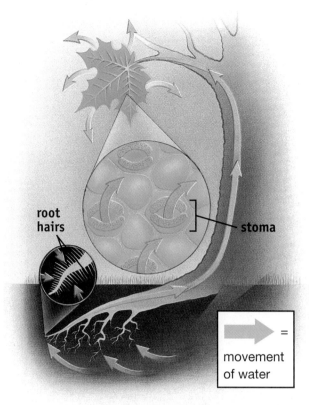

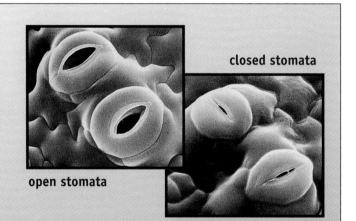

▲ A close-up view of open and closed stomata in a leaf

closed stomata

open stomata

root hairs

stoma

= movement of water

▲ A tree's pumping action is caused by transpiration of water vapor from the leaves.

straw, more juice enters the bottom of the straw and moves upward. As long as you keep sucking, a stream of juice fills the straw. Something like this happens in a plant.

When water evaporates from stomata, the water pressure in the leaf becomes lower because the cells contain less water. (Water pressure is higher in the xylem tubes in the stem.) The lower pressure creates a kind of suction pump that pulls more water up from the roots, through the stem, and into the leaf. In this way, transpiration helps keep water flowing toward the leaves. ■

INVESTIGATION 2

1. Describe a stoma, tell where it might be found, and explain its role in transpiration.

2. Explain why the processes of photosynthesis and respiration are both essential to the survival of plants and animals.

HOW DO PLANTS REACT TO LIGHT AND GRAVITY?

Have you ever planted a garden? If you have, did you worry about placing each seed so that the roots would grow down into the soil? Why isn't this a problem? In this investigation you'll explore the adaptations plants have for growing in the right direction and for getting as much sunlight as they can.

Activity

Ups and Downs

Imagine that you are doing plant experiments aboard a space shuttle. You want to know how a plant grows where there is no up or down. To plan for your shuttle experiment, you need to know how a plant grows right here on Earth.

MATERIALS
- goggles
- scissors
- blotting paper
- 2 small clear plastic cups
- water
- 8 soaked lima beans
- grease pencil
- *Science Notebook*

SAFETY
Wear goggles during this activity.

Procedure

1. Using scissors, cut two strips of blotting paper. Place the strips inside each of two clear plastic cups so that each strip snugly lines the inside of a cup. Fill each cup one-third full with water.

2. After the blotting paper is completely moistened, place four lima beans in a row, curved side up, in one cup. Make sure the beans are between the inside of the cup and the blotting paper. Using a grease pencil, write a letter (*A, B, C,* and *D*) on the outside of the cup above each lima bean.

3. In the second cup, place four lima beans—this time, curved side down—between the cup and the blotting paper. Using a grease pencil, write a number (*1, 2, 3,* and *4*) on the outside of the cup above each bean.

A48

4. Place both cups in a sunny spot. **Predict** how the seedlings will look when they sprout. **Discuss** your predictions with your group.

5. **Observe** the growth of your seedlings every day for at least two weeks. In your *Science Notebook*, set up a chart to record your data. **Record** your observations every day.

Analyze and Conclude

1. At the end of two days, what did you **observe** in the cup with the lettered seedlings? What did you **observe** in the cup with the numbered seedlings?

2. **Hypothesize** how roots respond to gravity.

3. **Infer** how these plant responses help the plant survive.

INVESTIGATE FURTHER!

EXPERIMENT

How will different conditions affect seedlings? Set up two cups with blotting paper. Moisten the blotting paper. Place two lima beans curved side down in each cup. Place one cup in a sunny spot and the other in a cardboard box with a lid. Predict what will happen to the seedlings. Discuss your predictions.

Plant Responses

In the activity "Ups and Downs," you saw how seedlings respond to one condition of their environment—gravity. Plant responses to conditions in the environment are called **tropisms** (trō′piz əmz). The word *tropism* comes from a Greek word that means "a turning." The plant response that you observed was geotropism, or a turning toward Earth. (*Geo-* means "Earth.")

Growth Toward Gravity

Roots respond to Earth's gravity by growing toward the center of Earth. Growing toward the center of Earth is a geotropic response. This growth response ensures that the roots will grow down into the soil, the plant's source of water and nutrients. Leaves and stems have the opposite response to gravity. They grow away from Earth's center. This response ensures that leaves and stems will be exposed to the sunlight that the plant needs to make its food.

Growth Toward Light

Leaves and stems tend to turn, or grow, toward a source of light. Growing toward light is a phototropic response, or a turning toward light. (*Photo-* means "light.") You have probably seen the leaves of houseplants turn toward a window. Stems may bend toward that window or the nearest source of light. The plants are not just bending—they

▲ Roots show a geotropic response, or a growth downward, toward the center of Earth.

▲ The stems and leaves of these plants are showing a phototropic response, or a growth toward light.

How do the roots of the two plants compare? What kinds of responses are the roots showing? ▼

are actually growing toward light. Such growth allows their leaves to capture the most sunlight for the process of photosynthesis.

Growth Toward Water

When plant roots are in soil that has lots of water, they grow toward the water. This kind of growth is a hydrotropic response. (*Hydro-* means "water.") However, roots do not "know" where the moisture is. They do not "try" to find the water. Instead, when roots come into contact with moist soil, they continue to grow toward the moisture. Roots touching only very dry soil may grow very slowly or not at all.

UNIT PROJECT LINK

Take a walk through a local park, woodland, or garden where there are plants that naturally grow well in your area. Bring along a field guide to identify the plants. List the plants that you find growing in bright direct sunlight. List also the plants growing in shade. Draw a picture of each plant and label each according to the best lighting conditions for that particular plant. Decide which plants from your list could grow in a terrarium.

The tendrils of (1) peas, (2) clematis, (3) morning glory, and (4) sugar-snap peas curl and twine around other objects.

Hanging On

Some plants have tendrils—thread-like parts of a climbing plant—that respond to objects they contact. The tendrils wrap around these objects, using the objects to support the plant as it climbs toward sunlight. This response to touch is still another kind of tropism. It is called a thigmotropic response. (*Thigmo-* means "touch.") Cucumbers, peas, morning glories, and grapes put out tendrils that curl around almost any object they touch. Tendrils help support plants. ■

INVESTIGATION 3

1. On a sunny kitchen windowsill, several potted plants appear to be bending toward the window. Explain what is happening.

2. A group of students grew lima-bean seeds in a plastic cup. After the seeds sprouted, the students turned them so that the roots pointed upward. Explain how the roots would develop between the third and the tenth days.

REFLECT & EVALUATE

WORD POWER

chloroplast   producer
consumer   starch
decomposer   stoma
food chain   tropism
food web
glucose
cell respiration
photosynthesis
transpiration

On Your Own
Use each term in a different sentence that tells the meaning of the term.

With a Partner
Make a word-search puzzle. See if your partner can tell you what each hidden term means.

PORTFOLIO
Draw a food chain that includes food you eat. Then use the information in your food chain to draw a labeled diagram of an energy pyramid.

Analyze Information
Study the drawing on page A34 that explains photosynthesis. Then explain the way in which photosynthesis occurs.

Assess Performance
Design and carry out an experiment to show transpiration in a plant. Compare your results with those of other students. What do the results tell you about plant transpiration?

Problem Solving
1. People sometimes refer to fertilizer as "plant food." You have learned in this chapter that plants do not eat food—instead they make their own food. Explain why it is not correct to refer to fertilizer as *plant food*.

2. The rain forests of South America and Central America are rapidly being cut down. Why do scientists consider this a problem for every living thing on Earth?

3. Have you ever planted flower bulbs, such as daffodil or tulip bulbs, upside down? What do you think would happen if you did? Explain your answer.

CHAPTER 3

PLANT REPRODUCTION

Do you know the saying "Tall oaks from little acorns grow"? Since prehistoric times, people have wondered about these little giants of the plant world. How can an acorn, maple seed, or pine cone produce a towering tree?

● ●

The Secret at Wollemi Park

Imagine the excitement when, in 1994, a grove of prehistoric pine trees was discovered in Wollemi Park, Australia. Newspapers told the story around the world. Everyone wanted to see the ancient trees.

With only 39 trees in the grove, the Wollemi pine is one of the world's rarest plants. The ancestors of these trees had withstood the nibblings of dinosaurs. But one carelessly tossed match from a tourist could cause the pine to disappear forever. How could its survival be assured?

Under the guidance of Barbara Briggs, the scientific director of Australia's parks, the location of the grove was kept secret. Scientists were sent to the grove to gather seeds to grow more of the trees. With their help the Wollemi pine will survive.

A54

Coming Up

◀ The Wollemi pine, one of the world's rarest plants

A55

INVESTIGATION ①

HOW DO PLANTS REPRODUCE?

An uncooked lima bean may seem lifeless. So does an onion. But perhaps you've planted bean seeds and watched them grow. Or you may have noticed that after several weeks, green leaves and roots begin to grow from an onion left in a paper bag. In Investigation 1 you'll find out where these new plants come from.

Activity
The Secret of a Seed

You put a seed in soil and keep it moist. In a few days a tiny new plant with roots, a stem, and leaves appears. How can a new living plant come from a seed that seems lifeless? Find out what secrets a seed holds!

MATERIALS

- soaked lima bean seeds
- soaked corn kernels
- plastic knife
- hand lens
- toothpicks
- *Science Notebook*

SAFETY

Use care in handling the knife.

Procedure

1. **Examine** and **compare** a lima bean seed and a corn kernel, which is actually a corn seed. **Record** your observations in your *Science Notebook*. **Make drawings** of the seeds.

2. Carefully peel off the thin outer covering of a lima bean and a corn kernel. **Observe** the covering with a hand lens. **Record** the differences and similarities you see.

3. Gently split open the bean seed with either your fingernail or a plastic

Step 3

A56

knife. Spread open the two halves of the bean seed and **examine** each half with the hand lens. **Draw** what you observe.

4. **Predict** what you will find inside the corn kernel. Then, with the knife, carefully cut the corn kernel in half lengthwise through one side and lay the halves flat. **Examine** each half with the hand lens. **Compare** the inside of the corn kernel with the inside of the bean seed. **Draw** the inside of the corn kernel. **Discuss** what you have observed with other members of your group.

5. Use a toothpick to scrape off a bit of the material that fills up each seed. **Examine** the material with the hand lens. **Compare** the material from the bean seed with that from the corn seed.

Analyze and Conclude

1. How was the covering of the lima bean seed different from the covering of the corn kernel? How was it similar? What purpose do you think this covering serves?

2. What structures did you find inside each seed?

3. **Hypothesize** the function of the material that fills up each seed.

4. What can you **infer** about seeds from this activity?

INVESTIGATE FURTHER!

EXPERIMENT

Line two clear plastic cups with moistened blotting paper. Place two soaked lima bean seeds between the blotting paper and the inside of one cup. Place two soaked corn kernels between the blotting paper and the inside of the other cup. Set the cups in a warm, sunny place. Keep the blotting paper moist. Relate what you observe over the next few days to the observations you made in the activity.

Activity

New Plants From Old

Can a new plant be reproduced from parts of an old plant? Find out!

Procedure

1. With the members of your group, decide how you can grow new plants from each of the plant parts you've been given. Should you use soil or water? Will the plant parts stand up by themselves, or will they need support?

2. With your group, decide how you will care for your plants. Will the plants need warmth? Will they need light and moisture?

3. Predict what might happen to each of the plant parts. **Record** your predictions in your *Science Notebook*.

4. Observe your plant parts over the next two weeks. **Record** your observations daily.

Analyze and Conclude

1. Describe what happened to each of your plant parts. How do your results compare with your predictions?

2. Compare your group's results with those of other groups. How could you account for any differences?

3. Classify the plant parts you used as *roots, stems,* or *leaves*. Why might a gardener want to grow new plants from plant parts rather than from seeds?

Step 1

A58

From Flower to Fruit

How would you encourage someone to come and visit you? You might prepare some food, put on your best clothes, and make sure you smell good. That's just what many flowers do to attract insects. When an insect visits a flower, however, the visit begins the process that produces seeds.

The flower is the reproductive organ of a flowering plant. Some kinds of plants have flowers that produce both male and female sex cells. Other kinds have flowers that produce either male or female sex cells.

When an insect, small bird, or bat visits a flower, that animal transfers the male sex cells from one flower to another. This transfer is part of the process of sexual reproduction in the flower. During **sexual reproduction** a male sex cell joins with a female sex cell to produce a fertilized cell. In flowering plants, this fertilized cell develops into a tiny plant enclosed in a seed.

In Chapter 1 you learned about the parts of a flower. The drawing below will help you recall the main flower parts. You may also want to refer to the flower on page A16.

THE PARTS OF A FLOWER

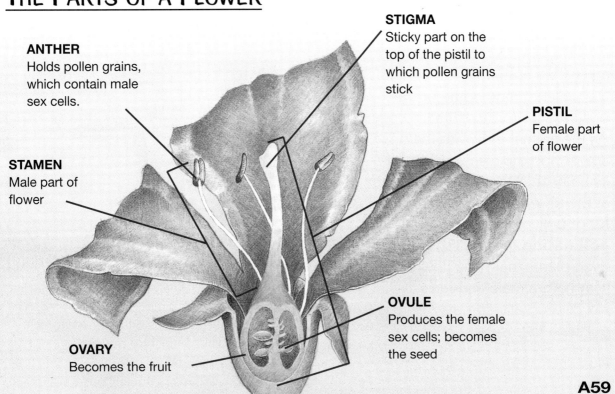

ANTHER
Holds pollen grains, which contain male sex cells.

STIGMA
Sticky part on the top of the pistil to which pollen grains stick

PISTIL
Female part of flower

STAMEN
Male part of flower

OVULE
Produces the female sex cells; becomes the seed

OVARY
Becomes the fruit

◄ **Pollen grains cling to a bee's body after it visits a flower. Pollen grains as seen with a microscope (*below*)**

Some flowers are pollinated when wind or rainwater carries pollen to them from another flower. Most flowers that are pollinated by the wind or rain are not scented or brightly colored. They do not need to attract insects.

Producing Seeds and Fruits

Follow the pictures on these two pages to see how seeds and fruits are formed. The first step in producing seeds is the transfer of pollen grains from the male part of a flower (the stamen) to the female part of another flower (the pistil). The pollen grains contain the male sex cells. When an insect, a bird, or even a bat brushes against an anther, which contains the pollen grains, some of the pollen sticks to the animal's body. As the animal moves to the next flower, some pollen brushes off its body onto the stigma, which is at the tip of the pistil. This transfer of pollen grains is called **pollination** (päl′ə nā′shən). Even plants that have flowers with both female and male sex cells usually do not pollinate themselves.

1 Pollen grain lands on the stigma of the pistil.

2 A tube grows down into the ovary. **Fertilization** (fʉrt ′l i zā′shən) takes place when a male sex cell from the pollen grain joins with the female sex cell inside the ovary.

A60

Pollination can take place only between plants of the same kind. If the pollen from an apple blossom lands on a tulip, for example, no pollination occurs. A tulip must be pollinated by pollen grains from another tulip.

Inside the ovule, the fertilized egg forms an **embryo** (em'brē ō), a tiny new plant. Other cells in the ovule produce a food supply for the embryo. The ovule then forms a protective **seed coat** around the embryo and its food supply, forming a seed. In the activity "The Secret of a Seed," you peeled the seed coat off bean and corn seeds. Inside each seed you found a tiny embryo and its food supply.

The ovary surrounding the seed or seeds enlarges and develops into a **fruit**. The fruit protects the seeds as they grow. Some fruits, such as plums and cherries, have only one seed; others, such as oranges and strawberries, have many seeds. Some fruits, such as tomatoes and apples, are soft

and moist; others, such as walnuts, wheat, and beans, are hard and dry. Some fruits, such as those on dandelions, have tiny parachutes that help spread the seeds over great distances. A bean pod and a corn husk look much different from the soft, moist inside of an apple, but the pod and husk are other forms of fruit that protect seeds as they grow. ■

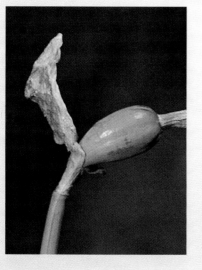

3 Following fertilization, the ovary enlarges and begins to form a fruit.

4 The ovary continues to enlarge, and seeds begin to form.

5 The fruit has ripened and has split open, releasing the seeds.

Growing Plants
Without Seeds

STS
SCIENCE
TECHNOLOGY
& SOCIETY

When you plant seeds, you are planting the result of sexual reproduction—the joining of male and female sex cells from parent plants. However, you found in the activity "New Plants From Old" that you can grow new plants without using seeds. Such plants are produced by asexual reproduction. In **asexual reproduction**, offspring are produced from one or more cells of a single parent.

In the activity you produced new plants from parts of other plants through a type of asexual reproduction

called vegetative propagation (vej ə-tāt'iv präp ə gā'shən). *Vegetative* means "growing." *Propagation* means "increasing in number." The new plants you grew are called **clones**. Clones are exact copies of the parent plants.

Tissue Culture

Another type of asexual reproduction is tissue culture. A group of cells that works together is called a tissue. *Culture* is another word for *growing*. Tissue culture involves growing new plants from the cells of healthy and disease-resistant plants in a laboratory.

Technicians preparing tissue culture in a laboratory (*below*) and a scientist observing the culture (*right*).

To grow plants from a tissue culture, technicians must work in a germ-free environment. They carefully select a parent plant and remove some of its cells. Then each cell is placed in a mixture where it can grow into an exact copy of the parent.

Through tissue culture, as many as 1 million plants can be grown in a year from a small piece of a parent plant. In the near future one laboratory in India expects to grow 20 to 25 million plants a year this way.

Leaves of the Pacific yew ▶

▲ **Bark of the Pacific yew, which is used to produce taxol**

Anticancer Drugs

Several laboratories in the United States are using tissue culture to try to create an anticancer drug called taxol. Taxol, which shrinks tumors in many patients and causes some tumors to disappear, is found only in the bark of the Pacific yew tree. These trees are becoming scarce because it takes the bark of three trees to produce the taxol for one treatment! Scientists are now trying to produce yew tree tissue through tissue culture. They hope to make taxol directly from this tree tissue without growing whole trees.

The Future

Tissue culture allows growers to raise valuable plants in a short time, year-round, and under disease-free conditions. Today the process is expensive. But farmers someday might be able to raise crops of potato, corn, or wheat that began with one perfect plant. It is hoped that these crops will be resistant to the diseases, insects, and drought that used to kill them. ■

═══════════════ **INVESTIGATION 1** ═══════════════

1. Describe how seeds and fruit form in a flower.

2. Describe two ways that plants can be reproduced asexually.

A63

INVESTIGATION 2

WHAT ARE THE STAGES IN THE LIFE CYCLE OF A SEED PLANT?

In Investigation 1 you saw how seeds were formed from male and female sex cells. But what happens after the seed falls from the plant? In Investigation 2 you'll find out the rest of the story of the life cycle of seed plants.

Activity

It's Just a Stage

Infant, child, teenager, adult: These are the stages of the human life cycle. In this activity you'll use Wisconsin Fast Plants™ to find out if plants have similar life cycle stages.

Procedure

1. Follow your teacher's instructions and have each member of your group fill a planter with soil, fertilizer pellets, and seeds. Then water the plants.

2. Place the planter under a good source of artificial light. If possible, keep the light on 24 hours a day. Water as needed.

3. In your *Science Notebook*, **make a chart** for recording height as the plants grow. **Measure** and **record** each plant's height each day. **Make a line graph** that shows the growth of each plant. Also **record** your observations about the appearance of each plant. **Make drawings** of the plants as they grow.

MATERIALS
- planter
- soil
- fertilizer pellets
- seeds of Wisconsin Fast Plants™
- water
- dropper
- good source of artificial light
- metric ruler
- red marker
- pollinating kit
- *Science Notebook*

SAFETY
Do not eat any seeds or soil!

Plant #	Height (cm)			
	Day 1	Day 2	Day 3	Day 4
1				
2				
3				

A64

4. When the stems are 5 cm tall, use a red marker to make a dot on the stem just below the leaves. Each day, **measure** and **record** the distance between the soil and the dot.

Step 4

5. If your plants have flowers, follow your teacher's instructions for transferring pollen from the flower of one plant to the flower of another plant. **Record** your method of pollination.

6. Continue to **observe** your plants. If fruits are produced, open several when they are ripe and **examine** the contents. What could you do with the contents?

Analyze and Conclude

1. Seedlings are the tiny plants that first appear above the soil. How many days after planting seeds did seedlings appear? If you saw flower buds, how many days after planting did they appear? If your plants formed fruits, how many days did it take for them to ripen?

2. What can you **infer** about stem growth from the measurements you made using the red marker?

3. What stages in the life cycle of a plant did you observe? What was the length of this life cycle?

4. What stage in the plant's life cycle is similar to the life cycle stage you are in? Explain your answer.

The Story of a Tree Seed

In the late spring the seeds of the red maple ripen and fall off the tree. The seeds are inside the fruit, connected in pairs. A paper-thin "wing" enables them to be carried by the wind.

As they fall to the ground, many seeds are eaten or hidden by small animals and insects. Some lie on the ground long enough for their fruits to open and release the seeds.

1 **GERMINATION** Water in the soil softens a maple seed. **Germination**, or sprouting, occurs. Inside the seed the embryo grows. As the root grows into the soil, it absorbs nutrients and water, and the rest of the embryo sprouts. The tiny plant uses food stored in the **seed leaves** that surround it.

2 **SEEDLING** As its stem appears above the ground, the plant becomes a **seedling**. True leaves develop in the familiar shape of the red maple. Then, with the cooler days of fall, the seedling stops growing. Chlorophyll in its leaves disappears, leaving behind the bright colors that were there all along.

3 **SAPLING** The following spring, buds appear on the stem and new leaves develop. As the stem becomes taller and thicker, bark forms. The roots grow deep and wide to support the growing plant and provide it with water and nutrients. Last year's seedling has become a **sapling**, or young tree.

The first spring that a young maple grows flowers, it is considered to be mature. A maple tree produces some flowers with female sex cells, other flowers with male sex cells, and a third kind of flower with both female and male sex cells. These flowers are pollinated when the wind carries pollen grains from the anther of one flower to the stigma of another flower. After fertilization occurs, the flowers produce the winged seeds that once more begin the red maple's life cycle. ■

4 **TREE** When its trunk measures 10 cm (4 in.) in diameter, the sapling is considered to be a tree. It will continue to get taller as the trunk, the tips of the branches, and the roots keep growing. A red maple may grow to be about 24 m (75–80 ft) tall with a trunk about 0.3–0.6 m (1–2 ft) in diameter.

Winged seeds of red maple ▶

The Life of a Bristlecone Pine

One of the oldest living things on Earth is a bristlecone pine named Methuselah. Methuselah has lived in Great Basin National Park in California's White Mountains for about 4,600 years! If this twisted, wind-battered tree could talk, what might it tell us about our history?

Today only a small portion of Methuselah is still alive. We know how old Methuselah is because scientists have learned how to use a tiny hollow drill to bore into trees and remove a thin core of wood. They can count the annual rings on the core and don't have to cut down the tree. How many other trees will live as long as Methuselah?

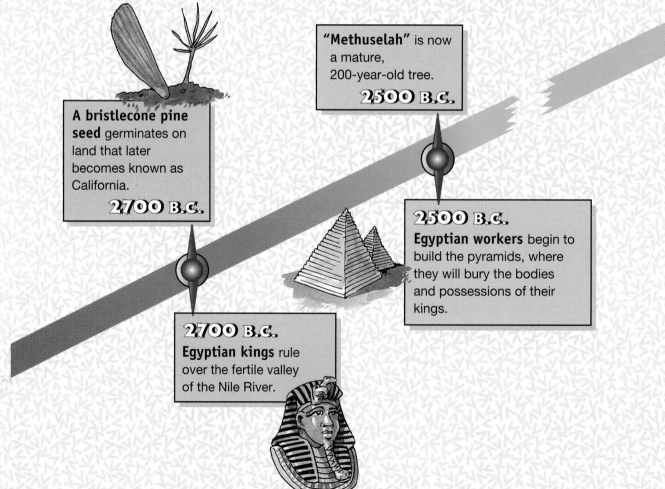

A bristlecone pine seed germinates on land that later becomes known as California.

2700 B.C.

"Methuselah" is now a mature, 200-year-old tree.

2500 B.C.

2700 B.C.
Egyptian kings rule over the fertile valley of the Nile River.

2500 B.C.
Egyptian workers begin to build the pyramids, where they will bury the bodies and possessions of their kings.

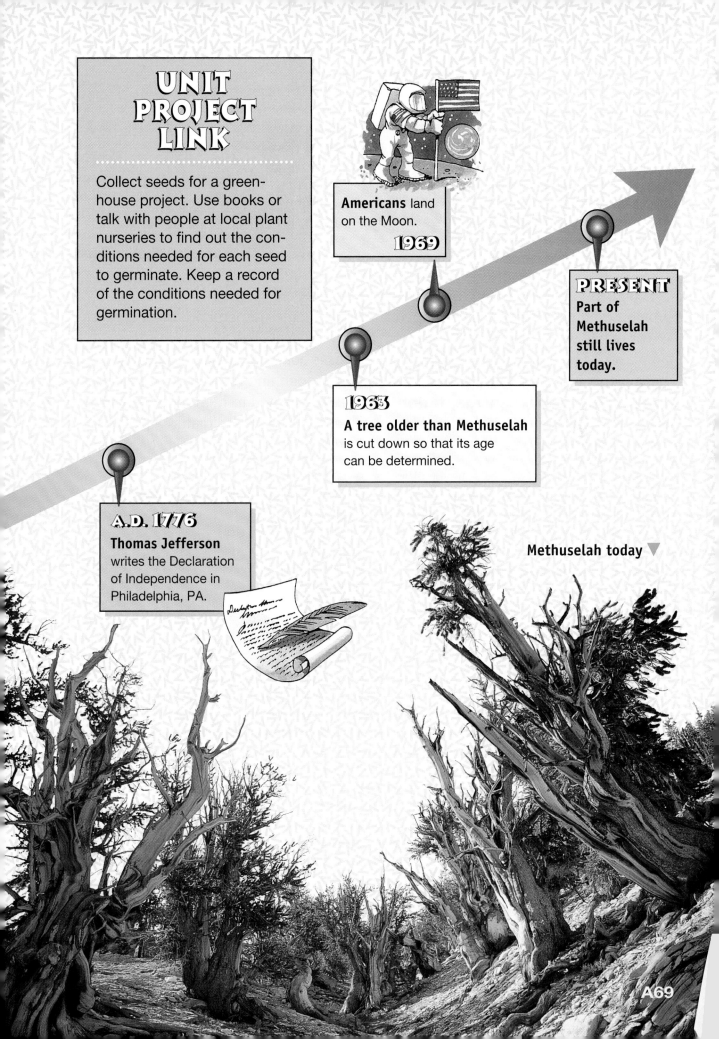

UNIT PROJECT LINK

Collect seeds for a greenhouse project. Use books or talk with people at local plant nurseries to find out the conditions needed for each seed to germinate. Keep a record of the conditions needed for germination.

Americans land on the Moon.
1969

PRESENT
Part of Methuselah still lives today.

1963
A tree older than Methuselah is cut down so that its age can be determined.

A.D. 1776
Thomas Jefferson writes the Declaration of Independence in Philadelphia, PA.

Methuselah today ▼

Timing Things Right

Why can't a cactus live in the Arctic? Why do pine trees have needle-shaped leaves, while water lilies have large flat leaves? The answer is that each of these plants is adapted for certain environmental conditions. An **adaptation** (ad əp tā′shən) is any trait that enables an organism to survive.

Cold Seeds

Seeds need the proper temperature to germinate. This temperature depends on the type of plant. Some seeds, such as those of the apple, peach, pine, and the ash tree shown here, need a period of cold before their seeds will sprout.

▲ Ash seeds must be exposed to cold before they can germinate.

Hot Seeds

Jack pines depend on forest fires for their survival. The life cycle of these trees is adapted to the fires. Their cones open and release seeds only after they are heated to high temperatures. The fire may kill the mature jack pine trees, but their seeds quickly germinate

▲ Lodgepole pines growing 5 years after a forest fire

in the charred soil. Lodgepole pines also produce cones that open after they are heated, but these trees also have a safety net. In case there are no fires, some of their seeds also sprout under ordinary conditions.

Blooming Desert

Some flowering desert plants have adapted to their dry, hot environment by developing very short life cycles. They sprout, burst into bloom, and produce seeds following a heavy rain. Many of these plants then die, but their seeds are ready to sprout during the next rain. In contrast to the ancient bristlecone pine called Methuselah, the desert bladderpod mustard plant sprouts from a seed, grows, blooms, produces its own seeds, and dies within as little as ten days.

▲ The bladderpod mustard plant's short life cycle is an adaptation to desert conditions.

SCIENCE IN LITERATURE

THE BLOSSOM ON THE BOUGH: A BOOK OF TREES
Written and illustrated by
Anne Ophelia Dowden
Ticknor & Fields, 1994

Do you like to draw and paint? If the answer is yes, then you might become a botanical artist—an artist who draws flowers and trees. Anne Ophelia Dowden has created watercolor paintings that not only are beautiful but also teach science. In *The Blossom on the Bough*, you'll see paintings of trees from all over North America.

The paintings show you parts of trees that may not be near each other on the real plant, such as male and female cones. The paintings also compare parts of trees that cannot be seen at the same time of year. That's what makes looking at botanical illustrations a great way to learn about plants.

Water-Storing Stems

Other desert plants adapt by storing water in their thick stems. On a rare rainy day, a large cactus can absorb and store 1,000 L (260 gal) of water. A giant saguaro cactus can store 9,000 L (2,340 gal) of water in its stem—enough to survive even if there is no more rain for three years! The spines on many cactuses reduce the surface area exposed to the dry desert air. This adaptation reduces the amount of water lost through transpiration.

▲ **A giant saguaro cactus can store enormous amounts of water.**

Food-Storing Roots

Longleaf pine seedlings, which look like clumps of grass, hardly grow at all during their first six years. Instead these pines store food in their roots. In their seventh year, they shoot up much faster than other pine trees and develop a thick bark that is resistant to fire. This quick growth and protective bark increase the seedlings' chances of survival. ■

▲ **The longleaf pine is adapted to areas that are rocky or sandy, and it even grows well in poor soil.**

INVESTIGATION 2

1. Give examples of ways that plants could survive a forest fire.

2. What kinds of adaptations do plants need to survive in your region?

REFLECT & EVALUATE

WORD POWER

adaptation   fruit
clone   germination
embryo   pollination
fertilization   sapling
asexual reproduction
seed coat
seed leaves
seedling
sexual reproduction

On Your Own
Review the terms in the list. Then use as many terms as you can in a paragraph that tells about sexual and asexual reproduction in plants.

With a Partner
Mix up the letters of each term in the list. Provide a clue for each term and challenge your partner to unscramble the terms.

PORTFOLIO

Draw the stages in the life cycle of a plant of your choice.

Analyze Information

Study the drawing. Then use it to describe and explain the environment for which the plant is adapted.

Assess Performance

Design and build a model of a flower that will be pollinated by bees and a model of a flower that will be pollinated by the wind or rain. Compare the models and explain why they differ.

Problem Solving

1. Throughout the world, basic foods in the human diet are seeds, such as rice, wheat, corn, and oats. Based on your knowledge of what a seed is, explain why seeds are nutritious.

2. Compare sexual reproduction and asexual reproduction in plants.

3. Explain how the short life cycle of the desert bladderpod mustard plant helps that species of plant survive. Explain how a plant might use a long life cycle to adapt to a difficult environment.

CHAPTER 4

A WORLD OF PLANTS

There are many kinds of plants. Some, like mosses, are tiny; others, like redwood trees, are huge. Some plants, like sunflowers, stand tall; others, like ivy, creep along the ground. In this chapter, you'll explore the rich variety of plant life.

Plant Animals

There's a leopard hanging around one of the gardens of the San Diego Zoo. Actually, the leopard is part of the garden! It is a piece of topiary (tō′pē er ē), or plant sculpture.

Linda Rodriguez is a topiary artist for the zoo. She makes some of her plant sculptures by allowing bushes to grow and then snipping them into different shapes. For faster results, Rodriguez designs a hollow mesh frame, packs it tightly with moss, and then roots ivy in the moss. The artist trains and cuts the growing plants to the shape of the frame.

Linda Rodriguez tries to make the sculptures lifelike. She knew she had succeeded when a strutting peacock at the zoo tried for days to get the attention of a topiary flamingo. What questions would you ask the topiary artist about her work with plants?

Coming Up

◄ Linda Rodriguez sculpts an ivy-covered animal. A lion with a spider-plant mane looms in the background.

HOW ARE PLANTS CLASSIFIED?

Imagine hang-gliding over a rain forest. From above, you observe a huge sea of green. Only up close can you see the individual plants that make up the forest. The forest has an amazing variety of plants. How is this huge variety of plants classified?

Activity

Looking at Leaves

How many different traits can you use to classify plants? In this activity, find out how you can classify plants according to the shape and arrangement of their leaves.

MATERIALS

- 5 pieces of paper
- pencil
- tape
- 5 sealable plastic bags
- "Leaf Characteristics and Classification" table
- *Science Notebook*

SAFETY

Wear clothing that covers your arms and legs if you'll be working in a forested area.

Procedure

1. With your teacher's permission, **observe** with a partner the variety of plants in your schoolyard. (If this cannot be done, your teacher will give you leaves to study.)

2. Look at the trees, shrubs, flowering plants, and nonflowering plants. Choose five very different plants to examine closely. **Observe** the whole plant. **Make a sketch** of each plant on a piece of paper.

3. For large plants, **observe** how leaves are arranged on their stems. Are the leaves opposite each other, or are they found on alternate sides along the stem? Do they grow in a circle around the stem? In your *Science Notebook,* make a "Classifying Leaves" chart like the one shown. **Record** your observations in this chart. Write each plant's name if you know it.

CLASSIFYING LEAVES		
Leaf Characteristics	Group Name	My Example

4. Carefully remove one whole leaf from each plant. Include the petiole if it has one. Tape each leaf to a separate piece of paper. Sketch the plant on the same paper. Place the paper in a plastic bag and seal the bag.

5. When you have collected five leaves, bring them back to class.

Analyze and Conclude

1. Look at the "Leaf Characteristics and Classification" table. Use the information in the table to **classify** each plant you studied into one of the major plant groups.

2. **Compare** your conclusions with those of other groups. **Discuss** any differences in the way the groups classified the plants.

3. Based on the class data, which plant group is most common? Are there any plant groups for which you did not find examples? If so, **infer** why.

INVESTIGATE FURTHER!

RESEARCH

Use field guides to trees, shrubs, flowering plants, and nonflowering plants that are written for your region of the country to try to identify the names of the plants you collected in the activity.

All Kinds of Plants

All plants are members of the **plant kingdom**. The plant kingdom family tree on this page shows that all plants are related. But as you saw in the activity on pages A76 and A77, different types of plants have different traits. Scientists use such differences to classify plants. For example, they divide the plant kingdom into two major groups: nonseed plants and seed plants. The **nonseed plants**—plants that do not reproduce with seeds—include mosses, ferns, and other less-familiar plants. The **seed plants**—plants that reproduce with seeds—include plants that have flowers or cones.

Mosses and Liverworts

If you walk through a forest, you may notice a spongy carpeting underfoot. This carpeting is formed of mosses. **Mosses** are small nonseed plants that lack true roots, stems, and leaves.

Like other nonseed plants, mosses reproduce by means of spores. Spores are one-celled structures that grow into new plants. Mosses also reproduce sexually, producing sperm cells and egg cells. However, no seeds are produced.

Liverworts are nonseed plants that lack true roots, stems, and leaves. They grow in moist places, such as along the banks of streams.

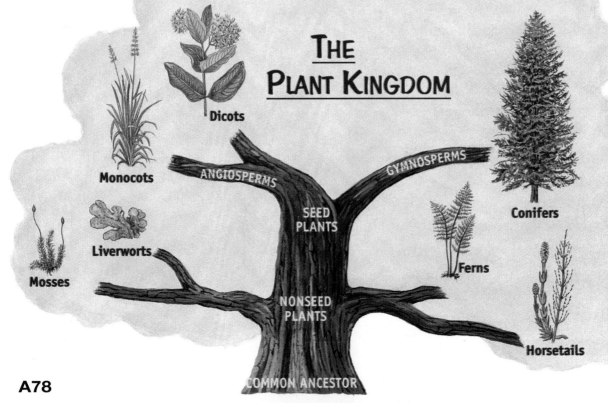

THE PLANT KINGDOM

Dicots

Monocots

ANGIOSPERMS

GYMNOSPERMS

Conifers

SEED PLANTS

Liverworts

Mosses

Ferns

NONSEED PLANTS

Horsetails

COMMON ANCESTOR

▲ Mosses produce spores at the tips of tall leafless stalks.

▲ The liverwort *Marchantia* produces spores on stalks with umbrella-shaped tops.

Mosses don't have xylem cells for carrying water. Because mosses lack structures to carry water, water must diffuse from cell to cell throughout the plant. This is why mosses are small plants that grow only in moist places.

Ferns and Horsetails

Ferns are spore-forming plants that have roots, stems, and leaves. Before the dinosaurs lived, giant ferns covered much of Earth. Today, ferns are not so common. But they still grow in many places that are not too hot or cold and that have lots of moisture.

Like mosses, ferns reproduce by spores. Ferns also reproduce sexually without producing seeds. Unlike mosses, ferns have xylem tubes to carry water from the roots throughout the plant. The roots of ferns anchor the plant in soil and carry water to the scaly, underground stems. These underground stems are called rhizomes.

The most obvious parts of ferns are their leaves, called fronds. At a glance, some fern fronds appear to be made of many leaves attached to several stems. Actually, all of the leaflike parts form one large fern frond. Spore cases, which look like dots, are often produced on the undersides of the fronds. Spore cases contain spores.

Horsetails, shown on page A81, look more like paintbrushes than the tails of horses. There are about 30 species of horsetails living in marshes and swamps around the world. Horsetails share some traits with ferns. For example, horsetails reproduce by spores and have underground stems.

The spots on the undersides of fern fronds are clusters of spore cases. ▶

A79

▲ A typical conifer

Conifers

Many plants, such as firs and the jack pine you read about in Chapter 3, produce seeds in cones. Cone-bearing plants are called **conifers** (kän'ə fərz). Like ferns, conifers have roots, stems, and leaves. However, conifers differ from ferns in the way they reproduce.

When conifers reproduce sexually, they form seeds. The seeds are located between the scales of protective cones. Unlike flowering seed plants, conifers do not form fruits.

Conifers may be small shrubs or tall trees. Huge forests of conifers blanket much of the northern part of the world. Unlike other kinds of trees, most conifers keep their leaves in autumn. Many conifers, such as pines, have needlelike leaves. Others, such as cedar trees, have leaves that look like overlapping scales.

Flowering Plants

Have you ever walked through a garden on a spring morning and been greeted by sweet odors and bright colors? The aromas and colors mean just

SCIENCE IN LITERATURE

A Pocketful of Goobers
A Story about George Washington Carver

by Barbara Mitchell
Illustrations by Peter E. Hanson

A POCKETFUL OF GOOBERS:
A STORY ABOUT GEORGE
WASHINGTON CARVER
by Barbara Mitchell
Carolrhoda Books, 1986

Honey-roasted peanuts. Peanut butter. Peanut oil. How many ways can you use peanuts? George Washington Carver, a plant scientist, discovered more than 300 uses for peanuts. He figured out how peanuts could be used to make milklike drinks, cheeses, shoe polishes, dyes, and even floor coverings.

To the poor farmers of the South at the beginning of the twentieth century, this former enslaved person was a hero. Find out how Carver's "goobers" saved the day when you read *A Pocketful of Goobers* by Barbara Mitchell.

**Hibiscus, a
flowering plant**

two groups—monocots and dicots. **Monocots** produce seeds with a single seed leaf, or food-storing leaf. A corn plant is an example of a monocot. Each kernel has one seed leaf used by the germinating seed for food. **Dicots** are plants that produce seeds with two seed leaves. A lima bean plant is an example of a dicot.

We couldn't get along without flowering plants. Each day, you eat parts of such plants—juicy oranges, dry grains made into bread and pasta, or corn made into oil or margarine—for breakfast, lunch, and dinner. On hot summer days, you cool off in their shade. You may sit on their wood either at a bench in the park or on a chair in your home. You might even use flowering plants as medicine when you are sick! ■

one thing—flowering plants are in bloom.

Most of the plants you are familiar with are flowering plants. **Flowering plants** are plants that have roots, stems, and leaves, and that reproduce by seeds formed in flowers. As the seeds are formed, a fruit develops to cover and protect them.

Flowering plants may be divided into

▲ **Water lilies, flowering plants**

◀ **Bird of paradise, a
flowering plant**

**Horsetails,
nonseed plants** ▶

Leaf Traits and
Classification

▲ **One species or two?**

Look at the flowering plants in the drawing above. Are the plants of the same, or different, species? If you said "different," congratulations! The plant on the top is a common dandelion. The one on the bottom is the prairie dandelion.

What clues suggest the dandelions are of different species? As you learned on pages A76 and A77, leaf traits help distinguish plant species. Different plant species have leaves of different shapes and sizes. The leaves are also arranged differently on the stems. Read on to find out how to classify broad-leaved plants.

Simple leaves

Compound leaves

Simple or Compound

The flat part of a leaf is called the blade. When a leaf blade is single, or undivided, the leaf is considered simple. Notice that simple leaves may have rounded lobes or points.

Many plants have leaf blades that are divided into leaflets. Each leaflet looks like an individual leaf. A leaf with two or more leaflets is a compound leaf. The number of leaflets may be three, five, seven, or many. The leaflets may join all in one point, or they may be spread out. Sometimes even leaflets have leaflets!

Where Do Leaves Attach?

Flowering plants can be classified by the way the leaves are attached to the stem. When two leaves are attached at the same position on opposite sides of the stem, the leaf attachment is called *opposite*. When leaves are attached on opposite sides of the stem but not directly opposite each other, the leaf attachment is called *alternate*. Some plants have leaves that are arranged in a circle around the stem, like spokes coming out from the center of a wheel. This kind of leaf attachment is called *whorled*. You can see examples of opposite, alternate, and whorled leaves in this box.

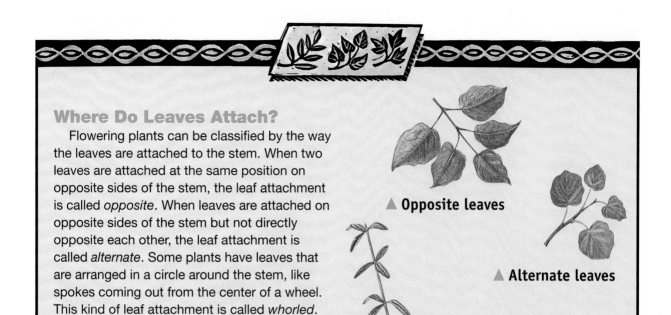

▲ **Opposite leaves**

▲ **Alternate leaves**

▲ **Whorled leaves**

On the Leaf Highways

Leaf veins are like "highways" that carry water to the cells of the leaf and carry the sugar made in the leaves to other parts of the plant. Some leaves have branched veins that spread through the leaf in all directions. Other leaves have parallel veins, which run side by side. Leaf vein patterns are used to distinguish the two major groups of flowering plants—monocots and dicots. Monocots have leaves with parallel veins. Dicots have leaves with branching veins.

▲ **Monocot**

▲ **Dicot**

INVESTIGATION 1

1. What are two traits you would look for to identify an unknown plant as a moss?

2. How can you distinguish between the two main kinds of seed plants? Give one example from each group.

HOW ARE PLANTS ADAPTED TO DIFFERENT ENVIRONMENTS?

You don't have to wait for it to rain to get a drink of water. People collect and store water in reservoirs to make sure that there is plenty of water when the faucet is turned on. Plants also have ways of getting enough water from their environments. You'll find out how in this investigation.

Activity

How Dry I Am

You know that plants need water to make food. You also know that plants live in many environments—including very dry deserts. How are plants adapted to getting—and keeping—the water they need?

MATERIALS

- 3 leaves: 1 each from a broad-leaved plant, a succulent, and a needle-leaved plant
- metric ruler
- pencil
- hand lens
- paper towel
- *Science Notebook*

Procedure

1. **Observe** the three leaves (especially their shapes) and, if possible, the plants from which they came. **Draw** the leaves in your *Science Notebook*.

2. Use a metric ruler to **measure** the approximate length, width, and thickness of each leaf. **Make a chart** and **record** this data in your *Science Notebook*.

Step 3

3. **Observe** the surfaces of each leaf with a hand lens to see if the leaf has small holes, or pores. Is there a covering on the leaf? **Record** your observations.

4. Place your leaves on a paper towel. Allow the leaves to remain in a sunny location for three days. **Predict** which leaf will show the greatest change from drying out. **Record** your prediction.

Step 4

Analyze and Conclude

1. Which of your leaves has a waxy covering? **Infer** the job of this covering.

2. The surface area of a leaf is the amount of area that is exposed to the air. Which of your leaves has the greatest surface area? How might surface area be a factor in a leaf's ability to conserve water?

3. Which leaf showed the most drying over the three days? Can you **hypothesize** why?

4. If you could measure the amount of water in each leaf, which do you think would have the most? Why? **Hypothesize** how a succulent leaf can survive a drought.

5. **Hypothesize** how conifer needles can live through the winter months when water in the ground may be frozen.

INVESTIGATE FURTHER!

· · · · · · · · · · · · · · · · · · ·

EXPERIMENT

Design an experiment to show how different kinds of plants conserve water. Share your findings with your class.

Plants and Water

All plants need water. However, some plants live in water, while others live where there is almost no water. How can plants live in such different environments?

Each kind of plant has structures or behaviors that help it survive in its environment. These structures or behaviors are called **adaptations**. The organism's adaptations are related to its habitat, or where it lives.

Root Adaptations

Most flowering plants absorb water through their roots. But not all root systems are alike. The mesquite (mes kēt') is a scrubby-looking tree that lives in dry areas. Its roots reach deep into the soil in search of water. Unlike the mesquite, many desert plants have long roots that spread in all directions just beneath the soil's surface. These roots absorb any

dew that collects and sinks into the top layer of soil.

Some plants growing high in the rain forest are not rooted in the ground at all. Instead, these plants have air roots. In some of these plants, the leaves gather water that falls as rain. These leaves then funnel the water to the roots, where it is absorbed.

Plant Conservationists

Many plants have adaptations to conserve the water they take in. In the activity on pages A84 and A85, you may have observed the stomata on the undersides of leaves. Plants take in carbon dioxide and give off oxygen and water vapor through stomata. Plants lose a great deal of water through their stomata. Many plants have adaptations to control the amount of water lost through their leaves.

A mesquite tree ▼

An aloe is a succulent. ▶

During winter, water in the soil may be frozen and unavailable. Many trees lose their leaves, an adaptation that allows them to overcome this lack of water. Trees that drop their leaves in fall are called deciduous (dē sij'ōō əs) trees. Dropping leaves reduces water loss through the stomata. These trees also go into a rest period and don't need as much water for their life processes.

Many conifers have needlelike leaves, which have a small surface area from which water can evaporate. Cactus spines and conifer needles also have waxy coatings that seal in moisture.

Succulents, such as the aloe shown here, are plants with fleshy leaves or stems and usually live in dry areas. After a rain, the leaves or stems swell with water that is stored and used slowly. Many succulents have tiny leaves, which reduces evaporation. Waxy or woolly leaf coverings on succulents keep in the much-needed moisture.

▲ **Water lilies have stomata on the tops of the leaves.**

Too Much Water

Why doesn't a water lily floating on water drown? Aquatic plants have adaptations for surviving in wet places. Water lily leaves are waxy to keep out water. Also, the stomata are on the tops, rather than the undersides, of the leaves. Many underwater plants don't have stomata at all. Such plants carry on gas exchange directly through the outer layer of their cells. ■

Deciduous trees drop their leaves in winter, which helps conserve water. ▼

The Story of Seed Dispersal

In 1883 a series of volcanic eruptions tore apart the small Pacific island of Krakatoa. When quiet returned, the island was completely barren of life.

Three years later, scientists counted 24 plant species growing on Krakatoa. By 1933 the island was green with plants. How did all these plants cross kilometers of ocean and get to Krakatoa?

Recall that many plants produce fruits, the plant part that holds seeds formed in the flower. When ripe, fruit drops from the parent plant. If all fruit fell straight to the ground, the seeds would be crowded together. The seedlings, lacking space and shaded from the Sun by the parent plant, would soon die. To survive, most seeds must be carried away from their parent plant. The scattering of seeds away from the parent plant is called **seed dispersal** (di spʉr′səl).

Most seeds cannot move by themselves. Instead, seeds have adaptations that allow other things to move them. Recall from Chapter 3 that agents such as animals and wind help pollinate flowers. As you can see from the photographs on this page and the next, these same agents help to disperse seeds. Seeds may also be dispersed by water or by being propelled from the parent plant much as a cannonball is shot from a cannon.

▲ Harvester ants disperse seeds by carrying them in their mouths.

▲ Burdocks, with their stick-tight hooks, are easily carried on animal fur.

▲ Birds that eat fruits may spread the seeds to new locations.

▲ Chipmunks often carry nuts far from the parent tree.

▲ The large seed of the coconut floats on water to a new location.

▲ Winged seeds of maple trees fly like helicopters through the air.

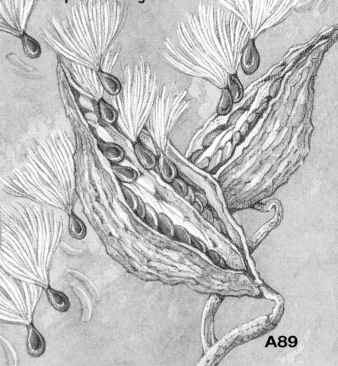

▲ The feathery seeds of milkweed are easily carried by the wind.

Plants of the Tundra

The tundra is a harsh environment with a cold, dry climate. Summer is very short in the tundra, but the number of hours of daylight is great, approaching 24 hours for a short time. Winter is cold and lasts up to nine months, with long nights for much of that time.

The short summer allows only the top few centimeters of frozen soil to thaw for a few weeks. Below this layer, the ground remains frozen. This permanently frozen soil is called permafrost.

Life in the Tundra

From a distance, the tundra appears barren and lifeless. However, during its short summers, the tundra comes alive. Large herds of reindeer and caribou wander the land. These large animals feed on small plants of the tundra.

Most trees and other deep-rooted plants cannot anchor in the permafrost layer. Trees that do grow, such as birch and willow, are severely bent and are small in size to withstand the high winds of the region. The black spruce creeps along the ground instead of growing upright.

The Arctic tundra is shown in violet. ▼

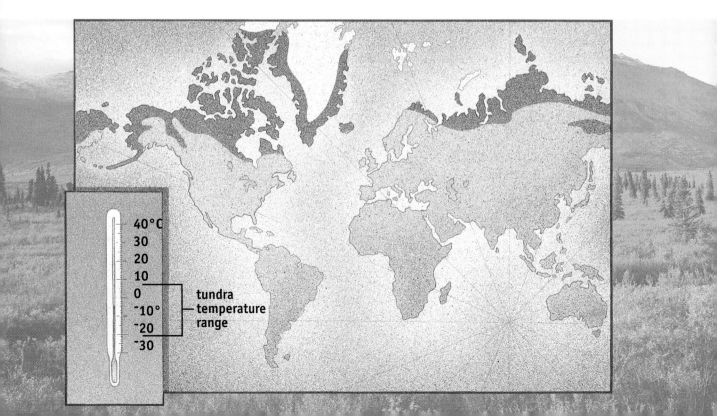

40°C
30
20
10
0
⁻10°
⁻20
⁻30

tundra temperature range

In terms of rainfall, the tundra resembles a desert. In this frigid land, the permafrost prevents melting snow from soaking into the ground. This water collects at the soil's surface to form bogs and puddles. In summer, these shallow pockets of water teem with plants such as sedges, grasses, and mosses. The puddles are also home to insects that serve as food for many migratory birds.

It's Been a Long Day

Recall that summer days in the tundra are long. The leaves of tundra plants are adapted to absorb the plentiful sunlight. The leaves are also small and grow low to the ground to help prevent the Sun from drying them out. Hugging the ground helps reduce evaporation. Many tundra plants also have tiny hairs or a waxy covering on their leaves to reduce water loss.

Tundra plants have many adaptations for staying warm. The petals of some flowers direct the Sun's rays inside the flower, keeping the air inside

several degrees warmer than the surrounding air. Tundra plants, such as the cloudberry, grow low to the ground in dense mats. Air pockets between the leaves of these plants heat up like a greenhouse. These hardy plants of the tundra are well adapted to life in their harsh surroundings. ■

UNIT PROJECT LINK

Collect plants from your area and try to include all plant parts—from roots to flowers. Press these plants in a plant press that you build, following your teacher's instructions. Classify and label each plant with its name and traits. Hang the mounted plants in your exhibit.

More than 600 plant species thrive in the tundra by rooting in the thin layer of thawed soil. ▼

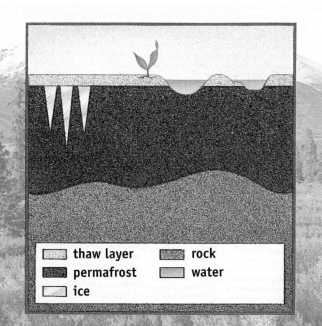

	thaw layer		rock
	permafrost		water
	ice		

Buttercups ▲

Cloudberries ▲

Plants in Peril

SCIENCE TECHNOLOGY & SOCIETY

You enter a time machine and zoom back to 360 million years ago. You find yourself in a forest of giant ferns and horsetails as tall as houses. There isn't a flowering plant anywhere to be seen!

The fern forests of the past are gone forever. Most plants that inhabited that ancient world have become extinct, or died out. These extinct organisms will never return to Earth.

Today many species of wild plants and other organisms are in danger of extinction. An endangered species is one with so few members that it is in danger of becoming extinct. A species that is declining in numbers is considered a threatened species.

Extinction is a natural process that has occurred almost since life began. However, human activity is speeding up the rate of species extinction. Some scientists warn that 680 endangered plants of the United States will be extinct by the year 2000. Worldwide, thousands of species face extinction.

Countdown to Destruction

A major cause of plant extinction is habitat destruction. Sadly, people have caused much of this damage. Each time land is cleared for roads and buildings, natural habitats are destroyed. When wetlands are filled to create more land, habitats are destroyed. More habitats are destroyed when farmers plow under sections of open land.

Extinction is a one-way street. Will these sixteen endangered plants survive? ▼

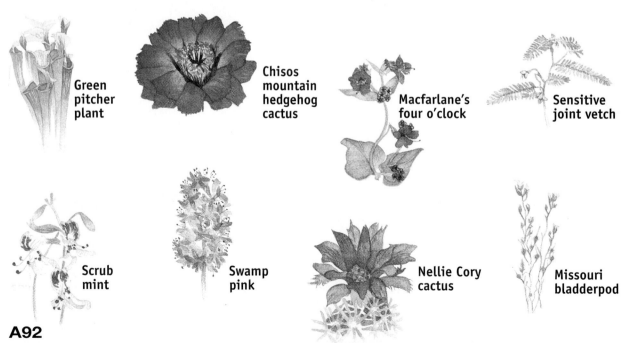

Green pitcher plant

Chisos mountain hedgehog cactus

Macfarlane's four o'clock

Sensitive joint vetch

Scrub mint

Swamp pink

Nellie Cory cactus

Missouri bladderpod

Of all Earth's environments, tropical rain forests are home to the greatest number of species. These forests, located in South America, Africa, and Asia, are disappearing. In 1950, 16 percent of Earth's land was rain forest. Then deforestation (dē fôr is tā'shən), or mass clearing of forest areas, began. By 1975, only 12 percent of Earth's land was rain forest. Scientists predict that only 7 percent of Earth's land will be rain forest by the year 2000. In just 50 years, more than half the world's rain forests will have been destroyed. Many plant species will be lost.

In North America, logging is destroying old forests faster than new trees can replace the old ones. Much of the wood becomes lumber. In some other countries, 50 percent of wood is used for heating and cooking.

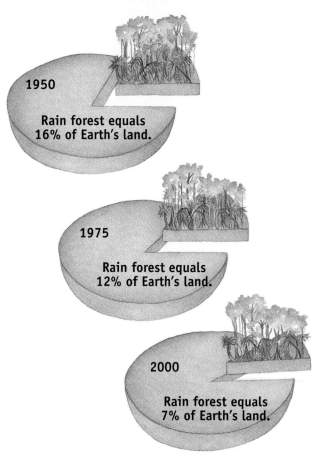

▲ Earth's rain forests are disappearing.

Other Paths to Extinction

Many cactuses and orchids are rare, valuable, and exotic plants. Over-collecting poses a serious threat to these and other species. Daffodils once covered much of Spain and Portugal. When merchants paid high fees for the bulbs, collectors nearly wiped out these plants.

Food production also endangers plants. People who grow food crops often kill native plants in the process.

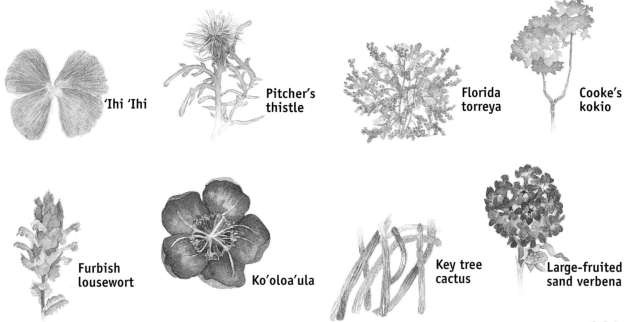

'Ihi 'Ihi

Pitcher's thistle

Florida torreya

Cooke's kokio

Furbish lousewort

Ko'oloa'ula

Key tree cactus

Large-fruited sand verbena

Grazing animals raised for food, such as sheep and cattle, can also destroy plants. These animals often nibble plants down to their roots.

Another danger is industrial pollution. Particles from smoke and exhaust block the stomata in plant leaves. When carbon dioxide and oxygen cannot be exchanged, the plant slowly dies. Rain falling through polluted air can become acidic. In North America and Europe, acid rain is destroying forests and turning lakes into lifeless pools of water. Excess use of fertilizers, insecticides, and other chemicals also harms plants and their habitats.

Saving the Green World

Governments around the world are beginning to take action to keep the world green. Some have passed laws prohibiting the collection or destruction of endangered plants. Laws have also been passed to protect habitats.

Governments alone cannot save endangered species from extinction. Through careful planning, developers can help prevent habitat loss while still providing land for homes and offices. Farmers can use natural enemies to kill insect pests and so reduce the use of insecticides.

People concerned about the environment may also take action to prevent species loss. Each time you recycle paper, you save trees. Each time you leave a flower unpicked, you save a wild plant. Each time you convince a friend to care about wild plants, you help to keep the world green. ■

The burning of rain forests threatens the survival of plants. ▼

INVESTIGATION 2

1. What are some adaptations of plants that enable them to survive in lakes and ponds, in deserts, and in the Arctic tundra?

2. Suggest some things a building developer might do to provide new office space in an area without destroying the habitats of native plant species.

A94

REFLECT & EVALUATE

WORD POWER

adaptation
conifer
dicot
ferns
flowering plants
monocot
mosses
nonseed plants
plant kingdom
seed plants
seed dispersal

On Your Own
Write a definition for each term in the list.

With a Partner
Use the terms listed to make a word-search puzzle. See if your partner can find the hidden terms and tell what each one means.

BUILD YOUR PORTFOLIO
Make a poster that shows the main characteristics of mosses, ferns, conifers, and flowering plants.

Analyze Information
Study the drawings. Explain what adaptations each seed has for dispersal, and then identify the agent of dispersal.

Assess Performance
Using materials such as pipe cleaners, tissue paper, and construction paper, design your own plant. Make adaptations for your plant that will allow it to survive in a desert, a tundra, or a lake. Explain how your plant is adapted to the area you have chosen.

Problem Solving

1. Imagine you have discovered a new kind of plant. Explain how you could use the appearance of the plant's leaves to decide if your plant is a moss, fern, conifer, or flowering plant.

2. Wax repels water. Using this knowledge, explain how a wax covering helps prevent water loss from a leaf. How does a wax covering prevent a water plant from taking in too much water through its leaves?

3. Would you expect a plant living in the Arctic tundra to have smaller, or larger, leaves than a plant living in a deciduous forest? Why?

A95

Throughout this unit you've investigated questions related to plants. How will you use what you've learned and share it with others? Here are some ideas.

Hold a Big Event
to Share Your Unit Project

Help restore native plants to your area. Contact an office of the Nature Conservancy, your state department of environmental conservation, a botanical garden, or a local environmental group. You might even help to change a vacant lot into a natural habitat. Invite students in other classes to join in.

Experiment

Obtain several live plants, both flowering and nonflowering. Carefully break apart each plant to separate its roots, stems, and leaves. Place each kind of plant part in a container of potting soil, labeling the container with the name of the plant and the plant part it contains. Water and observe each container, looking for growth once every week. Record what you observe. Which of the plant parts grew? Which did not? What can you conclude about vegetative propagation, or growing plants without seeds, from your observations?

Research

Since European settlers first came to North America, the landscape has changed greatly. Find out what plants once grew in your area but are no longer found there. Make a list of the plants you learn about. Choose one or two of the plants and create a mural that shows how the land looked when these plants grew in your area. Add to your mural a section that shows how the land has changed and add a caption explaining what caused the plants to disappear. Share your work with your classmates.

THE SOLAR SYSTEM AND BEYOND

Theme: Scale

GET READY TO

OBSERVE & QUESTION

How do the planets differ?

You can see several planets in the night sky with your unaided eyes. What does each planet look like up close? How big is each one compared to Earth? How far away is it? What is it made of? Does it have moons as Earth does—or perhaps even beautiful rings?

EXPERIMENT & HYPOTHESIZE

How do astronomers learn about space?

Astronomers use many different tools to study objects in space. In this unit you'll build your own telescope and observe distant objects through it. You'll also collect space dust, test the effects of weightlessness, and observe different colors that might be found in starlight.

INVESTIGATE!

RESEARCH & ANALYZE

As you investigate, find out more from these books.

- **The Illustrated World of Space** by Iain Nicolson (Simon & Schuster, 1991). From the nearby Moon to distant black holes, this book will tell you what's waiting to be explored in outer space.

The Illustrated World of
SPACE

IAIN NICOLSON

- **Stars, Clusters and Galaxies** by John Gustafson (Julian Messner, 1992). How are stars born? How do they die? How is the universe organized? Find out by reading this book.

- **The Wonderful Flight to the Mushroom Planet** by Eleanor Cameron (Little, Brown and Company, 1988). What would a visit to an alien planet be like? This book presents one possibility.

WORK TOGETHER & SHARE IDEAS

How would you live on board a space station?

Working together, you'll have a chance to apply what you've learned. You'll turn your classroom into a simulated space station and explore what life might be like there in free fall. Look for the Unit Project Links for ideas on how to design your station.

EXPLORING THE NIGHT SKY

In the daytime sky the Moon, when visible, is a pale ghost. Seen on a clear night, it's round and full at times. At other times it's a curved sliver that looks like a comma. And what about the stars? On a dark, clear night you'll see hundreds and hundreds of them twinkling. Many, many objects are visible in the night sky. What could you see with a telescope?

Saving the Planet

From a hill in southern California, Carolyn and Eugene Shoemaker scan the sky with a 46-cm (18-in.) telescope. They search for huge space rocks called asteroids that pass close to Earth. So far they've discovered more than 300. Gene works for the U.S. Geological Survey. Carolyn is an amateur astronomer who has discovered 28 comets.

One night in March 1993, the Shoemakers and David Levy, another comet hunter, spotted a comet. It was on a collision course with the planet Jupiter! The comet contained 21 separate chunks that measured up to 4 km (about 2.5 mi) across. When these slammed into Jupiter, it was the greatest collision ever observed.

You too can explore the night sky. You can study craters on the Moon with binoculars. You may even find a meteorite in your rainwater!

Coming Up

◀ David Levy (*left*) with Carolyn and Eugene Shoemaker (*center and right*)

WHAT CAN YOU SEE IN THE NIGHT SKY?

Star light, star bright,
First star I see tonight,
I wish I may, I wish I might
Have the wish I wish tonight.

Have you ever looked for the "first star" in this nursery rhyme? What do astronomers see when they look at the night sky?

Activity

Constellation in a Can

Individual stars are much easier to identify once you've learned to recognize star patterns called constellations. Learn a few of them now!

MATERIALS

- goggles
- black plastic 35-mm film canister
- tracing paper
- constellation patterns
- scissors
- tape
- pushpin
- *Science Notebook*

SAFETY

Wear goggles when punching holes.

Procedure

1. Place the bottom of a 35-mm film canister on a piece of tracing paper. Trace a circle around the canister.

2. Select one of the constellation patterns your teacher will provide. Then trace that pattern inside the circle you drew on the tracing paper.

Step 1

3. Cut out the circle, leaving about 2.5 cm of paper all the way around it.

4. Place the circle of tracing paper over the outside bottom of the film canister, with the drawing to the inside. Tape the paper to the canister.

5. With a pushpin, punch a small hole through the paper and the canister for each star in the pattern.

6. Hold the film canister up to the light and look through it. Turn the canister counterclockwise and **observe** the constellation pattern inside.

Step 5

7. Trade canisters with your classmates. Try to identify the other students' constellations by comparing what you see inside their canisters to the set of star patterns your teacher gave you.

Analyze and Conclude

1. In your *Science Notebook,* make a list of the patterns that you could identify and another list of the ones you could not.

2. Analyze how turning the canisters affects the way the constellations appear. **Draw** four pictures that show four different views of your own constellation as you turn your canister around.

3. **Hypothesize** why constellations might look different at different times of the night.

INVESTIGATE FURTHER!

RESEARCH

Look at pictures of constellations in an astronomy book. Identify three constellations that match images in the film-canister viewers that you and your classmates made. What person, animal, or object are the constellations named after?

Step 7

Activity
Making a Planisphere

Do the constellations always appear in the same positions in the sky? How can you predict when and where a particular constellation will be visible? Here's one way.

MATERIALS
- scissors
- horizon mask
- star wheel
- paper fastener
- cardboard
- glue
- *Science Notebook*

Procedure

1. Cut along the dashed lines on the horizon mask provided by your teacher. Be sure to cut out the large oval and the small slits.

2. Cut along the outer edge of the star wheel provided by your teacher.

3. With a paper fastener, punch a small hole in the center of the star wheel where the star Polaris is. Then use the fastener to attach the star wheel to the middle of a piece of cardboard, as shown.

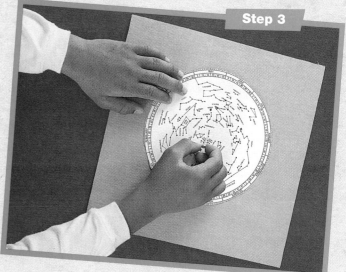

Step 3

4. Attach the corners of the horizon mask to the cardboard with glue, as shown, so that the outer portion of the star wheel is visible around the outer circular edge of the horizon mask. The wheel should turn freely behind the mask.

5. You have now made a planisphere, a map of the sky that can show the positions of the stars at different times. To use it, find the time of year you're interested in on the star wheel. Then turn the wheel until that date lines up with the hour you're interested in on the horizon mask. The stars in the sky at that time will have the same pattern as they do in the oval window of your planisphere.

Step 4

6. Use your planisphere to see how the Big Dipper and the Little Dipper will look at 8:00 P.M. tonight. **Draw** these star patterns in your *Science Notebook* and mark the compass directions to match those on the horizon mask. Label your drawing with today's date and the time 8:00 P.M.

7. **Predict** how the Big Dipper and Little Dipper will look at 11:00 P.M. tonight. Use the planisphere to check your prediction. **Draw** these star groups again with their compass directions, the date, and the new time. How will the two Dippers change during the three hours from 8:00 P.M. to 11:00 P.M.?

8. **Predict** how the Big Dipper and Little Dipper will look at 11:00 P.M. three months from now. Check your prediction. Then **draw** these star groups with their compass directions, the date, and the time. How will the two Dippers change during the next three months?

Analyze and Conclude

1. Based on what you learned in steps 6 and 7, **infer** how the appearance of the Big Dipper and the Little Dipper will change throughout the entire night tonight.

2. Based on what you learned in steps 7 and 8, **infer** how the appearance of the two Dippers would change throughout an entire year if you looked at them at the same time every night.

3. **Hypothesize** what might cause these changes. Do you think the stars are really moving in the way they appear to move in the sky? If not, what else might explain their apparent motion? Do you think the changes you see occurring nightly and the changes you see throughout the year are caused by the same thing? Explain your reasoning.

INVESTIGATE FURTHER!

EXPERIMENT

Go outside on the next clear night. Set your planisphere for the correct date and time. Hold it overhead, with the compass directions oriented correctly. Then identify the brighter constellations in the sky.

B9

Star Patterns in the Sky

Have you ever been out on a clear night and just looked up to see what you could see in the sky? Even if you live in a city with lots of bright lights, you can still spot dozens of stars. If you live in or visit the country, you can see literally thousands of beautiful, sparkling objects in the night sky.

So how do you find your way around that sky? It's easy to learn! In fact, if you've done the activities on pages B6 to B9, you already know a bit about what's up there.

Identifying Groups of Stars

The activities showed you pictures of constellations. A **constellation** (kän stə lā'shən) is a group of stars that forms a pattern in the night sky.

Throughout history, different cultures have identified and named such star patterns. Today's astronomers recognize a total of 88 constellations.

The constellations that can be seen from Earth's Northern Hemisphere received their names from Greek and Roman mythology. Leo, Pisces, and Taurus, for example, were named for a lion, two fish, and a bull. Orion (ō rī'ən) and Cassiopeia (kas ē ō pē'ə) are the names of a hunter and a queen in Greek and Roman myths.

The Southern Hemisphere's constellations probably aren't very familiar to you. These star patterns were named between the 1400s and the 1700s, when explorers from Europe first sailed south of the equator. The constellations they sighted were named for instruments they used and for objects and animals they encountered. Telescopium, for instance, was named for the telescope, and Tucana was named for

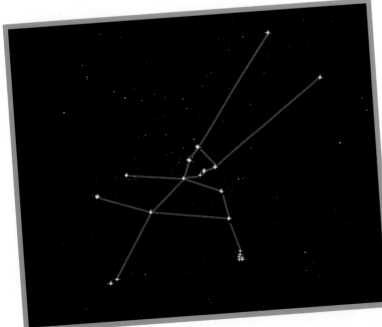

◀ **The constellation Taurus**

the South American bird called a toucan.

When *you* think of constellations, which ones come to mind first? The most recognized star patterns are probably the Big Dipper and the Little Dipper. These two are not really constellations by themselves at all, however, but are portions of two larger constellations. The Big Dipper is part of the constellation called Ursa Major, the Great Bear. The Little Dipper belongs to Ursa Minor, the Little Bear.

There's one important reason why the Big Dipper and the Little Dipper are so well known. It's not just because of their recognizable shapes. What's most important is that these two patterns can always be found in the same area of the northern sky. Polaris, the star at the tip of the Little Dipper's "handle," is known as the North Star because it always lies almost exactly above the North Pole. You'll learn why Polaris does this—and why other stars don't—later on in this investigation.

A Map of the Sky

Today's constellations no doubt started out just as pretty pictures in our ancestors' imaginations—the same way you might imagine you see castles or dragons in puffy clouds during

▲ **The constellation Orion**

the daytime. But constellations also serve an important practical purpose. They provide us with a map of the sky.

Since the sky is so huge, it could get complicated trying to tell someone where to find a certain object in it. But constellations divide the sky up into 88 imaginary sections, just as a map of the United States divides the country into 50 states. Astronomers use constellations to identify the "address" of a particular sky object, just as you use your state to identify where you live. We say that the bright reddish star Betelgeuse (bet'l-jōōz), for example, is located within the constellation Orion.

Now that you have a map, won't it be easier to find your way around the sky? Try it one night and see! ■

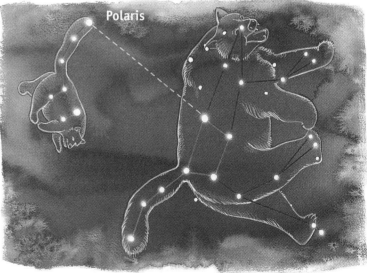

Polaris

▲ **The constellations Ursa Minor and Ursa Major**

Why the Stars Appear to Move

Consider the picture at right. What are all those rings in the photograph? They're the tracks of stars as they move throughout the night!

The tiny arc in the center of the photo is the track of Polaris, the North Star. This object hardly seems to move at all, while most of the other objects in the sky appear to revolve around it. If you point a camera at Polaris and leave the shutter open, you will take a photograph similar to this one.

While you can watch the northern constellations circle Polaris every night, other changes in the sky take place over many months. You simulated both types of changes when you did the planisphere activity on pages B8 and B9.

Orion is a good example of a constellation whose position shifts slowly with the seasons. On a late autumn evening, it can be seen low in the eastern sky. If you look for Orion on future evenings, you'll find that it appears to move higher and higher in the sky, reaching its highest position in mid-December. Then, on

▲ A time-exposure photograph of the northern night sky

winter evenings the constellation is found in the western sky. By early spring, it can only be seen on the western horizon. By late spring, Orion has disappeared altogether for the summer.

Two Kinds of Movement at Once

How can you explain the apparent daily and yearly movements of the constellations? To better understand what you're seeing, try this exercise.

Imagine you're a pitcher on the mound in a baseball game. You wind up and throw a curveball—a ball that spins as it flies through the air. Suppose that a housefly lands on your baseball and hangs onto its stitches as it races toward home plate. What will that insect see as the ball flies through the air?

Let's suppose you released the ball so that it spins from side to side, instead of from top to bottom. As the baseball rotates, the fly will see the player at third base appear to race by several times. But the girl playing third base hasn't really moved. She has only *appeared* to move, from the fly's point of view, because the ball on which the fly sits is spinning.

But the ball isn't just spinning. It's also traveling from the pitcher's mound toward home plate. As it does, the fly's view of the girl at third base changes. At first, the fly sees her from the side. But as the ball nears the plate, the fly is able to see the girl from the front.

The third-base player hasn't really moved. Instead, it's the fly who has moved. And yet, to that insect on the baseball, the girl has appeared to turn toward the fly and move backward, farther and farther away, as the fly's viewing angle and the distance between the ball and third base have changed.

Earth Rotates and Revolves

If you can imagine a fly on a baseball, you can imagine yourself standing on a planet. The planet is Earth, and just like the baseball, it moves in two ways at once.

First, Earth spins. To be more precise, it rotates on its **axis**, an imaginary rod stretching through the planet between the North and South poles. Earth takes 24 hours

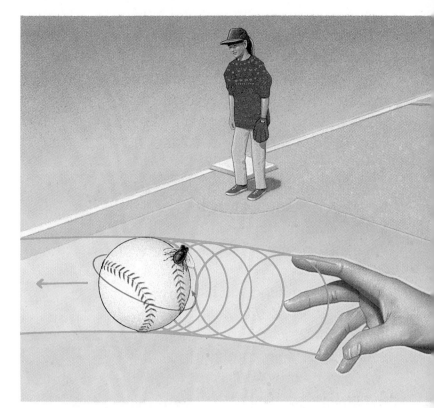

A curveball spinning and moving toward home plate in a baseball game (*above*) may be compared to Earth rotating and revolving in space (*below*).

to turn completely around and finish one **rotation**, even though our planet is spinning at a terrific speed.

Second, as Earth rotates, it also moves from one part of space to another. Rather than following a straight line, Earth follows a roughly circular orbit around the Sun. The distance Earth travels in its orbit is so great that each round trip—one **revolution**—takes about 365 days.

Earth is so huge and its gravity is so strong that you cannot feel the planet rotate or soar through space in its orbit. But evidence for both kinds of motion is all around you.

Earth's rotation, for example, makes the Sun appear to rise in the east and set in the west. When a particular spot on Earth rotates away from the Sun, then it's night for that location.

Earth's revolution around the Sun creates the seasons of the year. Because our planet's axis is tilted, the angle at which the Sun's rays strike Earth and the hours of daylight received by any part of Earth will change according to a regular pattern. We have seasons because different hemispheres tilt toward or away from the Sun at different times of the year.

▲ **Earth's rotation makes the stars appear to circle Polaris.**

The Stars' Apparent Motion

Can you now see why the stars appear to move? Think back to the imaginary fly on the baseball. Remember the third-base player, who seemed to be moving but was actually standing still? The stars are like that, and Earth is like the baseball. It's our planet's rotation that makes the stars appear to move each night from east to west.

(It's worth noting here that the stars are *not* in fact standing completely still. They're just so far away that they'd *seem* to be motionless if Earth itself weren't moving. But that's a story for Chapter 3!)

To us, only the North Star appears almost motionless. That's because Polaris lies directly above the North Pole— the northern tip of Earth's axis. This makes Polaris seem like the center of the sky, with all the other stars revolving around it.

Earth's revolution around the Sun means that different stars appear in the sky at different times of the year. The viewing "window" that we look through—the direction in space that the night side of Earth faces—keeps changing as Earth moves in its orbit. Different constellations wait to greet us as we sail along. ■

The Moving Bears
of the Native Americans

Scientists call it Ursa Major. Most people know it as the Big Dipper. To the Micmac Native Americans of eastern Canada, this pattern of stars is known as the Celestial Bear.

When the Micmacs look at the night sky, they see a bear in the four stars that we think of as the "dipper." Earth's daily rotation and yearly revolution make it appear that the bear is moving. The Micmacs have created a story about why the position of the bear keeps changing.

In early May, they say, the bear climbs out of her "den"—a circle of stars higher up in the sky—and is pursued by seven hunters. The three stars behind her that form the "handle" of the dipper are hunters named Robin, Chickadee, and Moose Bird. Following close by are hunter stars called Pigeon, Blue Jay, Hoot Owl, and Saw-whet.

In midsummer the bear runs across the northern sky trying to get away from her pursuers. In mid-autumn, she "stands up" to defend herself. At this time of year, the four stars near the Big Dipper set below the horizon, so that only three hunters remain to pursue the bear. In late autumn the bear falls on her back and the three hunters catch her. The bear's blood falls to Earth and turns the autumn leaves bright red.

This myth is the Micmacs' way of describing what they observed about the movement of the stars and the changing of the seasons. They created a story about the stars based on activities in their everyday lives. The Micmac story can help you remember how the stars appear to move. ■

The Big Dipper as seen by the Micmacs ▼

Wanderers
in the Night Sky

Other than the Sun and the Moon, most of the objects in the night sky look about the same to the unaided eye. They all seem to be just tiny points of light. Are all of those shiny objects stars? If not, what are they? And how can you tell which ones are which?

You can begin to answer these questions yourself by simply looking a little bit longer and a little more closely at those points of light in the sky. If you do, you'll soon realize that they are *not* all exactly alike.

A Different Sort of "Star"

Have you ever seen the object known as the "morning star"? This appears to be a very bright star that's only visible at certain times on the eastern horizon, just before the Sun rises.

▲ The "morning star"

If you look closely at this object, you'll see that it isn't just bright. The morning star seems to shine with a steady light, while almost all the other "stars" appear to twinkle.

If you observe the morning star through a telescope, it will no longer look like a tiny point of light. Instead you'll see a small round disk. This object, in fact, has phases like the Moon does, so you might see either a fairly full disk or a thin crescent.

If you use a more powerful telescope to observe the morning star, you'll see a larger disk. But no matter how powerful your telescope is, most of the other stars in the sky will still appear to be just tiny points of light.

If you look for the morning star several days in a row, you'll notice something else. It's moving! And it's moving not just *along with* all the other stars, but *in relation to* the other stars, including the Sun.

Over a period of weeks, you'll see the morning star move closer and closer to the Sun until it disappears in the Sun's glare. Then something even more interesting happens. The same object reappears in the west just after sundown as the evening star!

▲ **The Sun, Moon, and planets appear to move in the same narrow band across the sky.**

Of all the starlike objects easily visible to the unaided eye, only five have characteristics similar to those of the morning star—that is, they shine steadily rather than twinkling, appear in a telescope as disks rather than points of light, and move against the backdrop of the other stars.

These five objects have one other thing in common. They are only visible in a particular part of the sky. Although they all move, these strange "stars" appear only in a narrow band that roughly corresponds to the path of the Sun and the Moon across the sky.

The Wandering Planets

The ancient Greeks called these five special objects "wandering stars." In English, we call them *planets*—a name that comes from the Greek word for "wanderer." These five objects—and a few others like them that are not easily seen by the unaided eye—are really in a different class from stars.

A **star** is a huge globe of hot gases that shines by its own light. The Sun is a star similar to the other stars we see at night; it just appears bigger because it's much closer. A **planet**, on the other hand, is a large object that circles a star and does *not* produce light of its own. We can only see planets because they reflect sunlight.

The object we call the morning and evening star is really Venus, one of nine known planets that revolve around our Sun. So far, these nine—including Earth—are the only planets we know of in the universe. Finding such wanderers around another star would be a major discovery! ■

INVESTIGATION 1

1. Name two kinds of celestial objects you might see in a moonless night sky. How could you tell the difference between these objects?

2. Explain why the constellation Leo is visible in the east on a January evening but in the west on a July evening.

HOW DO ASTRONOMERS LEARN ABOUT SPACE?

How can you learn about objects that are as far away as stars and planets? This is a problem that has puzzled scientists for centuries. Two solutions to this problem are to use telescopes and to collect material that has fallen to Earth from space. You can do these things, too!

Activity
Making a Telescopic Camera

Astronomers use many tools to help them study the sky. In this activity you'll build a simple version of one of those tools.

Procedure

1. Hold a lens above a table and directly below a ceiling light. Adjust the lens's height above the table until it forms an image of the ceiling light on the table.

2. **Measure** the distance between the lens and the table. Then cut a cardboard tube so it's about three fourths of this length.

MATERIALS
- lens
- metric ruler
- 2 cardboard tubes
- scissors
- tape
- wax paper
- *Science Notebook*

SAFETY

Never look at the Sun through a magnifying lens. Your eyes could be injured. Do not focus sunlight on anyone or on any flammable object.

Step 1

3. Cut a second cardboard tube of the same length. Then cut this tube lengthwise. Overlap the edges and tape them so that this tube is slightly smaller in diameter than the other tube. This tube should slide smoothly inside the first tube, as shown.

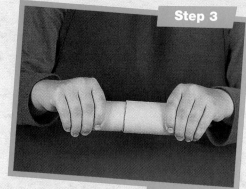

Step 3

4. Using tape, attach the lens to the open end of the larger tube. You may have to make a cardboard ring to hold the lens.

5. Cut a square of wax paper to cover the open end of the smaller tube. Tape the wax paper in place. You have now made a simple type of telescopic camera—a device that projects a magnified image of distant objects onto film (or, in this case, wax paper).

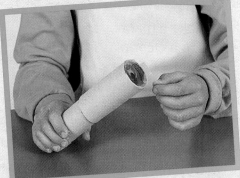

Step 4

6. Aim the lens of your camera toward a bright area—perhaps out a window. Look at the wax paper at the other end of the camera. Slide the tubes until you get a clearly focused image on the wax paper.

Analyze and Conclude

1. **Compare** the image on the wax paper with the real scene. In your *Science Notebook,* make a list of ways in which the image is different from the reality.

2. Astronomers and photographers place film where the wax paper is to create pictures. Make a list of other ways in which your cardboard-tube camera differs from a real camera on a telescope.

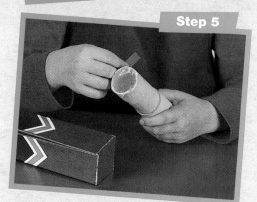

Step 5

3. Is your image on the wax paper brighter than the real object? **Hypothesize** what astronomers might do to make their images of faint stars brighter.

UNIT PROJECT LINK

Astronauts often navigate by identifying stars through the windows of their spacecraft. You can do the same thing by creating a navigation pod for your space-station simulator. Draw windows for your station on large sheets of paper. Within the windows, draw the stars of several constellations that are near each other in the sky. Then use your telescopic camera to take sightings on particular stars.

Activity
Mining for Meteorites

Have you ever seen a "falling star"? Do you know what one looks like up close? Find out!

Procedure

1. Take a magnet and place it inside a clear plastic bag. Then run the covered magnet through the rainwater your teacher has collected.

Step 1

2. Use a hand lens to look carefully at the outside of the bag. If you find any small round balls there, use a tongue depressor to scrape them onto a microscope slide.

3. **Observe** the objects through a microscope. If they still look like round spheres, what you probably have are meteorites— pieces of space dust that came to Earth as "falling stars"!

Analyze and Conclude

1. Infer what material your meteorites are made of. What part of the activity provided you with this information?

2. Hypothesize what might cause most meteorites to be rounded in shape.

3. Hypothesize how small meteorites could wind up in rainwater. In your *Science Notebook*, **draw** a picture of Earth that shows where you think your meteorites were before they fell to the ground during a rain shower.

Step 2

Telescopes:
How They Work

Imagine that you're living hundreds of years ago. All that you know about the stars and planets is based on what you can see with your unaided eyes. But you've just learned about a new device called a telescope—a viewing instrument that can magnify distant objects. After focusing this device on faraway buildings, mountains, and sailing ships, you think it might be interesting to look through it at the sky.

So you aim your telescope at the speck of light called Jupiter. Until now, Jupiter just looked to you like a very bright star. But what you see today astonishes you! Instead of appearing as a tiny point of light, Jupiter can now be clearly seen as a round disk. Not only that, but four smaller points of light—previously invisible to you—can now be seen close to Jupiter. As you watch through the telescope each night, it becomes obvious that the four smaller objects are moons that circle Jupiter, just as our own Moon orbits Earth. What an amazing discovery!

The person who actually made this discovery, in the seventeenth century, was the great Italian scientist Galileo Galilei. What he found revolutionized people's views of the universe. He made his observations using one of the most useful devices ever developed by human beings—the telescope.

The two main types of telescopes are pictured on the next page. A **refracting** (ri frakt'iŋ) **telescope** looks like a long, narrow tube, such as a sea captain might use. You look directly through the tube. Light from a distant object is focused by a large lens and then magnified by a smaller lens before it reaches your eye.

  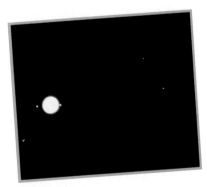

▲ Galileo discovered four moons of Jupiter by viewing scenes like these through his telescope.

A refracting telescope ▼

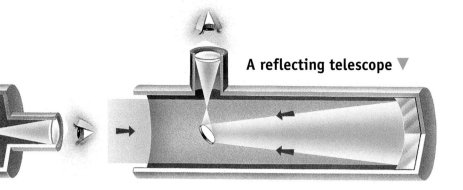

A reflecting telescope ▼

The camera you made in the activity on pages B18 and B19 used a simple single-lens refracting system.

A **reflecting telescope** gathers light in a curved mirror at the back of its tube. It then reflects and focuses the light on a smaller mirror near the front. The small mirror is often angled to send the image out through an eyepiece on the side of the tube. The eyepiece contains lenses that can usually be changed to give you different magnifications.

The largest telescopes in the world are reflectors, because it's easier to build large mirrors than large lenses. A mirror has only one surface that must be precisely made. A lens must be shaped per-fectly from top to bottom! Since a mirror reflects light, a mirror's bottom surface can rest on a supporting structure. Light must pass through a lens, so a lens has to be supported around the edge. The nation's largest reflecting telescope, at Mount Palomar, California, has a 5-m (200-in.) mirror. By comparison, the lens of the world's largest refractor, at Yerkes Observatory in Wisconsin, is only about 1 m (39 in.) in diameter.

Wonders in the Heavens

No one is sure who made the first tele-scope, although many historians believe it was a Dutch spectacle-maker named Hans Lippershey. Whoever was respon-

The observatory at Mount Palomar, California ▶

▲ **The Hubble Space Telescope, about to be released from an orbiting space shuttle**

sible, the Dutch had learned by the early 1600s how to line up two curved lenses in a tube and look through them to make faraway objects appear closer.

As soon as Galileo heard about the Dutch invention, he immediately set out to make his own telescope. Soon he built another, and then another, each one more refined and more powerful than the last. Then he did something no one else had ever done. He took his most powerful telescope outside and looked up.

Galileo's telescope could bring the heavens only 30 times closer, yet what he saw astounded him! The Moon became an alien wonderland covered by deep craters and towering mountains. And there were many more stars than he had ever imagined, some gleaming with newly visible colors.

Called "Galileo's ladder" for many years, the telescope was soon improved. An important advance came from the English scientist Sir Isaac Newton. The simple lenses of his day distorted color, but a mirror did not. So he designed a reflecting telescope that would collect light in a mirror before passing it through a lens.

Since Newton's time, astronomers have learned new ways to use telescopes to see things the human eye cannot see. For example, by attaching a camera to a telescope's eyepiece and exposing the film for long periods of time, astronomers can capture pictures of very faint objects that would not otherwise be visible.

Putting Telescopes in Space

Today we even have large telescopes in orbit around Earth. The Hubble Space Telescope is positioned beyond our planet's atmosphere, so it does not have to deal with distortions caused by looking through the air. It can see more clearly and see objects that are fainter and farther away than telescopes on the ground can see. Space telescopes can even see in wavelengths of light that aren't visible from Earth's surface.

Imagine what you might discover if you could use the Hubble telescope to see seven times farther into space than humans have ever seen before! ■

Meteorite
Messengers

Pretend that you're a giant. Build yourself a huge snowball, about 5 km (3 mi) wide. Stuff some dirt and rocks in with the snow. Let the whole thing freeze rock-hard. Then send it hurtling through space at about 250,000 km/h (155,000 mph).

Aim your snowball so that it will swing in toward the Sun, go completely around it, and then head back out into the most remote regions of the solar system before it returns. The snowball's path should look like a long, thin oval.

Congratulations! You have now created your own **comet** and launched it into an elliptical (e lip'ti kəl) orbit around the Sun.

Snowballs That Melt in the Sun

A comet can look like a ball of fire. Yet real comets begin just as your imaginary one did, as giant chunks of ice. At the core, comets are mostly frozen water, ammonia, and methane, mixed with enough dust and debris to create what you might call a "dirty snowball."

Each comet spends most of its lifetime drifting through the cold outer reaches of the solar system. But when its orbit brings it in closer to the Sun, that's when the show begins!

Because the main body of a comet is made of frozen material, it is doomed to slow destruction by the Sun's heat. Yet the "fire" you see is really not fire at all. Instead, as the comet approaches the Sun, its body begins to melt, releasing its frozen gases into space. These gases spread out to form a huge misty head around the comet's front end.

A comet's tail is made of gases and grains of dust—the "dirt" streaming off the dirty snowball. A stream of charged particles given off by the Sun, called the

◄ Halley's comet—shown at the top of this page as a telescope on Earth would see it—follows an orbit similar to this one.

solar wind, causes a comet's tail to point away from the Sun, no matter in which direction the comet is moving.

Some comets with very long orbits have only appeared once during recorded history. Others have reappeared regularly many times. The most famous one, Halley's comet, revolves around the Sun once every 76 years.

Comets: The Meteor Makers

Throughout history, millions of tiny chunks of comets have broken off and been captured by Earth's gravity. These dust particles then speed into our atmosphere and burn up there as "shooting stars," or **meteors**.

Most meteors don't survive to reach the ground. Only rarely does one land

▲ **A close-up of the head of Halley's comet, photographed by a passing space probe**

that's large enough to do any damage. If a meteor does fall to Earth, the remaining material is called a **meteorite** (mē′tē ər īt). Not all meteors come from comets, but comets do appear to cause many large meteor showers.

SCIENCE IN LITERATURE

The Illustrated World of
SPACE

IAIN NICOLSON

THE ILLUSTRATED WORLD OF SPACE
by Iain Nicolson
Simon & Schuster Books for Young Readers,
1991

How will the Big Dipper look 100,000 years from now? What does it mean when a star winks? How bright would the Sun appear if you could see it from Pluto? You can look up the answers to these space questions, and more of your own, in *The Illustrated World of Space* by Iain Nicolson.

To find out more about how meteorites and comets are related to the beginning of our solar system, read pages 28–29 in *The Illustrated World of Space*. What role might ancient "dirty snowballs" have played in forming the planets?

▲ **Barringer meteor crater in Arizona**

Collisions between comets and planets are rare—but when they do occur, the results can be spectacular! You may have seen pictures of such an event that took place in 1994, when a comet called Shoemaker–Levy 9 struck the planet Jupiter.

Some scientists hypothesize that Earth's dinosaurs became extinct because a comet struck our planet in prehistoric times. But the chances of something like that happening today are very, very small. Most brushes with comets have good results. They help scientists get their hands on material from space in the form of meteorites.

Meteorites can be made of either metal or rock. The tiniest ones—like those in the activity on page B20—are so light that they often remain sus-

pended in the atmosphere until a rain shower brings them to Earth.

Astronomers think that material from comets may date back more than 4 billion years, to the time of Earth's beginnings. By studying meteorites, scientists can learn about both comets and the origins of the solar system. ■

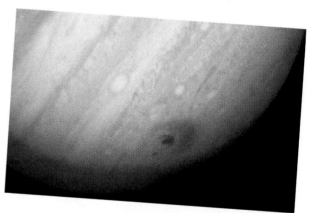

▲ **One of the impact sites of Comet Shoemaker–Levy 9 on the planet Jupiter**

INVESTIGATION 2

THINK IT WRITE IT

1. Describe how a comet can produce material that scientists collect and study on Earth.

2. Suppose you could build a telescope anywhere on Earth. Where would you build it, and what kind of telescope would it be? Explain the reasons for your choices.

REFLECT & EVALUATE

WORD POWER

axis
comet
constellation
meteorite
meteor
planet
reflecting telescope
refracting telescope
revolution
rotation
star

On Your Own
Write a definition for each term in the list.

 With a Partner
Mix up the letters of each term in the list. Provide a clue for each term and challenge your partner to unscramble the terms.

BUILD YOUR PORTFOLIO

Make a poster that shows what your favorite constellation looks like. Beside your drawing, write a short story that explains how the constellation got its name.

Analyze Information

Copy this drawing of the Little Dipper as it appears at 7:00 P.M. in the February sky. Then redraw the picture to show how it will appear at 1:00 A.M. the same night. Label Polaris in each drawing and add an arrow to show the direction in which the constellation appears to be moving. Explain why the constellation appears to move.

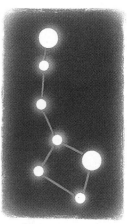

Assess Performance

Make a model to show Earth's rotation and revolution. Use two balls of different sizes and any other materials you wish. Use your model to show how Earth's motions make the stars appear to move during the night and throughout the year.

Problem Solving

1. Use what you have learned about the apparent motion of the stars to explain how stars might be used as a navigational tool.

2. You see an object in the night sky. To your unaided eye, it looks like a bright point of light. How would you go about identifying this object?

3. Suppose you want to learn all you can about a particular comet. Describe the different tools and methods you might use to study this object.

CHAPTER 2

THE SOLAR SYSTEM

Venus is called both the morning star and the evening star. It's the brightest of all the planets, and it's the closest planet to Earth. But Venus is shrouded in clouds, and its surface was a mystery until recently.

● ●

Visiting Our Next-door Neighbor

The Magellan spacecraft was launched from the space shuttle *Atlantis* in May 1989. Sixteen months later it reached Venus and began using radar to create pictures of the planet's surface and send them back to Earth. An international group of scientists gathered at NASA's Jet Propulsion Laboratory to process the billions of pieces of electronic data received from Magellan. The result was a startlingly clear picture of the planet's surface.

Hundreds of scientists and engineers worked on the Magellan project for 20 years. They gave us the first good look at our "sister" planet. Since Venus is similar to Earth in size and density, we increase our knowledge of Earth's development by visiting this unusual neighbor. How else do we learn about our solar system?

Coming Up

◀ Magellan scientists use special
glasses to view three-dimensional
pictures of Venus's surface.

WHAT IS THE SOLAR SYSTEM MADE OF?

Our solar system's diameter is about 11.6 billion km. You can't picture that? Start walking at a rate of 5 km/h. Don't stop! You will walk a distance equal to the solar system's diameter in about 275,000 years. Now learn about the objects that make up our solar system and how they came to be.

Activity

When to Go Planet Watching

You've learned that the planets in our solar system seem to move across a narrow band in the sky. In this activity you'll discover how the planet Mars really moves in space—and how that motion affects how Mars looks in Earth's night sky.

MATERIALS

- small objects to use as planet models
- pencils or pens of different colors
- metric ruler
- *Science Notebook*

Step 1

Procedure

1. **Make a drawing** in your *Science Notebook* like the one on this page. Your drawing should show the Sun, Earth's orbit around the Sun, and the larger orbit of the planet Mars around the Sun.

2. Choose two different small objects to represent the planets Earth and Mars. Place each object on top of your drawing at any location along its planet's orbit.

3. Use another color pencil or pen to **draw** a circle underneath each object and show its position in your drawing. Label the two circles *Earth* and *Mars*.

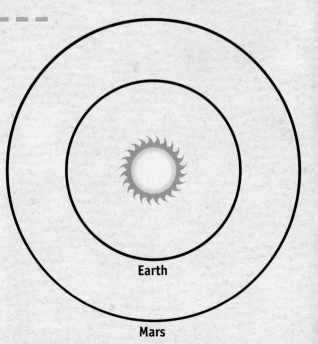

Earth

Mars

4. With a ruler, **measure** how far apart the two planets are in your drawing. **Record** that measurement.

5. Move both planet models along their orbits until you have them as close together as you can. **Draw** these positions, using a third color. Then **measure** and **record** the new distance between the two objects.

6. Move both planet models along their orbits until you have them as far apart as you can. **Draw** these positions, using a fourth color. **Measure** and **record** the distance between the objects.

Analyze and Conclude

1. Look at the locations of the Sun, Earth, and Mars when Mars is as close to Earth as it can be. **Predict** what time of day you'd look for Mars in Earth's sky when the real planets are positioned this way. Would Mars be visible from the daytime or nighttime side of Earth?

2. Look at the locations of the Sun, Earth, and Mars when Mars is as far from Earth as it can be. **Predict** what time of day you'd have to look for Mars when the real planets are positioned this way. Would the daytime or nighttime side of Earth be facing Mars? Where would Mars appear to be in Earth's sky in relation to the Sun? Would you be able to see Mars from Earth at this time?

3. Look at the first positions you chose for the Earth and Mars objects. **Predict** whether you'd be able to see Mars from Earth if the planets were positioned in this way.

INVESTIGATE FURTHER!

RESEARCH

For planets such as Mars that are farther from the Sun than Earth is, the point of closest approach to Earth is called opposition. At this time the planet is at its brightest. Call a planetarium to find out when each planet is at opposition. Plan one or more outdoor sessions to observe the planets in the nighttime sky.

Step 4

Activity
Comparing Planetary Distances

How far from Earth and from the Sun are the other eight planets? How can you better understand such large distances in the solar system? Here's one way to do it.

MATERIALS
- 400-sheet roll of toilet paper
- *Science Notebook*

Step 3

Procedure

1. To create a model of planetary distances, go with nine other students to a long hallway, a gym, or an outdoor playground on a dry, still day. Choose one student to represent the Sun and have each of the others represent one of the nine planets.

2. Have the Sun student sit on the ground with one hand holding down the end of a roll of toilet paper.

3. Have the planet students unroll the toilet paper and count the tissue sheets, until each student comes to the sheet number that's listed on the table for his or her planet. At that point the student should sit beside the line of unrolled paper with a hand on the sheet representing his or her planet's average distance from the Sun.

Planet	Sheet Number
Mercury	3
Venus	between 5 and 6
Earth	between 7 and 8
Mars	between 11 and 12
Jupiter	40
Saturn	74
Uranus	149
Neptune	233
Pluto	305

4. Back in the classroom, **calculate** the shortest distance between each two neighboring planets in terms of toilet paper sheets. To get the distance between Mercury and Venus, subtract Mercury's sheet number from Venus's sheet number. (When the table says Venus is between sheets 5 and 6, count that as sheet $5\frac{1}{2}$.) Do the same calculations for the distance between Venus and Earth, between Earth and Mars, and so on. **Record** the answers in your *Science Notebook*.

5. **Calculate** and **record** the distance in sheets between each planet and Earth, at the time when each planet is closest to Earth.

Analyze and Conclude

1. **Compare** the distances between neighboring planets. Which two are closest together? Which two are farthest apart? As a group, which set of planets is closest together— those nearest the Sun or those farther out?

2. With other students, **hypothesize** about the effects of a planet's distance from the Sun. Which planets would be hottest? Which would be coldest? What would the Sun look like from each one? How long would a year be on each planet? **Compare** your ideas with those of your classmates.

3. Suppose you want to send a radio signal from Earth to each of the other planets, at the time when each planet is closest to Earth. Which planet would receive a signal fastest? Which would take the longest to get a signal? Use the results of step 5 to make a list of the planets according to their distance from Earth.

UNIT PROJECT LINK

Future trips to other planets may begin from an Earth-orbiting space station. Create a docking port for your simulated space station. Begin to collect information so that you can decorate the docking port area with travel posters of different planets and moons. Which ones would you and your classmates like to visit most?

Earth's Neighborhood:
The Solar System

Do you remember how the resource on star patterns on pages B10 and B11 compared each constellation to the state in an address? If you continued this comparison, you might call a solar system a neighborhood.

A **solar system** consists of a star and the objects that revolve around it. A model of our own solar system—the only one we've been able to detect so far—is shown here. In addition to the Sun itself, our solar system includes nine known planets, the moons that orbit those planets, and many smaller objects such as comets and the small rocky bodies known as asteroids. The four inner planets and five outer planets are separated by a belt of asteroids that orbit the Sun.

When you did the activity on pages B32 and B33, you learned how large the distances are between planets. The planets themselves are tiny compared to those distances. The objects in this model are shown much larger than they should be, compared to the size of their orbits, so that they can be seen better. ■

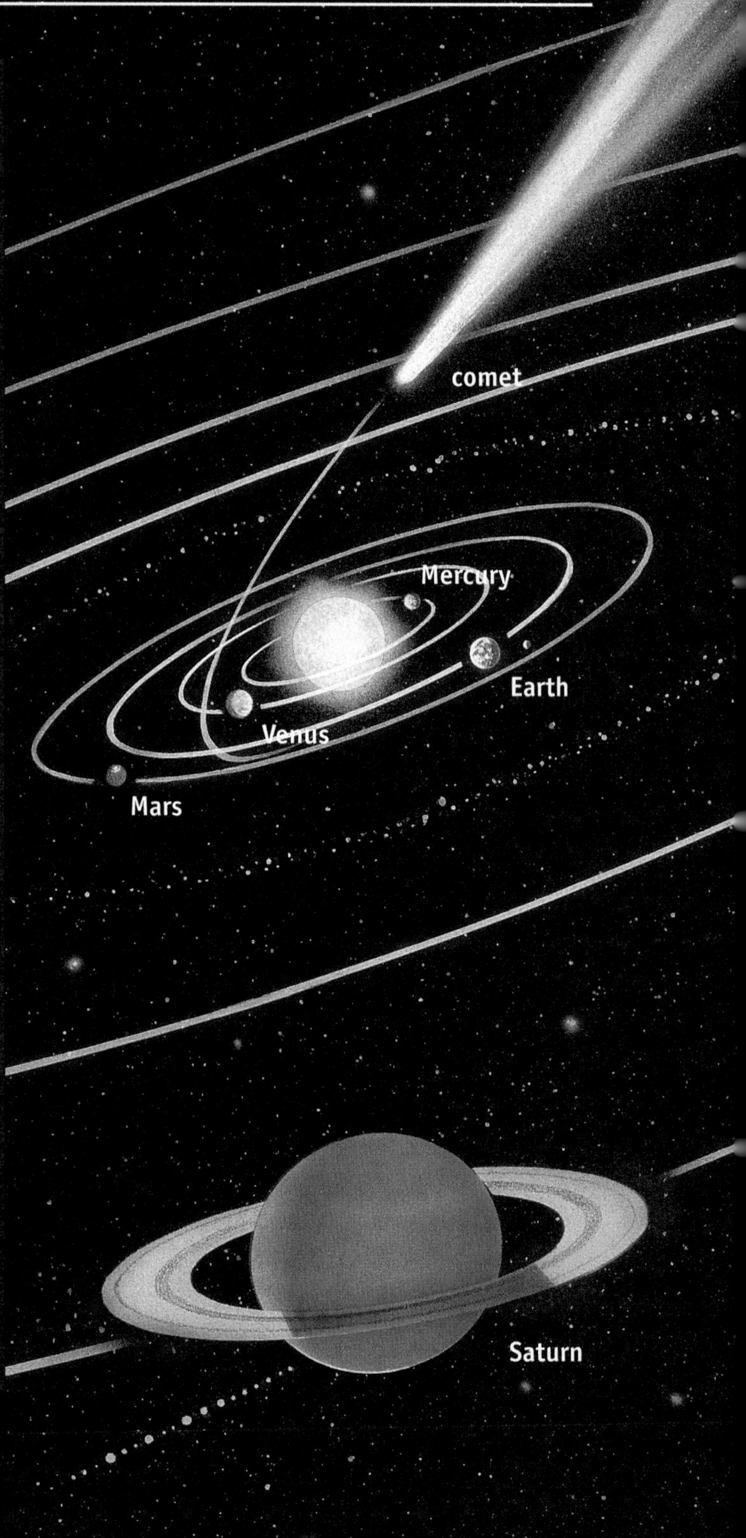

comet

Mercury

Earth

Venus

Mars

Saturn

Neptune

Pluto

Uranus

asteroid belt

Jupiter

Planet	Average Distance From the Sun (in millions of km)	Period of Revolution (in Earth years)	Number of Known Moons
Mercury	58	0.24	0
Venus	108	0.62	0
Earth	150	1.00	1
Mars	228	1.88	2
Jupiter	778	11.86	16
Saturn	1,429	29.46	18
Uranus	2,875	84.01	15
Neptune	4,504	164.79	8
Pluto	5,900	248.60	1

Ptolemy
Was Right–and Wrong!

TIME Capsule

"Pygmies placed on the shoulders of giants see more than the giants themselves." It may seem to you that this saying has little to do with science. But consider how it applies to two giants in the world of astronomy. One of these men was totally wrong about a major principle, yet his work prepared the way for later astronomers to arrive at a better understanding of the universe.

That man's name was Ptolemy, and he lived in Egypt in the second century A.D. Ptolemy tried to understand why the planets seem to wander across the sky. After charting their movements, he worked out a model that seemed to explain what he was seeing.

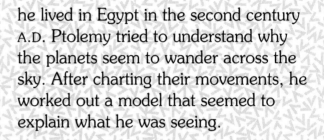

The Maya in Central America use astronomical observations to create the most accurate calendar in the world. **300**

Greek philosopher Aristarchus proposes that Earth and the other planets are spheres that revolve around the Sun.

260 B.C.

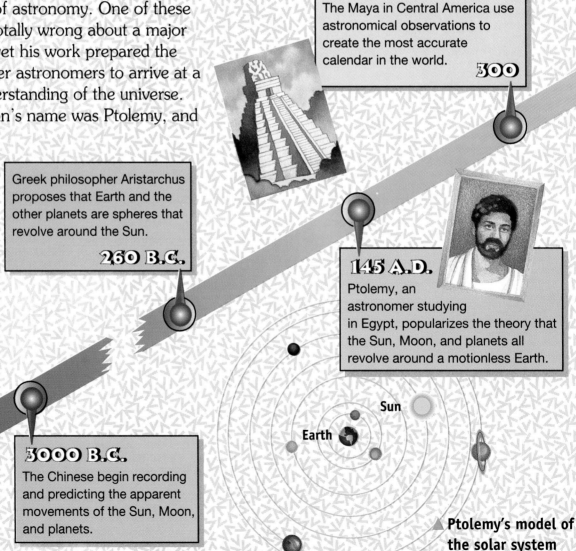

145 A.D.
Ptolemy, an astronomer studying in Egypt, popularizes the theory that the Sun, Moon, and planets all revolve around a motionless Earth.

3000 B.C.
The Chinese begin recording and predicting the apparent movements of the Sun, Moon, and planets.

Sun

Earth

▲ **Ptolemy's model of the solar system**

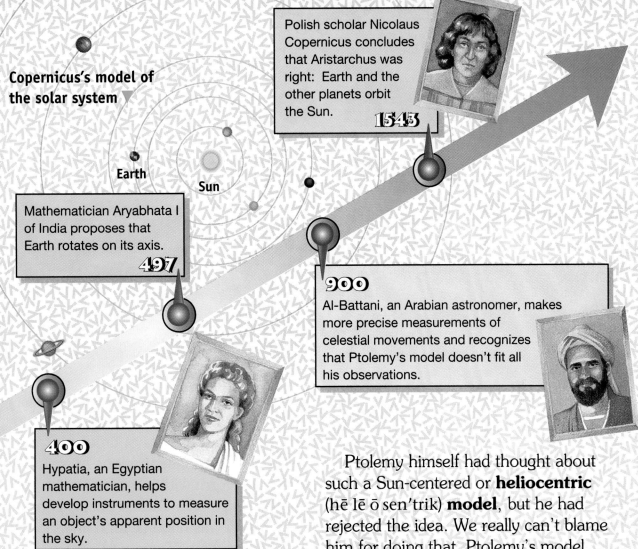

Copernicus's model of the solar system ▼

Earth

Sun

Polish scholar Nicolaus Copernicus concludes that Aristarchus was right: Earth and the other planets orbit the Sun.
1543

Mathematician Aryabhata I of India proposes that Earth rotates on its axis.
497

900
Al-Battani, an Arabian astronomer, makes more precise measurements of celestial movements and recognizes that Ptolemy's model doesn't fit all his observations.

400
Hypatia, an Egyptian mathematician, helps develop instruments to measure an object's apparent position in the sky.

Ptolemy's model was an Earth-centered or **geocentric** (jē ō sen'trik) **model**. To him that seemed perfectly logical, since Earth appeared to Ptolemy to be steady and unmoving. To explain the motions of the Sun, Moon, and planets, he reasoned that they all must revolve around Earth.

Ptolemy's model was used for more than a thousand years. But in 1543 a Polish clergyman named Nicolaus Copernicus put forth a different idea. Copernicus positioned the Sun at the center of the universe and suggested that all the planets, including Earth, revolve around it.

Ptolemy himself had thought about such a Sun-centered or **heliocentric** (hē lē ō sen'trik) **model**, but he had rejected the idea. We really can't blame him for doing that. Ptolemy's model explained the solar system based on the best data available to him at the time. It's a basic principle in science that you can't get the right answer if you don't have all the necessary information. But you can't always wait for everything to be discovered before you try to use what you know, either.

That's where "standing on the shoulders of giants" comes in. When Copernicus came along, he had a head start because he was able to build on Ptolemy's work. By adding his own observations to Ptolemy's, Copernicus could create a more accurate hypothesis that would form the basis for all of modern astronomy. ■

Birth of the Solar System

▲ **The Big Bang Theory**

Where did the solar system come from? This is one of the biggest questions that human beings have ever asked. The answer may never be completely discovered or proved to everyone's satisfaction. But based on all the evidence people have uncovered over the centuries, here is what most scientists consider the best explanation so far.

The Big Bang

All the matter and all the energy that have *ever* existed or will *ever* exist in the universe were once concentrated in an incredibly tiny, extremely hot, unbelievably dense ball. In this case, the word *dense* means very closely packed.

Then all at once, at least 10 billion years ago, this churning ball of matter and energy exploded. The explosion sent a vast cloud of matter swirling out in all directions into space.

Time passed—*lots* of time. As it did, little by little, concentrations of matter began to form within the massive, expanding cloud. Each separate concentration was huge beyond anything we can imagine. Together they must have been millions of times bigger than Earth and all the planets combined, to have contained enough material to condense into all the objects that now exist.

But condense they did, thanks to the force of gravity. Very slowly, each individual clump of material began to contract. Different clumps joined together, forming bigger clumps. And as these clumps contracted, they began to spin. At the same time, each clump continued to move outward, away from all other clumps.

These huge spinning concentrations of matter would eventually become galaxies—the giant clusters of stars that you'll learn more about in Chapter 3.

The Sun and Planets Form

More time went by—more billions of years. Then, within one of the galaxies, one particular collection of matter began to condense. This was an event of special importance to us, for this material would eventually form our solar system!

As this cloud of matter rotated and flattened, most of the material collected in the center, where it would become our Sun. At the same time, in the swirling clouds surrounding this future Sun, separate eddies or "whirlpools" also began condensing to form the different planets, including Earth. By about 4.6 billion years ago, the major objects in our solar system were finally in place.

What was happening in our own neighborhood was just one tiny chapter in a much larger story. For throughout the billions of kilometers of emptiness that make up outer space, other concentrations of matter were also condensing to form other galaxies, other stars, and even—scientists think—other planets around those stars.

How Do We Know It's All True?

The story you've just read is commonly known as the **Big Bang Theory** of the origin of the universe. How do scientists know it all happened this way? Well, they don't, not for certain. But the evidence continues to mount as we gather more and more data about the universe. Piecing together the cosmic puzzle of our origins is the biggest job ever—and maybe, someday, you can help solve the puzzle! ■

▲ **Three stages in the formation of the solar system**

INVESTIGATE FURTHER!

RESEARCH

Find out about different theories regarding the origins of particular objects in the solar system. Go to the library and look up some of these subjects in a recent encyclopedia or astronomy book: the Moon, the satellites of Mars, the asteroid belt, Saturn's rings, Pluto, comets.

Trajectory to the Planets

SCIENCE
TECHNOLOGY
& SOCIETY

Distances between the planets are *huge!* Remember that figure at the beginning of this investigation—the one that said the solar system is more than 11 billion km (7 billion mi) wide? Well, it would take more than a decade for even our fastest space probe to travel that far.

Furthermore, a spacecraft doesn't travel in a straight line from Earth to another planet. It begins by traveling along with planet Earth in orbit around the Sun. As the space probe passes planets, their gravity causes its path to curve. This curved course is called a trajectory (trə jek'tə rē).

Remember, both Earth and the spacecraft's target planet are constantly moving. To calculate a craft's trajectory, its builders must use powerful computers that take into account the different bodies' movements, their gravity, and all the other factors that might influence the spacecraft's course. The probe must be aimed at the point in space where its moving target will be *when the probe gets there*.

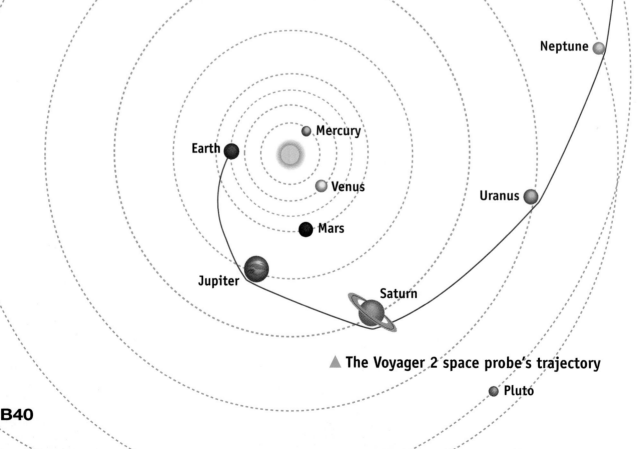

▲ The Voyager 2 space probe's trajectory

A spacecraft carries fuel that can be used to make small changes in its course. But major changes in direction use up a lot of fuel. Often, mission planners use a technique called a gravity assist. In such a maneuver, a probe uses the gravitational pull of a planet to change its direction and even its speed. Instead of using up its own fuel, when the spacecraft passes near a planet, it lets the gravity of that body fling it in a new direction. By coming up "behind" a moving planet and letting the planet's gravity pull it along, a probe can wind up leaving the planet's neighborhood with more speed than it had coming in.

Perhaps the best example of a spacecraft using this "slingshot" technique was a probe that was launched by the United States in 1977, Voyager 2. As it left Earth, Voyager 2 was traveling at about 40,000 km/h (25,000 mph). Because its targets, the four giant outer planets, happened to be lined up in just the right way, Voyager 2 was able to visit Jupiter, Saturn, Uranus, and Neptune in turn. At each planet the spacecraft was tar-

▲ **Voyager 2 at Jupiter**

geted to receive a gravity assist that would send it on to the next planet.

By the time Voyager 2 completed its "grand tour" in 1989, it had attained a speed of about 97,000 km/h (60,000 mph)—making it the fastest object ever built by human beings to date! ■

INVESTIGATION 1

1. Name five kinds of objects that exist in our solar system. Explain where each kind may be found in relation to one of the other kinds.

2. Explain why we never see the planet Venus in the sky at midnight.

INVESTIGATION 2

HOW DO THE PLANETS DIFFER?

My Very Elegant Mother Just Served Us Nine Pickles.
This sentence is a tool that will help you remember the names of the planets in order of their distance from the Sun. Each word's first letter is the first letter of a planet. Now learn what distance from the Sun has to do with the characteristics of each planet.

Activity

Measuring Planet Sizes

Which planets are the biggest? Which are the smallest? How large is the difference between them? Find out!

MATERIALS
- sheet of paper
- *Science Notebook*

Step 2

Procedure

1. Make an Earth ruler like the one pictured on the facing page. Place the edge of a sheet of paper just below the picture. **Draw** lines on the paper's edge at exactly the same places as the lines in the picture. Number the spaces on your ruler as shown.

Pluto   Neptune   Uranus   Saturn

2. Place your Earth ruler over the picture of each planet on these two pages. Use the ruler to **measure** the distance across the middle of each planet in terms of Earth diameters. **Record** each measurement in your *Science Notebook*.

3. Make a list of the planets that ranks them from smallest to largest.

4. **Make a bar graph** showing the diameters of the nine planets. List the planets' names on one side of the graph and the number of Earth diameters on the other.

Analyze and Conclude

1. With a group of classmates, **hypothesize** about the differences between the larger planets and the smaller ones. For example, how strong might each planet's gravity be compared to Earth's gravity? Do you think each planet could hold onto an atmosphere? **Discuss** and **compare** your ideas.

2. Imagine that you lived on a moon around each planet in turn. Assume that each moon is about the same distance from its planet as Earth's Moon is from Earth. **Predict** how big each planet would look in the sky from its moon. About how much of the sky would each of the planets fill up?

3. **Compare** the pictures of large planets with those of small planets. Besides size, what differences do you observe? Make a list of those differences.

INVESTIGATE FURTHER!

RESEARCH

Look at the order of the planets. Are the biggest planets close to the Sun or far away? Can you hypothesize why those giant planets are located where they are? Look in an astronomy book that tells about the origins of the solar system to find out scientists' theories about this.

EARTH RULER

(Earth diameters)

| 1 | 2 | 3 | 4 | 5 | 6 | 7 | 8 | 9 | 10 | 11 | 12 | 13 | 14 | 15 | 16 | 17 | 18 | 19 | 20 |

Jupiter

Mars   Earth   Venus   Mercury   Sun

The Inner Planets

The inner planets are Mercury, Venus, Earth, and Mars. These four have something else in common besides being close to the Sun. They all resemble Earth in size, in density, and in their mainly rocky composition. Because of this, they are known as **terrestrial** (tə res'trē əl) **planets**, meaning those that are Earth-like.

Two of the inner planets and all of the outer ones have satellites. Astronomers use the terms **moon** and **satellite** interchangeably when they refer to natural objects that revolve around a planet. (The word *satellite* can also mean an orbiting object built by humans.) Now let's look at each of the inner planets. ■

☿ MERCURY

MERCURY is the closest planet to the Sun and the second smallest of the nine planets. It looks a lot like Earth's Moon, with a rocky surface covered by craters. Mercury has almost no atmosphere, just faint traces of helium and one or two other gases that it probably "captured" from the Sun. Surface temperatures on Mercury get hot enough to melt lead. This speedy planet takes just three months (measured in Earth time) to revolve around the Sun.

♀ VENUS

VENUS is the second planet from the Sun. Although it's named after the Roman goddess of beauty, it's not a very pleasant place. The Venusian (vi nōō'-shən) atmosphere consists mainly of carbon dioxide with sulfuric acid clouds. It's so dense that the atmospheric pressure on the planet's surface is tremendous. Temperatures there reach about 500°C (900°F).

Venus's clouds appear featureless in normal light, but certain cameras reveal swirling patterns (above right). Radar provided this computer-generated view of the surface (right). ▶

⊕ EARTH

EARTH is the only planet in the solar system on which life is known to exist. It's the third planet from the Sun and the largest of the four inner planets. Earth has a vast core of molten metal and rock, with a thin crust of solid rock. Our planet's atmosphere is about 78 percent nitrogen and 21 percent oxygen, plus traces of other gases. As seen from space, Earth is one of the most beautiful planets, with bright blues indicating the abundant water and swirling whites, its scattered clouds.

▲ **The Moon** is Earth's only natural satellite. A rocky, cratered body with no atmosphere, it's one of the largest satellites in the solar system.

▲ **The features on Venus** range from smooth plains to volcanic mountain ranges. A computer created this false-color ground view from radar data.

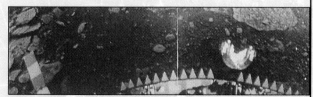

▲ **Venus's surface** was photographed by a Russian probe that landed on the planet but survived only a few minutes in its harsh conditions.

♂ MARS

MARS, the fourth planet from the Sun, resembles Earth more than any other planet. Mars is smaller and less dense than Earth, which gives it less gravity and a thinner atmosphere. But the Martian day is only 41 minutes longer than the Earth day, and the planet has four seasons similar to those on Earth. Surface temperatures on Mars dip down to −90°C (−200°F) and seldom rise above 0°C (32°F). Iron oxide gives Martian soil the reddish color of rust. There are also white polar caps that grow and shrink with the seasons, and dark patches that were once mistaken for canals or vegetation. We now know that these dark areas come and go as dust storms cover and uncover darker rock.

MARS continued

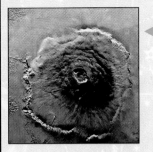

◄ **Olympus Mons**
(ō lim′pəs mänz) is a huge extinct volcano on Mars, nearly three times the height of the tallest mountain on Earth.

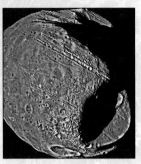

◄ **Phobos** (fō′bəs) is a Martian satellite just 27 km (17 mi) long. Its companion moon Deimos (dī′məs) is even smaller. Many scientists think these rough-shaped objects are asteroids that were captured by Mars's gravity.

◄ **The Martian surface** was photographed by a U.S. lander that scooped up and analyzed soil samples.

SCIENCE IN LITERATURE

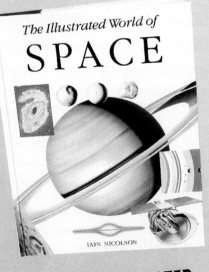

The Illustrated World of
SPACE

IAIN NICOLSON

THE ILLUSTRATED WORLD OF SPACE
by Iain Nicolson
Simon & Schuster Books for Young Readers, 1991

Reference books like *The Illustrated World of Space* are fun to read because you can pick them up and start reading on any page. They are also the perfect place to find the answers to specific questions.

Use the index in *The Illustrated World of Space* to look up each of the planets in our solar system. Read about the planets and examine the illustrations that show the layers of each planet. Then make a chart to summarize what you find out about the compositions of the planets. In your chart, include columns for the planets' cores, mantles, crusts, and atmospheres. Share your chart with your classmates.

The Outer Planets

Four of the five planets farthest from the Sun are very much alike. They're quite large in comparison to the inner planets, they have ring systems, and they're made up mostly of substances that would be gases on Earth. Jupiter, Saturn, Uranus, and Neptune are therefore often referred to as the **gas giants**. The outermost known planet, Pluto, seems to be more like the inner terrestrial planets in size and composition. Let's take a closer look at this planet and its neighbors. ■

♃ JUPITER

JUPITER is the fifth planet from the Sun and the largest planet in our solar system. When the solar system was forming, Jupiter almost became a star. It couldn't sustain the nuclear reactions that keep the Sun burning, however, so Jupiter cooled and became a planet instead. It's composed mainly of gaseous and liquid hydrogen and helium, probably surrounding a small rocky core. The planet's upper atmosphere features swirling cloud bands and the Great Red Spot, a huge circular storm that's lasted for centuries. Jupiter has a set of rings, but they're so thin and dark that they're practically invisible in natural light.

Io (ī′ō), a satellite of Jupiter, is the most volcanically active object we know of in the solar system. This rocky moon's volcanoes regularly recoat the satellite's surface with lava. ▶

Io's volcanoes send up towering plumes of gas, like this one seen in a false-color view. ▶

♄ SATURN

SATURN is the sixth planet from the Sun and the last planet you can easily see with your unaided eye from Earth. It's almost as big as Jupiter, with a very similar composition and banded atmosphere. Strong winds sweep across Saturn almost constantly, reaching speeds of 1,800 km/h (1,100 mph). The planet's spectacular rings are its most distinctive feature.

▲ **Saturn and some of its moons** are shown in this composite photo. Saturn has the most known satellites of any planet. Some have rocky surfaces and others are ice-covered.

▲ **Saturn's rings** are shown in a false-color view that brings out their details. A planet's ring system is made up of countless ice and rock fragments. These fragments orbit so closely together that the rings look solid from a distance.

▲ **Titan**, the largest of Saturn's satellites, is the only moon in the solar system with a dense atmosphere. Its haze is shown clearly in this false-color photo. Titan's atmosphere may resemble that of early Earth.

♅ URANUS

URANUS (yʊʊrʹə nəs), blue-green in color, is the seventh planet from the Sun. It has thin, dark rings like those of Jupiter that are too faint to be easily photographed. Since this planet can't readily be seen from Earth without a telescope, its existence was recognized only in the 1700s. Because of its distance from the Sun, Uranus is very cold, with temperatures near −150°C (−300°F) in the cloud tops.

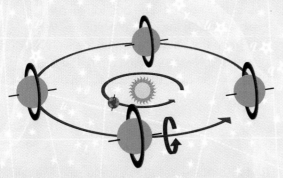

▲ **The tilt of Uranus's axis** is the most unique feature of this planet. Compared to Uranus's orbit, the axis is tilted way over on its side, so that the poles take turns pointing toward the Sun.

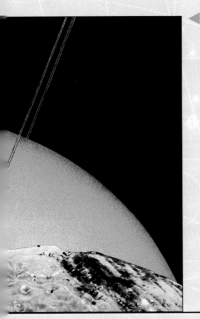

◄ **Uranus and its moon Miranda** (mə ranʹdə) are seen in this computer-generated photo. The picture shows what Uranus's faint rings might look like from nearby. Miranda has been called the most bizarre object in the solar system. Scientists think the patchwork appearance of this satellite's surface resulted when the moon was torn apart by collisions and then reassembled by its own gravity.

♆ NEPTUNE

NEPTUNE was discovered in the 1800s. It's a planet very similar to Uranus, but it doesn't share the feature of a severely tilted axis. Neptune's rings, like those of Uranus, are too faint to be seen from a distance. While Uranus's cloud tops present a pretty bland face, Neptune's atmosphere has swirling blue and white features.

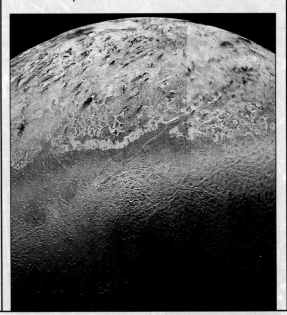

Triton is a rocky, ice-covered moon of Neptune that seems to be active despite being very cold. It has geyserlike features that send up plumes of material into Triton's thin atmosphere. ▼

♇ PLUTO

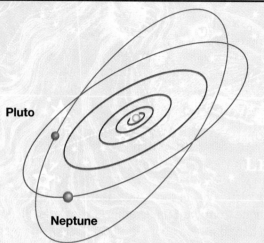

PLUTO is the most remote planet in the solar system— at least, it usually is! It's also the smallest planet, about the same size as Earth's Moon. Not much is known for sure about Pluto, since no space probe has ever visited it. Indeed, Pluto is so small and so far away that only Earth's most powerful telescopes can see it at all. The Hubble Space Telescope took this photo (*above*), which shows the planet and its one known moon, Charon (ker'ən). It's cold beyond imagination on Pluto, probably never warmer than −175°C (−350°F).

Pluto

Neptune

▲ **Pluto's unusual orbit** makes it the ninth planet most of the time but sometimes brings it inside the orbit of Neptune. When that happens, Pluto becomes the eighth planet and Neptune is the ninth! Pluto is closer to the Sun from 1980 to 1999.

◀ **Pluto's surface** may look something like this artist's view. Scientists think that Pluto's rocky ground is covered with a frost of frozen gases, under a very light atmosphere of methane and nitrogen. The artist has pictured the moon Charon and the tiny-looking Sun in Pluto's sky.

═══════ **INVESTIGATION 2** ═══════

THINK IT WRITE IT

1. List some differences and similarities between the inner planets and the outer planets in our solar system.

2. Suppose you could establish a scientific outpost on any planet or satellite in the solar system. Where would you build it and why? List some advantages and disadvantages of your choice.

REFLECT & EVALUATE

WORD POWER

Big Bang Theory
gas giants
geocentric model
heliocentric model
moon
satellite
solar system
terrestrial planets

 On Your Own
Review the terms in the list. Then use as many terms as you can in a paragraph that tells how our ideas about the planets have changed over time.

 With a Partner
Write a definition for each term in the list. Have your partner match each definition to the correct term.

Make a solar system album. Find photos of the planets in magazines. Cut out the photos and paste them in an album. Write captions for your photos.

Analyze Information

Use the information in the following table to arrange the planets in order of increasing distance from the Sun.

Planet	Period of Revolution (in Earth years)	Planet	Period of Revolution (in Earth years)
Saturn	29.46	Jupiter	11.86
Mars	1.88	Earth	1.00
Pluto	248.60	Mercury	0.24
Venus	0.62	Neptune	164.79
Uranus	84.01		

Assess Performance

Make a model that illustrates the differences between Ptolemy's and Copernicus's views of how the solar system is organized. Use yarn, plastic-foam balls of different sizes, glue, and posterboard. Add labels that show the locations of Earth and the Sun.

Problem Solving

1. How does the makeup of the planets change as their distance from the Sun increases? How does their size change? How is temperature related to a planet's distance from the Sun?

2. Use sketches to illustrate how scientists think the solar system formed.

3. A friend tells you that Mars is the planet most similar to Earth. Explain why you agree or disagree with this statement.

CHAPTER 3

STARS AND GALAXIES

The main entrance to an ancient ceremonial hall in New Mexico faces the North Star. The ceilings of some caves in Arizona are covered with drawings of stars. Native Americans identified and located stars and planets thousands of years ago. Why did they do it? How accurate were they?

Ancient Astronomers

Two thousand years ago in Mexico, a large city was laid out according to knowledge of the Sun, Moon, planets, and stars. A pyramid was built facing the point in the sky where the Pleiades star cluster set. A hall was built so that it would align a distant point with the Sun on the first day of spring.

Carved rocks found throughout the Americas were used to mark the rising and setting of stars. From their knowledge of the positions of stars, early Native Americans designed a 365-day calendar. They determined the four compass directions and decided when to plant crops. As you study stars and galaxies, you'll learn more about these objects that the ancient astronomers observed so carefully.

◄ An ancient Native American rock carving of stars, from New Mexico

WHAT ARE STARS AND HOW DO THEY DIFFER?

When you look at the stars at night, do they all look the same? The next chance you get, look carefully at the night sky. You might be surprised at some of the differences you can observe among the stars.

Activity
Capturing Colors

Stars come in many colors. Find out how astronomers observe the colors in starlight.

MATERIALS

- lamp with a clear-glass bulb
- red and green filters
- spectroscope
- colored pencils
- *Science Notebook*

SAFETY

Do not touch the bulb.

Procedure

In a dark room, view a glowing light bulb. **Describe** what you see in your *Science Notebook*. **Observe** the bulb through a red filter, then through a green filter. **Describe** what you see through each. **Observe** the bulb through a spectroscope. **Draw** a color picture of the band of light, or spectrum, that you see. Place the red filter over the opening of the spectroscope, view the bulb, and **draw** a color picture of what you see. Do the same with the green filter.

Analyze and Conclude

1. How did the filters and the spectroscope affect the appearance of the bulb? Based on your observations, what can you **infer** about white light?

2. Brainstorm how astronomers might use filters and spectroscopes to help them obtain information about the stars.

Activity

How Big Is Betelgeuse?

Stars come in many sizes. Betelgeuse (bet'l jōoz) *is a giant red star. Our Sun is a medium-sized yellow star. What would our solar system be like if Betelgeuse were our star? Find out!*

MATERIALS

- large piece of drawing paper
- string
- metric ruler
- red pencil or crayon
- *Science Notebook*

Procedure

1. On a large sheet of paper, **draw a model** of the solar system out to Jupiter. First, place a dot in the center of the paper. This dot represents the Sun in your model.

2. Next, use a string as shown in the picture to **draw** the orbits of the planets. The information in the table tells you how large to make the orbits. Label each one.

Step 2

3. Finally, **draw** a circle 12 cm in diameter around the Sun in your model. Shade everything inside this circle red. This circle represents Betelgeuse.

Analyze and Conclude

1. What does your model indicate about the relative sizes of the Sun and Betelgeuse?

2. In your *Science Notebook*, **hypothesize** what would happen to Earth if our Sun were to grow to the size of Betelgeuse. Use your model to support your hypothesis.

Planet	Distance From the Sun
Mercury	1.2 cm
Venus	2.2 cm
Earth	3.0 cm
Mars	4.6 cm
Jupiter	15.6 cm

How Stars Differ
From One Another

When Galileo first looked through his telescope at the night sky, he began to notice differences among the stars. Some were so dazzling they took his breath away, but others seemed dim and plain. Scientists now know that stars differ from one another in a great many ways. Four of the most obvious differences have to do with brightness, size, temperature, and color.

The Characteristics of Stars

You don't need a telescope to know that some stars are brighter than others. Stars also range in size from dwarfs to supergiants. The largest body in our solar system, the Sun, is an average-sized star with a diameter of about 1.4 million km (865,000 mi). A supergiant can have a diameter up to 1,000 times that of the Sun. Some dwarf stars have diameters less than half that of Earth.

The temperature and color of a star are closely linked. In fact, temperature determines a star's color, as it sometimes does with materials here on Earth. A furnace that glows with a white light, for example, is hotter than one that glows with an orange light.

Stars exhibit a wide range of colors, indicating a variety of temperatures. Astronomers use spectroscopes to study the light given off by stars, just as you used a spectroscope to study light in the activity on page B54.

The surface temperature of the hottest stars may be as high as 50,000°C (90,000°F). These stars shine with a bluish light, while the coolest stars shine with a red light.

Star Color	Surface Temperature	Examples
Blue	11,000°–50,000°C	Regulus, Rigel
Blue-white	7,500°–11,000°C	Deneb, Sirius
White	6,000°–7,500°C	Canopus, Procyon
Yellow	5,000°–6,000°C	The Sun, Alpha Centauri
Orange-red	3,500°–5,000°C	Aldebaran, Arcturus
Red	2,000°–3,500°C	Betelgeuse, Proxima Centauri

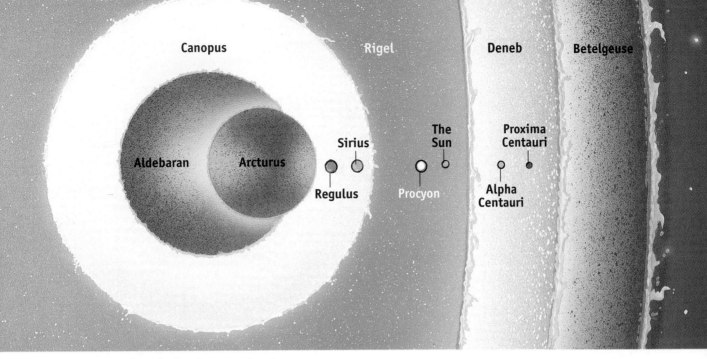

Canopus Rigel Deneb Betelgeuse

Sirius

The Sun

Proxima Centauri

Aldebaran Arcturus

Regulus Procyon Alpha Centauri

▲ **Stars of various sizes and colors**

The table on the left shows the relationship between star color and temperature.

The picture above shows the relative sizes of the stars in the table. Find the red star Betelgeuse, which you drew in the activity on page B55. Now find the red star called Proxima Centauri. These two stars are the same color and so have similar surface temperatures. But stars of the same color can vary greatly in size.

How a Star Gets Its Energy

Although stars have different visible features, they all have one thing in common: the way they produce energy. A star is a gigantic ball of hot gases—so hot that the gases at the star's surface glow. Energy is generated by nuclear reactions that convert hydrogen into helium in the center of the star. It's as if millions of hydrogen bombs were detonating there every second.

Unlike a hydrogen bomb, a star doesn't explode and fly apart. It has so much mass that it's held together by its own gravity. So the energy released by the nuclear reactions moves throughout the star, generating heat and light. ■

═══════ **INVESTIGATION 1** ═══════

1. Identify four ways in which stars may differ from one another.

2. A red star and a blue star appear from Earth to be equally bright. What other inferences could you make about these two stars?

INVESTIGATION 2

HOW FAR AWAY ARE THE STARS?

If you traveled beyond our solar system at the speed of light, you could reach the closest one of these objects in about four years. What are these objects? They are stars.

Activity
Making a Paraffin Photometer

Can you tell how far away a star is by looking at it? Do all stars shine with the same brightness? In this activity you'll make a photometer to help you measure brightness and relate it to star distances.

Procedure

1. Measure and cut out a 12 × 12 cm piece of aluminum foil.

2. Fold the foil in half, shiny side out, to form a 12 × 6 cm rectangle.

3. Make a "sandwich" by placing the aluminum foil between two blocks of paraffin. Use rubber bands to hold the sandwich together. You have now made a simple photometer (fō täm'ət ər).

Step 3

4. Stand your photometer on a flat surface and darken the room. Have another group member shine a flashlight beam on one side of the photometer. **Observe** how the lighted side of the photometer compares with the side away from the light. **Record** your observations in your *Science Notebook*.

5. **Predict** how the lighted side of the photometer will change when the light is moved closer to it and farther from it. Have the group member with the light move it and check your predictions. **Record** your observations.

6. Have a third group member shine another flashlight on the other side of the photometer. One of the two flashlights should be held still. The other flashlight should be moved toward or away from the photometer until both paraffin blocks shine with the same brightness. Then **measure** and **record** the distance between the photometer and each flashlight.

Analyze and Conclude

1. **Describe** how the distance between a flashlight and the photometer affects the brightness of the paraffin.

2. In step 6, what did you **observe** about the distances between each flashlight and the photometer? From this information, what can you **infer** about the brightness of the light given off by each flashlight?

3. Brainstorm how techniques like those used in this activity might be used to study light from different stars.

4. Besides measuring a star's *apparent* brightness, **infer** what else astronomers need to know about that star to determine its *actual* brightness.

INVESTIGATE FURTHER!

EXPERIMENT

Light bulbs are rated by wattage. The higher the wattage, the brighter the light that is produced. Use your photometer to compare the brightness of bulbs of different wattages.

Measuring
Distances in Space

Incredibly large distances separate stars from Earth. Scientists can't run a tape measure across space to measure these distances. Instead, they measure something called parallax (par'ə laks).

To understand parallax, try this exercise. Close one eye. Hold up one finger at arm's length. Line up your finger with a reference point, such as a mark on a chalkboard. Keeping your finger and head still, open your closed eye and close the eye that was open. Observe how your finger *appears* to move in relation to your reference point.

In this exercise, nothing actually moved. But your finger appeared to shift position because you were viewing

it from a slightly different location when you changed eyes. Such an apparent shift in position is called parallax.

Astronomers use parallax to figure out distances to nearby stars. As shown below, they view a star from two different places in Earth's orbit. Then they measure how far the star appeared to move in relation to other, more distant stars. They use this information to calculate the distance to the star.

Distance and Brightness

The measure of a star's brightness is called magnitude (mag'nə to͞od). Astronomers use photometers—devices similar to the one in the activity on pages

▲ A student's finger appears to shift due to parallax, just as a star's position against more distant stars appears to shift.

B58 and B59—to measure how bright a star *appears* to be. That is the star's **apparent magnitude**, and it depends on two things: (1) how far away the star is, and (2) the star's absolute magnitude. **Absolute magnitude** is the amount of light a star actually gives off.

Imagine looking at a bonfire and a match. If these two sources of light are the same distance from you, the bonfire will seem brighter. However, if the bonfire is a kilometer away and the match is at arm's length, the match will appear brighter. The "absolute magnitudes" of the two light sources won't have changed—but their apparent magnitudes will vary with distance.

Astronomers can determine the absolute magnitude of a star if they know the star's apparent magnitude (which can be measured) and its distance from Earth (from the parallax method). They can also use magnitude to estimate the distance to faraway stars, where parallax cannot be used.

Because distances between stars are so great, astronomers measure these distances using units called light-years. A **light-year** is the distance that light travels in one year. Since the speed of light is about 300,000 km (186,000 mi) per second, a light-year is about 9.5 trillion km (5.9 trillion mi). Imagine having to write out numbers such as these! ■

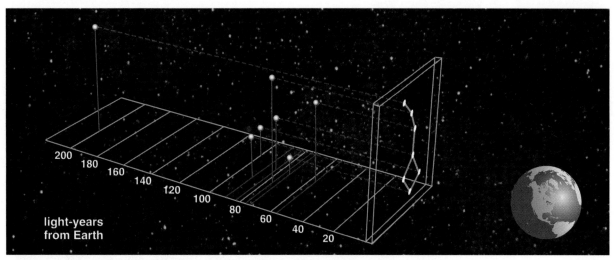

light-years
from Earth

200 180 160 140 120 100 80 60 40 20

▲ **The stars in the Big Dipper lie at different distances from Earth.**

INVESTIGATION 2

1. Why is the light-year a useful unit for measuring distances to stars?

2. The star Sirius (sir′ē əs) appears to be about ten times brighter than the star Deneb. Yet scientists have found that Deneb gives off much more light than Sirius does. How can you explain this puzzling situation?

INVESTIGATION 3

WHAT IS THE LIFE CYCLE OF A STAR?

The stars that you see today are the same ones that ancient astronomers viewed thousands of years ago. But stars do change over very long periods of time. In this investigation you'll discover the different stages a star can go through.

MATERIALS
• *Science Notebook*

Activity

Studying Nebulas

A nebula (neb′yə lə) *is a cloud of gases and dust in space. In this activity you'll learn about the role nebulas play in the life cycles of stars.*

▲ A nebula in Vela   ▲ The Orion Nebula   ▲ The Horsehead Nebula

Procedure

1. Each of the six photographs below includes a nebula. Study the photos carefully and **describe** each one in your *Science Notebook*.

2. Astronomers think that stars form from the gases and dust that make up nebulas. **Identify** the photo or photos that show evidence that stars may have recently formed or may be forming now. **Describe the evidence** you see.

3. It is thought that the gases and dust in nebulas come from old stars that have exploded. **Identify** the photo or photos that support this hypothesis. **Describe the evidence** you see in those photographs.

4. Evidence indicates that, under certain conditions, stars may form in groups or clusters. **Identify** the photo or photos that provide such evidence. **Explain the evidence** you see.

Analyze and Conclude

1. Compare the nebulas in the photographs. What characteristics do they have in common? How are they different?

2. Many of the photographs show some dark areas. What can you **infer** about the nature of such dark areas?

3. Explain why you think astronomers study nebulas to learn about the life cycles of stars.

INVESTIGATE FURTHER!

RESEARCH

On a star chart in an astronomy book, locate the types of objects you studied in this activity. Find out which objects, if any, might be visible in the sky over where you live. Go outside and see if you can spot any of these objects. If binoculars are available, they will make your task easier.

▲ **The Helix Nebula**

▲ **The Lagoon Nebula**

▲ **The Pleiades**

The Life Cycle of a Star

Although a star is not a living thing, it has a "life cycle." Like a living thing, a star passes through several stages as it ages. These stages include "birth," growth and development, middle age, old age, and "death."

The life cycle of a star covers a huge span of time. For example, our Sun is a middle-aged yellow star of average size and temperature. It has been shining just as it does today for more than 4.5 billion years. It should continue to shine for another 4.5 billion years before it begins to change very much.

The Birth of a Star

Huge clouds of gases and dust, called **nebulas**, are scattered through many regions of space. Nebulas provide the raw materials from which stars form. Under certain conditions, portions of a nebula begin to contract, forming clumps of spinning gases. Over millions of years, gravity causes these clumps to shrink, or condense, into dense pockets of matter within the nebula. These pockets of matter form the beginnings of stars and are called **protostars** (prō'tō stärz).

Stages in the life cycles of stars. Each star's fate depends on its mass. ▼

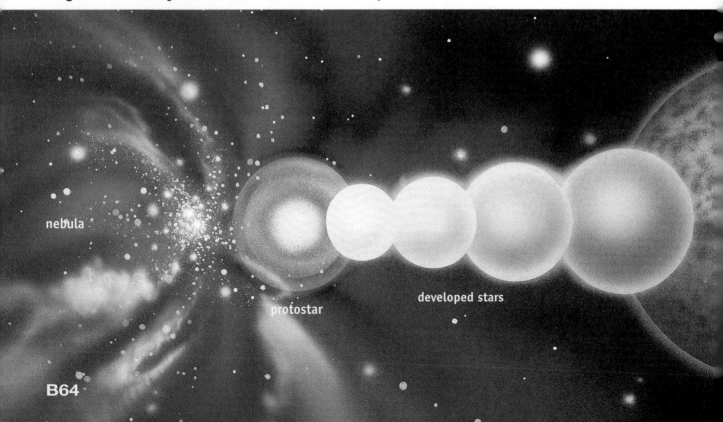

nebula

protostar

developed stars

As a protostar continues to condense, its particles are squeezed closer and closer together, creating enormous pressure at the center. This pressure causes the core of the protostar to become very hot. When the core's temperature reaches about 15,000,000°C, nuclear reactions begin, releasing tremendous amounts of energy. At this point, the protostar stops shrinking and begins to shine. It is now a full-fledged star.

The Life of an Average Star

How long does a star "live"? The main factor that determines a star's life span—and the kind of death it will have—is the star's mass. A star of medium mass, like our Sun, shines for billions of years by converting its hydrogen into helium.

Eventually, though, the star's hydrogen fuel begins to run out. The star's core, now made up mostly of helium, shrinks and releases energy as it collapses. This energy, when added to the energy of the remaining nuclear reactions, causes the outer layers of the star to expand far out into space, swelling the star to many times its original size.

As the outer layers expand, they move farther from the star's central furnace. The outer layers then cool, the light they give off reddens, and the star becomes a **red giant**. This is what will happen to our Sun, though not for billions of years.

After a long period as a red giant, the last traces of fuel will run out, and the Sun will collapse one final time. It will become a **white dwarf** star, not much larger than Earth is now. At this stage, the Sun will still be shining, but only dimly. Its atoms will be packed tightly together at a density a million times greater than that of water. Finally

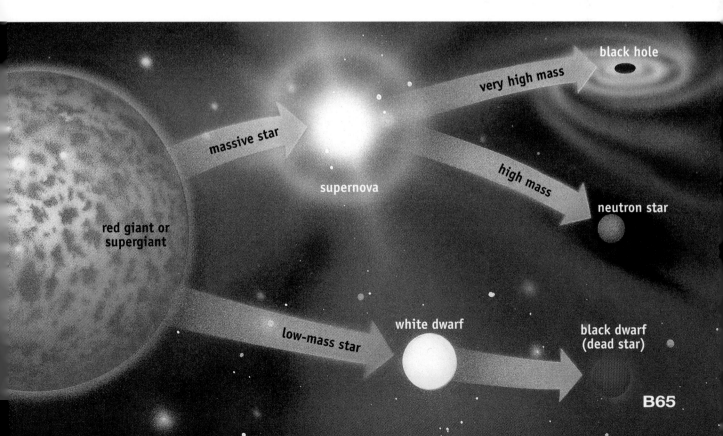

red giant or supergiant

massive star

supernova

very high mass

black hole

high mass

neutron star

low-mass star

white dwarf

black dwarf (dead star)

the Sun will die completely and become a cool, darkened **black dwarf**.

How Massive Stars Die

Stars that begin with much greater mass than our Sun live shorter lives. They also end their careers in a much more spectacular fashion.

When a massive star forms, much greater pressure is created as it condenses. Although the early part of a massive star's life is much like that of an average star, the larger star reaches the red giant stage much sooner.

After that, the star's life is a constant battle between two opposing forces. The outward pressure caused by ever-increasing core temperatures continues to fight against the inward push of gravity. As this battle is waged, the star may expand and contract several times.

When the star's fuel is finally used up, the outer layers of the star fall back into the core at tremendous speeds. The great pressure created by the star's rapid contraction can result in a gigantic explosion known as a **supernova**. This is one of the most dazzling events in the universe. A supernova can appear as a bright "new" star in Earth's sky. It can produce as much light as an entire galaxy. The material released by a supernova may include elements from which future stars can be created.

SCIENCE IN LITERATURE

STARS, CLUSTERS AND GALAXIES
by John Gustafson
Julian Messner, 1992

When is a star not a star? When it's a double, or binary, star. You can find out more about these interesting objects by reading pages 7–10 in *Stars, Clusters and Galaxies* by John Gustafson. Then if you'd like to see a binary star for yourself, follow the instructions on page 46. Binoculars are helpful, but you'll find out about a binary star in the Big Dipper that can be spotted with the unaided eye.

Stars, Clusters and Galaxies is more than a reference book full of amazing photographs of the night sky. It's also a great how-to guide for star-watching.

▲ The Crab Nebula is what remains of a supernova observed by Chinese astronomers nearly 1,000 years ago.

much as a billion tons on Earth!

The gravitational pull in the collapse of a massive star may be too strong for the collapse to stop at the stage of a neutron star. So, the star may keep shrinking until it has collapsed to a tiny region, or point, with a very strong gravitational field. This region or point is called a **black hole.** The gravitational attraction of a black hole is so strong that absolutely nothing can escape it—not even light! ■

Neutron Stars and Black Holes

The life of a massive star doesn't necessarily end with a supernova. If enough of its original mass remains after the explosion, the surviving shrunken core of the star can become either a neutron star or a black hole.

In a **neutron star,** the collapse of the core is so powerful that it crushes the star's remaining matter. A typical neutron star is less than 20 km (12 mi) in diameter. Its material is so tightly packed that only a spoonful would weigh as

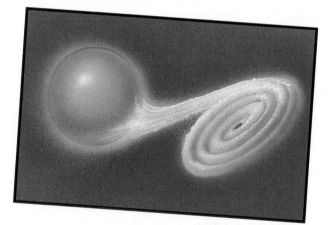

▲ A black hole—normally invisible—might be detected if material from a nearby star is pulled into it.

INVESTIGATION 3

1. Compare the life cycle of an average-sized star with the life cycle of a very massive star.

2. The elements that make up a star today may have been part of another star that lived and died billions of years ago. How can this be?

B67

INVESTIGATION 4

WHAT ARE GALAXIES AND HOW DO THEY DIFFER?

Sometimes an object in the night sky that looks like a single star is actually a huge group of stars, so far away that their light seems to come from a single source. Find out about these star collections called galaxies.

Activity

MATERIALS
• *Science Notebook*

Classifying Galaxies

Each night, astronomers study distant galaxies. In this activity you can observe and compare some, too.

- -

Procedure

1. The photographs on these pages show several different galaxies. Study each galaxy carefully and **describe** it in your *Science Notebook*.

▲ The Large Magellanic Cloud   ▲ Galaxy NGC 7217   ▲ The Whirlpool Galaxy

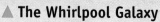

▲ Galaxy NGC 1365

▲ The Centaurus A Galaxy

▲ The Small Magellanic Cloud

2. Different galaxies may have characteristics in common that can be used to classify galaxies into groups. Study the photos on these pages again and **classify** the galaxies into two or more groups.

Analyze and Conclude

1. Based on your observations, **identify** one or more characteristics that all galaxies have in common.

2. Identify the characteristics you used to classify the galaxies. How many different groups did you have?

3. Astronomers recognize three general classes of galaxies: spiral, elliptical, and irregular. Use these terms to **identify** each of the galaxies on these pages.

4. Before galaxies were properly identified, astronomers thought that such objects were nebulas. **Compare** the characteristics of galaxies with those of nebulas.

UNIT PROJECT LINK

Create a space telescope for your space-station simulator. On large sheets of paper, draw what your space telescope might look like as seen through a station window. Draw computer consoles that would receive the telescope's pictures. Draw some of the stars, galaxies, and other objects you have studied and display their pictures around your telescope area.

The Milky Way
and Other Galaxies

If a visitor from outer space asked you your address, what would you say? You'd probably mention a house or apartment number, a street, a city or town, and a state. You could then add a country and even a planet—Earth. But how could you tell the visitor the location of your planet?

Earth and eight other planets are members of a solar system, all revolving around a star we call the Sun. The solar system belongs to a gigantic cluster of stars known as the **Milky Way Galaxy**.

Our Sun is just one of more than 100 billion stars that make up the Milky Way.

Is there anything bigger than a galaxy? Yes! You, your planet, your solar system, and your galaxy are all part of the **universe**, which includes absolutely everything that exists.

"Building Blocks" of the Universe

A **galaxy** is a huge collection of stars. A typical galaxy may contain hundreds of billions of stars, all revolving

The Milky Way Galaxy as seen in Earth's sky (*right*) and as it might look from outside (*below*)

location of our solar system

▲ An elliptical galaxy   ▲ A spiral galaxy   ▲ An irregular galaxy

around a central core. Why can galaxies be thought of as building blocks of the universe? The reason is that they're the largest single structures that astronomers have identified so far. There may be as many as 100 billion galaxies in the universe.

Edwin Hubble (1889–1953)—the man for whom the Hubble Space Telescope is named—was a well-known American astronomer who spent many years studying galaxies. He found that they can be classified into three basic groups, based on their shapes. You tried classifying galaxies yourself in the activity on pages B68 and B69.

The most common type of galaxy is elliptical in shape—that is, it's shaped like a slightly flattened sphere, with no clear features. The second most common type is a spiral galaxy, with arms that make it resemble a pinwheel spinning in space. The third type of galaxy is irregular, having no definite shape.

The Milky Way Galaxy

The Milky Way is not a "special" galaxy in any way—except, of course, that you and everyone you know live inside it! The Milky Way is a spiral galaxy with at least two arms that

extend out from a central bulge. This bulge is some 20,000 light-years in diameter and 10,000 light-years thick. A trip from one side of our galaxy to the other, traveling at the speed of light, would take about 100,000 years.

From our vantage point in one of the galaxy's arms, the Milky Way appears as a broad band of light stretching across Earth's night sky. You can see this band for yourself if you're out in the country, away from bright city lights, on a clear, moonless night. The stars and dust clouds of our galaxy seem to form a milky-white path across the sky, giving the galaxy its name.

How Do Galaxies Move?

Every galaxy, in addition to rotating around its own imaginary axis, is also moving in another way. It was Edwin Hubble, about 80 years ago, who discovered the second way that galaxies move.

While studying the light given off by distant galaxies, Hubble came to an amazing conclusion. He found that most galaxies seemed to be moving away from planet Earth. What would explain such an observation?

Hubble was smart enough to realize that his findings didn't mean that Earth lay at the center of the universe. He wasn't about to become another Ptolemy! Instead, Hubble realized that *all* galaxies, including our own Milky Way, are moving rapidly away from *one another*.

For help in visualizing this expanding universe, imagine a deflated balloon with lots of small dots on its surface. What happens to the dots as you inflate the balloon? They all move away from

one another. This is similar to what's going on in the universe. If you pretend you're looking out from a dot that represents the Milky Way Galaxy, all the other dots on the balloon will appear to be moving away from you—even though you too are moving!

▲ **The expanding universe can be compared to a balloon that's being inflated.**

Hubble's discovery of the expanding universe later became a cornerstone of the Big Bang Theory, which you learned about in Chapter 2. Hubble helped astronomers realize that the universe isn't just a big place right now. In fact, it's getting bigger and bigger all the time! ■

═══════════════ **INVESTIGATION 4** ═══════════════

1. Name three types of galaxies and describe the differences between them. What type is our own Milky Way Galaxy?

2. In the past, many astronomers thought that the universe was steady and unchanging, with no beginning and no end. How did Edwin Hubble's discoveries disagree with that view of the universe?

REFLECT & EVALUATE

WORD POWER

black dwarf
black hole
galaxy
light-year
nebula
neutron star
absolute magnitude
apparent magnitude
Milky Way Galaxy

protostar
red giant
supernova
universe
white dwarf

 On Your Own
Review the terms in the list. Then use as many terms as you can in a paragraph about stars.

 With a Partner
Make up a quiz using all the terms in the list. Challenge your partner to complete the quiz.

PORTFOLIO

Make a poster that traces the life of a star. Include captions that explain each stage. Note where different things might happen, depending on the star's mass.

Analyze Information

Study the pictures. Identify each type of galaxy and describe its characteristics.

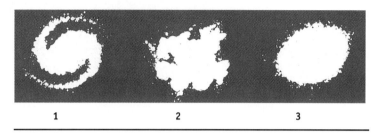

1   2   3

Assess Performance

Design a model that shows how distance affects the apparent brightness of a lighted object. Use three lamps with bulbs of different wattages and a metric tape measure. Make a drawing of your completed model, identifying the wattage of each bulb and the distance between each lamp and the viewer when the three lamps appear to be equally bright.

Problem Solving

1. Suppose you're studying two stars that are blue. What else do those stars have in common? With the information you now have, what can you tell about the sizes of these stars?

2. If a star is 100 light-years from Earth, how long does it take the light from this star to reach Earth? If you could travel to the star in a spaceship that moved at the speed of light, how long would it take you to reach this star?

3. Suppose you could view the Milky Way Galaxy from a distance and measure its movement. What would this object look like? How would it be moving?

CHAPTER 4

LIVING IN SPACE

"Houston? This is *Freedom*. We have just received a signal that may have been sent by extraterrestrials! Request advice."
Will space station *Freedom* send this kind of message some day?
What should we be doing to prepare for such an event?

Space Kids

Every week, the U.S. Space Camp in Huntsville, Alabama, welcomes a new bunch of campers. They will experience a hands-on course in space technology. The campers participate in a simulated two-hour flight of the space shuttle *Endeavour*, complete with authentic ground control. Launch, Earth orbit, and landing are realistically simulated. Student astronauts perform various tasks in space, solve in-flight emergencies, and experience simulated weightlessness.

During the five days at camp, participants study the Apollo 16 spacecraft that flew to the Moon. They build model rockets and tour the camp's missile park and model space station. As you study living in space, you'll have many experiences that could help you design your own space camp program.

Coming Up

◀ A camper at U.S. Space Camp

B75

WHAT IS IT LIKE TO TRAVEL IN SPACE?

Imagine floating as if you had no weight at all. This is what you would experience if you were in orbit on a space shuttle. In this investigation you'll learn what causes the experience of "weightlessness" and how it can make many everyday activities unique.

Activity

Free Falling

What does free fall mean? How does it affect astronauts? Find out!

Procedure

1. Hang a paper cup from a loop of string. Tie a shorter loop of string to the top of the big loop, as shown, with a metal washer hanging from the short string. When you hold the cup and washer up by their strings, the washer should be hanging about even with the top of the cup.

2. Hold the cup in one hand. Hold the strings up above the cup with the other hand. Release the strings and **observe** what happens. **Record** the result in your *Science Notebook*.

3. Hold the cup up as high as possible by the two strings. Then let the cup and washer drop.

4. With members of your group, watch the objects fall. Listen for the sound of the cup hitting the floor and the sound of the washer hitting the bottom of the cup. When do you hear each sound?

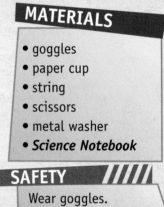

Step 1

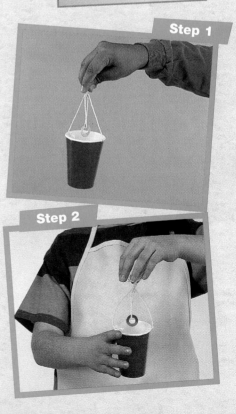

Step 2

5. Repeat steps 3 and 4 at least three times. Make sure the objects fall straight to the ground without hitting each other on the way. Make sure you can tell when the two sounds occur. Does each sound always occur at about the same time?

6. Draw four pictures showing the stages of the experiment in steps 3 and 4. Show what the experiment looks like (a) just before you let it drop, as you hold it up by the strings; (b) when it's falling in midair; (c) at the moment the cup touches the ground; and (d) at the moment the washer touches the bottom of the cup.

Step 3

Analyze and Conclude

1. Compare how the washer fell in step 2 with the way the washer and cup fell in steps 3 and 4. **Suggest a hypothesis** to explain the differences you observed.

2. Pretend you are a tiny bug sitting on the washer. How would you feel when the washer is released? How would the cup below you look as both objects fall toward the ground in steps 3 and 4? Would the cup appear to stay the same distance away from you or not? At what point would you start to move closer to the cup?

3. An astronaut in a spaceship orbiting Earth is said to be in free fall, with both the astronaut and the spaceship "falling" around Earth. **Infer** how this activity might relate to astronauts feeling weightless in orbit. If the imaginary bug on the washer represents an astronaut, what does the cup represent?

4. Infer some ways that free fall would affect an astronaut. Discuss your inferences with your group.

INVESTIGATE FURTHER!

EXPERIMENT

Punch a small hole in the side of a plastic-foam coffee cup, down near the cup's bottom. Fill the cup with water and lift it over a sink. What happens? Refill the cup with your finger over the hole. Observe the hole as you drop the cup into the sink from as great a height as possible. What happens? Suggest a hypothesis that would explain your observations.

Activity

Eating and Drinking in Space

Can you swallow in space if you are in free fall? Try this activity and see.

Procedure

1. Pour water into a sealable plastic bag until the bag is about half full. Insert a plastic straw into the top of the bag.

2. Seal the bag around the straw. Wrap tape around the straw where it enters the bag to keep water from escaping.

3. Prop up one end of a bench by placing books under the legs, so that this end is 7 or 8 cm higher than the other. Lie on your stomach on the bench, with your feet at the high end and your head extending out over the low end.

4. Have a group member hold the plastic bag so that it is several centimeters below your head. Try to suck water into your mouth through the straw.

Analyze and Conclude

1. In your *Science Notebook*, **describe** the path of the water from the bag to your stomach. Is it going uphill or downhill?

2. **Hypothesize** whether gravity is necessary when you eat. Does gravity move food from your mouth to your stomach? How do you know?

3. Based on your experiment, **infer** whether astronauts can drink from a squeeze bottle in space.

Step 4

Living in Free Fall

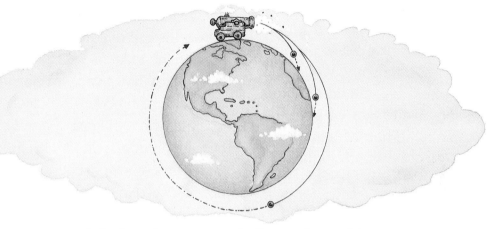

▲ **An imaginary cannonball goes into orbit.**

Imagine that you had a huge cannon, like the one sitting on planet Earth in the picture. If you shot a cannonball like the first ball that's shown, it would arc down toward the ground because of Earth's gravity. If you shot a second ball with more speed, it would go farther before it fell. If you could shoot a third cannonball with so much speed that the arc of its fall matched Earth's curvature, the ball would go into orbit.

The third cannonball would still be falling because of Earth's gravity, but Earth's gravitational pull would keep the cannonball from flying off into space. All other things being equal, the imaginary ball would keep falling forever around and around Earth. That's what it's like to be in orbit and experience **free fall**.

Coasting "Weightless" in Space

People often refer to free fall as "weightlessness" or "zero gravity." Although these terms describe the way objects appear to behave in free fall, they are not completely accurate.

You're not really totally weightless in space—you just feel that way because you and the spaceship are falling. Have you ever gone high up on a swing and felt weightless for a split second at the top? You weren't *really* weightless—but you *were* in free fall for a moment!

There's still plenty of gravity present in an orbiting spacecraft. You'd have to be millions of kilometers farther away to escape the influence of Earth's gravity. It's just that you don't feel the effects of gravity in free fall, because there's nothing resisting your fall.

Most of the time, an orbiting space-craft coasts with its engines off, literally just falling around planet Earth. Astronauts inside the ship are falling along with it, just as the washer fell along with the cup in the activity on pages B76 and B77. Like the imaginary bug on the washer, the astronauts feel weightless as they fall.

On Board the Space Shuttle

For a space shuttle crew, weightlessness is both enjoyable and challenging. Imagine being able to float all over the shuttle's cabin, with hardly any effort! All you need to get around is a little push—and a little practice in how to avoid bouncing wildly off the walls!

Most astronauts experience a little motion sickness at the beginning of a space flight, but then they adjust to life in zero gravity. Soon they can eat, drink, sleep, and do just about anything else they might do on Earth.

Food and drink must be kept in sealed packages and consumed carefully so that pieces and droplets don't float around the cabin. Each crew member has a sleeping bag that can be tied to the wall, floor, or ceiling. If the bag weren't tied down, the dozing astronaut would float around the spacecraft.

Taking showers or baths in space is difficult, so shuttle astronauts wash by wetting a cloth with a water gun. They use a toilet with handles designed to hold them down. Instead of plumbing that relies on gravity, the toilet uses suction to draw the waste away like a vacuum cleaner.

The human body is conditioned to operate where the pull of gravity is resisted by Earth's surface. In free fall the body undergoes many changes, some of which are described in the picture on page B81.

When astronauts return to Earth, it generally takes just a short time for their muscles to adjust to gravity again. But weightlessness for long periods could have far-reaching and permanent effects on the human body. Many questions must be answered before humans can travel on trips to other planets that could last years at a time. ■

An orbiting space shuttle and the astronauts inside it are in free fall. ▼

When free fall begins, blood moves from your legs toward your head. Your face swells and you feel like you have a stuffed-up nose. You must drink extra liquids to replace lost fluids until your body reaches a new fluid balance.

Your heart has less work to do to pump blood in free fall. It may become a little smaller—and a lot lazier—until it resumes its normal workload on Earth.

Your waistline gets thinner as your body's fluids are redistributed. Because gravity no longer compresses your spine, you'll be about 2.5 cm (1 in.) taller in space.

Your bones lose calcium in space. Doctors aren't sure if the body can fully recover from the calcium loss caused by a very long space flight.

All the muscles of your body have much less work to do in space. You should exercise as much as possible to keep your muscles in shape.

▲ **How the human body adjusts to free fall**

INVESTIGATION 1

1. Explain why the term *zero gravity* is not completely accurate in describing conditions in an orbiting spacecraft.

2. In training, astronauts simulate weightlessness by riding in an airplane that flies steeply upward and then arcs down into a dive. Explain why conditions during that arc are similar to those in orbit.

INVESTIGATION 2

HOW DO HUMANS SURVIVE IN SPACE?

What would you pack for a trip to another planet? You'd need more than just a change of clothing! What would you eat and drink? What would you breathe? What would you use for shelter? In this investigation you'll think about what humans need to survive and then explore some answers to these questions.

Activity

MATERIALS

• *Science Notebook*

Requirements for a Space Mission

How much food, oxygen, and water would you need to survive in space? You may be surprised to find out.

Procedure

1. Imagine you're planning a space mission. **Calculate** how much food you'll need to eat each day, using the following table as a guide. How many total grams of food will you require daily? How much energy will you get from that food? **Record** your calculations in your *Science Notebook*.

Type of Food	Mass Requirement	Energy Requirement
Carbohydrates	416.7 g/person/day	1,682 Calories/person/day
Proteins	124.7 g/person/day	505 Calories/person/day
Fats	90.7 g/person/day	834 Calories/person/day

2. Using the second table, **calculate** and **record** how much oxygen you will need each day. Plan on taking one daily extravehicular (eks trə vē hik′yo͞o lər) activity, or EVA—a trip outside the spacecraft. You must use the air lock once when you leave the spacecraft and once when you return.

Oxygen Use	Requirement
Breathing	0.8 kg/person/day
EVA	0.6 kg/person/8-hour EVA
Leakage	1.0 kg/day
Air lock losses	7.0 kg/air lock use

3. Using the third table, **calculate** and **record** how much water you will need each day.

Water Use	Requirement
Drinking	1.9 kg/person/day
Food preparation	1.2 kg/person/day
Washing clothes	12.5 kg/person/day
Washing hands	1.8 kg/person/day
Showering	3.6 kg/person/day
Flushing toilet	0.5 kg/person/day
EVA	4.4 kg/person/8-hour EVA

Analyze and Conclude

1. Suppose you're part of a crew of eight astronauts going to Mars. Your round trip to Mars will take two years. **Calculate** how much food, oxygen, and water your crew will need if nothing can be recycled. (Don't include EVAs.)

2. **Identify** the items on your list that could be recycled. **Describe** how you might recycle these things.

3. **Identify** the items that could be produced on board your ship. **Describe** how they could be produced.

Activity

Survival on the Moon

What are the most important supplies you'd need to survive on the Moon? Pretend you're a stranded astronaut and figure out the answer.

first aid kit containing bandages, medicines, injection needles, and related items

packages of food concentrate

solar-powered portable heating unit

self-inflating life raft

magnetic compass

map of the stars

box of matches

2 large tanks of oxygen

parachute silk

2 pistols

packages of powdered milk

solar-powered radio receiver and transmitter

nylon rope

signal flares

5 containers of water

Procedure

1. Imagine that your spaceship has just crash-landed in daylight on the Moon. You were scheduled to rendezvous with a mother ship 320 km (200 mi) away on the lighted surface of the Moon, but the rough landing has ruined your ship and destroyed all the equipment on board except for the 15 items listed to the right. Your crew's survival depends on reaching the mother ship. Some supplies will be critical for the long trip, but you don't want to carry the extra weight of items you cannot use.

2. In your *Science Notebook*, make a list of the 15 items on the facing page. Number the items in order of importance, with the number 1 indicating the most important item for survival and the number 15 indicating the least important. **Discuss** your choices with your group before assigning each number. Keep in mind that you might wish to use some items for purposes other than those originally intended.

▲ **A U.S. astronaut on the Moon**

Analyze and Conclude

1. Identify the objects that are most critical to your survival. Why are they so important?

2. Identify the objects that are useless. Why?

3. Identify any objects you could use in ways for which they were not originally intended. How would you use them?

4. Compare your group's rankings with the rankings provided by your teacher, which come from NASA—the U.S. space agency. Subtract to find the difference between each item's NASA ranking and your own group's ranking for it. Add up all the differences to find your total score.

5. Compare your score to these figures to see how well your group did.

0–25	Excellent	46–55	Fair
26–32	Good	56–70	Poor
33–45	Average	71–112	Stay home!

UNIT PROJECT LINK

Create two more areas in your space-station simulator—life-support storage and the kitchen. In the life-support storage area, use large sheets of paper to create the fronts of make-believe storage lockers for water and oxygen tanks. On the front of these lockers, indicate how much water and oxygen you will need for a one-month mission. In the kitchen area, decide what foods you would store for the mission. Plan a space meal, using only foods that astronauts can store and consume easily while in free fall.

Keeping Humans Alive in Space

On flights into space, the biggest problem is providing everything that people need to survive. You yourself got a taste of this problem when you did the activities in this investigation. Space is not a friendly place—no restaurants, no bathrooms, and not a single tow truck in sight if anything breaks down.

Some people think we should send only robot probes into space. But a trained scientist seeing something first-hand can often learn much more than a machine can. An astronaut can also deal better with unexpected problems and opportunities. So how can humans stay alive when they do go into space?

The Cycles of Life

When people go into space, they must bring along all the food, water, oxygen, heat sources, and other supplies they need to sustain them throughout their mission. To keep themselves alive and healthy, they must duplicate in space the natural cycles that operate on Earth. The key to doing this is to *recycle* as much as possible.

One important natural cycle is the **oxygen–carbon dioxide cycle**. When living things breathe, they take in oxygen and give off carbon dioxide. When plants carry out photosynthesis, they change carbon dioxide and water into food and in turn release oxygen.

The water cycle and the oxygen–carbon dioxide cycle ▼

water

carbon dioxide

oxygen

water

Another key cycle is the **water cycle**. Living things take in water and give off waste products, including water. On Earth, waste water winds up in rivers and oceans, then evaporates into the atmosphere to be recycled as rain. Other waste products wind up in soil, where organisms break them down into nutrients that plants can use.

Creating Biospheres in Space

All the living and nonliving parts of planet Earth work together to form a **biosphere**, a self-contained and self-sustaining natural system. For humans to survive in space, they must bring along a version of their biosphere.

On short trips, astronauts don't need to worry about recycling—they just carry enough food, water, and oxygen to last the length of their flight. But for longer voyages, they need to think about recycling water, carbon dioxide, and other waste products.

Future astronauts will probably need to carry plants with them that can convert some waste products back into oxygen and food. Otherwise, they'd have to carry large amounts of bottled oxygen and packaged food—and they'd have to dispose of large amounts of waste. Imagine what a year's supply of food for one astronaut would look like—or a year's supply of garbage! ■

Humans may someday be living in biospheres built inside orbiting space stations. ▼

=== INVESTIGATION 2 ===

1. Describe the biosphere around your home and two major cycles that occur in it.

2. The residents of a future space colony have decided to establish a large greenhouse. List some of the benefits they'd gain by doing this and some of the problems they'd face in setting it up.

IS THERE OTHER LIFE IN THE UNIVERSE?

Have you ever watched a science fiction movie about aliens from outer space? How did the movie maker imagine they looked? In this investigation you'll learn what astronomers think the possibilities are for finding life beyond planet Earth.

Activity

A Postcard From Earth

If intelligent life exists beyond Earth, that life could be very different from intelligent life as we know it. How would you communicate with a being from another planet? Give it a try!

Procedure

1. On the front side of a blank postcard, **draw** a scene of Earth. Use your scene to tell about Earth and about yourself. Be careful not to draw things that might confuse an alien being who is unfamiliar with Earth.

2. On the back side of the card, **draw** a diagram or map that might tell another civilization where your planet is located. Remember that residents of another planet will not be able to read English or any other Earth language. Use symbols that might mean something to another civilization.

Step 2

Analyze and Conclude

1. Exchange postcards with a classmate.

2. In your *Science Notebook*, make a list of all the things you are able to learn about Earth from your classmate's post-card. Look for as many things as possible.

3. Make a second list of all the things in the postcard that could be misinterpreted. Look at the card as if you were from another planet and another civilization. You wouldn't even know when a picture was right side up!

4. **Share** your lists with your classmate. See if the two of you can think of ways to improve both postcards. Make a third postcard with ideas that you've thought up together.

5. **Infer** how easy or hard it might be for humans to communicate someday with beings from another planet. What might some of the problems be? What ways of communicating might work best? What things might our two civilizations have in common that could help us understand one another?

▲ How would you try to communicate with another species here on Earth?

INVESTIGATE FURTHER!

RESEARCH

Find out how people have tried to communicate with other species here on Earth. Look in books about animal behavior and animal communication. Discover what techniques humans have used with such animals as chimpanzees, gorillas, and dolphins. How might such methods be applied to communication with beings from another planet?

Messages to the Stars

How would you talk to an extraterrestrial (eks trə tə-res'trē əl)? What would you say and how would you say it? And just what *is* an extraterrestrial, anyway?

The word **extraterrestrial** can be used to describe anything that comes from beyond Earth. Meteorites, for example, are said to be of extraterrestrial origin. But when many people say *extraterrestrial*, what they really mean is a living being from outer space.

Humans tend to think a lot about the possibility of life on other worlds. Some people even believe that Earth has already been visited by aliens riding around in unidentified flying objects, or UFOs—although no proof exists that anything like this has *ever* happened.

Even though scientists are skeptical about the idea that aliens have visited Earth, many scientists do think it's possible for life to exist beyond our own planet. Some scientists have even gone so far as to try to send a message to any extraterrestrial civilization that might be out there, waiting.

One method of communicating with an alien civilization would be by using pictures, as you did in the activity on pages B88 and B89. That's what the

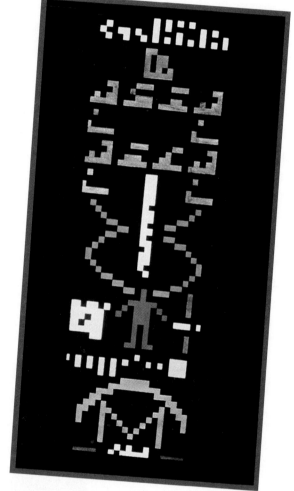

▲ **Frank Drake's radio message**

scientists did who launched the Pioneer 10 and 11 space probes back in 1972.

Each Pioneer spacecraft was equipped with a gold plaque, which was designed to tell any extraterrestrials it might encounter what the creatures were like who made it and where it came from. On each plaque is a drawing of a man and a woman and a map of our solar system. A line shows the probe's course away from Earth.

Another way to communicate is to use radio or television signals. Without meaning to, humans have been broadcasting this kind of message for decades! Ordinary radio and TV signals travel at the speed of light out into space. If there are any aliens out there, the first sign they get of intelligent life on Earth could be a broadcast of rock music!

Scientists have also consciously used a radio telescope to send out messages to extraterrestrials. In 1974, astronomer Frank Drake sent out a signal whose pattern of on-and-off signals could be decoded into pictures of a human, a DNA molecule, and our solar system.

The most elaborate message yet is one that relies heavily on a third method of communication—namely, sound. This message was placed in 1977 on board the Voyager 1 and 2 probes, including the spacecraft you learned about in Chapter 2.

Each Voyager probe carries a 30-cm (12-in.) disk made of gold-plated copper, designed to operate like an old-fashioned phonograph record. Called *The Sounds of Earth,* each disk includes greetings spoken in 54 different Earth languages. There also is music that ranges from Beethoven to African and Mexican folk songs to jazz and rock. There are natural sounds such as a barking dog, the song of a whale, and the cry of a newborn baby.

Each Voyager record was encased in a metal jacket engraved with instructions on how to play it. Before they can receive their message, aliens will have to figure out how to build their own record player! ■

▼ **The Voyager message disk**

▲ **A Voyager space probe receives its message disk.**

The Search for Intelligent Life

Men and women from *every era* have spent time dreaming about the possibility of life existing on other worlds. So far, scientists haven't found a single living cell from another planet, much less a civilization of intelligent beings. But every time we get a clearer peek into the universe, we come closer to answering our questions about extraterrestrial life.

How We Search for Life

Radio telescopes are one of the major ways we get that clearer peek. A **radio telescope** is not a telescope in the visual sense at all. You can't look through one and see anything. Instead, radio telescopes are gigantic antennas that receive radio signals.

The first radio telescope was built in 1931 as an aerial for studying static

SCIENCE IN LITERATURE

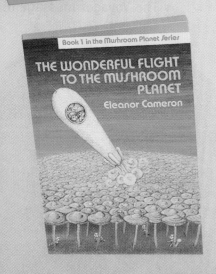

Book 1 in the Mushroom Planet Series

THE WONDERFUL FLIGHT TO THE MUSHROOM PLANET

Eleanor Cameron

THE WONDERFUL FLIGHT TO THE MUSHROOM PLANET
by Eleanor Cameron
Little, Brown and Company, 1988

Science is made up of "what ifs." "What ifs" are also the stuff of fantasy. Put the two together and you have science fiction! You live in a time when space shuttles launch and return to Earth several times a year. *The Wonderful Flight to the Mushroom Planet* was first published back before the first artificial satellite, Sputnik, was launched into space in the 1950s. That was long before humans went into space and explored the Moon.

Yet, you can still enjoy this story 40 years later. As you read, use the science you have learned to separate fact from fantasy. Which parts could be true? Could this story really happen?

▲ The Drake equation

The Odds of Hearing Something

What are the chances that we might communicate someday with an alien civilization? Multiplying each of these estimates may help us find an answer.

1 Estimate the total number of stars that will ever be born.

2 Estimate the percentage of those stars that will have planets.

3 Estimate what proportion of planets will have environments capable of supporting life.

4 Estimate what fraction of potentially habitable planets actually *will* develop life.

5 Of those planets that develop some form of life, estimate what percentage will develop *intelligent* life.

6 Of those planets with intelligent life, estimate what proportion will develop the technology to communicate across space.

7 Estimate the life span of an average civilization after it gains the ability to communicate across space.

that was interfering with radio transmissions. Scientists found that this "static" was coming from the Milky Way. They soon discovered that radio waves are generated naturally by stars, planets, and other objects in space.

Astronomers interested in the possibility of extraterrestrial life realized that radio might be a good way to detect a distant civilization. If humans have been unintentionally sending radio signals out into space since the 1920s, perhaps other civilizations have also been broadcasting news of their existence.

In the 1960s, astronomer Frank Drake began monitoring radio signals from nearby stars that resemble the Sun. This was the beginning of what we now call the search for extraterrestrial intelligence, or SETI. Today, SETI involves radio telescopes as large as 304 m (1,000 ft) in diameter that can pick up faint signals from as far away as 15,000 light-years.

Frank Drake has considered the odds that SETI might someday be successful. The equation he developed to estimate those odds is shown in the box above.

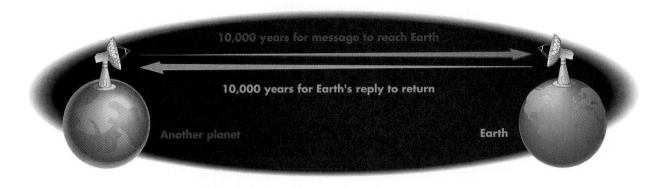

▲ Communicating with a planet 10,000 light-years away

Look especially at the last factor in the equation. Factor 7 may seem out of place with the rest, but it's one of the most important pieces of the puzzle.

Remember how large the distances between stars are? What if a civilization 10,000 light-years from Earth were to send a radio message in our direction? Traveling at the speed of light, that message would take 10,000 years to reach us. If aliens sent the message out today, would humans still be here to receive it in 10,000 years? If we were, and we immediately sent a reply, would the civilization that sent the first message still be around to get our answer after another 10,000 years—20,000 years after they sent their first signal?

What if aliens had sent a message out 20,000 years *ago*? After a 10,000-year trip, the message would have reached Earth around 8000 B.C. Would anyone have had a radio back then to pick up the signal?

When you look at the Drake equation on the previous page, it should be clear to you that there are no firm numbers for any of its steps. Nobody knows how often planets develop or how often intelligent life evolves. Many scientists think it's probable that life exists elsewhere in the universe, but the chance that we'll have a two-way conversation with that life appears slim. If we keep on trying, however, someday we may just get lucky! ■

INVESTIGATION 3

THINK IT WRITE IT

1. Describe several ways in which humans have tried to send messages to and receive messages from other worlds.

2. Suppose you're an astronomer and you receive a signal from outer space. Is it likely or unlikely that this is a communication from extraterrestrials? Would you respond to it? Explain your answers.

REFLECT & EVALUATE

WORD POWER

biosphere
extraterrestrial
free fall
oxygen–carbon dioxide cycle
radio telescope
water cycle

 On Your Own
Write a definition for each term in the list.

With a Partner
Mix up the letters of each term in the list. Provide a clue for each term, and challenge your partner to unscramble the terms.

BUILD YOUR PORTFOLIO

Make a model of a biosphere on the Moon. Include and label various items that will be necessary to support life from Earth.

Analyze Information

Study the drawing. Describe how the two natural cycles shown are important when planning space travel.

Assess Performance

Design your own packaging for three food products you would take on a trip into space. Work with water, cereal, and a carrot. Test different materials to package these items. Explain the reasons for your final packaging choices.

Problem Solving

1. What causes objects to seem weightless in space? Use your answer to explain how gravity affects an orbiting spacecraft.

2. What are some advantages and disadvantages of sending people to do research in space? What are some reasons for sending robot probes instead of people?

3. Suppose that scientists received a radio signal and determined that it came from another inhabited planet. Do you think that humans would be able to communicate back and forth with those who sent the signal? Why or why not?

Throughout this unit you've learned about the solar system and objects beyond the solar system. How will you use what you've learned and share that information with others? Here are some ideas.

Hold a Big Event
to Share Your Unit Project

Invite parents, friends, and other classes to view your completed space-station simulator. Plan and conduct a simulation that will show your visitors what each part of the space station does and what life is like in space. Have different students play different roles, such as chief engineer, medical officer, and astronomer. Include an exciting event in your simulation that might really happen in space.

Experiment

Extend one of the activities in this unit by using different materials or adding new elements. You might expand on your film-canister viewer to make a miniature planetarium. You might develop an improved telescopic camera or use the old one in new ways. You might create new experiments to investigate free fall or to observe light through a spectroscope. Set up a plan for your experiment and show it to your teacher before you begin.

Research

Find out more about a particular object or group of objects in space. You might choose a constellation, a planet or moon, a star or galaxy, or any other object in this unit. Use reference materials to learn as much as you can about your subject. Make a scrapbook highlighting what you discover. If the object can be seen in the sky where you live, locate it and observe it. Use binoculars or a telescope if you can. Describe and sketch what you see and add this to your scrapbook.

ENERGY, WORK, AND MACHINES

Theme: Systems

GET READY TO

OBSERVE & QUESTION

What are work and friction?

Are the people in this picture working, or playing? It might surprise you to learn that work is being done as the toboggan races down the hill. But who or what is doing the work? How would this picture be different if it was summer instead of winter?

EXPERIMENT & HYPOTHESIZE

How can energy be changed to other forms?

Studying the behavior of a bouncing ball will help you learn about different kinds of energy and about how energy changes from one kind to another. This activity can also help you learn how energy is stored in different kinds of matter.

C2

INVESTIGATE!

RESEARCH & ANALYZE

As you investigate, find out more from these books.

- ***Racing the Iditarod Trail*** by Ruth Crisman (Dillon Press, 1993). This book traces the history of a famous sled dog race. It also describes a sport in which a great deal of energy is used to do work.

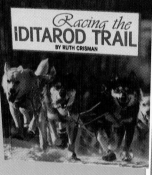

- ***The Winter Room*** by Gary Paulsen (Dell, 1991). What kinds of tools were used on a Minnesota farm years ago? How are these tools related to simple machines that we use every day? Read this book to find out.

WORK TOGETHER & SHARE IDEAS

How can you model the building of an Egyptian pyramid using simple machines?

Working together, you'll have a chance to apply what you've learned to an ancient project—the building of the pyramids in Egypt. Find out if your group can use energy, work, and machines to overcome some of the obstacles faced by the Egyptians as they were constructing the Great Pyramid at Giza.

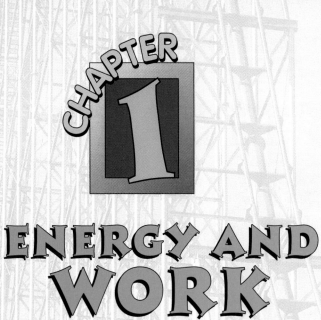

CHAPTER 1

ENERGY AND WORK

You're climbing ever so slowly upward. As you look skyward, your heart pounds, and you tightly clutch the safety bar over your lap. You finally reach the top, pause for one agonizing moment, and then hurtle downward with terrifying speed! You're on a roller coaster, a ride that zooms with energy.

Designing for Speed

Ron Toomer is a mechanical engineer who designs roller coasters. President of Arrow Dynamics, Inc., of Clearfield, Utah, Toomer has designed some of the highest roller coasters in the world.

When Ron Toomer begins to design a roller coaster, he builds a model to help him visualize the ride. Then, using a computer, he determines how to construct an exciting, but safe, roller coaster whose cars will have enough energy to speed over the entire track. What gives a roller coaster energy? Find out through the Investigations in this chapter.

Coming Up

◀ One of Ron Toomer's roller coasters

WHAT ARE SOME DIFFERENT FORMS OF ENERGY?

Make a list of all the things in your classroom that contain energy. In this investigation you'll discover what forms of energy these things contain, how energy changes, and how it travels.

Activity

It's a Stretch

Do you know how to store energy? In this activity you'll see how to store and release energy—just by working with a balloon and a rubber band.

MATERIALS

- goggles
- 2 small balloons
- large rubber band
- pencil
- *Science Notebook*

SAFETY

Wear goggles during this activity. When snapping rubber bands, be sure the bands are directed at the intended target only.

Procedure

1. Blow up a balloon and tie its neck so that no air escapes.

2. Hold the balloon firmly out in front of you with your fingertips while your partner pushes the eraser end of a pencil into the balloon. Release the balloon. In your *Science Notebook*, **describe** what happens to the balloon.

Step 2

3. Place the balloon on a flat surface. Make a fist with your thumb pointed up and place a rubber band over the tip of your thumb.

4. Stretch the rubber band back and aim it at the balloon as shown. **Predict** what will happen if you release the rubber band. Release it and **describe** what happens.

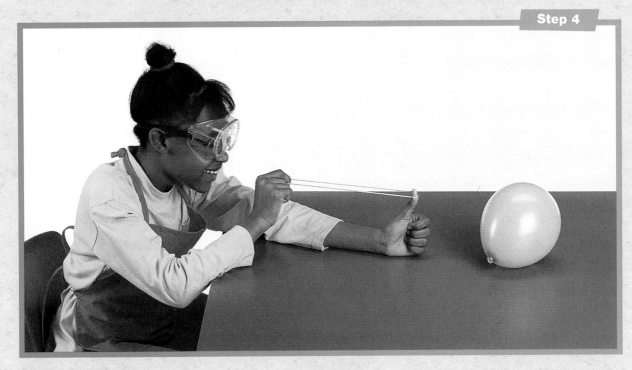

Step 4

5. Blow up a second balloon. Hold the neck tightly, but don't tie it off. **Predict** what will happen if you release the balloon. Release it and **describe** what happens.

Analyze and Conclude

1. How did you store energy in the balloon in step 2? in the rubber band in step 3?

2. Releasing stored energy often causes something to move. In this activity, **tell what evidence** you used to determine that stored energy was released.

3. Moving objects have energy. **Tell what evidence** you observed that indicated that stored energy can be changed to energy of motion.

INVESTIGATE FURTHER!

EXPERIMENT

Create your own experiment with a rubber band and a balloon. Be sure to wear your goggles. Describe the energy forms you observe.

Activity
Using Stored Energy

A battery stores energy. In this activity, you can release some of the energy stored in a battery and find out what forms of energy you can get from it.

Procedure

1. Use a small piece of tape to connect one of the stripped ends of a piece of wire to the bottom of a battery.

2. Tape the other bare end of the wire to the small cap on the top of the battery. Carefully feel the wire by holding a section of the coated wire between your fingers. **Record** your observation and then disconnect the wire from the battery.

3. Connect two wires to the bulb holder. Then touch the unconnected ends of the wires to the top and bottom of the battery as shown. **Observe** what happens.

4. Remove the wires from the battery and **record** your observations in your *Science Notebook*.

Step 3

Analyze and Conclude

1. What kind of energy did the battery supply in this activity?

2. What type of energy did you observe in step 2 of the activity?

3. What type of energy did you observe in step 3?

4. Based on this activity, what can you **infer** about various forms of energy?

Energy and Change

As thousands of people roar, an athlete races down a narrow runway. At the end of the runway, she leaps upward and forward. A fraction of a second later, her heels dig into a soft pit. Sand flies in all directions. The roar of the crowd becomes louder as fans in the stands realize that the athlete has broken a world record.

How did the athlete achieve her great feat? For one thing, she used energy to make things happen, or change. As a matter of fact, this is one way to describe energy: **Energy** is the ability to cause change.

Changes Caused by Energy

If you were to watch a replay of the athlete's record-breaking leap, you might discover some of the changes caused by the energy she produced. Look at the picture on this page. What changes do you see?

Energy can cause an object to change position. The athlete used energy in her muscles to move down the runway. That's a change of position.

Energy can make things change speed or direction. The athlete changed speed as she dashed down the runway. She changed her direction when she

What changes are caused by the athlete's energy? ▼

C9

Sound energy can shatter glass (*left*) and damage eardrums (*right*).

jumped into the air.

Energy can also cause temperature to change. If you could have taken the athlete's temperature, you would have found that it went up while she was running and leaping. Energy released in her body made this happen.

Kinds of Energy

There are many kinds of energy, and each kind can cause things to change. The athlete used mechanical energy to make things change. Mechanical energy includes everything having to do with an object's motion.

If you watched the track event on television, you used electricity, another form of energy. In most power plants, coal or oil is burned to produce heat energy, which is used to make electricity. The burning of fuel releases energy that has been stored in the fuel's chemicals for millions of years. This kind of stored energy is called chemical energy.

You have already seen chemical energy being used. In the activity on page C8, the electricity in the wires came from chemical energy that was stored in the battery.

It doesn't have to take millions of years to store energy in something. In fact, you can store energy in this book just by lifting it up and holding it steady. "Come on," you might say, "there's nothing in this book but pages." OK, then let go of the book. What happens? The book moves toward the floor. All of a sudden, it has energy of motion. Where did the book get that energy? You put it there when you picked up the book. And the energy of motion in the falling book is about equal to the energy you used to lift it.

Let's return one last time to the track star. The energy she used in running and jumping came from chemical energy stored in food she had eaten earlier. Now it's time for the woman to "recharge her batteries." With a little rest and a balanced meal or two, she'll be ready to take another shot at the long-jump record. ■

Energy Transfer

A farmer shades his eyes from the blinding light of a summer day. Waves of heat rise up from the fields around him. Sweat trickles down his tanned neck as he glances at a nearby thermometer. The thermometer reads a sizzling 35°C (95°F).

High in the sky over the farmer's head—150,000,000 km away—is the source of his discomfort. It's the Sun, a blazing star. Deep within the Sun, tremendous amounts of energy are produced continuously. This energy leaves the Sun and travels outward through space in the form of waves. Such energy is called electromagnetic (ē lek′trō-mag net′ik) energy.

Energy Travels in Different Ways

Light is electromagnetic energy you can see. There are other kinds of electromagnetic energy you can't see, such as X-rays, ultraviolet radiation, and infrared radiation.

Electromagnetic energy can travel through empty space. You know this, because energy from the Sun reaches Earth. And there is little between Earth and the Sun except empty space. As stated earlier, electromagnetic energy travels as waves. The transfer of energy by waves is called **radiation**.

If you hold your hand near a hot object—a radiator, for example—you can feel the heat without touching the

Energy from the sun can make you squint and make your skin feel hot. ▼

How does heat travel from the radiator to your hands? ▼

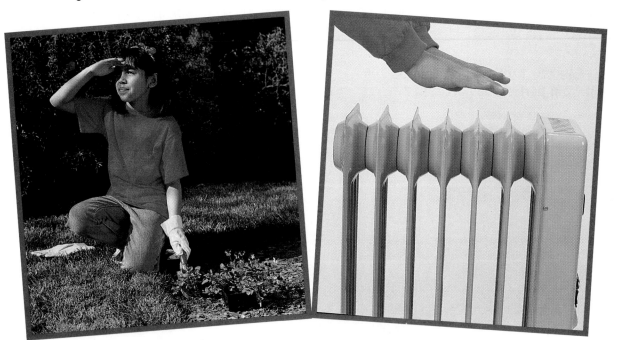

▲ **Why does the last penny move from the row?**

object. Some energy leaves the radiator as infrared radiation. When this invisible form of electromagnetic energy reaches your hand, it is absorbed and changed to heat energy.

All forms of energy can travel from place to place. However, electromagnetic energy is the only form that can travel through empty space. Every other form of energy needs a *medium* of some kind to carry, or transfer, it. A medium may be matter in any of its familiar states—solid, liquid, or gas.

Disturbing Particles

Energy can travel through solids, liquids, and gases by disturbing the particles that make up these mediums. In solids, energy causes the particles to vibrate a bit. But the particles don't go anywhere. They simply transfer energy from one particle to the next. In this way, the energy moves through the mediums as waves.

To get an idea of how this transfer of energy works, lay eight pennies down in a row on a flat surface. Each penny should touch the next penny in line, as shown in the picture. Now take a ninth penny and snap it against a penny at one end of the row. What happens to the eight pennies?

Only the last penny moves. The energy that you gave to the penny you snapped is transferred through the line of pennies to the last penny. The other pennies serve as the medium for the transfer of energy.

Heat and other forms of energy can be transferred through different mediums. Let's say you want to fry eggs in a pan with a metal handle. You place the pan on a hot stove burner. Soon the pan is hot. You drop in butter and eggs, and they begin to sizzle.

If you continue to hold the handle of the pan, soon something besides eggs might begin to sizzle—your hand! This

Heat travels through the metal of the pan from particle to particle. ▼

Warm air rises.

...cools and sinks.

Air is heated.

Cool air moves toward the stove.

Cool air pushes up warm air.

▲ **Air in the room is heated by convection.**

happens because heat is transferred through the metal pan to its handle.

Energy is transferred through solids such as the pan by conduction (kən-duk'shən). **Conduction** is the transfer of energy by direct contact between particles. The particles in a solid are packed close together. Energy is simply conducted, or passed along, from one particle to the next.

Energy can also be transferred through fluids—liquids and gases—by the movement of particles. The transfer of heat energy through fluids by moving particles is called **convection** (kən-vek'shən). The picture at the top of this page shows how heat energy from a

stove on one side of a room can warm the air on the other side of the room by convection.

Convection can occur in fluids because the particles in fluids can move about quite freely, carrying heat energy with them. Energy can't be transferred through solids by convection, because the particles remain in fixed positions.

Solids, liquids, and gases can also carry energy as waves. Think about the energy carried by ocean waves, for example. Sound energy travels through air as waves. Unlike electromagnetic waves, however, sound waves can't travel through empty space. Sound travels by "making waves" of air. ■

INVESTIGATION 1

1. Name three kinds of energy and give examples of how each kind can cause a change to occur.

2. Explain why astronauts used radio waves (electromagnetic waves) rather than sound waves to communicate with each other on the Moon.

HOW CAN ENERGY BE CHANGED TO OTHER FORMS?

Where does your body's energy come from? On a sheet of paper, make a drawing of a person. Around the person, draw pictures that show where the person gets energy. Add to your diagram to show where the energy in these sources comes from. Use arrows to show where you think energy changes form.

Activity

To Bounce or Not to Bounce

A flashlight has energy stored in its chemicals. How can an object placed on a high shelf also have stored energy? How can that energy change?

MATERIALS
- small rubber ball
- clay
- meterstick
- *Science Notebook*

SAFETY //////
Be careful not to lose your balance when standing on a chair.

Procedure

1. Hold a ball in front of you at a height of 1 m. Release the ball and have another student **measure** how high the ball bounces. **Record** the height of the bounce in your *Science Notebook*.

2. Stand on a chair and hold the ball at a height of 2 m, as shown. **Predict** how high the ball will bounce after it hits the floor. Release the ball and have a group member **measure** and **record** the height of its bounce.

3. Shape the clay into a ball about the size of the rubber ball. Drop the clay ball from a height of 1 m. **Describe** how the clay looks after hitting the floor.

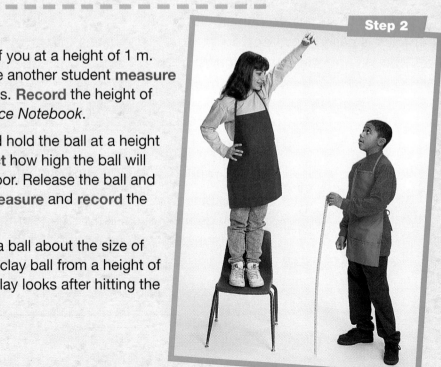
Step 2

C14

4. Reshape the clay into a ball and drop it from a height of 2 m. **Describe** how the clay looks after it hits the floor.

Analyze and Conclude

1. **Tell what evidence** you observed that the rubber ball and the clay ball at a height of 1 m had stored energy.

2. What happened to the amount of energy stored in the balls as you raised them from a height of 1 m to a height of 2 m? How do you know?

3. What happened to the energy stored in the balls when you released them? How do you know?

4. Some materials can store energy as they change shape when striking a surface. Which material, rubber or clay, stores more energy this way? How do you know?

Steps 3 and 4

INVESTIGATE FURTHER!

EXPERIMENT

In this activity you discovered that a rubber ball bounces differently than does a clay ball. Now get together with your group members and design an experiment to find out how balls made of other materials respond to being dropped from different heights. You might also design an experiment to find out if the mass of a ball affects how high it will bounce. After you have designed your experiment and described it in writing, show it to your teacher. If your teacher approves, carry out your experiment and record your results.

Activity
Roller Coaster Energy

A roller coaster car has stored energy as it sits at the top of the first hill. How does the energy change as the car speeds down this hill and up the next?

MATERIALS
- aquarium tubing (about 3 m)
- BB or small marble
- masking tape
- *Science Notebook*

Procedure

1. Place a BB inside a piece of aquarium tubing and seal the ends of the tubing with tape.

2. Let the BB roll to one end of the tubing. Raise that end of the tubing and release the BB. **Observe** how its speed changes as it rolls down the tubing. **Record** your observations in your *Science Notebook*.

3. Arrange the tubing in a series of hills (at least two) to model the form of a roller coaster track. The beginning of your model should be the top of a hill. **Sketch your model** roller coaster in your *Science Notebook*.

4. Place the BB at the starting point of your model and release it. **Observe** and **record** how the speed of the BB changes as it moves through the tubing.

5. If the BB doesn't make it all the way to the end, reshape the tubing and try again.

Step 3

C16

Analyze and Conclude

1. **Compare** the potential energy of the BB with its energy of motion just after you released it.

2. At what point in its journey does the BB have the most energy of motion?

3. When does the BB speed up during its trip? When does it slow down?

4. When is the BB traveling the fastest in the tubing? When is it traveling the slowest?

5. The energy of the BB changes from stored energy to energy of motion as it travels through the tubing. **Describe** the BB's trip along your model roller coaster in terms of the energy changes that take place.

INVESTIGATE FURTHER!

EXPERIMENT

Shape the tubing so that it has a loop in it. First draw the shape of the track. Then experiment with the track until the BB can make it through the entire loop. What factor seems to determine whether the BB moves all the way through?

Energy Changes

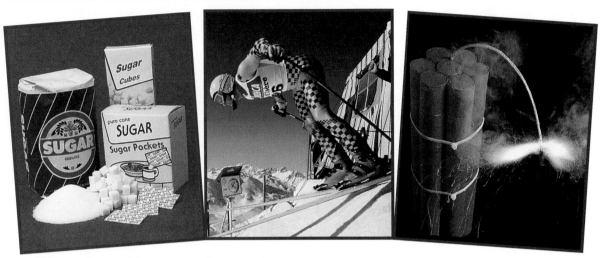

▲ **All of these objects contain stored energy.**

Look at the pictures on this page. What do the sugar, the dynamite, and the skier at the top of a steep hill have in common? They all have energy stored in them.

Sugar is a source of quick energy that can help you do something like dash around a basketball court. Dynamite can blow rocks out of a mountainside. And when a skier moves onto the slope of a hill, he or she has enough energy to speed swiftly to the bottom of the hill.

So the sugar, the dynamite, and the poised skier contain enough energy to cause something to change position, or to move from one place to another. However, the energy in these things isn't being used. It's just sitting there, waiting for something to set it loose. This energy-in-waiting is called potential energy. **Potential energy** is stored energy.

Chemical Storehouses

Energy is stored in different ways. Consider a packet of sugar and a stick of dynamite. Although one of these materials is harmless and the other can be very destructive, both materials store energy in the same way.

The energy in sugar and dynamite is stored in the chemical bonds that link their atoms. A bond can be compared to the rope in a tug of war. The atoms are like people pulling on opposite ends of the rope. The energy the people exert is stored in the rope. The rope holds the people together. But if the rope breaks, the people go flying in opposite directions. When this happens, the energy that was stored in the rope is released.

When you eat sugar, the chemical bonds that

store energy in the sugar are broken down by chemicals in your body. This action releases energy for you to use. With dynamite, the bonds are broken down by a spark or a jolt of electricity. When these bonds break, a great deal of energy is released very quickly. Because the energy in sugar and dynamite is stored in chemical bonds, it is called chemical potential energy.

How Much Energy?

How much energy is stored in that packet of sugar you read about earlier? If you read the label on a packet, you'll find that the sugar contains 16 Calories. But what does that tell you about the amount of stored energy in the sugar?

A Calorie is a measure of energy. One Calorie is the amount of heat energy needed to raise the temperature of 1 kg of water 1°C. So if changed to heat energy, the stored energy in a packet of sugar could raise the temperature of 1 kg of water 16°C.

The Calorie is a useful unit for finding the stored energy in different foods. But scientists deal with many different forms of energy, and they need a unit of measure that can be applied to all of

▲ Food is burned in a calorimeter (kal ə rim′ət ər) to find out how many Calories the food contains.

them. The **joule** (jo͞ol) is the basic unit of energy used by scientists.

The joule is named after an English scientist who studied the relationship between heat and other forms of energy. One joule is the amount of energy that is needed to raise the temperature of 1 g of water 4.18°C.

Transfer of Energy

Look at the photograph on page C20. A couple of seconds before the picture was taken, the two acrobats on the end of the seesaw were standing up on the platform to their right. The acrobat flying through the air was standing on the other end of the seesaw.

Energy stored in the rope is released when the rope breaks. ▼

▲ **Where did the flying acrobat's energy come from?**

While standing on the platform, the two acrobats had potential energy because of their position above the ground. They had stored that energy as they climbed up to the platform. Energy stored in an object because of its position above the ground is called gravitational potential energy. Such an object can be set in motion by Earth's pull of gravity on the object.

As the two acrobats stepped off the platform, their potential energy was changed to kinetic (ki net'ik) energy. **Kinetic energy** is energy of motion. When the acrobats landed on the seesaw, their kinetic energy pushed one end of the seesaw down. The other end was pushed up, launching the third acrobat into the air. The kinetic energy of the two acrobats had been transferred through the seesaw to the third acrobat.

Energy on a Roller Coaster

The thrills of a roller coaster ride depend on repeated changes in energy—from potential to kinetic and back again. These changes are similar to the changes that the BB experienced as it moved through the plastic tubing in the activity on pages C16 and C17.

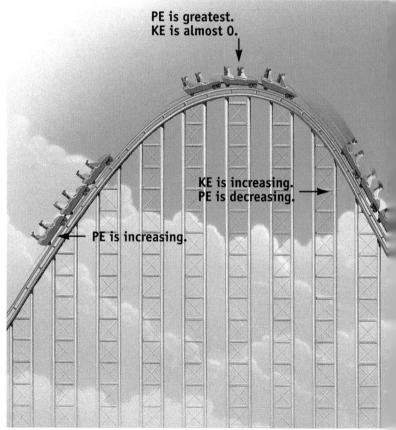

PE is greatest.
KE is almost 0.

KE is increasing.
PE is decreasing.

PE is increasing.

C20

As a roller coaster ride begins, energy supplied by a motor hauls the roller coaster car up a track. As the car goes up, it gains potential energy. At the top of the hill, when its potential energy is greatest, the car is set loose.

What happens now? The car begins to roll down the hill. It gains kinetic energy. The potential energy the car had due to its position at the top of the hill is changing to energy of motion.

As the seconds flash by, more and more potential energy is changed into kinetic energy. How do you know this is happening? The roller coaster moves faster and faster down the track.

When the car reaches the bottom of the hill, all the potential energy it had at the top of the hill has been changed to kinetic energy. At this point the car is moving so fast it has enough kinetic energy to carry it all the way up to the top of the next hill.

As the car climbs, it slows down. Kinetic energy is being changed back to potential energy. When the car reaches the top of the hill, it begins a new plunge. Once again, potential energy changes into kinetic energy. Engineers design roller coaster rides so that repeated changes from potential to kinetic energy and back to potential will keep the cars in motion for the entire trip. And the changes will keep you screaming all the way. ■

Energy changes in a roller coaster ride ▼

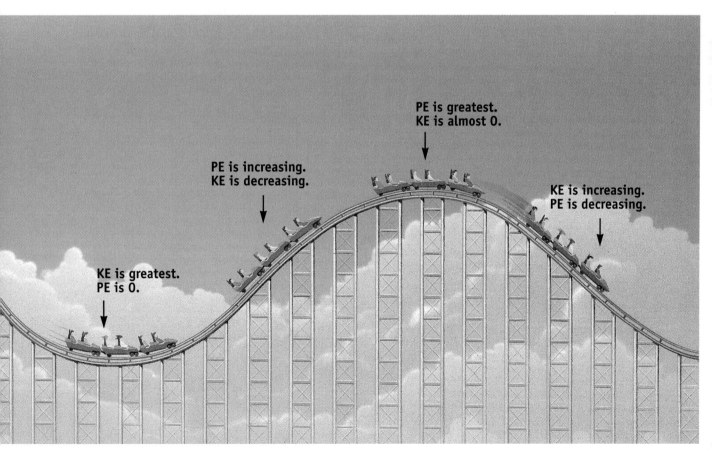

PE is greatest.
KE is almost 0.

PE is increasing.
KE is decreasing.

KE is increasing.
PE is decreasing.

KE is greatest.
PE is 0.

Green Plants: Energy Factories

Every country in the world is dotted with silent factories. In some places these factories cover the land as far as the eye can see. You may be thinking that these factories must be idle if they are silent, that no useful products are being made.

These factories, however, aren't idle—they make a product without which you and all the world's people could not live. That product is food. And the food contains the stored energy all living things need to carry out their life activities.

Unfortunately, in many countries of the world there aren't enough of these factories to keep all the people healthy

or even alive. What's more, many scientists fear that the situation may get worse as the years pass. Later you'll find out why scientists think this is true. But first let's take a brief tour of one of these energy factories to find out what it is and how it works.

The factories are green plants. Green plants make their own food. That food is also used by all living things that eat green plants. The plants are not actually single factories. Rather, the plants contain millions of tiny factories called chloroplasts (klôr′ə plasts).

The chemical chlorophyll gives chloroplasts their green color. Inside a chloroplast, water from the soil and carbon dioxide from the air are combined

The product made in this factory is sugar. ▼

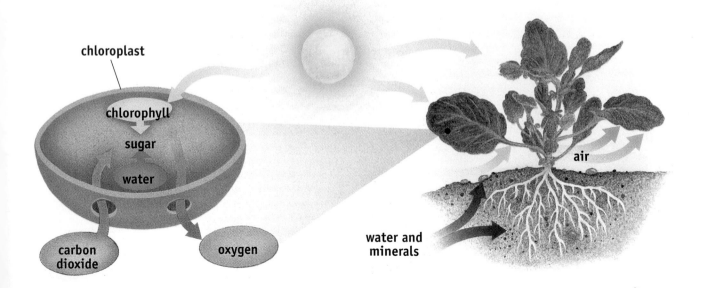

chloroplast

chlorophyll

sugar

water

carbon dioxide

oxygen

water and minerals

air

to make a sugar called glucose (glōō′kōs). In this process, called photosynthesis (fōt ō sin′thə sis), some of the sun's energy gets stored in the glucose.

When you eat a leaf of spinach, a slice of bread, or any other plant product, you're taking in energy stored in glucose. In your body, your cells are able to break down the glucose and release its stored energy. You're using some of that energy right now. You're using energy to move, to think, and to do all the other things that keep you alive.

This thought brings us back to the problem that faces many people— hunger! Of the almost 6 billion people in the world, more than half a billion don't get enough food. Many millions of people die every year from starvation.

In some places the human population is growing faster than farmers are able to grow the crops needed to feed the people. In a sense the energy factories aren't keeping up with the people factories. The reasons can be summed

▲ **Bad weather can lead to crop failures.**

up in a few words—bad weather, poor soil, and increasing populations.

Scientists and farmers all over the world are seeking solutions to the problem of hunger. New methods to increase crop production have been successful in some countries. But further efforts are needed to find ways to adequately feed all the people in the world. ■

INVESTIGATION 2

1. Trace the energy you get from eating an apple back to the Sun.

2. You give a friend on a playground swing one hard push. Describe the energy changes that the swing undergoes until it stops moving.

C23

INVESTIGATION 3

WHAT ARE WORK AND FRICTION?

List all the work you've done since you got up today. A scientist's list might be quite different from yours. To a scientist, *work* has a special meaning. Check your list again after this investigation. Then you'll know how many of your activities involve "real" work and why work isn't easy.

Activity

A Lifting Experience

How much work do you do when you lift things? Take some measurements in this activity.

MATERIALS

- spring scale
- small cloth bag or plastic bag
- meterstick
- assorted objects to be weighed
- *Science Notebook*

Procedure

1. Make a chart in your *Science Notebook* like the one shown here.

Object	Force (Newtons)	Distance (Meters)	Work (Joules)

2. The force needed to lift an object is equal to the weight of the object. Weigh each object by placing it in a small bag and hanging the bag from a spring scale, as shown. Use the weight unit labeled *Newton* on the scale. **Record** the weights in your chart under the heading *Force*.

Step 2

3. Use a meterstick to **measure** the heights of two different tables in your classroom.

4. Place on the floor all of the objects you weighed. Lift half the objects onto the lower table. Then lift the rest of the objects onto the higher table. **Record** the height an object is lifted in the *Distance* column of your chart.

Step 4

5. Find the amount of work done on each object by multiplying the weight of an object by the distance you lifted it. **Record** the results in the *Work* column of your chart.

Analyze and Conclude

1. Describe the relationship between the weight of an object and the work you do to lift it.

2. Describe the relationship between the height that you lift an object and the work that you do to lift it.

3. Suppose you lift an object that weighs 3 newtons onto a shelf that is 2 m high. Then you lift an object weighing 6 newtons onto a bench that is 1 m high. How would the amount of work done on the first object compare with that done on the second object? How do you know?

Activity
Sliding Along

Sometimes when you have to move something that's too heavy or bulky to lift, you slide it along the floor. Then you notice that a force seems to push against you. Discover the nature of that force.

MATERIALS

- goggles
- smooth board
- sandpaper
- thumbtacks
- thin rubber band
- 2 blocks of wood
- string
- metric ruler
- *Science Notebook*

SAFETY ///////

Be careful when using thumbtacks. Wear goggles during this activity.

Procedure

1. Tack a piece of sandpaper to one half of the board, as shown.

2. Rub your finger across the smooth part of the board and then across the sandpaper. In your *Science Notebook*, **describe** the differences you feel.

3. Stick a tack in the top of one of the wooden blocks. Place the block on the board and loop the rubber band around the tack.

4. **Measure** and **record** the length of the unstretched rubber band. Then slowly pull on the rubber band until the block moves along the smooth part of the board at a steady speed. Have a group member **measure** and **record** how much the rubber band stretches as you pull the block.

Step 1

5. **Predict** how the sandpaper will affect how much the rubber band will stretch. Then pull the block across the sandpaper. **Measure** and **record** how much the rubber band stretches as the block is pulled.

6. Use string and thumbtacks to attach two wooden blocks, as shown. Use the rubber band to pull the blocks across a smooth surface—a desktop, for example. **Measure** and **record** how much the rubber band stretches as you pull the blocks.

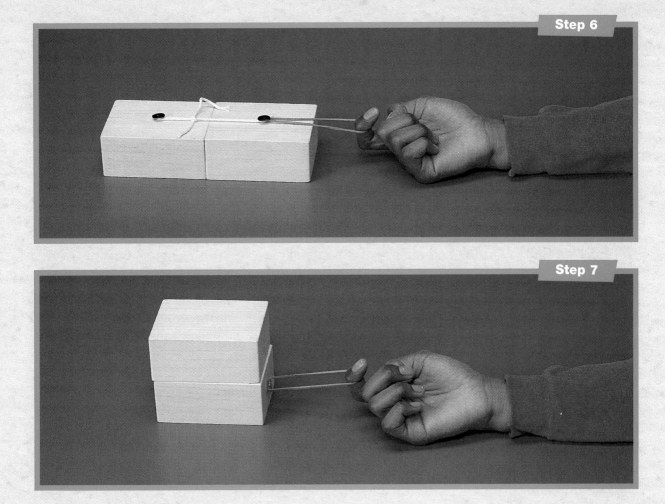

7. Now place one block on top of the other. Again, use the rubber band to pull the blocks along the smooth surface. **Measure** and **record** how much the rubber band stretches.

Analyze and Conclude

1. Does it take more force to move the block over the smooth surface or over the rough surface? **Tell what evidence** you used to draw your conclusion.

2. **Compare** the forces needed to move the blocks in steps 6 and 7. What is different about the two setups?

3. **Friction** is a force that opposes motion. What **inferences** can you make about friction, based on this activity?

UNIT PROJECT LINK

Each block used in the Great Pyramid of Giza was transported several kilometers over land and then moved up a sloping side of the pyramid. Design methods to decrease the effort needed to move each block by reducing friction between the block and the surface over which it moves.

When It's Work and
When It's Not

You might think that reading a difficult book is hard work. A scientist might say, "Well, it all depends." You might answer, "Depends on what?" "Depends on whether or not you turn the pages," the scientist would reply.

You *see*, the word *work* has a special meaning for scientists. Specifically, **work** is done if a force moves an object. If there's no movement, no work is done. So merely reading, no matter how difficult the subject matter, isn't work. On the other hand, turning the pages of a book *is* work.

When you turn a page, you apply a force to the page with your fingers. A **force** is a pull or push. That force moves the page a certain distance. The amount of work you do depends on the size of the force you exert on the page and the distance the page moves. This idea can be expressed by the statement: *Work equals force times distance.* Scientists use a shorthand formula to express the amount of work done. This formula is

$$W = F \times D$$

Energy and Work

Energy is needed to do work. For example, the energy released when dynamite explodes underground is transferred to the rocks as work is done on them by the force of the explosion. This force makes the rocks fly some distance through the air. So energy produces a force that moves an object through some distance. And that's doing work.

Getting Tired Without Doing Work

Imagine you and some friends are collecting large rocks to build a wall around a summer camp. You come upon a perfect rock in the middle of a narrow trail. You bend down and pull on the rock, but it doesn't move. You

No work is done. ▼

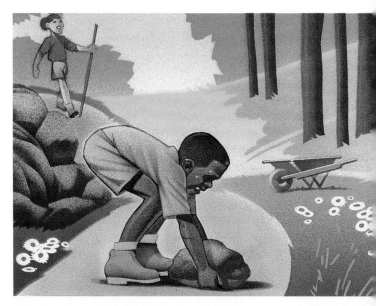

get a better grip and pull even harder, but still no luck.

You don't give up. You keep pulling, your muscles begin to ache, and sweat begins to roll down your head and into your eyes. Finally, you can't pull anymore. You've used up a lot of energy, and you're very tired. But you still haven't done any work on the rock. The force you exerted on the rock didn't move it any distance.

While you're catching your breath from your exertion, a friend comes along and offers to help you move the rock. Acting together, the two of you are able to exert enough force to lift the rock. Once the rock has been lifted, your friend tells you to hold it while she goes for the wheelbarrow you left at the side of the trail.

You get a good grip on the rock and your friend lets go. And you hang on for dear life! Although it only takes your friend a few seconds to get the wheelbarrow and bring it back, it seems like forever. By the time you lower the rock into the wheelbarrow, your muscles are

shaking and your knees are weak.

Surely you did some work on the rock while you were holding it. Wrong again! Even though you exerted a lot of force to keep the rock from falling, you didn't move the rock. Once again, you're tired and sore, but you didn't do any work on the rock.

How Work Is Measured

As you discovered earlier, work can be calculated by multiplying the force exerted on an object by the distance the object moves, or $W = F \times D$.

You know how distance is measured. You measure distance in a familiar unit called the meter (m). But you may not be familiar with the unit used to measure force. This unit is called a **newton** (N). Scientists named this unit in honor of Sir Isaac Newton, a famous British scientist who studied force and motion about 300 years ago.

Since force and distance units are multiplied to get work, the unit for work turns out to be the newton-meter (N-m). You might think this is a clumsy unit.

Work is done. ▼

No work is done. ▼

And scientists have agreed with you. They simplified the unit by calling it a joule (J). Recall that a joule is a unit for measuring energy. Since doing work on an object transfers energy to the object, it makes sense to measure both work and energy in the same unit.

Now you can figure out how much work you and your friend did in lifting the rock 1 m. Let's say that the rock weighed 200 newtons.

Use the formula:

$$W = F \times D$$
$$= 200\ N \times 1\ m$$
$$= 200\ N\text{-}m,\ \text{or}\ 200\ J$$

How much work would you and your friend have done if the rock had weighed 250 N and was lifted 0.5 m above the ground? Figure it out.

Why Doing Work Isn't Easy

To get any work done, you always have to overcome some force. For example, gravity is a force you have to overcome to lift something. Friction is another force you have to overcome to do work, especially when you're trying to move an object along the ground. You learned about friction in the activity on pages C26 and C27.

Friction and gravity are forces that resist, or oppose, certain motions. Forces that resist motion are called **resistance forces**. The force you have to exert on an object to get it to move is called the **effort force**. In order for work to be done on an object, the effort force must always be greater than the resistance force. ■

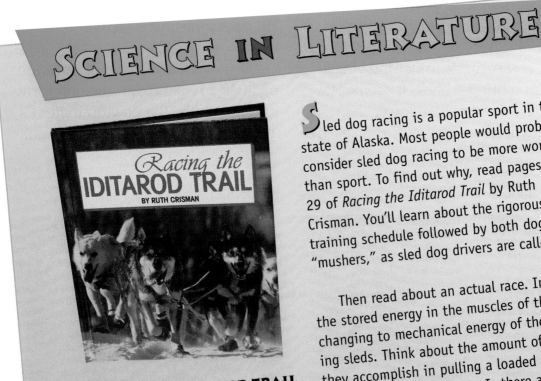

SCIENCE IN LITERATURE

RACING THE IDITAROD TRAIL
by Ruth Crisman
Dillon Press, 1993

Sled dog racing is a popular sport in the state of Alaska. Most people would probably consider sled dog racing to be more work than sport. To find out why, read pages 27-29 of *Racing the Iditarod Trail* by Ruth Crisman. You'll learn about the rigorous training schedule followed by both dogs and "mushers," as sled dog drivers are called.

Then read about an actual race. Imagine the stored energy in the muscles of the dogs changing to mechanical energy of the moving sleds. Think about the amount of work they accomplish in pulling a loaded sled over the 1,600-km course. Is there any doubt that sled dogs are among the best-conditioned athletes in the world?

Friction and Work

You're speeding down a snow-covered hill on a toboggan. As you near the bottom of the hill, you expect to slow down and come to a stop. But to your surprise and amazement, your toboggan doesn't slow down. It keeps on moving at a constant speed over long stretches of flat ground.

Towns and cities flash by. You cross one state border after another. The snow is gone, but your toboggan keeps gliding over grass, sand, concrete, and gravel. You wonder if you will ever stop moving. And you won't—the force of friction has been suspended!

Suddenly, the sound of your alarm clock intrudes into your fantasy. Your dream is over, and friction is back.

Sometimes a lack of friction is good . . . ▼

▲ **. . . sometimes it's not!**

Friction: The Antimotion Force

A world without friction is only possible in a dream or a science fiction story. Any time that matter rubs against other matter, there is friction.

The matter could be any of these things: the runners of a sled and the snow under them, the soles of your shoes and a sidewalk, the tires of a car and the concrete of a road.

Friction is a force that acts against other forces, like pushes and pulls. Since pushes and pulls tend to produce motion, you might think of friction as being an antimotion force. *Anti-* means "against" or "opposed to."

C31

If there were no friction, walking would be impossible. And if, somehow, you did manage to get yourself moving, how would you stop? You couldn't grab onto anything, because grabbing requires friction. You'd have to crash into something, like a fence or a tree.

As you can see, there are times when friction is useful. There are also times when it is not. It's not useful if you want to glide a long way on a sled. It's very useful, however, if you want to play basketball without falling down every time you cut toward the basket. And, of course, it's extremely useful if you want to stop a moving car.

The Friction Story Heats Up

Friction slows a moving object by changing some of its kinetic energy to heat energy. That is, the energy of motion is changed to heat energy. This heat is wasted energy. As more of a moving object's kinetic energy is turned to heat, the slower the object moves.

How do you know that friction produces heat? If you've ever seen a speeding car screech to a stop, you may have seen a puff of smoke and smelled something unpleasant. The smoke came from the car's tires rubbing against the road. And burning rubber has an unpleasant smell.

But you don't have to recall a near accident to experience the heat produced by friction. Just rub your hands together. What do you feel?

Friction: More or Less

It's a cold winter day and your front walk is a sheet of ice. You have friends coming over, and you're afraid that someone might slip on the ice and get hurt. So you go out and spread some sand over the ice.

Recall how the sandpaper in the activity on pages C26 and C27 increased the friction between the blocks and the board. Spreading sand over the walk will make the surface of

Friction at work ▼

▲ Sliding friction can be difficult to overcome.

Wheels, rollers, and ball bearings are all used to reduce sliding friction. Imagine trying to move a freight train without wheels, and you'll get a clear idea of the advantages of rolling friction over sliding friction.

Skating on Water

Another way to reduce sliding friction is to place some fluid between the surfaces that rub against each other. *Lubricants* (lo͞o′bri-kәntz), such as oil, grease, and wax are probably the most familiar fluids used to reduce friction. For example, you can apply wax to the runners of a sticky drawer, or oil to a squeaky hinge. In addition to making work easier, lubricants extend the life of moving parts of machines that rub against other parts.

the ice rougher. This will increase the friction between your friends' feet and the ice, thereby making the ice less slippery.

Now let's change seasons. It's spring and you've been asked by your parents to haul a carton of trash to the curb. The carton is too bulky to carry, so you try pushing and pulling it across the ground. The carton barely budges.

After a few minutes of shoving and hauling, you decide that there's too much friction between the carton and the ground. You're up against something called sliding friction. How can you reduce this friction?

You think for awhile and come up with an idea. You put the carton on a skateboard and push. The carton moves easily. How come? You substituted rolling friction for sliding friction. A carton that moves by rolling on wheels produces less friction than one that moves by sliding.

You can roll along with rolling friction. ▼

▲ **This girl is skating on "thin water."**

You probably think that ice is slippery enough, right? Well, if you've ever been ice skating, your skate blades have actually made the ice even more slippery. As the blades of your skates slide across the ice, heat is produced. This heat melts the ice beneath your skate

blades. So the blades glide over a thin film of water. This fluid lubrication reduces the friction between the blades of your skates and the ice.

Friction and Work

You know from experience that it takes more force to slide an object over a rough surface than over a smooth one. You also know that rough surfaces produce more friction than smooth surfaces. So you can infer that it takes extra force to overcome friction. How does this need for extra force affect the amount of work you do?

For a clue to the answer to this question, take another look at the formula for work: $W = F \times D$. This formula tells you that the work done in moving an object is equal to the force used times the distance the object is moved. What happens if friction makes you exert extra force to move the object? You have to do more work to move the object the same distance.

Friction, then, is sort of a mixed bag. Friction can make work harder, and it can wear out your shoes. But friction also makes moving about possible. And without it, you couldn't lick an ice-cream cone. ■

─────── **INVESTIGATION 3** ───────

1. Explain why you wouldn't wear basketball shoes to go bowling.

2. Imagine that you pick up a book from the floor and place it on a shelf 1.5 m high. If the book has a weight of 10 N, how much work do you do?

REFLECT & EVALUATE

On Your Own
Write a definition for each term in the list.

With a Partner
Make up a quiz, using all the terms in the list. Challenge your partner to complete the quiz.

PORTFOLIO

Cut out a picture of a roller coaster from a magazine, or draw your own roller coaster. Glue your picture to a sheet of posterboard. Add labels to your poster to show how a roller coaster makes use of potential energy and kinetic energy.

Analyze Information

Study the drawings. Then use the drawings to explain how much work each person will do in moving her rock the distance shown.

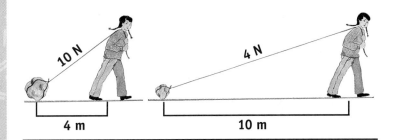

10 N   4 N

4 m   10 m

Assess Performance

Design an experiment to determine the effect of oil on friction. Work with the materials you used in the "Sliding Along" activity and salad oil. Predict how the oil will affect friction. Then conduct your experiment and check your prediction.

Problem Solving

1. Samantha used a match to light the candles on her brother's birthday cake. Describe all the energy changes that were involved. What role did potential energy play in the lighting of the candles?

2. Suppose you put a pot of water on the stove to boil. Describe how heat is transferred from the stove burner to the water.

3. Imagine that you pick up a carton of books that weighs 20 N and lift it to a height of 1 m. You carry it 12 m across the room and place it on a shelf 2 m high. How much work do you do on the carton of books?

CHAPTER 2

WORK AND MACHINES

Some words just go together: *salt* and *pepper*, *day* and *night*, *hot* and *cold*, *on* and *off*. What words seem to go with *knife*, *hammer*, and *tennis racket*? You might answer *fork*, *nails*, and *tennis ball*. However, in this chapter you'll find *one* word that goes with *knife*, *hammer*, and *tennis racket*. That word is *machine*.

What a Racket

During a two-week period that begins in late August, the U.S. Open Tennis Championships are held at the National Tennis Center in New York City. This tournament features the top tennis players in the world. Among them is Zina Garrison Jackson, a professional American tennis player who is among the very best. To play tennis at Zina's level, an athlete must have stamina, quickness, and the ability to hit a tennis ball with great accuracy. Of course, one other item is essential: A TENNIS RACKET!

Through countless hours of practice, Zina Garrison Jackson has developed techniques for hitting winning shots with power and precision. She has mastered the machine of tennis. That's right—a tennis racket is a type of simple machine known as a lever. In this chapter, you'll learn how levers and other machines help you do work.

Coming Up

◄ Zina Garrison Jackson,
tennis professional

HOW DO RAMPS HELP US DO WORK?

Imagine that you are planning to hike to the top of a mountain, and you have the choice of two trails. One trail winds around the mountain at a gentle slope to the top; the other follows a straight path up the side of the mountain. Both trails start at the same point and end at the same place. Yet one trail is much easier to climb. Why? Which trail would you take?

Activity

Ramps and Rocks

The mountain trails are types of ramps. Suppose that, after returning from your hike, you had to move a heavy rock from the ground onto the back of a truck. Would it be easier to lift the rock straight up or slide it up a ramp?

MATERIALS

- goggles
- string
- small rock
- paper clip
- thin rubber band
- metric ruler
- smooth board
- 3 books
- *Science Notebook*

SAFETY

Wear goggles during this activity

Procedure

1. Tie a piece of string around a small rock. Bend a paper clip into a double hook. Connect it to the rock, as shown.

2. Measure the length of an un-stretched rubber band and record the length in your *Science Notebook*. Hook the rubber band to the paper clip and rock. Use the rubber band to lift the rock. Have a group member measure and record the length of the stretched rubber band.

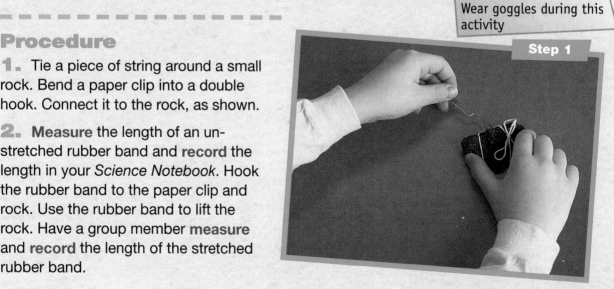

Step 1

3. Make a ramp by placing one end of a smooth board on a pile of books. Place the rock at the bottom of the ramp.

4. Predict how much the rubber band will stretch when you pull the rock up the ramp. Slowly pull on the rubber band until the rock starts to move up the ramp. Continue to pull at a slow, steady rate so that the rubber band remains stretched at a constant length. Have a group member **measure** and **record** how far the rubber band stretches as you pull on it.

Analyze and Conclude

1. What force does the stretching of the rubber band measure?

2. How do you know that you are doing work in step 1 and in step 4?

3. Did you have to exert more force to lift the rock or to pull it up the ramp? Explain your answer.

4. How does using a ramp make the job of raising a heavy object easier?

INVESTIGATE FURTHER!

RESEARCH

Look for a construction project underway around your school or neighborhood. See if a ramp is in use there. Prepare a report explaining how the ramp is being used.

Step 4

Activity

Different Slants on Doing Work

Some ramps are steeper than others. How does a ramp's steepness affect the force needed to move things along it?

MATERIALS

- metric ruler
- 3 books
- 3 boards of different lengths
- small heavy object
- small cart with wheels
- spring scale
- *Science Notebook*

Procedure

1. In your *Science Notebook*, **make a chart** like the one shown here.

Length of Ramp	Height of Books	Force

2. **Measure** the lengths of the three boards. **Record** these lengths in the first column of your chart. Stack three books. **Measure** and **record** the height of the stack.

3. Use the longest board to make a ramp up to the top of the stack of books.

4. Place the object to be moved in a cart, and use a spring scale to pull the cart up the ramp at a steady speed, as shown. Have a group member **observe** the reading on the spring scale and **record** it in the *Force* column of your chart.

5. **Predict** what effect the use of shorter boards would have on the force needed to pull the cart up the ramps. To check your prediction, repeat step 4, using the other boards as ramps.

Analyze and Conclude

1. **Make a bar graph** of your data. Plot ramp lengths on the *x*-axis and plot force along the *y*-axis.

2. Describe the relationship between the length of a ramp and the force needed to move a load up the ramp.

Step 4

3. What is the advantage of using a ramp with a gentle slope? a steeper slope?

C40

Activity
Ramp with a Twist

Long ramps take up a lot of room. But can a long ramp be redesigned so that it takes up less space?

MATERIALS
- metric ruler
- crayon or colored pencil
- sheet of unlined paper
- scissors
- tape
- unsharpened pencil
- screw
- *Science Notebook*

Procedure

1. With a ruler and a crayon, **draw** a diagonal line across a sheet of paper from corner to corner. Cut the paper along this diagonal and keep one triangle.

2. Notice that the colored line is like a ramp. **Measure** the length of this line and **record** the length of the line in your *Science Notebook*.

3. **Brainstorm** with members of your group to come up with a way to make the line on the paper produce a "ramp" that winds around a pencil. Then carry out your plan. In your notebook, **draw a sketch** of your model ramp.

Step 3

4. **Measure** and **record** the length of the pencil.

5. **Compare** the ramp on the pencil with the threads on a screw.

Analyze and Conclude

1. How does the length of the diagonal line compare with the length of the pencil? How did you make the "ramp" take up less space?

2. Which part of the screw is similar to the ramp that winds around the pencil?

3. When a screw is twisted down into a board, what "travels" along the ramp part of the screw?

A Barrier-Free
Environment

STS
SCIENCE
TECHNOLOGY
& SOCIETY

The next time you're out walking around your community, notice where there are ramps. In many cities and towns, the curbs at street corners are gentle ramps rather than steps. And gently sloping ramps lead from streets to the entrances of theaters, schools, office buildings, and other public places.

In such cases, steps have been replaced by ramps to make it easier for people in wheelchairs to get around. The ramps have also proved to be a great help for people pushing wheeled vehicles such as shopping carts and strollers.

Some buildings have ramps inside, as well as stairs. An example of a building famous for its ramps is the Solomon R. Guggenheim Museum in New York City. A great spiral ramp encircles the inside of this unusual building, which is home to the works of many of the world's great modern artists.

▲ **Inside the Guggenheim Museum**

As you might guess, engineers who design ramps for people in wheelchairs must make sure that the slopes of such ramps are gradual enough to allow wheelchair users to comfortably climb the ramp. To accomplish this, engineers have found that a ramp must be ten times as long as the height to which it climbs. You could also say that for every meter a ramp rises, it must be 10 meters long. ■

INVESTIGATE FURTHER!

TAKE ACTION

Let's say you're an engineer. You're asked to design a ramp to be installed beside a staircase. The staircase rises 3 m from one floor to the next. How long must you make the ramp? What if the foot of the staircase is too close to a wall for you to make a ramp as long as you need it to be? How might you redesign the ramp? Hint: Think Guggenheim.

Simple Machines

The place is Africa. The time is 2 million years ago. A hunter crouches over an antelope he has just killed. The hunter begins to skin the animal with a sharpened rock. A short distance away, a second hunter uses a stone ax to chop a slender branch from a tree. He will make a spear from the branch.

The First Machines

The sharpened rocks used by these early hunters are tools. They are the first machines invented by humans. A **machine** is a device that makes work easier. One way that some machines make work easier is by reducing the amount of force needed to do a job. In effect, such machines multiply the force you apply to them.

Inclined Planes

The sharpened edge of each stone tool is a type of inclined plane. An

▲ Ancient stone tools were the earliest machines

inclined plane is a simple machine with a sloping surface. A ramp is a familiar example of an inclined plane. As you learned in the activity on pages C38 and C39, it is easier to raise objects from one level to another using a ramp than it is to simply lift the objects directly.

Look at the drawings below. Use the drawings and your observations from the activity, "Different Slants on Doing Work," to infer the answer to the caption question.

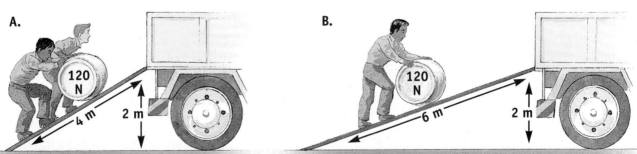

A. | B.
120 N — 4 m — 2 m | 120 N — 6 m — 2 m

▲ How does the slope, or angle, of the ramp affect the force needed to move the barrel up to the platform?

Sometimes it isn't practical to use a straight inclined plane to do a job. For example, suppose you wanted to ride your trail bike to a campsite at the top of the mountain shown in the picture. Both trails are ramps. Which trail would make the job of pedaling up to the campsite easier?

Inclined Planes That Move

A wedge is a special type of inclined plane that moves. Wedges are used to push objects or materials apart. Recall the stone tools used by the hunters on page C43. The edges of such tools are examples of wedges.

A screw is another example of an inclined plane that moves. When a screw is driven into a board, the wood actually travels along the threads of the screw. A screw can also be used to raise or lower something, like the seat of a piano stool.

One Advantage of Using a Machine

A machine helps to make work easier. A machine does not, however, reduce the *amount* of work that is done. Look again at the drawings on page C43. The work being accomplished is moving the barrel from the ground onto the truck.

▲ A wedge is two inclined planes placed back-to-back. What part of a screw is like an inclined plane?

Using the formula $W = F \times D$, the amount of work required to lift the barrel straight up can be calculated as

120 N × 2 m = 240 N × m, or 240 joules

The amount of force needed to move the barrel up either of the ramps is less than 120 N. However, the force is exerted through a greater distance. Because of friction, you will do more work when you use a machine than when you don't use one! The actual work done when you move the barrel up either ramp is greater than 240 joules!

A machine doesn't reduce the amount of work done, but it does help make work easier. An inclined plane is one type of machine that makes it possible to reduce the force a person needs to exert in doing work.

The number of times that a machine multiplies the effort force is called the **mechanical advantage** (MA) of the machine. To find the mechanical advantage of an inclined plane (while ignoring friction), divide the length of its sloping surface by its height.

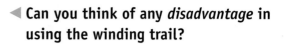

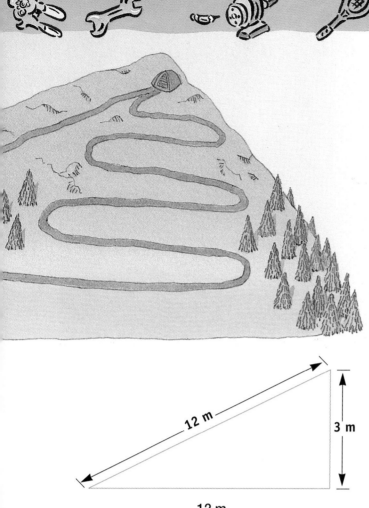

$$MA = \frac{12 \text{ m}}{3 \text{ m}} = 4$$

In drawing *A* on page C43, the length of the inclined plane is 4 m and its height is 2 m. So the mechanical advantage of this inclined plane is

$$MA = \frac{4 \text{ m}}{2 \text{ m}} = 2$$

◀ **Can you think of any *disadvantage* in using the winding trail?**

This inclined plane multiplies the effort force two times. So by using it, the workers exert about one-half as much force to move the barrel up onto the platform as they would have used to lift the barrel straight up. Keep in mind that the mechanical advantage is really a bit less than 2—friction makes it impossible to have a maximum mechanical advantage.

Now find the mechanical advantage of the inclined plane in drawing *B* on page C43. Would you have to exert more force to move the barrel using this ramp or the other ramp?

The advantage of using a ramp to raise an object is that you can use less force. Is there any disadvantage? Like the winding mountain trail, the disadvantage is you have to travel a greater distance. The gentler the slope of a ramp, the longer the ramp must be.

The next time you use an inclined plane, keep in mind that you're making your work easier. You may end up doing a little more work, but you won't need to use as much force to do it. ■

INVESTIGATION 1

1. How much work must you do to move a box of books weighing 2 N from the floor onto a shelf 0.8 m above the floor?

2. You use a ramp 4 m long to move the box of books onto the shelf. How does the ramp help you? How does it affect the actual amount of work you do? Explain.

INVESTIGATION 2

WHAT ARE LEVERS AND PULLEYS?

Imagine that you are rowing across a lake. You pull on the oars in one direction, and the rowboat moves in the opposite direction. An oar is a type of simple machine called a lever. You might be surprised at the number of levers you use every day.

Activity

The Ups and Downs of a Seesaw

A seesaw is a type of lever. To make your end of the seesaw go up, you need someone to push down on the other end. How much force does that person have to use? Where should he or she sit? Let's find the answers to these questions.

Procedure

1. Tape three pencils together to make a triangle, as shown. Tape a paper cup to each end of a metric ruler.

2. Place the ruler on the pencils so that the middle of the ruler (the 15-cm mark) rests on the top of the triangle. You have made a lever. The point where the ruler touches the pencils is called the **fulcrum**.

3. Place a piece of clay the size of a large marble in the cup attached to the zero end of the ruler.

4. Add paper clips, one at a time, to the cup at the other end until the zero end of the ruler is lifted.

Step 1

5. In your *Science Notebook*, **make a chart** with two columns. In the first column, **record** the distance between the cup of paper clips and the fulcrum; in the second column, **record** the number of paper clips needed to lift the clay.

6. Take the paper clips out of the cup. Move the ruler so that the fulcrum is at the 10-cm mark of the ruler. Repeat step 4 and **record** the data.

7. Take the paper clips out of the cup and move the fulcrum to the 5-cm mark. **Predict** how many paper clips it will take to lift the cup containing the clay. **Record** your prediction; then repeat step 4 and **record** the data.

Analyze and Conclude

1. Describe the relationship between the distance of the clay from the fulcrum and the number of paper clips needed to lift the clay.

2. Talk with members of your group and **predict** how many paper clips you would need if the fulcrum were at the 8-cm mark. Then check your prediction.

3. Predict how many paper clips you would need if the fulcrum were at the 20-cm mark. Try the experiment and check your prediction.

4. What can you **infer** about how a lever makes the job of lifting the clay ball easier?

INVESTIGATE FURTHER!

EXPERIMENT

Suppose you and a friend are going to ride on a seesaw. Predict how you would adjust your position on the seesaw if you were using it with a friend who weighs less than you do. How about if your friend weighs more than you do? The next time you're on the playground, check your predictions.

Step 3

Activity

The Pulley—A Special Kind of Lever

Have you ever raised a flag to the top of a flagpole? How did you get the flag up there? How did you get it down?

MATERIALS

- several books
- wooden ruler
- single pulley
- heavy string or twine
- small heavy object
- spring scale
- *Science Notebook*

Procedure

1. **Study** the pulley setup shown and **discuss** it with the members of your group.

2. Use the materials listed above to **set up** a similar pulley. A pulley arranged this way is known as a single fixed pulley. **Sketch** this arrangement in your *Science Notebook*.

3. Use a spring scale to **measure** the weight of a small heavy object. **Record** the weight.

4. Tie one end of a piece of heavy string to the heavy object. Place the object on the floor below the pulley. Thread the other end of the string through the pulley and tie it to the spring scale, as shown below.

Step 4

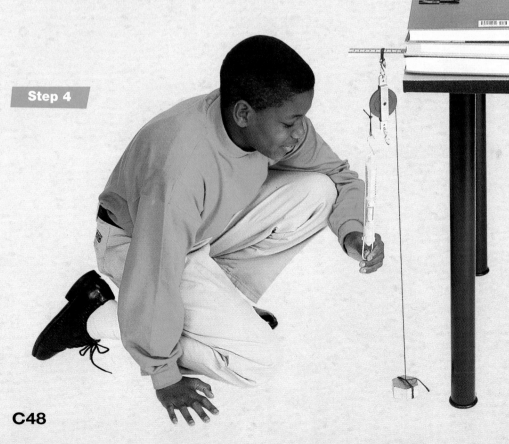

C48

5. **Predict** what will happen to the object if you pull down on the spring scale. Gently pull down on the spring scale and use the pulley to lift the object at a steady speed. **Record** the reading that is on the scale.

6. Remove the pulley from the ruler. Rearrange the pulley, string, and object as shown in the pictures. This arrangement is known as a single movable pulley.

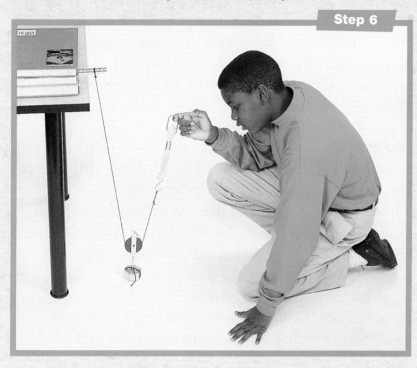

Step 6

7. Gently lift up on the spring scale, again using the pulley to lift the object. **Record** the reading on the scale.

Analyze and Conclude

1. When you used a fixed pulley, in what direction did you pull on the string? In what direction did the object move?

2. **Compare** the weight of the object with the force you used to lift the object with a fixed pulley.

3. **Compare** the weight of the object with the force you used to lift it with a movable pulley.

4. How did each pulley arrangement help you do work on the object?

INVESTIGATE FURTHER!
. . . .
RESEARCH

Look around your school for pulleys. Investigate flagpoles and blinds in particular. Write a description of the pulleys you find. Include sketches to show how the pulleys operate.

Levers

If you've ever pried a rock from the ground with a crowbar, moved dirt with a wheelbarrow, or swung a baseball bat, you've used a lever. A **lever** is a simple machine made up of a bar that turns, or pivots, around a fixed point.

What All Levers Have in Common

Basically all levers are bars, although they don't all look like bars. The fixed point around which the bar is free to move is called the **fulcrum**.

You apply a force called the effort force on one part of a lever. The effort force causes the lever to pivot, or turn, around the fulcrum. At some other point on the lever is a force called the

resistance force. This force must be overcome if work is to be done.

The resistance force might be the weight of an object to be moved, or it might be friction to be overcome, as when a nail is removed from a board.

How Levers Differ

Study the pictures showing the three classes of levers on these pages. Notice that a first-class lever has the fulcrum between the effort force (E) and the resistance force (R).

Suppose that you want to use a lever to move a heavy rock. A first-class lever will reduce the force you exert and make it easier to move the rock. A first-

1ˢᵗ CLASS LEVER

When the fulcrum of a first-class lever is close to the resistance, a small effort on one end of the lever will move a large resistance at the other end.

C50

class lever also changes the direction of the force. However, the effort force must be exerted through a large distance to move the resistance a small distance.

In a second-class lever, the resistance force is between the fulcrum and the effort force. A second-class lever can reduce the force you have to exert, but it can't change the direction of that force. Notice that the nail shown will move in the same direction as the effort force.

In a third-class lever, the effort is exerted between the resistance and the fulcrum. A third-class lever does not reduce the force you exert or change its direction.

2ᴺᴰ CLASS LEVER

A hammer that is used to pull a nail from a board is an example of a second-class lever. As shown in the picture, the effort force is exerted at the end of the handle. The fulcrum is located where the hammerhead turns against the board. The resistance is offered by the nail. What causes this resistance force?

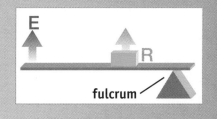

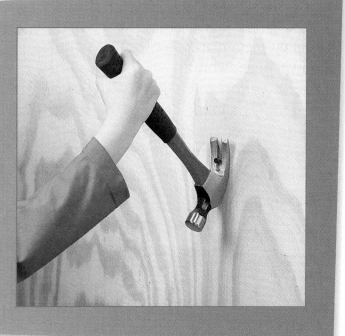

3ᴿᴰ CLASS LEVER

When the player pushes the hockey stick, she exerts the effort through a short distance. The curved end of the stick moves a greater distance. This means that the resistance force moves farther and faster than the effort force. This advantage can be used to make an object, such as a field hockey ball, move away from the stick at great speed.

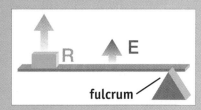

▲ Bottle opener

▲ Wheelbarrow

▲ Oars

Look at the picture of the field hockey player on page C51. When the player pushes on the stick, she exerts a strong effort force that doesn't move very far. The curved end of the stick exerts a force on the ball. This resistance force is not as strong as the effort force, but it moves much farther and faster than the effort force moves.

You use different kinds of levers every day, often without thinking about it. The pictures above show a variety of ways that people use levers to make their work easier to do. Study the pictures and identify the class of lever shown in each. ■

SCIENCE IN LITERATURE

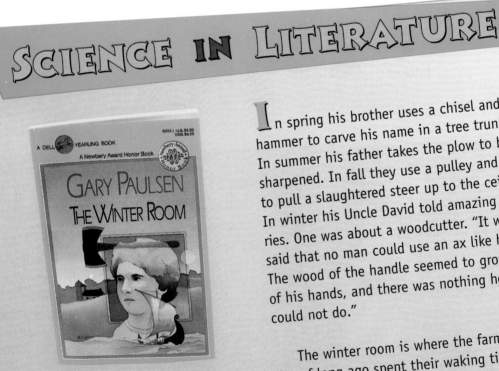

THE WINTER ROOM
by Gary Paulsen
A Yearling Book, Dell Publishing, 1991

In spring his brother uses a chisel and hammer to carve his name in a tree trunk. In summer his father takes the plow to be sharpened. In fall they use a pulley and rope to pull a slaughtered steer up to the ceiling. In winter his Uncle David told amazing stories. One was about a woodcutter. "It was said that no man could use an ax like him. The wood of the handle seemed to grow out of his hands, and there was nothing he could not do."

The winter room is where the farm families of long ago spent their waking time on long dark evenings. Through the eyes of a Minnesota farm boy, observe the change of seasons and their relationships to simple machines when you enjoy *The Winter Room* by Gary Paulsen.

Pulleys

How can you move a bag of cement from the ground to a roof 10 m above your head without moving your feet? Sounds impossible, doesn't it? But there is a simple machine that can make what seems like an impossible task possible. The simple machine is a pulley.

A **pulley** is a wheel around which a rope or chain is passed. If you attach an object to one end of the rope or chain and pull down on the other end, you can lift the object. And you can do this without moving your feet.

A Single Fixed Pulley

The drawing below shows a single fixed pulley similar to the one you set up in the activity on pages C48 and C49. The word *fixed* means that the pulley can't change position. It is attached to one place. In the drawing, the bag of cement is the resistance. A person is supplying the effort by pulling down on the rope.

A single fixed pulley is similar to a first-class lever with its fulcrum halfway between the effort and the resistance. In a pulley, the wheel is the fulcrum, and the rope supports the resistance that is to be moved.

A single fixed pulley doesn't change the effort force. It changes the direction of the force. When you pull down on the rope, the bag of cement goes up. This is certainly easier than carrying the bag of cement up a staircase.

A Single Movable Pulley

Do you recall the other single pulley you set up in the activity on pages C48 and 49? As shown in the drawing below, the arrangement of this pulley is different from that of the single fixed pulley just discussed. The pulley below is free to move. It is a single movable pulley. One end of the rope is fixed, and the other end is loose. If a person pulls on the loose end of the rope, the

A single fixed pulley ▼   **A single movable pulley** ▼

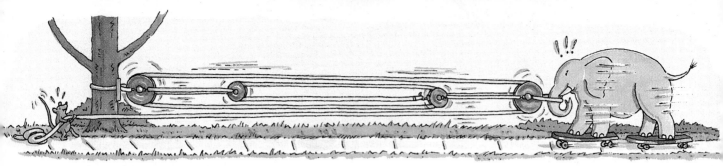

▲ You'd be surprised how much work can be done
with the right pulley combination.

pulley and the bag of cement will move
in the same direction as the effort force.
In this case, the person pulls up, and
the pulley and the cement both rise
toward the roof.

What advantage is there to using
such a pulley? It cuts the effort force
exerted in half. This force is halved
because the cement is supported by two
lengths of rope instead of one.

What price do you pay for cutting
the effort force in half? You have to
exert that force through twice the distance that the resistance moves. In this
case, for every meter that you raise the
cement, you have to pull 2 m of rope
through the pulley.

Pulley Combinations

The drawings at the bottom of the
page show pulley systems that reduce
effort three times, four times, and seven

times. You can tell how much a pulley
system will reduce effort by counting
the lengths of rope that support the
resistance. However, you don't always
count the "effort" rope—the length of
rope you're pulling on.

You only count the effort rope when
the effort is exerted in the same direction that the resistance is moved. So if
you pull down on a length of rope to lift
a resistance, you don't count that
length of rope.

Look at the pulley system below that
reduces the effort three times. This system has two fixed pulleys and one movable pulley. The resistance moves in the
opposite direction to the effort force. So
you count the three ropes supporting the
resistance, but not the effort rope.

To reduce the effort force by four,
you would need a system that has four
lengths of rope supporting the resistance.

Pulley combinations ▼

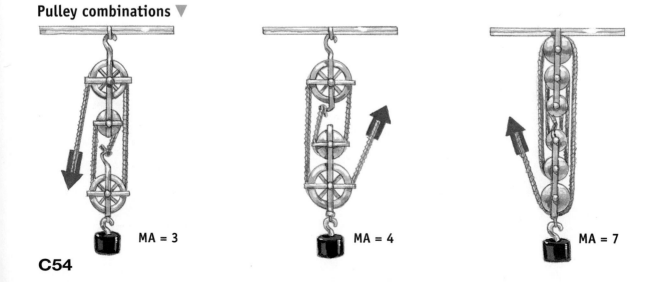

MA = 3

MA = 4

MA = 7

C54

The pulley system shown in the middle is such a system.

Distance Makes the Difference

As the picture at the right shows, machines make it possible to do certain tasks that would be very difficult to accomplish otherwise. Because machines make work easier, it often seems as if they reduce the amount of work that is done.

If you ever find yourself thinking that a machine reduces work, recall this formula: $W = F \times D$. If you discount friction, W doesn't change when using a machine. For example, the work done in raising the piano from the ground to the window is always the same, no matter how you get it up there.

Most machines reduce the amount of force you have to exert to do work. To get this reduction, you sacrifice distance. So, if the F in the formula gets smaller, the D gets bigger, and W stays the same. For every meter that the workers raise the piano, they have to pull 4 m of rope through the pulley system.

Sometimes it takes longer to get work done using a machine. But distance and time are small prices to pay to get a job done. After all, how else are

▲ **Lifting a heavy object is no problem with a combination of pulleys.**

you going to get that big, heavy piano from the sidewalk up to the second floor of that apartment building? ■

INVESTIGATION 2

1. How is a single fixed pulley like a first-class lever? How are the two machines different?

2. You use a wheelbarrow to remove a pile of rocks from a vacant lot. What class of lever is the wheelbarrow? How do you know?

WHAT IS A WHEEL AND AXLE?

Suppose someone removed the handlebars from your bicycle. Could you turn the front wheel by gripping the small shaft your handlebars were attached to? How do the handlebars help you do work on the front wheel?

Activity

Wheel and Axle

In this activity you'll find out how a wheel and axle work together to make a machine.

- -

Procedure

1. **Draw a circle** with a diameter of 6 cm on a piece of posterboard. Cut it out and use the scissors to make a small hole in the center of the circle.

2. Insert a pencil through the hole in the center of the circle. The pencil is now the axle of your wheel and axle. Mark one point on the edge of the wheel.

Step 2

MATERIALS

- goggles
- drawing compass
- ruler
- posterboard
- scissors
- round pencil
- screwdriver
- screw in a board
- *Science Notebook*

SAFETY

Wear goggles. Use caution when working with scissors, screwdriver, and compass.

C56

3. Roll the wheel along the table top. Notice that the pencil turns once when the wheel turns once.

4. In your *Science Notebook*, **measure** and **record** the distance that the wheel travels in making one complete turn along the table top.

5. Remove the pencil from the wheel and roll the pencil on the table. **Measure** and **record** how far it travels in one complete turn.

6. Now grip a screwdriver by its metal shaft. Try to remove a screw from a board while gripping the screwdriver in this way.

Step 6

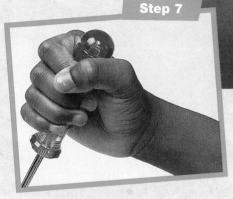
Step 7

7. Repeat step 6 while gripping the screwdriver by its handle, as shown.

Analyze and Conclude

1. How does the circumference of the posterboard wheel **compare** with that of the pencil "axle"? [Hint: You determined the circumference of each in steps 4 and 5.]

2. Suppose you were to grip the pencil axle and use it to turn the posterboard wheel. Through what distance would the axle have to turn to make a half-turn of the wheel? How does this type of machine help do work?

3. **Compare** the diameter of the screwdriver handle with the diameter of the shaft. Which is the wheel and which is the axle? Was it easier to turn the screw when you gripped the screwdriver by its shaft or by its handle?

4. How does a wheel and axle make work easier when force is applied to the wheel?

UNIT PROJECT LINK

The ancient Egyptians used some simple machines to help them move the pyramid blocks. Use wood blocks as model pyramid blocks. Design and build some simple machines to help you move the blocks across a flat surface and to raise them some distance above the surface.

Wheels Turning Wheels

When you hear the word *wheel*, what pictures spring into your mind? Pictures of cars, buses, bicycles, skateboards, and numerous other things that move from one place to another on wheels might come to mind.

But many wheels don't go anywhere! Instead, they stay in one place and help you do work. A doorknob is a wheel that doesn't go anywhere. So is the faucet on a sink. And a Ferris wheel is, of course, a wheel.

Double Your Wheels

Actually, all these devices are made of two wheels, one large and one small, connected to each other. The combination is called a wheel and axle.

A **wheel and axle** is a simple machine made up of two wheels that

The circle turned by the wrench is the wheel. What "axle" does the wheel turn? ▶

turn, or pivot, around the same point. Effort is usually applied to the larger wheel. This force causes the smaller resistance wheel, called the axle, to turn in the same direction.

Where Are the Wheels?

Does a wrench look like a wheel to you? With many wheel-and-axle systems, you have to imagine the wheel part. If you've ever tried to remove a nut from a bolt with your bare hands, you know that a wrench makes the job easier. The wrench turns in a circle, causing the smaller nut to turn also. The wrench handle acts as the wheel in a wheel-and-axle machine.

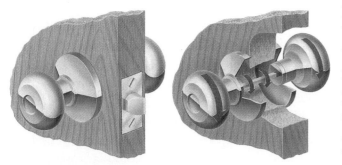

▲ The doorknob is the wheel; it turns the axle that runs through the door.

▲Turning the handle causes the axle to turn. Rope attached to a bucket winds around the axle, raising the bucket of water. With each turn, the effort force exerted on the handle travels much farther than the resistance, which is the bucket of water.

Now look at the picture above of the wheel and axle used to raise a bucket of water from a well. The effort force applied to the handle (wheel) is less than the force needed to raise the bucket directly. So a wheel and axle is another simple machine that makes work easier by reducing the amount of effort force that a person exerts to do work.

You could reduce your effort force still more by increasing the size of the wheel. Of course, as you increase the size of the large wheel, you have to turn it through a greater distance to raise the bucket. And this will take more time. So you lose speed as you reduce your effort force.

Speed's the Thing

What would happen if effort were applied to the smaller wheel of a wheel and axle? That's what happens in a Ferris wheel. A force is applied to the axle of the Ferris wheel, causing it to turn. Each time the axle moves through a short distance, the cars near the outer edge of the large wheel move through a much greater distance, and move much faster.

When effort is applied to the small wheel of a wheel and axle, distance—and speed—are gained. What's sacrificed? Force. A great effort force must be applied to the small wheel. Fortunately, in a Ferris wheel the effort force is supplied by an engine.

A wheel and axle is a simple machine. It helps make work easier. It is not the same as the wheels that spin *around* an axle. Those kinds of wheels only reduce friction. ■

▲ In a Ferris wheel, a large force is applied to the axle, causing the outer rim of the wheel to move at high speed.

Gearing Up

On an old-fashioned bicycle, the pedals are attached to the large front wheel. When the rider pushes on the pedals, the force exerted makes the large wheel turn. This is an example of a wheel and axle in which the effort force is applied to the smaller wheel. Recall that when a force is applied to the smaller wheel, the larger wheel moves a greater distance at a greater speed.

Today's bicyclists still apply force to a bike's pedals. However, the pedals of a modern bicycle are not connected to either of the bicycle's wheels. The pedals are connected to a gear. A gear is a wheel with teeth.

Transferring Force

Gears transfer force. In other words, a force applied to one gear is "sent" somewhere else, usually to another gear. In a bicycle the pedals are part of a wheel and axle, which is connected to a large gear. A chain connects this gear to a smaller gear, which is attached to the back wheel. When the pedals are turned, the front gear turns, moving the chain that turns the rear gear. When the rear gear turns, the back wheel turns—and off you go.

▲ **On a multispeed bicycle, the gearshift lever is used to switch the chain from one set of gears to another.**

When pedaling up a steep hill, a bicyclist shifts the chain to the larger rear gears. This shift makes it easier to pedal. You apply less force over a greater distance. When riding on level ground, the bicyclist shifts the chain to the smaller rear gears. This makes it harder to pedal, but it increases the distance the bicycle moves with each pedal stroke.

Does all of this sound complicated? It probably is, especially if you try to imagine all the gears working at once. However, if you think about one pair of gears at a time, it's much simpler. Fortunately, when you're out riding your bike, you don't have to think about how the gear system works. When you come to a hill, you just have to know when to shift. ■

Compound Machines

The ringing of your alarm clock announces that morning has arrived. You yawn, hardly noticing the rumble of a truck outside your window. You peek out and see three workers unloading a crate from a truck.

The crate holds a washing machine that your parents have ordered. You watch as the men deposit the crate at the foot of the stairs leading to your front door and then drive off. Suddenly you remember something your mother told you yesterday. The workers are not allowed to carry the crate up the steps and into the house. Your mother also told you it would be your job to find a way to get the crate into the house. Impossible! That crate must weigh more than you do.

Making the Job Easier

As you dress, you think of a possible solution. You remember that a simple machine makes a job easier. Perhaps you can use a simple machine to get the crate up the stairs.

To start, you lay a board against the stairs. The slanted board is an inclined plane. And you know that moving an object up an inclined plane is easier than lifting it. You try to push the crate up the board, but it won't budge. Even after you put rollers under the crate to reduce friction, you can only move it a few centimeters. Do you give up?

Machine Team

You try to think of other machines that might make the job easier. What

▲ A simple machine helps to make work easier.

▲ Sometimes one simple machine isn't enough to get the job done.

▲ **When you combine simple machines, you also combine their mechanical advantages.**

about a lever? No, a lever won't work. How about a pulley? Pulleys can make work easier by reducing the effort you need to exert.

You set up a single, movable pulley system as shown. Then you stand at the top of the stairs and pull. Much to your surprise, the carton moves slowly but surely up the ramp. By combining a couple of simple machines—a ramp and a pulley—you have accomplished a task that you thought was impossible.

Multiplying Forces

Do you realize that you have built a compound machine? A **compound machine** is a machine that's made up of two or more simple machines. Your compound machine is made up of two kinds of simple machines—an inclined

plane and a pulley system. By combining these machines you did a job you could not otherwise have done.

Each machine gave you an advantage; each multiplied your effort force on the crate. The combination of machines multiplied your effort enough to enable you to raise the crate to the top of the steps.

Compound Machines All Around You

Most of the machines that make life easier are compound machines. The truck that delivered the crate is a very complex compound machine. It's made up of wheel-and-axle systems, levers, and gears. Even your bicycle combines many simple machines.

Most compound machines used in and around a home are much simpler machines than a truck or a bicycle. Can openers are made up of at least two simple machines. How many simple machines make up the can opener in your home? Hint: Remember that a wedge is a kind of inclined plane.

Search your home for compound machines. Identify the simple machines that make up each of these compound machines. ■

INVESTIGATION 3

1. Explain why a water faucet is a type of wheel-and-axle machine.

2. Using a short screwdriver that has a thin handle, you try unsuccessfully to remove a screw from a board. Would you try using a screwdriver with a thicker handle or a screwdriver with a longer shaft? Explain your answer.

REFLECT & EVALUATE

WORD POWER

fulcrum   lever
machine   pulley
compound machine
inclined plane
mechanical advantage
wheel and axle

 On Your Own
Review the terms in the list. Then use as many terms as you can in a paragraph about simple machines.

With a Partner
Mix up the letters of each term in the list. Provide a clue for each term and challenge your partner to unscramble the letters and name each term.

BUILD YOUR PORTFOLIO

Make a chart that describes four types of simple machines, explains how each makes work easier, and shows common examples. Use pictures cut from magazines or your own drawings to illustrate the chart.

Analyze Information

Identify the type of simple machine shown in each diagram. Then explain how each machine makes work easier.

A   B   C

Assess Performance

Design an experiment using several different types of screws to determine how the distance between the threads affects the amount of force needed to drive the screws into a material. Use screws with different distances between the threads. Relate your observations to the formula for finding the mechanical advantage of an inclined plane.

Problem Solving

1. Patricia wants to use an inclined plane to move a large box onto a platform 2 m above the ground. She has two boards—one is 4 m long and the other is 6 m long. Which board will provide the greater mechanical advantage if used as a ramp up to the platform? Explain.

2. A shovel is an example of a lever. Decide whether a shovel is a first-class, second-class, or third-class lever, and explain your reasoning.

3. Imagine you work at a construction site. You want to move a roll of roofing paper to the roof of the building you are working on. Will the job be easier using a single fixed pulley or a single movable pulley? Explain.

Throughout this unit you've investigated questions related to energy, work, and machines. How will you use what you've learned and share that information with others? Here are some ideas.

Hold a Big Event
to Share Your Unit Project

After you have designed machines to help you move large wooden blocks, use them to build a pyramid. Better yet, work with a group to design your own building or structure. Draw up plans and show them to your teacher for approval. Then use your machines to build it. Invite your parents and friends to visit your classroom to view the machines your group has made and to learn about how ancient Egyptians might have used similar devices in building the Great Pyramid at Giza.

Experiment

Plan a long-term project based on an activity in this unit. You might want to build a scale model of a real roller coaster or a compound machine that combines all the different simple machines. Set up a plan for your experiment and show it to your teacher before you begin.

Research

Read one of the books mentioned in this unit. You might want to learn about what life was like on a farm years ago and compare the machines used then with the types of machinery used on a modern farm.

Take Action

Did you design a new, breathtaking roller coaster ride? Did you figure out how a simple machine can make some task at school or home a little easier? Choose one of these ideas or develop one of your own and take action. Share your information with others.

UNIT D

POPULATIONS AND ECOSYSTEMS

Theme: Systems

GET READY TO

OBSERVE & QUESTION

What is biodiversity and how is it changing?

Think this brown tree snake is at home in any old rain forest? Think again! Each place on Earth has organisms and conditions that make it special. In this unit you'll find out about these places and learn what makes them unique.

EXPERIMENT & HYPOTHESIZE

How are living things in an ecosystem related?

What can an organism's lunch tell you about where and how it lives? Why is it important to learn? Activities in this unit will show you!

INVESTIGATE!

RESEARCH & ANALYZE

As you investigate, find out more from these books.

- **The City Kid's Field Guide** by Ethan Herberman (Simon & Schuster, 1989). There are ecosystems everywhere! Whether you live in or visit a city, you'll want to take this book with you to learn what life is like for organisms in cities around the world.

- **Bears** by Joni Phelps Hunt (Silver Burdett Press, 1995). There are only eight species of bears in the world and all of them are in danger of becoming extinct. Find out what the future may hold for them, and for the ecosystems they inhabit.

WORK TOGETHER & SHARE IDEAS

How would you show how your ecosystem has changed over the years?

Working together, you'll have a chance to create an exhibit like those displayed at a science museum. The exhibit will portray your local ecosystem as it existed in the past and exists today. Look for the Unit Project Links for ideas on how you can build this science exhibit that will teach people about how ecosystems change.

CHAPTER 1

LIVING THINGS AND ENVIRONMENTS

Nature—it's amazing! Everything works together so smoothly. In every environment, each plant and animal finds what it needs to survive. Together with other organisms in the environment, plants and animals form a busy, healthy community.

The Nature Fixer

What can be done when the environment of a community of plants and animals is in trouble? Companies that clean up the environment can help restore it to health. Mark Smith works for a company like that.

Question: What stops organisms from getting what they need?

Mr. Smith: It is often something that people put into the environment. Oil is an example. When oil is spilled, it can harm plants and animals and ruin ground water.

Question: How can an oil spill be removed?

Mr. Smith: Until recently, all we could do was dig up the oily soil. But now we have learned to put tiny organisms that eat oil into the spill area. They eat all the oil! Find out how you can be a nature fixer.

Coming Up

◀ "Nature fixers" help make environments better for living things.

WHAT IS AN ECOSYSTEM?

Do you need living things to survive? Do you need nonliving things? If you answered "yes" to both questions, then you are part of an ecosystem. In this investigation you'll find out what an ecosystem is.

Activity

A Local Ecosystem

All ecosystems include living and nonliving things. How do these parts of an ecosystem affect each other, or interact? Study a plot of soil to find out.

- -

Procedure

1. Use a meterstick to **measure** a plot of ground that is 1 m square. Mark off the square by pushing a wooden stake into the ground at each corner. Tie string around the four stakes to complete the square.

2. **Predict** the kinds of living and nonliving things you'll find in your plot and how they'll interact. **Record** your predictions in your *Science Notebook*.

3. **Make a chart** like the one shown. Leave enough room to record your observations. **Describe** the location of your plot.

	Living Things	Nonliving Things	Not Sure Whether Living or Nonliving	Interactions
Plot				
Soil Sample				

MATERIALS

- gloves
- meterstick
- 4 wooden stakes
- string (5 m long)
- garden trowel
- aluminum or plastic tray
- paper towel, moistened with water
- hand lens
- toothpick or probe
- *Science Notebook*

SAFETY //////

Wear gloves during this activity. Do not touch any plants until they have been identified as safe by your teacher. Some plants—poison ivy, for example—can cause skin rashes.

D6

4. In your chart, **list** the number and kinds of living things that you see in your plot. Also list nonliving things you see.

5. **List** any interactions you see between living things and between living and nonliving things in your plot.

Step 7

6. Place a moist paper towel in the bottom of a tray. Use a garden trowel to take a small sample of soil from the plot. Spread the soil on the paper towel.

7. With a hand lens and a toothpick or probe, **examine** the soil for living and nonliving things. Be sure to use the probe gently. Do not injure any living things you find. In your chart, **list** living and nonliving things in your soil sample and **describe** any interactions between them that you observe. **Record** your observations.

8. Empty the tray in the same spot from which you took the soil sample.

Analyze and Conclude

1. **Write a paragraph** that describes which living and nonliving things make up the plot you observed.

2. How did your predictions about what you would find in your plot compare with your observations?

3. What evidence do you have that living things in the plot interact with one another?

4. How do living things in the plot depend on and interact with nonliving things?

5. *Eco-* means environment. A *system* is made up of parts that interact. Was your plot an example of an ecosystem? **Provide evidence** to support your answer.

INVESTIGATE FURTHER!

TAKE ACTION

Ecosystems work well until they are disrupted by things that are foreign to them. Did you find anything in your plot that didn't belong there—anything that might harm the ecosystem? Compare your results with those of others in your class. Come up with ways to remove harmful objects from your study plot and ways to prevent it from being disrupted again.

Activity
Ladybugs in the Garden

Ladybugs are good for a garden ecosystem because they eat insects that eat plants. How would a scientist find out if there were enough ladybugs in a garden to keep harmful insects under control?

MATERIALS

- unlined paper
- metric ruler
- seeds in cup
- colored pencils
- *Science Notebook*

Procedure

1. On a sheet of white paper, **draw** a grid like the one shown. Each of your squares should be 2 cm × 2 cm. The grid represents a garden with an area of 100 m². Each square represents 1 m².

2. Choose 15 squares at random from the grid and color them in. Scatter the seeds on the grid. Imagine that the seeds represent a population of ladybugs in a garden. **Estimate** how many ladybugs are in this "garden."

3. Pretend that you are a scientist collecting samples from different places in the garden. Count the number of ladybugs in each of the colored squares. **Record** this data in your *Science Notebook*.

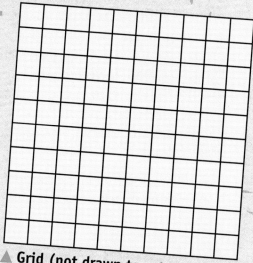

▲ Grid (not drawn to actual size)

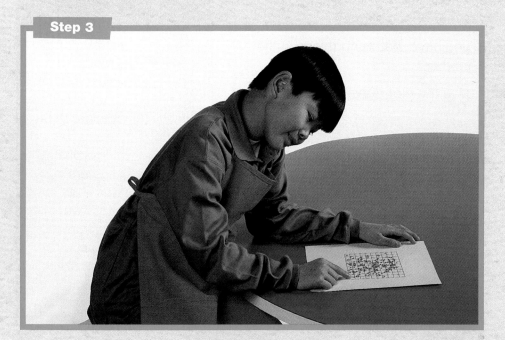

Step 3

4. Use this data to find the average number of ladybugs in a square. **Record** this number.

5. Multiply the average number of ladybugs in a square by the total number of squares. **Record** this calculation of the estimate of the size of the ladybug population based on the samples you collected.

Analyze and Conclude

1. Your cup contained 100 "ladybugs." Does your calculated population size match your actual population size? Give two reasons why the numbers might be different.

2. How could you have made your estimate more accurate?

3. Why might a scientist want to find out approximately how many ladybugs or other organisms live in an ecosystem?

4. Why might a scientist choose to use a sampling method rather than to do a complete count?

UNIT PROJECT LINK

How many different kinds of living things share your neighborhood? 10? 100? 300? more than 300? Work with other students to brainstorm a list of living things you might find in your neighborhood. Then devise a chart and carry out a plan to survey the area, marking the location of all living things you find. Next analyze your data and compare your findings with others. What plants and animals appeared on most lists?

The Nature of an Ecosystem

Imagine that you have spent the night camping out in the woods. As the Sun rises, you are warm and cozy in your sleeping bag on the forest floor. With your eyes still closed, you listen to the sounds around you. Insects drone. Squirrels chatter. A woodpecker hammers at a hollow tree. You open your eyes, and you view the broad green leaves overhead that filter the morning sunlight. On a nearby log, you see a striped chipmunk scurry for cover.

What you see and hear from your sleeping bag is your environment. An organism's environment is made up of all the living and nonliving things around it. The forest—and everything in it—is the natural environment of organisms such as squirrels, birds, worms, and plants. As you may remember from the activity on pages D6 and D7, organisms interact with their environment. In the forest, for

example, birds eat insects and worms. Insects and worms feed on dead leaves and decomposing animals in the soil. Dead trees fall and rot, adding nutrients to the soil. Raccoons and skunks nest in hollow trees, and white-footed mice burrow underground. Organisms interacting with one another and with their physical environment make up an **ecosystem**.

The living (and once-living) things in an ecosystem are called the biotic factors. Biotic factors include trees, birds, insects, and all other organisms. The nonliving things in an ecosystem are called abiotic factors. Abiotic factors include soil, rocks, rain, snow, temperature, and sunlight.

Ecosystem Dwellers

Organisms that live together in an ecosystem make up a **community**. A community contains many different populations of organisms. Each **population** contains all the organisms of the same kind in a community. In a forest, there are populations of squirrels, maples, woodpeckers, worms, and so on. In the activity on pages D8 and D9, the "ladybugs" are a population in a garden ecosystem. Together with other populations, such as aphids, they form a community. All the members of a population are members of the same species (spē'shēz). Organisms of the same species have the same general physical characteristics and can mate, producing offspring of the same kind. For example, male and female redheaded woodpeckers can mate with each other to produce baby redheaded woodpeckers.

Ecosystem Size

An ecosystem may be small, containing only a few interacting species. A puddle that forms on the sidewalk after a heavy rain is a small ecosystem. It may contain three or four species of microscopic organisms. An ecosystem may be large, such as a rain forest, which stretches for thousands of kilometers. It may contain millions of different species, from monkeys to beetles, from long creeping vines to microscopic algae. Most ecosystems are made up of many smaller ecosystems in which living and nonliving things interact.

A Watery Ecosystem

Now imagine that you climb out of your sleeping bag and begin to explore your environment. You ramble through the forest and come upon a large pond. The Sun is now overhead, warming your face as well as the pond. You hear the plop of jumping fish. You see turtles sunning themselves on a fallen log and lily pads floating on the water. This ecosystem is different from the forest you have left. Plants and animals are living in and on water rather than land.

Changing Ecosystems

You continue to explore. You come to a place where the pond meets the cornfields of a farm. Human activity has changed this landscape—the cornfield was once part of the forest. The cornfield, like the forest, is an ecosystem.

Logging, farming, road construction, industries, and homes all change ecosystems. Marshes can be filled in, and houses, cars, and children can replace muskrats and mice. Forests can make way for factories. What did humans do to change the ecosystem below from a forest to a warehouse?

Humans aren't responsible for all changes to ecosystems. Ecosystems change naturally, too. Lightning strikes, starting a forest fire. An earthquake cracks open the ground. These natural events change physical environments and as a result change ecosystems. At first such events may appear to be disastrous—in fact, they are often called natural disasters. With time, however, the number of populations in these communities will increase again.

▲ The ecosystem of Mount St. Helens changed drastically—but naturally.

The Mount St. Helens volcanic eruption proved how suddenly an ecosystem can change without human interference. On the morning of May 18, 1980, the evergreen-covered slopes of Mount St. Helens in Washington State fell strangely still. The birds stopped singing. The squirrels ceased their constant chatter.

Suddenly the mountain burst apart. Hot rock, ash, and steam billowed into the air, then rained down on the forest.

▲ A forest ecosystem may be replaced.

▲ The new ecosystem may not support the earlier community.

▲ What used to be living trees looked like giant toothpicks after the eruption.

▲ But the regrowth soon began.

Boiling mudflows surged down the mountain. Within minutes, trees were flattened and wildlife disappeared. From the air, the once-lush mountainside looked gray and lifeless.

Natural disaster? To the people who lived in the area, it surely was. But the land, although it looked dead, was really just "napping." Before long, plants protected by a layer of unmelted snow began to grow. Shoots from underground roots poked through the ash. Frogs, salamanders, and crayfish, sheltered by a layer of ice, swam in mountain lakes. Ladybugs, springtails, and

beetles, hidden safely inside rotting logs, returned to the soil and air. Bacteria thrived in pockets of water. Each year since the eruption, the number of organisms and species on Mount St. Helens increased. More seeds and insects blew in with the breeze. Large mammals wandered in, carrying hitchhiker seeds that sprouted. Small animals that survived in underground tunnels ventured out and produced offspring.

Ecosystems are constantly changing. Some changes might be hardly visible. Other changes, whether caused by nature or by humans, are dramatic. ■

INVESTIGATION 1

THINK IT WRITE IT

1. Pretend that you are a reporter covering a natural disaster affecting an ecosystem near your school. Write an article about it for the local paper. Tell the community why the ecosystem is not really "dead."

2. What makes both the pond and cornfield you observed ecosystems? What are the main differences between these ecosystems?

HOW ARE LIVING THINGS IN AN ECOSYSTEM RELATED?

How did you get energy this morning—eat a bowl of cereal? Different kinds of organisms have different ways of getting energy. In this investigation you'll see how the members of an ecosystem are related by the ways they get energy.

Activity

A Meal Fit for an Owl

Many organisms eat to get energy. By examining the remains of an owl's meal, you can find out a lot about how owls are related to other organisms in their ecosystem.

MATERIALS

- goggles
- owl pellet
- paper towel
- hand lens
- tweezers
- toothpick
- *Science Notebook*

SAFETY

Wear goggles during this activity.

Procedure

Unwrap an owl pellet and place it on a paper towel. **Observe** the outside of the pellet with a hand lens. **Predict** what you will find inside the pellet. **Record** your predictions. Use your fingers, tweezers, and a toothpick to separate the pellet's contents. **Examine** the parts carefully with the hand lens. **Record** your observations.

Analyze and Conclude

1. How did your findings compare with your predictions?

2. Based on your observations, **infer** what an owl eats. What kind of an ecosystem would this owl live in?

D14

Activity
Lunch Time!

If you don't get something to eat at lunch time, you probably won't have enough energy to have fun after school. In this activity you'll find out how the members of an ecosystem get their energy.

MATERIALS
- marker
- paper
- hand lens
- *Science Notebook*

Procedure

1. With your group, go to the area that your teacher has selected. Look for every organism in the ecosystem.

2. Have one member of your group copy and fill in a chart like the one below with the data the group collects.

Organism	How It Gets Energy

3. Have another member carry the hand lens and do "close-up" studies of the organisms you see. Have another member of your group make sure that every organism seen is recorded.

4. Using what you have just learned about ecosystems, have your group discuss how the organisms obtain energy.

5. Back in the classroom, copy your observations into your *Science Notebook*. Share with other groups what your group observed.

Step 3

Analyze and Conclude

1. **Infer** how most of the organisms that were studied by members of your class got energy for life processes.

2. Name any organisms in the ecosystem that produced energy for other organisms in the ecosystem you observed.

The Sun:
Life's Energy Supply

▲ **The Sun provides energy for Earth's organisms.**

You've probably heard people say, "It's so hot outside, you could fry an egg on the sidewalk!" Fry an egg? Don't you need a stove for that?

No, you don't need a stove. You just need plenty of heat energy. And sometimes, when it's extremely hot and sunny out, it can feel as though there is enough heat energy from the Sun to fry an egg.

Energy from the Sun reaches Earth as light and other forms of wave energy, such as infrared rays. Much of this energy is converted to heat energy in Earth's air, land, and oceans. Day after day, year in, year out, the Sun illuminates and warms Earth. Even on cloudy days, energy from the Sun reaches Earth.

Plants Convert the Sun's Energy

What do you think would happen to Earth's ecosystems if the Sun's energy were blocked? If you said that most life on Earth would soon disappear, you would be correct. Almost all life on Earth depends on the Sun for energy, either directly or indirectly. All plants depend directly on the energy of the Sun. Certain groups of plantlike microscopic organisms also depend on the Sun. Included in this group are organisms called algae (al´jē).

Plants and plantlike organisms use light energy from the Sun to make food through a process called photosynthesis (fōt ō sin'thə sis). These living things take in water and carbon dioxide, a gas that is in the air and water, and convert

D16

them to sugar and oxygen. The sugar is the plant's food and contains stored energy. So a plant actually "stores" the Sun's energy. When animals eat plants, they also use the solar energy stored in the sugar.

Organisms that undergo photosynthesis contain a chemical called chlorophyll. Chlorophyll (klôr′ə fil) is the substance in plants that gives leaves and stems their green color. It also captures light energy from the Sun for use during photosynthesis. Organisms that do not contain chlorophyll can't capture light energy and therefore can't produce food from carbon dioxide and water.

What About Nongreen Organisms?

What would happen to nongreen organisms—such as you and your friends, your dog or cat, or a mushroom—if the Sun's energy were blocked? You may think that you and these other organisms could get along just fine—after all, none of you contains chlorophyll or makes your own food. But think again! Even though animals and many other organisms can't use the Sun's energy directly, they still depend on the Sun. To obtain their energy, animals eat plants, or they eat other animals that eat plants. Fungi

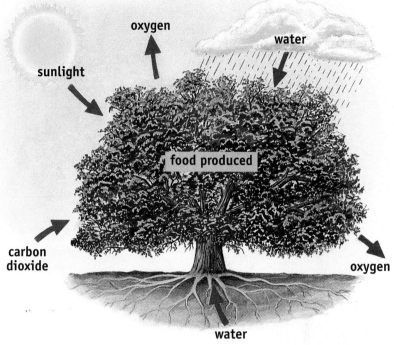

▲ During photosynthesis, plants turn the energy in sunlight into food energy— the kind of energy that we need in order to live.

(fun′jī), such as mushrooms, get their energy by breaking down dead animals and plants. All these organisms depend on the Sun for energy. ■

INVESTIGATE FURTHER!

RESEARCH

The Sun is important to you in many ways. Find out whether solar power is used in your area. Hypothesize why it is a common or uncommon source of energy. In the library, research *solar power* and decide whether a completely solar-powered house could be built in your area.

What's to Eat?

▲ **Great horned owls prey on small animals for food energy.**

It is mid-autumn, and the Sun is setting in the forest. A gray squirrel scuttles around the base of a sycamore tree, searching for food. Few acorns remain on the forest floor, so the squirrel ventures into a nearby clearing to nibble on fallen berries.

High above, a great horned owl perches on the branch of a red oak tree. The owl has begun its nightly search for prey. It hears the squirrel scurrying in the clearing and focuses its eyes in preparation for attack.

The owl spreads its wings and in one swift silent swoop seizes the squirrel in its powerful talons.

Everyone Needs Food

Great horned owls thrive in forest ecosystems, where they find plenty of small mammals to feed on. In all ecosystems, each organism has its own way of getting food energy. Some organisms can use the Sun for food because they can carry on photosynthesis. These organisms are called **producers**. In forest ecosystems, producers include trees, vines, low-growing shrubs, ferns, and mosses.

▲ **Deer are herbivores.**

D18

▲ **Box turtles will eat plants or animals—whichever are available.**

Organisms that obtain energy by eating other organisms are called **consumers**. To get energy, consumers must eat producers or other consumers. Both owls and squirrels are consumers in a forest ecosystem. Squirrels eat acorns, fruit, berries, tree sap, and more than 100 kinds of plants. Owls eat squirrels, many other small mammals, and sometimes insects.

Another kind of consumer, called a **decomposer**, feeds on the wastes of living organisms and on dead, decaying organisms, such as rotting plants and dead trees and animals. Fungi, bacteria, and worms are forest decomposers that release nutrients from animal waste and decaying matter and return those nutrients to the soil.

Three Kinds of Consumers

Consumers can be classified by the kinds of food they eat. Plant-eating consumers are called **herbivores** (hʉr′bə vôrz). Meat-eating consumers are called **carnivores** (kär′nə vôrz). Consumers that eat both plants and animals are known as **omnivores** (äm′ni vôrz).

Squirrels, deer, rabbits, mice, and most insects are examples of forest herbivores. Carnivores feed on herbivores and other carnivores. In the activity on page D14, you probably saw that owl pellets contain fur, bones, and other animal remains that owls cannot digest. You might be surprised to know that some owls can capture mammals as large as cats, rabbits, and skunks!

Omnivores can eat either plants or animals. They often eat whatever is available. The forest-dwelling box turtle, for example, eats strawberries, blackberries, and mushrooms. It also eats insects and spiders. Other common omnivores include woodpeckers and tree creepers.

Other ecosystems contain different organisms, but all ecosystems contain producers, consumers, and decomposers. ■

Wolves are meat eaters, or carnivores. ▶

Eat or Be Eaten

The cycle of organisms eating and being eaten is a major part of life in an ecosystem. Every consumer has to eat in order to live. An organism that hunts and eats other organisms is called a predator (pred'ə tər). An organism that is hunted and eaten is called the prey. The interaction between a predator and its prey is called a predator-prey relationship. Predator-prey relationships occur between animals and other animals or between microscopic animal-like protists and other protists.

The Lynx and the Hare

In the evergreen forests of North America, the lynx and the hare have a predator-prey relationship. The lynx

feeds on the hare. The lynx population increases when hares are abundant and decreases when hares are scarce. The graph below shows the relationship between the lynx and hare populations over a period of time.

Similar relationships take place between plants and animals. Elephants may eat so many plants in an area that the environment no longer contains enough food. The elephants move on, allowing the plants in the environment to recover.

For Better or for Worse

Predator-prey relationships are only one kind of interaction between organisms in an ecosystem. Some species

◄ **Predators and Prey** As a predator population increases, it consumes more and more prey. Eventually the predators consume so much prey that the prey become scarce. As a result the predators have trouble finding food. Some starve, so the predator population declines. This gives the prey a chance to increase again.

Population graph: y-axis Population (5, 40, 80, 120, 160); x-axis years (1850, 1875, 1900, 1925). Hare (in thousands) ——— Lynx (in thousands) ———

form long-term close relationships with other species. This kind of relationship is called symbiosis. Symbiosis can occur between plants and microscopic organisms, animals and microscopic organisms, animals and plants, and animals and other animals. The three kinds of symbiosis are explained below.

Ouch! That Hurts!

In **parasitism** (par′ə sīt iz əm), one organism lives off of, feeds upon, and harms another organism. An organism that feeds on other organisms is called a parasite; the organisms that are fed upon are called hosts.

A familiar example of parasitism is the relationship between a dog (host) and fleas and ticks (parasites). Fleas and ticks live and feed upon dogs and other animals. The fleas and ticks benefit, and the dogs are harmed—and irritated!

Parasites harm their hosts, but they rarely cause them to die. Death of the host would lead to death of the parasite; the parasite would eventually have nothing to feed upon.

No Harm Done

In **commensalism** (kə men′səl iz-əm), one species benefits while the other species seems to be unaffected. Many animals have such relationships with plants. The animals resemble a certain part of a plant and can thus hide from predators. For example, some crab spiders resemble flower petals. The spiders sit in flowers, hidden from

SCIENCE IN LITERATURE

The City Kid's Field Guide

Ethan Herberman

THE CITY KID'S FIELD GUIDE
by Ethan Herberman
Simon & Schuster, 1989

Do species live in harmony in cities, too? Of course! If you don't think that wild creatures live in cities, you need to read *The City Kid's Field Guide* by Ethan Herberman. You'll find out that drains, basements, kitchens, back yards, vacant lots, and even downtown skyscrapers are home to an amazing variety of living things.

Do you want to see animal predators in the city? Look in your basement for centipedes or on tall buildings for peregrine falcons or hunting pigeons! Are you wondering what other city animals eat? Read how omnivores such as pigeons, raccoons, rats, and cockroaches find the city a feast because they eat foods that people throw away or spill! Let *The City Kid's Field Guide* be your guide to watching wildlife in *your* favorite city.

D21

▲ Can you see where the crab spider is hiding?

▲ Make way for egrets!

▲ Lichens, lichens . . . everywhere!

the view of pollinating insects. When an insect lands on a flower, the insect is quickly eaten by the spider. While the spider profits, the flower is not benefited or harmed (although the flower's pollen is not being spread at that moment).

On the African savanna, the routine of the wildebeest greatly benefits the egret. As a wildebeest grazes, its sharp hooves loosen the soil. Hungry egrets walk eagerly behind the wildebeest, feasting on the insects stirred up from the ground. The wildebeest, of course, is completely unaffected by the actions of the egrets.

The closest relationship of all is **mutualism** (my$\overline{oo}$'ch$\overline{oo}$ əl iz əm), in which all species that take part benefit. Probably the most familiar example of mutualism is the pollination of flowers by bees. Bees and certain small birds, such as hummingbirds, drink nectar from flowers and in the process carry away pollen to pollinate other flowers. The bees benefit by getting food, and the flowers benefit by being pollinated. Some forms of mutualism are so close that two species become physically linked together. Lichens, which look like colored patches on rocks and trees, are separate organisms—fungi and algae—that live together. The algae produce sugars that the fungi can use, and the fungi supply the algae with nutrients and water. ■

INVESTIGATION 2

1. Consumers and producers are the two most basic categories of organisms in an ecosystem. How can they be distinguished from one another? Where do decomposers fit in?

2. Classify an organism near your school or in a nearby park as a consumer, decomposer, or producer. Explain how the organism gets its energy. Describe its diet and the place where it lives.

REFLECT & EVALUATE

WORD POWER

carnivores   producers
community   herbivores
consumers   mutualism
decomposer   omnivores
ecosystem   parasitism
population
commensalism

 On Your Own
Review the terms. Then write one new thing you learned about each term.

With a Partner
Make up a quiz, using all the terms in the list. Challenge your partner to complete the quiz.

PORTFOLIO

Make a chart with the following heads: *Producers, Consumers*, and *Decomposers*. Divide the Consumers column into these sections: *Herbivores, Carnivores*, and *Omnivores*. Illustrate your chart with pictures of three organisms in each group.

Analyze Information

Study the photograph. In your own words, identify the type of relationship shown and explain whether the organisms benefit or are harmed by the relationship.

Assess Performance

Observe a small natural area, such as a park or a forest. Make a drawing of the types of organisms you see there. Make a list of the names of the organisms under the heading *Biotic Factors*. Make a second list, under the heading *Abiotic Factors*, of the nonliving things you found.

Problem Solving

1. Like other organisms, you interact with your environment and are part of an ecosystem. Give three examples of ways that you interact with the living and nonliving parts of your environment.

2. Think about the foods you eat. Would you classify yourself as an herbivore, a carnivore, or an omnivore? Explain your answer.

CHAPTER 2

ENERGY AND MATTER IN ECOSYSTEMS

An ecosystem is like a bustling city. Producers are busy capturing energy. Consumers are always "shopping" for energy. And decomposers keep the city clean. The citizens of this "city" are plants, animals, and other living things.

• •

Visiting an Ecosystem

Would you like to visit a real "energy city," where there is always something exciting going on? The kids at Byram Intermediate School in New Jersey have discovered such a place. For them, it is a neighborhood river called Lubbers Run. The Run is a sleepy old waterway that crawls, not runs, past their school. With their teacher, Wayne McGarva, the Byram students have discovered the fascinating watery world of beavers, turtles, and long-legged wading birds.

They have also discovered something else. They have found out that the recent growth of their little town has affected the Run. Now, with Byram's Environmental Commission, the students are measuring and studying those effects.

Somewhere near you is an ecosystem teeming with life. Perhaps it is a salt marsh, a wooded park, or a creek that appears only in rainy seasons. Whether it is large or small, it's worth exploring. Use this chapter as your tour guide!

Coming Up

◀ Wayne McGarva
and his students
at the Byram
Intermediate
School

D25

HOW DOES ENERGY FLOW IN AN ECOSYSTEM?

Energy moves through an ecosystem by being transferred from one organism to another. How does this happen? Find out in Investigation 1!

MATERIALS

• strip of paper (100-cm long)
• metric ruler
• scissors
• *Science Notebook*

Activity

Energy in a Pond

A food chain shows the path that energy takes from the Sun through producers and consumers. You can trace some of the paths energy takes in a pond.

- -

Procedure

1. The table to the right lists pond organisms and their sources of food or energy. Use the information in the table to **identify** which organisms are producers and which are consumers. **Draw** a pond food chain. **Record** the data and the drawing in your *Science Notebook*.

2. You will work with three other students. Each person will play the role of one of the organisms in the food chain. One of you will be a producer, another will be the first-order consumer, a third will be the second-order consumer, and a fourth will be the third-order consumer. As you do this activity, remember that the organism you choose represents an entire population of these organisms.

Organisms	Food or Energy Source
Pondweeds	sunlight
Algae	sunlight
Snails	pondweeds
Waterfleas	algae
Dragonflies	waterfleas
Minnows	snails, waterfleas
Perches	snails, minnows

3. The energy captured by a producer is stored in the food made by the producer. A 100-cm strip of paper represents this captured energy. If you are the producer, **measure** and cut 90 cm of the paper strip. This represents the amount of captured energy you use for growth and other activities.

4. If you are the consumer eating the producer (the first-order consumer), take the 10 cm left from the 100-cm strip. This is the amount of captured energy available to you. **Measure** and cut 9 cm from the 10-cm strip. This represents the energy you use.

5. If you are the consumer eating the first-order consumer (the second-order consumer), take the 1-cm strip from the first-order consumer. **Measure** and cut 9 mm from the 1-cm strip. This represents the energy you use. Pass the 1-mm strip on to the third-order consumer. This is the amount of captured energy left to pass on to that consumer.

Analyze and Conclude

1. Identify the producer and the consumers in your food chain.

2. About what percentage of the energy captured by producers is available to first-order consumers?

3. About what percentage of the energy obtained by first-order consumers is available to second-order consumers? by second-order consumers to third-order consumers?

4. Do you think this food chain could support a fourth-order consumer? Explain.

5. There are usually more producers than consumers in an ecosystem. **Suggest a hypothesis** to explain why this is so.

INVESTIGATE FURTHER!

RESEARCH

Visit a pond or a nature study center in your area and collect some organisms for study. Using tools, such as a hand lens and a garden trowel, look for organisms that live in the pond water and in the mud. Observe the actions and interactions of these organisms. Are producers or consumers more in evidence? Return samples to the environment when you are finished.

Activity
Weave a Food Web!

What happens when food chains overlap in an ecosystem? Do this activity and see for yourself!

MATERIALS
- construction paper
- markers
- scissors
- bulletin board
- pushpins
- tape
- string
- *Science Notebook*

Procedure

1. Look at the table, which identifies feeding relationships in a grassland ecosystem. You and your group should choose two food sources and **predict** what would happen if they were removed from this ecosystem.

2. **Draw** and **label** all the different grassland organisms. **Draw** a picture of the Sun. Cut out the drawings and attach them to the bulletin board with pushpins. Leave space between the drawings.

3. Tape one end of a piece of string to any one of the drawings. Using the information in the table, connect the other end of the string to an organism that either eats it or is eaten by it.

4. **Draw** and cut out an arrow. Attach it to the string to indicate the flow of energy from one organism to another.

5. Use string to connect all the organisms according to their feeding relationships. Use arrows to show the direction of the energy flow. You and your group have just created a model of a food web.

Analyze and Conclude

1. Why is the term *food web* a good name for what you have just made?

2. Which organisms in your food web are the producers? Which organisms are the consumers?

3. List three paths that the Sun's energy takes in this food web.

4. Suppose a disease killed all the grasshoppers. To show this, cut the strings that connect grasshoppers to all other consumers and producers. **Predict** how the death of the grasshoppers would affect the other organisms in the ecosystem.

Organism	Food or Energy Source
Prairie dog	roots of grass grasshoppers
Snake	mice, prairie dogs
Grass	sunlight
Clover	sunlight
Hawk	snakes, mice, prairie dogs
Grasshopper	grass, clover
Mouse	grass seeds, shoots, grasshoppers
Fungi	dead plants
Bacteria	dead plants

The Cycle of Food

Why do you eat lunch? If you didn't eat, you'd get really hungry, right? You'd probably also have trouble concentrating during the afternoon. You might even fall asleep in class!

All living things need energy to survive. This energy comes from food. The food you eat gives you the energy you need to move, breathe, and even think. But how does energy get into your food? The source of most life-giving energy is the Sun.

Capturing the Sun's Energy

Animals cannot capture the Sun's energy to make food. Plants and other producers have that job. Only producers can change solar energy— energy from the Sun—into food energy.

As you may remember from Chapter 1, producers convert solar energy into food energy through a process called photosynthesis. Much of this energy is used for the producer's growth and reproduction. Some of this energy, however, is stored in the producer's cells for later use.

When a consumer eats a producer, some of this stored energy is passed on to the consumer. (You saw this for yourself in the "Energy in a Pond" activity.) The consumer, in turn, uses this energy for its bodily functions. If this consumer is eaten by another consumer, energy stored in the first consumer's cells is passed onto the second consumer. This transfer of energy creates a food chain. A **food chain** is the flow of energy from one organism to another.

Moving Up the Line

Plants are often the first link in a food chain. Because plants convert the Sun's energy into a usable form that can be passed on to other organisms,

◄ **People are consumers in food chains.**

plants are called producers. Organisms that eat producers are called first-order consumers. Second-order consumers eat first-order consumers, and so on.

Let's trace the energy path in the salt marsh ecosystem shown on the next page. When the crickets eat grass, they get only part of the energy that the grass received from the Sun. When the mice eat the crickets, the mice get only part of the energy that the crickets received from the grass. This pattern continues up to the hawks or owls. Since less energy is available at each higher level in the food chain, there are fewer organisms at each higher level. So this ecosystem can support more mice than owls or hawks.

Starting Over Again

All food chains include decomposers. Decomposers are organisms that get their energy by breaking down dead plant and animal matter. Many decomposers, such as bacteria, fungi, and worms, live in the soil and enter the food chain when organisms die. Where might

Fungi such as mushrooms are decomposers. ▼

decomposers be found in the salt marsh ecosystem?

Overlapping Food Chains

Most consumers and decomposers can obtain energy from more than one kind of food. Thus, an organism can be part of many food chains. This causes food chains to overlap. In the activity on page D28, you learned that overlapping food chains form a **food web**. In a food web, an organism can be a first-order consumer in one food chain and a second- or third-order consumer in another food chain. What organisms in the salt marsh ecosystem are both second- and third-order consumers?

What About Us?

You may be wondering about your place in the world of food chains and food webs. Humans differ from many other consumers because of what we eat. **Herbivores** eat only plants. **Carnivores** eat only animals. Humans, however, are omnivores. **Omnivores** eat both plants and animals.

As an omnivore, you can eat "high" or "low" on the food chain. If you eat animal foods, such as meat, eggs, and fish, you are eating high on the food chain—you are consuming other consumers. If you eat mostly plant foods, such as grains, fruits, and vegetables, you are eating low on the food chain—you are eating producers.

Many countries, including the United States, have abundant crops and the means to transport them. This enables

Rail

Owl

Hawk

Cricket

Shrew

Grass

Duck

Mouse

Rat

Sticklefish

Prawn

Heron

Algae

▲ **Energy path in a salt marsh ecosystem**

people to eat many fruits and vegetables, as well as meat, all year long. In contrast, the climate of some regions, such as the Arctic, is harsh. Soil there does not support much plant growth. Because of the climate and the poor soil, these areas do not produce abundant crops. Unless fruits and vegetables are imported, people in these regions tend to eat foods mostly from animals. In some places, then, location and climate result in a shortage of plant foods, and energy is obtained high on the food chain. ■

INVESTIGATION 1

1. Describe a food web of which you are a part. What other organisms does your food web include?

2. Make a drawing that shows what happens to the amount of available energy in an ecosystem as the energy flows from producers through several levels of consumers.

INVESTIGATION 2

HOW IS MATTER CYCLED IN AN ECOSYSTEM?

Matter matters in ecosystems! Energy, although not used up, becomes unavailable as it moves through an ecosystem. Matter does *not* become unavailable. Instead, it cycles between living and nonliving portions of the ecosystem. How is this cycling done? Find out in Investigation 2.

Activity
Where's All the Water?

Water is matter. Plants help water cycle through an ecosystem. Find out how.

MATERIALS
- bean plant (in cup) with 4 or 5 leaves
- water
- small plastic bag
- rubber band
- *Science Notebook*

Procedure

Your teacher will give you a bean plant in a cup. Add water to the plant so that the soil is moist. Loosely cover two or three of the leaves of the plant with a plastic bag. Place a rubber band around the bag and stem to hold the bag in place.

Leave the cup in a sunny spot for two days. Each day, **record** in your *Science Notebook* any changes to the plant. Note how the inside of the bag looks. Note how the leaves that aren't covered by the plastic bag look.

Analyze and Conclude

1. What happened to the water in the soil over the two days?

2. Plants take in water and return some of it to the air through their leaves. What evidence do you have of this process?

Activity

Every Breath You Take

Your body uses the oxygen you inhale to release energy from the food you eat. You exhale one of the waste products, carbon dioxide. How is that carbon dioxide cycled back into oxygen?

Procedure

1. Fill a beaker about two-thirds full with water. Use a dropper to add enough BTB to turn the water blue.

2. Using a plastic straw, blow into the water. **Record** in your *Science Notebook* what happens after you blow into the water.

3. Put an *Elodea* plant in a test tube. Completely fill the test tube with the BTB solution from the beaker. Completely fill another test tube with the BTB solution from the beaker.

4. Place your thumb over the mouth of the first test tube to seal it. Turn the test tube upside down and put it in a beaker, as shown. Do not let air get into the test tube. Do the same thing with the second test tube. Wash your hands.

5. Put the test tube setups in a sunny place for one hour. **Predict** what changes, if any, will take place. **Record** your predictions. After one hour, **observe** both test tubes and **record** your observations.

Analyze and Conclude

1. How did the BTB change when you blew through the straw? (The carbon dioxide that you breathed out caused this change.)

2. How did the BTB solution change after you left the *Elodea* plant in it for one hour? Compare it with the BTB in solution in the other test tube. What can you **infer** about the carbon dioxide you breathed into the BTB solution?

3. In what way are you and plants cycling matter?

Step 4

The Carbon Dioxide–Oxygen Cycle

1 During cell respiration, living things use oxygen that plants give off to break down food and obtain energy. When organisms carry out this process, carbon dioxide is given off into the air and the water.

▲ **How carbon dioxide and oxygen are cycled in ecosystems**

Take a deep breath. As you inhale, you take in oxygen, as well as nitrogen, carbon dioxide, and water vapor. When you exhale, you breathe out mostly carbon dioxide—*more* than you took in! Each time you breathe, you take part in the worldwide **carbon dioxide–oxygen cycle**. Follow the steps in this cycle in the drawing.

Into the Soil

Did you know that soil is a major part of the carbon dioxide–oxygen cycle? Plant roots deep in the soil take in water. The water is combined with carbon dioxide to make sugar, a carbon compound rich in energy. Fallen leaves and other plant matter contain these carbon compounds. Carbon is released as carbon dioxide when decomposers break down plant and animal matter. The use of oxygen to break down carbon compounds and release energy is called **cell respiration** (res pə rā′shən). You saw evidence of this process in the activity "Every Breath You Take."

Into the Ocean

Carbon dioxide and oxygen cycle through ocean ecosystems, too. For

2 During photosynthesis, plants use carbon dioxide, water, and energy from the Sun to make food in the form of sugar. They give off oxygen as a waste product.

4 As plants decay, they add carbon compounds to the air and soil.

3 A plant breaks down some food for energy and stores the rest. This stored energy is passed from one organism to another in the food chain.

▲ **Shells are storehouses of carbon and oxygen on the ocean bottom.**

instance, in ocean food chains, algae are producers. Algae are plantlike organisms that carry out photosynthesis. The oxygen released may be used by other sea creatures to break down carbon-containing compounds to obtain energy. So carbon dioxide is released into the water.

The ocean acts as a storage site for carbon dioxide and oxygen. Some ocean organisms use carbon and oxygen along with calcium to make their shells. When these organisms die, their shells settle on the ocean floor, trapping carbon.

The carbon dioxide–oxygen cycle is important to organisms in ecosystems on land as well as in water. Without the delicate balance of both carbon dioxide and oxygen, organisms could not survive. ■

The Water Cycle

2 As water vapor rises, it cools and changes back into a liquid. forming clouds. Eventually the clouds release this water as precipitation.

1 An evaporating puddle is only a very small part of the world-wide cycling of water. The Sun's energy causes liquid water to evaporate from all over Earth's surface.

▲ **How water is cycled in ecosystems**

Like carbon dioxide and oxygen, water moves in a continuous cycle among Earth's land and seas, the air, and living things. This constant movement of water is called the **water cycle.** The Sun is the main engine driving the water cycle.

Have you ever watched a puddle disappear after the Sun came out? Where does the water go? Some of it seeps into the ground. Much returns to the air as water vapor. The process by which liquid water changes to water vapor is **evaporation** (ē vap ə rā'shən).

Much of the water that evaporates from Earth's surface—about 84 percent—comes from the ocean. When water vapor reaches the cool air above Earth, it changes back into a liquid. The process by which water vapor is changed to liquid water is called **condensation** (kän dən sā'shən). After water has condensed in the clouds, it falls back to Earth in the form of precipitation (prē sip ə tā'shən).

Living things form an important link in the water cycle. All living things need water to survive. Water carries

3 Much precipitation falls into the ocean, lakes, and streams. Some water runs along the ground and ends up in bodies of water. Water also seeps into the ground.

4 Organisms take in water for their daily activities. Through transpiration, plants return some water back to the atmosphere. Both plants and animals also release water as a result of respiration.

nutrients, flushes away wastes, and is needed for life processes. Animals drink water or take in water in the food they eat. Some of this water is released back to the environment as waste products of digestion and cell respiration.

Plants also cycle water through ecosystems. Precipitation that seeps into soil may be taken in by plants through their roots. Recall that plants use some of this water, along with carbon dioxide and sunlight, to carry out photosynthesis and

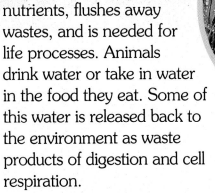

▲ **Condensation or precipitation?**

produce sugars. When the plants break down the sugars through cell respiration, water is formed as a waste product. Water is released through leaves in a process called transpiration (tran spə rā′shən).

In places with a great many plants, such as tropical rain forests, as much as 90 percent of the rainfall is cycled back to the air by the plants. You saw this process for yourself in the activity on page D32. What happens to the water once it is again in the air? ■

Recycling Waste Water

Water—we drink it, cook with it, and bathe in it. We flush our toilets with it. We wash our clothes, dishes, and cars with it, and sprinkle our lawns with it. Farms and factories also use large quantities of water. An average of 2,000 L (500 gal) of water per person every day is used for all of these activities. How can we get along without water?

The answer is we can't. The human body is about two-thirds water. In this regard, we are similar to most organisms. As you know from the activity on page D32, plants also need water. In fact, all living things contain and need water.

In addition to being essential to life, water is useful in many ways. And there's a lot of it around. In fact, about three fourths of Earth's surface is covered by water.

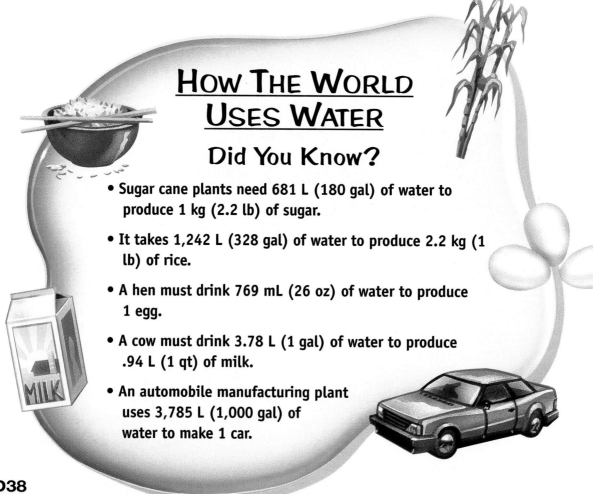

HOW THE WORLD USES WATER

Did You Know?

- Sugar cane plants need 681 L (180 gal) of water to produce 1 kg (2.2 lb) of sugar.

- It takes 1,242 L (328 gal) of water to produce 2.2 kg (1 lb) of rice.

- A hen must drink 769 mL (26 oz) of water to produce 1 egg.

- A cow must drink 3.78 L (1 gal) of water to produce .94 L (1 qt) of milk.

- An automobile manufacturing plant uses 3,785 L (1,000 gal) of water to make 1 car.

With all of the water on Earth, you might think that people never need to worry about having enough water. But this is not the case. Not all of Earth's water is usable. Much of it is salt water. Some water is frozen in polar ice caps or locked up in soil. Also, when we use water, we get it dirty with soaps and detergents. When water combines with food wastes and wastes from our bodies, this used water becomes sewage.

When people dump sewage into rivers and lakes, these bodies of water get dirty. Soon there's less clean water for all organisms to use. That's why towns and cities now have sewage treatment plants—places that clean up waste water.

Sewage treatment plants can't cure all sewage problems. For one thing, it may not be possible to remove all types of wastes that get added to water as it is used. Some microscopic organisms present in sewage may not be removed during the sewage treatment process. Also, sewage treatment plants are expensive to build and maintain. They can break down and spill untreated sewage back into Earth's waterways. Some towns are running out of money to treat their sewage.

Many people are trying to find new ways to solve sewage treatment problems. They have found that they can use natural processes of plants and microscopic organisms called bacteria to do so.

SCIENCE IN LITERATURE

THE CITY KID'S FIELD GUIDE
by Ethan Herberman
Simon & Schuster, 1989

Would you like to see up close how important water is to an ecosystem? Just get permission to explore a vacant city lot. On pages 38–41 of *The City Kid's Field Guide* by Ethan Herberman, you'll find helpful hints about how to observe and record the flow of energy in any vacant lot.

So get a notebook and pencil and bring some caution and patience. As you examine the plants and the creatures that live among them, you'll begin to see how they relate to one another. Draw some food chains and even a food web of your vacant lot.

▲ **Marshes are used in sewage treatment in Arcata, California.**

One Town's Solution

The town of Arcata, California, has found a solution to its sewage treatment problems. Instead of using a huge sewage treatment plant, Arcata uses marshes that teem with wildlife to clean its water.

Arcata's sewage flows first into a holding tank. Next, it moves into a huge concrete tub, where solid materials settle to the bottom. The waste water is then drained from the tub into a large pond with no vegetation. Here, bacteria begin to break down the harmful compounds in the water. When the water leaves the pond, it is treated with chlorine to kill disease-causing organisms. (The chlorine does not stay in the water long, because it soon evaporates.)

Next the water enters a series of marshes. These marshes are filled with many kinds of aquatic plants, including duckweed, cattails, and bulrushes. Bacteria and other small organisms cling to the underwater stems of these aquatic plants. These bacteria filter and clean the waste water. By the time the water flows into a nearby bay, it is cleaner than the bay water itself.

The people of Arcata have a sewage treatment facility that doesn't smell bad and doesn't break down. It's also not expensive to maintain. It's a recreation area and wildlife preserve, attracting wildlife, joggers, and birdwatchers. (Look at the photo above.) Most importantly, the facility cleans waste water very well. ■

UNIT PROJECT LINK

How have populations of living and nonliving things changed in your neighborhood over the past 200 years? Do research to learn about how people lived, learned, and had fun. Consider how these activities affected both living and nonliving things in the neighborhood. Also consider how the cycles of energy and matter may have changed over the years. Then create a display that highlights what you discovered.

The Nitrogen Cycle

You know that living things need energy, oxygen, and water. Living things also need proteins. **Proteins** are compounds that act as the building blocks of living things. Some proteins control chemical processes that take place in the human body. Other proteins make up body structures such as hair, cells, and nails.

Nitrogen is needed to make proteins. Earth's atmosphere is about 78 percent nitrogen gas. With all this nitrogen, you might think that your body could use the nitrogen that you inhale. But that isn't so. Nitrogen gas can't be used directly by most organisms. Before nitrogen can be used, it must be "fixed," or changed into nitrogen compounds.

You can see from the illustration on the next page that dead organisms and the wastes that organisms produce are sources of nitrogen. Decomposers feed on dead organisms and waste products. The nitrogen they release from the wastes is in the form of ammonia, which plants can use. Ammonia is changed into other compounds that may be used by plants. Unused compounds are broken down by bacteria that release nitrogen gas back to the air.

Inhaled and exhaled air have the same percentage of nitrogen, showing that nitrogen in air is not used directly to form protein. ▼

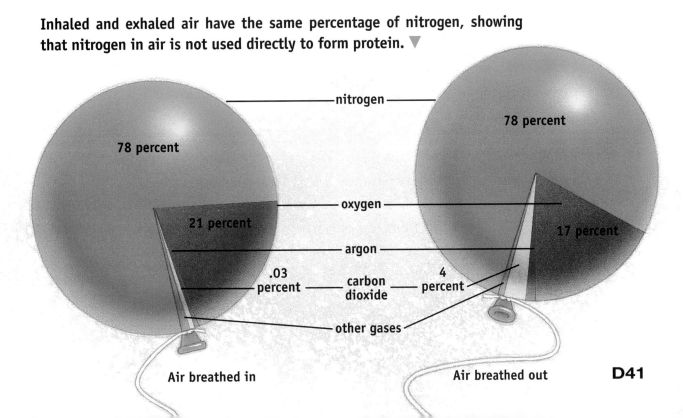

nitrogen

78 percent

78 percent

21 percent

17 percent

oxygen

argon

.03 percent

carbon dioxide

4 percent

other gases

Air breathed in

Air breathed out

1 In the **nitrogen cycle**, nitrogen gas is converted to a usable form and eventually returned to the atmosphere as nitrogen gas.

2 Lightning changes some nitrogen gas into nitrogen compounds. These compounds are washed to Earth in rain. Some of the nitrogen compounds enter the soil with rainwater.

5 When organisms die, the proteins in their bodies are broken down by decomposers to ammonia, nitrites, and nitrates. These compounds are used by plants or break down into nitrogen gas, which passes into the air.

3 Nitrogen is made usable by bacteria that grow on the roots of plants such as beans and peas. These bacteria turn nitrogen into ammonia. Other bacteria change ammonia into nitrates that can also be used by plants.

4 Plants use ammonia and nitrates to make proteins. Animals get nitrogen by eating plants or other animals.

▲ **How nitrogen is cycled in ecosystems**

INVESTIGATION 2

1. Modern farming practices speed up the decomposition of matter in soil. How might this affect the nitrogen cycle?

2. A compost pile is made from grass clippings, leaves, and food wastes that can be broken down for use as fertilizer. What organisms must be part of a compost pile?

REFLECT & EVALUATE

WORD POWER

carnivores
condensation
evaporation
food chain
carbon dioxide–oxygen cycle
cell respiration
nitrogen cycle
water cycle

food web
herbivores
omnivores
proteins

On Your Own
Write a definition for each term in the list.

With a Partner
Make up a quiz, using all the terms in the list. Challenge your partner to complete the quiz.

BUILD YOUR PORTFOLIO

Obtain pictures of at least ten different kinds of plants and animals that live in your community. Use the pictures to create a bulletin-board display or poster showing a possible food web for the organisms.

Analyze Information

Study the drawing. Then explain each organism's role in food chains and food webs.

Assess Performance

Add a small amount of food coloring to water. The food coloring represents a poison in sewage. Using only water and a plastic jar, show how a small amount of material in sewage can pollute water.

Problem Solving

1. Imagine that Earth stopped receiving light from the Sun. What effect would the lack of sunlight have on food chains and food webs? What effect would it have on the carbon dioxide–oxygen cycle? the water cycle? the nitrogen cycle?

2. Suppose you work on a farm. Identify three ways that you could improve the nitrogen content of the soil. What are the advantages and disadvantages of each of your proposed improvements?

CHAPTER 3

DIFFERENT KINDS OF ECOSYSTEMS

Do you live in the American Southwest? If so, you may see cactuses outside your window. Perhaps you live somewhere else. You may see the Northeast's maple trees or the Southeast's palms. Wherever you live, you are part of one of the large ecosystems on this planet. If your ecosystem changes, your life and the life of every other organism will change, too.

A Daring Rescue

If you had visited Kenya in 1977, you would have seen a land stripped of trees. Ninety percent of Kenya's forests had been cut down. As the forests disappeared, so did Kenya's streams and wildlife. Wood for fuel had nearly vanished. Without fuel, it was difficult to cook healthful foods. As a result, children were not eating well. The natural ecosystem was being destroyed. Every organism in the ecosystem suffered.

That same year a Kenyan biologist named Wangari Maathai began to save the ecosystem. She started a tree-planting project called the Green Belt Movement, in which young trees are given to women farmers to plant. Maathai's idea has been a great success. In just the first ten years of the project, the Green Belt planted 5 million trees!

As you read this chapter, think about how a movement like Maathai's might save other ecosystems.

▲ Wangari Maathai's Green Belt Movement helped restore Kenya's ecosystem.

HOW DO EARTH'S MAJOR ECOSYSTEMS DIFFER?

Some ecosystems, like the plot you studied near your school, are very small. Others, such as deserts or oceans, cover vast areas of Earth's surface. Find out the characteristics that make each of Earth's major ecosystems unique in this investigation.

Activity
Make a Mini-Biome!

Ecosystems that cover large areas of Earth's land surface are called biomes. In this activity you can make a model of the biome of your choice and see how abiotic factors affect it.

Procedure

1. From the table on the next page, choose the kind of plant you wish to grow. Your teacher will give you several of these plants.

2. Cover the bottom of a jar with a layer of activated charcoal 0.5 cm thick. Use the table to find the kind of soil your plants need—potting soil, sand, or a potting soil/sand mixture. Place a layer of this soil, 3 cm thick, on top of the charcoal.

Step 2

MATERIALS
- newspaper
- gardening gloves
- plants (several of the same kind)
- large plastic jar
- activated charcoal
- metric ruler
- potting soil
- sand
- grass seed
- water in a spray bottle
- *Science Notebook*

SAFETY
Use gardening gloves to handle plants that have needles or spines.

D46

PLANTS FROM DIFFERENT BIOMES

Kind of Plant	Soil Type	How Often to Water
Broad-leaved	potting	every 2–3 days
Cactus	sand	lightly, every 2 weeks. Let soil dry completely between waterings.
Grass	potting	every other day
Needle-leaved	potting/sand mixture	weekly

3. Carefully lift the plants out of their pots, making sure that most of the soil clings to the roots. Place the plant roots in the soil. Be sure the roots are completely covered so that the plant is well anchored. If you choose to grow grass, scatter the seeds on the soil and cover them with a thin layer of soil.

4. Place your mini-biome in a sunny spot. Use a spray bottle to moisten the soil. Use the table as a guide to watering the plants.

5. Observe your mini-biome daily. Record your observations in your *Science Notebook*.

6. Observe the mini-biomes of the other students. Compare the various biomes represented in your class.

Analyze and Conclude

1. The biomes varied as to the kind of plants, type of soil, and amount of watering. What abiotic factors were the same for all the biomes represented?

2. Which two biomes had the most similar growing conditions? Which two had the least similar conditions? What would happen if you switched the plants growing under the least similar conditions?

3. What is the relationship between abiotic factors in a biome and the kind of plant life found there?

Step 3

Land Ecosystems—
Earth's Biomes

The abiotic characteristics of an area include things such as climate and soil type. Along with the biotic factors, such as plants and animals, abiotic characteristics determine an area's ecosystem. Ecosystems that cover large areas of land are called **biomes**.

The major biomes on Earth are the deciduous forest, the desert, the grassland, the taiga, the tropical rain forest, and the tundra. This map shows you where these biomes are found. Humans live in all biomes, but some biomes support human populations better than others do.

UNIT PROJECT LINK

Which biome do you live in? How can biomes change? Work with others to create a model of your biome as it might have looked before any people inhabited it. Include any extinct plants and animals that once lived there.

The human population is greater in biomes that have abundant plant and animal resources and in biomes with milder climates, such as temperate and tropical regions. Temperate and tropical regions are those that lie close enough to the equator to benefit from the Sun's energy for most of the year.

On the next two pages, find out what the abiotic and biotic factors are that make each biome unique.

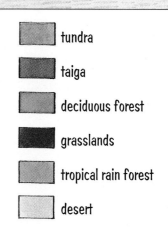

- tundra
- taiga
- deciduous forest
- grasslands
- tropical rain forest
- desert

Equator

Toucan

◀ **TROPICAL RAIN FOREST**
Tropical rain forests are lush and green year-round. Heavy rainfall and a warm climate create an environment in which an amazing variety of plants and animals thrive. These plants and animals live in "layers" of the forest, from the ground to the tops of trees. Tree branches form one layer known as the canopy.

GRASSLAND   Grasslands are ▶ wide-open fields of grass that once covered vast expanses of every continent except Antarctica. The amount of rainfall affects the particular grasses that will thrive in a grassland. Wetter areas have taller grasses; drier areas have shorter grasses. Grasslands attract grazing animals and rodents, as well as their predators.

Field mouse

◀ **DESERT   Deserts** can be either hot or cold, but they are always very dry. So desert plants and animals have to survive without much water. As a result, few types of plants grow in desert ecosystems. Animal populations also are not diverse.

Horned lizard

DECIDUOUS FOREST Deciduous (dē sij′o͞o əs) **forests** grow where winters are cold and summers are warm and wet. The large leaves of deciduous trees—maple, oak, and birch, for example—carry out photosynthesis. Their leaves are lost in autumn. There is plenty of food for insects, birds, rodents, and other animals.

Beetle

TAIGA The **taiga** (tī′gə) contains coniferous forests—evergreens such as spruce, pine, and fir trees. These trees grow in areas where the winters are long and cold. On the forest floor are low-growing mosses and lichens. Many birds and mammals prey on needle-eating insects and seed-eating rodents.

Lodgepole pine cone

TUNDRA The **tundra** is the Arctic grassland north of the taiga where the subsoil is frozen year-round. The tundra has long, cold winters and cool summers. There is little precipitation. A thin layer of snow and ice covers the ground most of the year. The few plants and animals that live in the tundra survive a growing season that is only two to three months long.

Saxifrage

D51

Water Ecosystems

Look back at the map on pages D48 and D49. Two thirds of Earth's surface is covered by water! There are two main kinds of water ecosystems: freshwater ecosystems and saltwater ecosystems. Each of these ecosystems includes a number of smaller ecosystems in which a great variety of organisms live.

Freshwater Ecosystems

Only 3 percent of the water on Earth is fresh. Of that 3 percent, about three fourths is locked in ice at the North Pole or the South Pole or at the tops of mountains. Most of the rest of the water has soaked into the ground. The remaining fresh water is surface water.

Fresh water fills all the lakes, ponds, rivers, streams, swamps, marshes, and bogs of the world. A great variety of organisms live in freshwater ecosystems. The variety of living things in a fresh-water community depends on whether the water is still or flowing, slow-moving or fast-moving. It also depends on other abiotic factors, such as what the water temperature is, whether the water is clear or cloudy, and how much oxygen the water contains. All these factors are connected. Cold water, for example, holds more oxygen than warm water; fast-moving water holds more oxygen than slow-moving water. The illustration on this page will introduce you to the variety of life forms freshwater ecosystems support.

great blue heron

RIVER A river is running water that empties into a lake, an ocean, or another river. Some rivers are wide and slow-moving. Others are narrow and fast-moving. The underwater ecosystems of rivers vary a great deal. Rivers support freshwater fish, shrimp, plants, birds, and other life forms.

cattail

pickerelweed

deciduous trees

WETLAND A **wetland** is an area where land and water meet. The soil of a wetland is watery and the concentration of oxygen is less than in a river or lake. Many types of wetlands exist. A marsh is dominated by grasses and cattails. A swamp is similar to a marsh but is dominated by trees and shrubs. A bog consists primarily of mosses.

LAKE A **lake** is a large standing body of fresh water. Lakes range in size from huge expanses, such as Lake Superior, to small bodies of water. A lake contains a variety of habitats, but each lake is different. Lake fish include perch and bass. Lakes also support frogs, insects, and other water life.

blue-winged teal

waterlily

leopard frog

ghost crab

gray seal

SHORELINE The **shoreline** is where the ocean meets the land. It may be only a narrow strip of land, but it circles every bit of land on Earth! Tides and waves affect the organisms that live along the shoreline, as does the type of shore—rocky, sandy, or pebbly.

sponges

jellyfish

COASTAL OCEAN The coastal ocean is home to kelp, jellyfish, and many kinds of fish—as well as whales. The coastal ocean is shallow enough that sunlight can shine all the way down to the coastal floor. Plankton—the organisms that form the basis of the food chain in coastal ocean ecosystems—abound.

corals

Saltwater Ecosystems

Ninety-seven percent of Earth's water is salty ocean water. If you look at a globe, you'll see that the oceans actually are one continuous body of water. The forms of life this ecosystem supports vary from tiny one-celled organisms to mammals as large as any animals that ever lived. In general, different organisms are found at different depths.

Ocean water generally contains about 3.5 percent salt, but this amount can vary. This variation is important. The amount of salt in water can either support or kill organisms. Other factors such as water pressure, temperature, and light affect the types of organisms that live in salt water. So there are really several different saltwater ecosystems.

So the next time someone talks about the ocean as if it were one big ecosystem, you can tell him or her that saltwater ecosystems are not as simple as they seem. They require a lot of close-up study and observation. ■

sailfish

Atlantic mackerel

hammerhead shark

gray whale

sunfish

OPEN OCEAN The **open ocean** is the vast expanse you see over most of the globe. In fact, the open ocean forms the largest ecosystem on Earth. In the upper layers of open ocean water, plankton and the organisms that feed on it are plentiful. Many species of fish swim in the open ocean, as do whales and squid. Organisms that live on the ocean floor survive by manufacturing their own light or live without light.

white shark

squid

anglerfish

viperfish

lantern fish

manta ray

INVESTIGATION 1

1. Deciduous forests and grasslands have been able to support a large human population. Why do you think this is so? Have humans really adapted to these biomes, or have humans forced the biomes to adapt to them?

2. What abiotic factors determine the type of water ecosystem found in an area?

WHAT IS BIODIVERSITY AND HOW IS IT CHANGING?

Earth's ecosystems are home to millions of species of living things. Each species in an ecosystem plays a role. In this investigation you'll find out how diverse ecosystems are in the species they support, and how changes in this diversity affect an ecosystem.

Activity
Vanishing Species

When ecosystems change, many species are displaced or may even die out. See if you can determine one factor that has led to the decline of a rain forest in Ecuador by doing this activity.

Procedure

1. Locate the country of Ecuador on a globe.

2. Look at the maps to the right, which show how the area covered by forests in Ecuador has changed since 1938. Forested areas are green on the map. In your *Science Notebook*, **describe** what has happened between 1938 and 1988.

3. Refer to the table on the next page. **Draw a bar graph** that shows the change in Ecuador's forested area based on data from the years 1961, 1971, and 1991 (the years for which precise figures are available). Use the figures provided for the square kilometers of forest and woodland.

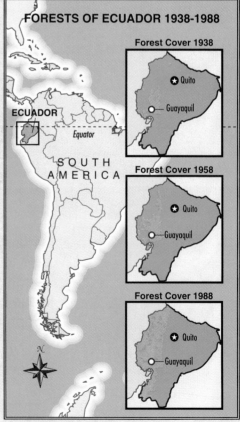

FORESTS OF ECUADOR 1938-1988

Forest Cover 1938

Forest Cover 1958

Forest Cover 1988

4. During those 30 years, the human population in Ecuador had grown. **Draw a bar graph** that shows the change in Ecuador's population based on data from the years 1961, 1971, and 1991 (the years for which census figures are available). Use the figures provided.

ECUADOR			
	1961	**1971**	**1991**
Forest & Woodland	173,000 km^2	153,000 km^2	112,000 km^2
Population	5,162,000	7,035,000	10,782,000

Analyze and Conclude

1. **Compare** the graphs you drew. What relationship has there been between the change in the human population and the change in the amount of forested land in Ecuador? What reasons are there for this relationship?

2. There are no census or forestation figures for 1981. Based on your bar graphs, **infer** what happened to Ecuador's population and forested area between 1971 and 1991.

3. Based on your knowledge of food webs, what do you think happens to a rain forest community when the primary producers—trees—are cut down?

SCIENCE IN LITERATURE

BEARS
by Joni Phelps Hunt
Silver Burdett Press, 1995

"Polar, Panda, Brown, Black, Sloth, Moon. All may soon be gone . . . ." The world's eight species of bears are in danger of becoming extinct. You'll begin to see that for yourself at the beginning of *Bears* by Joni Phelps Hunt. A map shows where brown bears used to live and the smaller area that they now inhabit.

In *Bears* you'll find spectacular close-up photos of these intelligent mammals. You'll also read about how bears live, what they eat, and how they raise their young. Find out what animals are predators of bears and what threats humans pose to bears' survival.

Variety in Ecosystems

Try to imagine 1,000 beetles, each a different species. Tough, isn't it? But if you go to the forests of Central and South America, you can find more than 1,000 different beetles on a *single* tree. Now try to imagine *300,000* different species of beetles. Impossible! Can there really be that many? Yes, there can. There probably are at least that many. But scientists think they have actually identified only a tiny fraction of all the species of beetles in the world.

Scientists believe our planet may be home to as many as 100 million different species of organisms. Only about 1.4 million of them have been identified!

The great abundance of different life forms is called **biodiversity** (bī ō də-vur′sə tē). *Biodiversity* is a combination of the words *biological* and *diversity*. The term refers to the millions of species that can live in Earth's many ecosystems. Biodiversity refers not only to the variety of species on Earth but also to diversity within a single species. Think about all the earthworms you might find in a plot of soil. They are not all exactly the same length, the

same color, or the same diameter. In fact, each one is a little different, just as you are different from your mother, brother, neighbor, and classmates. Yet, just as humans are all members of the same species, *Homo sapiens*, earthworms are all members of the same species, *Lumbricus terrestris*. Yet each earthworm is slightly different from every other earthworm.

Diversity—A Lot or a Little?

The amount of biodiversity varies among ecosystems. One ecosystem may contain thousands of different species; another, fewer than 50. What makes the difference? The biodiversity of an ecosystem depends on three major factors: its size, its terrain, and its latitude, or distance from the equator.

Large ecosystems support a greater number of species than smaller ecosystems. Over a larger area, abiotic factors are more variable. For example, suppose a 1,000-km^2 island covered with forests is home to 50 different species of butterflies. Another island, also forested, but covering 10,000 km^2, may contain 100 kinds of butterflies. Why? Perhaps a tall mountain rises on the larger island. Mountains can cause the amount of rainfall and the temperature to vary across the island. The result? The larger island has many more different ecosystems than the smaller one. And different ecosystems have different populations of organisms. Thus, the larger island, with more variable abiotic factors and more ecosystems, also supports more species of butterflies.

Latitude also affects abiotic factors. Away from the equator, temperatures are not consistently high, sunlight is intense only part of the year, and precipitation is not as steady. These conditions become more extreme the farther an ecosystem is from the equator.

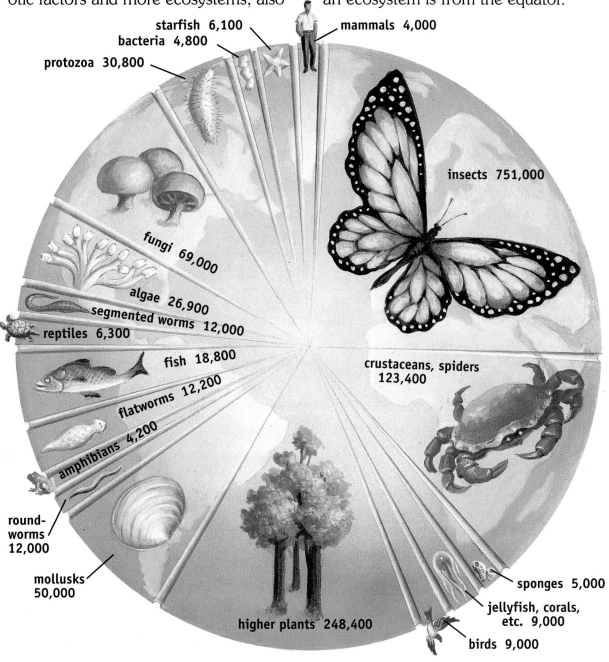

starfish 6,100
bacteria 4,800
protozoa 30,800
mammals 4,000
insects 751,000
fungi 69,000
algae 26,900
segmented worms 12,000
reptiles 6,300
fish 18,800
flatworms 12,200
amphibians 4,200
crustaceans, spiders 123,400
round-worms 12,000
mollusks 50,000
higher plants 248,400
sponges 5,000
jellyfish, corals, etc. 9,000
birds 9,000

▲ **VARIETY ON EARTH** This is a "species-scape." The number of known species of each major group of organisms is listed. The sizes give a rough approximation of the abundance of each group.

Close to the equator, temperatures are high, sunlight is intense, and rain is plentiful. Plants can grow all year. As a result, producers in tropical ecosystems are abundant and varied. They also can support more consumers, of a greater variety, than the producers in a colder or drier climate. Most rain forests are in tropical locations. Thus, rain forests have the highest biodiversity of any ecosystem. Remember the activity on pages D56 and D57? In the forests of Ecuador, Colombia, and Peru—just 2 percent of the world's land surface—there are more than 40,000 species of plants!

The stable climate of the tropics has led to interesting relationships among organisms, which also increases biodiversity. As you know, a single tree rooted in the ground is part of a forest. The tree also supports another whole ecosystem in its canopy layer. The canopy is laden with plant life—mosses, ferns, orchids, and even small trees. In turn, this miniature forest is home to a great many consumers, from one-celled organisms to snakes, tree-dwelling frogs, mammals, and beetles, of course!

Tinkering With Biodiversity

Do you think the dandelions in your back yard, the tumbleweed that rolls across the prairie, and the Norway maple are "all-American"? Like most of us, you'd probably think so. But you'd be wrong! Dandelions, tumbleweed,

▲ **The brown tree snake**

and Norway maples are three of the more than 3,000 species of plants that were introduced to the United States by accident or on purpose. Animal species have been introduced from other places, too. For example, the fierce brown tree snake was introduced to Hawaii from Guam in 1991. Scientists believe the snake survived a plane flight wrapped around the aircraft's wheels.

Native species can be driven out of their habitats by introduced species. Ecologists are trying to restore some ecosystems to their native biodiversity. ■

The rain forest canopy ▶

The Challenge of Biodiversity

Have you ever seen a dinosaur? Did you ever hear of a dusky seaside sparrow? Have you ever used the expression "dead as a dodo"?

Neither you—nor anyone else—has ever seen a live dinosaur, and none of you ever will. You may have heard of a dusky seaside sparrow, but you will never see one alive. Both dinosaurs—all kinds—and dusky seaside sparrows are as dead as dodos. These species are **extinct**. None remains alive. They are gone forever.

Some species, such as the giant panda, are not *yet* extinct. However, many species are **endangered** or threatened. Endangered species are those in danger of becoming extinct. Threatened species are in danger of becoming endangered. Eleven percent of the world's bird species are endangered.

The greatest threat to biodiversity is habitat destruction. For centuries, habitats have been destroyed in many ways, for many reasons. Early farmers cut down Europe's forests many centuries ago, destroying their native ecosystems.

Will the highly endangered panda (*right*), meet the same fate as the the passenger pigeon (*top right*)?

Settlers plowed under the prairies of the midwestern United States and planted crops. Developers fill in the wetlands to build suburban housing developments. Habitats can also be harmed without being destroyed. Pollution can poison a healthy habitat. The introduction of species can drive out native organisms.

But why do we have to care about biodiversity? Why should we care what happens to plants and animals, as long as we're all right? Why should we stop destroying habitats, as long as our homes are safe?

▲ The dodo is extinct. Are all the species in the rain forests headed in the same direction?

Humans cannot live alone on Earth. As you know, plants and animals provide us with food, raw materials for clothing, and building materials. More than 40 percent of all medicines come from living organisms. The complex web of plant life on Earth provides us with oxygen for life processes. Decomposers keep the soil fertile for growing crops. Bacteria and other microscopic organisms break down wastes and purify water. The diversity of life on Earth is inspiring and awesome.

Aside from all these reasons, many people feel that human beings have a responsibility to preserve Earth. We have the power to destroy ecosystems and drive species to extinction. We also have the power—and the knowledge—to save ecosystems and encourage species' survival. We know the consequences of doing both. What will we do? ■

INVESTIGATION 2

THINK IT WRITE IT

1. Identify a favorite species you have read about that you fear is in danger of becoming extinct. Why is it endangered? Can we do anything to save it?

2. What is biodiversity and why does it vary among ecosystems?

REFLECT & EVALUATE

WORD POWER

biodiversity
biomes
deserts
endangered
extinct
grasslands
coastal ocean
deciduous forest
open ocean
tropical rain forest

lake
river
shoreline
taiga
tundra
wetland

 On Your Own
Review the terms in the list. Then use at least five terms in a paragraph about Earth's biomes.

With a Partner
Write each term in the list on one side of an index card and the definition on the other. Use the cards to quiz your partner.

PORTFOLIO

Imagine you are building a zoo. Make a drawing of a biome to include in your zoo. Obtain pictures of plants and animals for your biome. List the abiotic factors needed.

Analyze Information

Study the table below. Based on the data, which two biomes are farthest north? Which biome shows the greatest temperature range? Which shows the smallest temperature range?

Biomes	Average Temperature Range (yearly)
Tundra	-26°C to 4°C
Taiga	-10°C to 14°C
Deciduous forest	6°C to 28°C
Tropical rain forest	25°C to 27°C
Grassland	0°C to 25°C
Desert	24°C to 32°C

Assess Performance

Build a simple ecosystem, either land or water. Choose some organisms to include in the ecosystem. Identify the biotic and abiotic factors in the ecosystem. Vary one of the factors and note any effects on the ecosystem.

Problem Solving

1. Many scientists hypothesize that dinosaurs became extinct after an asteroid struck Earth. Earth's atmosphere was filled with dust that blocked out the Sun's rays. Discuss this theory in terms of concepts from this chapter.

2. Compare the variety of ecosystems in the ocean and on land. Suggest reasons why there is greater variety on land than in the ocean.

3. How has Earth's biodiversity been affected by the development of civilization?

Throughout this unit you've investigated questions related to populations and ecosystems. How will you use what you've learned and share that information with others? Here are some ideas.

Hold a Big Event
to Share Your Unit Project

Turn your classroom into a museum exhibit about the history of your ecosystem. Divide your classroom into two sections. Using your knowledge of what organisms currently live in your ecosystem and what organisms used to live in your ecosystem, develop posters, dioramas, and videotapes showing how organisms, energy, and matter have interacted in your ecosystem over time. Group the displays on the history of your ecosystem in one section of the classroom; in the other section set up your showcase of what your ecosystem looks like now. Invite others to view your display. Have on hand a brochure or tape to guide them through the ecological history of the community.

Experiment

What kind of water ecosystem is found near you—shoreline, river, ocean, lake, or wetland? Choose one of these areas and then conduct some field tests, as environmental engineers do. Some examples:
- Use a pH strip to find out if the water is acidic, basic, or neutral.
- Evaporate a little bit of water to see what materials are in it.
- Note the organisms living in and around the ecosystem.
- Catalog any signs of pollution or other problems.
- Talk to people who have lived in the area for many years to find out how the ecosystem has changed.

Take Action

Your class can "adopt" an acre of rain forest. To find out how, write or call a rain forest protection agency such as: The Nature Conservancy Adopt An Acre Program, 1815 North Lynn Street, Arlington, VA 22209, 1-800-628-6860

UNIT E

THE SOLID EARTH

Theme: Constancy and Change

GET READY TO

OBSERVE & QUESTION

How do rocks bend?

Rocks are used by people to make buildings and monuments. In nature, rocks may also build hills and mountains. How do forces both inside Earth and on its surface create structures such as the one shown?

EXPERIMENT & HYPOTHESIZE

How can fossils help tell us how old a rock is?

Make your own series of rock layers—with fossils in the layers. The order of the layers along with the fossils they contain are clues to the ages of the rocks.

INVESTIGATE!

RESEARCH & ANALYZE

As you investigate, learn more from these books.

- *Rocks, Minerals, and Fossils* by Keith Lye (Silver Burdett Press, 1991.) Ever wonder how you can tell the difference between jewelry made of glass and that made of real diamonds? This book will tell you how to find out.

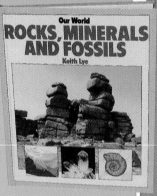

- *My Side of the Mountain* by Jean Craighead George (Puffin Books, 1991). What would it be like to live in the mountains? Read this book for one person's story.

WORK TOGETHER & SHARE IDEAS

How can you build an organized mineral collection?

Working together, you'll begin a collection of rocks, fossils, and minerals. Then you will share your new knowledge with others by creating a museum-type display of your collection and by publishing a guide to local rocks, fossils, and minerals.

CHAPTER 1

MINERALS

Have you ever visited a jewelry store or a museum and admired jewelry containing gemstones such as rubies or diamonds? Have you ever seen bracelets or necklaces made of shiny metals such as silver or gold? Both gemstones and metals have something in common. They are *minerals*.

Prospecting for Gold

The Alaska gold rush of 1898 brought a flood of hopeful prospectors to the North. Alaska still boasts of some hardy individuals who search for gold in rugged, remote areas. Three such people are Paul and Grace Byrd and their daughter, Blyss. During the summer, the family prospects for gold in Bonanza Creek, a stream in southeastern Alaska's Wrangell-St. Elias National Park. The Byrds use a portable suction machine to suck up stones and sand from the creek bottom. The reward for their hard work is finding about 28 g (1 oz) of gold per day.

Gold is just one of a group of substances called minerals. Minerals vary greatly in appearance and texture. Sparkling diamonds, gleaming gold, and graphite are all minerals. What properties make something a mineral? Through the investigations in this chapter, you'll find out.

Coming Up

◄ The Byrd family prospecting for gold in Alaska

INVESTIGATION 1

HOW CAN YOU IDENTIFY MINERALS?

A mineral is a solid element or compound from Earth's crust that has a definite chemical composition and crystal shape. Now see if you can name this mineral. It is most often black or brown. It's used in tools for drilling. It's highly prized when it is colorless or blue-white. If you said diamond, you are right!

Activity

The Way Minerals Look

Think about it—you identify most things just by looking at them. Minerals aren't any different. When you get to know them, you'll be able to look at them and name them. The key is getting to know them.

Procedure

1. Use your egg carton to store your mineral specimens. Open the carton and use the marker to number the pockets from 1 through 12.

2. **Observe** each mineral specimen. Does each look like it is made up of all the same kind of material? Is there any evidence of crystal structure in the minerals? **Record** your observations in your *Science Notebook*.

Step 1

3. **Make a chart** like the one shown, with 8 columns and 12 rows. Any columns you don't fill in during this activity will be filled in during later activities.

MINERAL PROPERTIES CHART							
Mineral Number	Luster	Color	Streak	Hardness	Cleavage	Special	Name

4. The way a mineral reflects light is called **luster** (lus′tər). Some minerals reflect light well—they appear shiny. They have a *metallic* luster. Those that don't have a metallic luster have a *nonmetallic* luster. Separate your mineral specimens into two sets, one set that looks shiny like metal (such as brass, gold, or iron) and the other that doesn't look like metal.

Step 5

5. Put each mineral in your egg carton. As you do it, write on your chart *metallic* or *nonmetallic* under *Luster* and opposite the number of the pocket.

6. Inspect each mineral specimen and write its color in the next column of your chart. If needed, use more than one word, such as *yellow-brown* or *brass yellow*.

7. When a mineral is ground to a powder, its color is called its **streak**. **Predict** each mineral's streak. With each mineral, try to make a mark (like a pencil mark) on the tile. The color of the mark is the color of the streak. **Record** each mineral's streak in your chart.

Analyze and Conclude

1. **Compare** the color and streak of each mineral in your collection. What conclusions can you draw about the color and streak of a mineral?

2. How are the properties of streak and luster useful in getting to know minerals?

INVESTIGATE FURTHER!

RESEARCH

You use two minerals every day in your classroom. In fact, you use them for their streak. Find out what they are.

Activity
Scratching Minerals

You may have noticed that some minerals are harder than others. Hardness is an important property in identifying minerals. Geologists test a mineral's hardness by seeing what objects will scratch or be scratched by the mineral. Try this scratch test yourself.

MATERIALS

- goggles
- mineral set in egg carton from previous activity
- Mineral Properties Chart
- pane of glass, 8-cm square
- steel nail
- copper wire, 10 cm in length
- *Science Notebook*

Procedure

1. Try scratching one mineral with another; do just a little scratch. Don't scrub the minerals together or you'll damage them. Can you find the hardest mineral in your set? How about the softest? **Record** your findings in your *Science Notebook*. Remember to return each mineral to its numbered pocket.

2. Geologists often use a set of tools to judge the hardness of a mineral. The tools include a piece of glass, a fingernail, a steel nail, and a piece of copper. **Predict** which of these items will be the hardest. Then scratch each tool with the others to rank the tools from softest to hardest.

3. Try to scratch each mineral with the edge of your fingernail. Always rub your finger over a mark to make certain it's a scratch and not a streak. A streak will rub off, but a scratch won't. If your fingernail scratches the mineral, write $H < F$ ("hardness is less than a fingernail") for that mineral in your chart.

SAFETY

Put on goggles. When using the glass, keep it flat on the desk. Press the mineral specimen onto the glass and pull it across the glass. DO NOT HOLD THE GLASS IN YOUR HAND.

Step 3

Step 4

4. Find out if the copper wire will scratch the minerals that your fingernail did not scratch. For those that the copper scratches, write $F < H < C$ ("hardness is greater than a fingernail but less than copper").

5. Now try the steel nail on those minerals that the copper didn't scratch. If the nail scratches the mineral, write this in the chart, using an S for "steel": $C < H < S$.

6. Finally, try scratching the glass plate with any mineral that was not scratched by the steel. **Record** those that scratch the glass as $H > G$ ("hardness is greater than glass").

Analyze and Conclude

1. What was the order of hardness for your hardness tools?

2. Did your predictions match your results? Which mineral did you find to be the hardest? Which was the softest? **Compare** your results with those of your classmates. Did your classmates get the same results? If not, repeat the test and compare.

INVESTIGATE FURTHER!

RESEARCH

One of the important properties of gemstones is that they are hard. After all, you wouldn't want to wear a gem if it scratched easily. Look up the hardness of diamonds, rubies, sapphires, emeralds, topaz, and garnets. How do they compare? What scale is used to compare hardness?

Activity

Minerals That Break Funny

MATERIALS
- salt
- hand lens
- mineral set
- Mineral Properties Chart
- *Science Notebook*

If you have ever broken some glass, you were probably more concerned with cleaning it up than with how the glass broke. However, the way something breaks can tell us something important. Find out how minerals break.

Procedure

1. **Observe** some salt with a hand lens. Can you see the flat sides? They are called **cleavage** (klēv′ij) planes. The salt crystals always break along their cleavage planes. Pick out a large crystal and try to crush it with your pencil. How are the pieces like the original crystal? **Record** your observations in your *Science Notebook*.

Step 1

2. **Observe** some large salt crystals with a hand lens. Can you see cleavage planes inside the crystals? They often look like cracks. The cracks look as though the crystal might break along them. Sometimes you can see cleavage planes inside a crystal when you can't find them on the outside.

3. **Observe** your mineral samples. Can you find any that have flat surfaces where the mineral has broken? The surfaces are probably cleavage planes. Can you see cleavage planes inside the mineral? If you find one or more cleavage planes on a mineral, write *yes* under *Cleavage* in your chart.

Analyze and Conclude

1. **List** the minerals that have cleavage planes.

2. **Compare** your mineral observations with those of your classmates. Do you agree on which minerals show cleavage? **Hypothesize** why you did or did not get the same results.

Activity
Name That Mineral

Now that you can recognize mineral properties, you can find out the name for each of the minerals in your mineral set.

MATERIALS
- mineral set
- Mineral Properties Chart
- *Science Notebook*

Procedure

1. Take mineral number 1 from its pocket in the egg carton. Use your chart to review the properties of the mineral.

2. Refer to the "Properties of Minerals" table on page E19. Look at the left column. Notice that it divides the table into two sections, minerals with metallic luster and minerals with non-metallic luster. In which section of the table does your mineral belong? **Record** your observations in your *Science Notebook*.

3. Now move to the second column in the table. It is for hardness. How hard is your mineral? Find the part of the column that describes the hardness of your mineral. Remember to stay in the section for the luster of your mineral when finding the hardness.

4. Move from left to right through the columns of the table. Information about streak and cleavage is sometimes in the column labeled *Special*. You should find the name of the mineral in the right-hand column. Write its name in the last column of your chart.

5. Repeat steps 1–4 for all the other minerals in your set.

PROPERTIES OF MINERALS					
Luster	Hardness	Color	Streak	Special	Name
Metallic	Harder than glass	Black	Black	magnetic	MAGNETITE
Metallic	Harder than glass	Brassy yellow	Black	"fools gold"	PYRITE
Metallic	Softer than glass	Steel gray	Red or reddish brown	may have reddish patches	HEMATITE
Metallic	Softer than glass	Brassy to gold yellow	Black	often has blue, red & purple tarnish	CHALCO-PYRITE
Metallic	Harder than a fingernail	Silver gray	Gray to black	heavy, shows cleavage	GALENA
Luster	Hardness		Color	Special	Name
Non-metallic	Harder than glass		white, pink, gray	hardness is very close	FELDSPAR
Non-metallic	Harder than glass	yes ( )			AMPHIBOLE
Non-metallic	Harder than glass	yes (2)			PYROXENE
Non-metallic	Harder than glass	no			
Non-metallic	Softer than steel	yes (6)			
Non-metallic	Softer than steel	yes (4)	purple, yellow		
Non-metallic	Softer than copper	yes (3)	white, pink	crystal faces are usually curved	
Non-metallic	Softer than copper	yes (3)	colorless, white, yellow	cleavage planes make parallelograms	CALCITE
Non-metallic	Softer than a fingernail	yes (3)	colorless, white	tastes salty, breaks in cubes	HALITE
Non-metallic	Softer than a fingernail	yes (1)	colorless, white	sometimes transparent	GYPSUM
Non-metallic	Softer than a fingernail	yes (1)	colorless, silvery black	peels in thin sheets, can be green	MICA
Non-metallic	Softer than a fingernail	yes (1)	light green to white	usually flakey	TALC
Non-metallic	Softer than a fingernail	no	yellow to brown	looks like rust	LIMONITE
Non-metallic	Softer than a fingernail	no	red	earthy	HEMATITE

Analyze and Conclude

1. Were you able to find the name of each of your minerals? **Hypothesize** why you were or were not able to find all of the minerals' names.

2. How are properties useful in identifying minerals?

Mineral Properties

Did you know that the "brain" of a computer, called a computer chip, is made from a mineral found in beach sand? A **mineral** is a solid element or compound from Earth's crust that has a definite chemical composition and crystal shape. Minerals can look very different from one another—colorless like quartz, silver or red like hematite, or shiny like gold and silver—but we find ways to use them all.

Look around and you'll see minerals being used. People may be wearing jewelry made of a gemstone like a ruby, an emerald, or an opal. The walls in your home are probably made of wallboard, which is gypsum sandwiched between layers of paper. The windows in your classroom are made from quartz. The body

powder you use may be made from the mineral talc. When you talk to a friend on the telephone, copper wires transmit your voice. Your lunch may be wrapped in aluminum foil, made from the mineral bauxite. Perhaps you can think of other minerals you use every day. How many are there?

Why are minerals used in so many ways? They have different properties that make them right for many different uses. These same properties help scientists tell minerals apart, just as they helped you in the activities. What are some of the properties of minerals you examined in the activities?

▲ The mineral gypsum is used to make wallboard, or drywall.

▲ Talc is a mineral that you may sprinkle on your skin after a shower.

E12

▲ A mineral's luster is a clue to its identity. Silver, at left, has a metallic luster. Fluorite, right, has a nonmetallic luster.

Luster

Luster is one property that can be used to classify minerals. **Luster** refers to the way light reflects from the surface of a mineral. Look at the graphite in your pencil or at a piece of silver or gold jewelry. The shiny appearance of these minerals is called metallic luster. Any mineral that reflects light like polished metal has a metallic luster. All other minerals have nonmetallic luster. Minerals that have nonmetallic luster vary in the way they look. For example, the luster of a nonmetallic mineral may be dull like cinnabar, pearly like mica, or glassy and brilliant like diamond.

Hardness

A mineral's **hardness** is a measure of how easily it can be scratched. Talc is the softest mineral. It can be scratched by all other minerals. Diamond is the hardest mineral. It can scratch the surface of any other mineral, but no other mineral can scratch a diamond.

You can estimate a mineral's hardness by using Mohs' scale, shown in the table below. This scale lists the hardness of

MOHS' SCALE OF MINERAL HARDNESS		
Mineral	**Hardness**	**Simple Test**
Talc	1	easily scratched by fingernail
Gypsum	2	scratched by fingernail
Calcite	3	barely scratched by copper
Fluorite	4	easily scratched by steel knife
Apatite	5	scratched by steel knife
Orthoclase feldspar	6	scratches glass with difficulty
Quartz	7	scratches glass and steel
Topaz	8	scratches quartz
Corundum	9	no simple test
Diamond	10	no simple test

ten common minerals. To test a mineral for hardness, find out which mineral on the scale is the hardest one that your mineral scratches. For example, a mineral that can scratch calcite but can't scratch fluorite has a hardness between 3 and 4. Also, just as you did in the activity on page E8, you can use your fingernail, copper, steel, glass, and the simple scratching tests listed in Mohs' scale to estimate hardness. What would be the hardness of a mineral that can be scratched by copper but not a fingernail?

Hardness is caused by the arrangement of matter in a mineral. For example, both diamond and graphite consist only of carbon. One arrangement produces the hardest natural mineral (diamond), and the other arrangement produces one of the softest minerals (graphite).

Color

Another mineral property is color. The elements making up a mineral determine its color. For example, chromium gives ruby its unusual red color. Although color is the easiest mineral property to observe, it's not the most reliable for identifying minerals. Many different minerals have similar colors. Some minerals vary in color due to the presence of tiny quantities of other substances. Pure quartz is colorless, but traces of other substances can make it become white, pink, or purple.

Streak

Most minerals aren't as hard as a ceramic tile. When you scratch a mineral against a tile called a streak plate,

SCIENCE IN LITERATURE

Our World
ROCKS, MINERALS AND FOSSILS
Keith Lye

ROCKS, MINERALS AND FOSSILS
by Keith Lye
Silver Burdett Press, 1991

Read about fool's gold and true gold on page 25 of *Rocks, Minerals and Fossils* by Keith Lye. Make a table to summarize all the tests that can be done to tell these two minerals apart. Make sure you include the expected results of each test.

When you're done, browse through this colorful reference book. You'll find it's easy to locate information that interests you by looking at the pictures, reading the large titles, or using the index. For example, if you're not sure what makes a mineral different from a rock, look on page 13. There's a photo of a rock, called granite, and the four kinds of minerals that make it up.

some minerals crumble off as a powder. The color of this powder is the mineral property called **streak**.

The streak of most minerals is either colorless or the same color as the mineral. However, for a few minerals, the color of the mineral and the color of the streak aren't the same. For example, if you scratch silver-colored hematite on a streak plate, you find its streak is red! Apatite is a dark mineral with a white streak. Pyrite is brassy yellow and leaves a greenish-black streak. Which of the minerals that you tested had a colored streak?

▲ **A mineral's streak may be different from its color.**

Cleavage

Some minerals split easily along flat surfaces, a property called **cleavage**. If you have ever handled mica, you know how easily it splits apart. Mica breaks along cleavage surfaces that are all in the same direction. Some minerals have cleavage surfaces in more than one direction. The salt you observed in the activity on page E10 is the mineral halite. Its cube shape occurs because halite splits along cleavage surfaces in three directions.

You may think that gemstones break naturally along several cleavage surfaces. But most gemstones do not break along cleavage surfaces. Therefore, gem cut-

▲ Calcite can be cleaved in three directions, or planes.

▲ Rubies, like many other gemstones, have no cleavage.

▲ Mica cleaves along one plane, and peels in thin sections.

ters must grind the gems to create the flat, shiny faces, called facets, that give gems their different shapes.

Using Mineral Properties

How are mineral properties useful? If you were a gold miner, using the properties you just learned about might make you a fortune! You would need mineral properties to tell gold from other minerals you find.

Compare the samples of gold and pyrite shown. At first glance they may seem alike. Notice that they both have a brassy yellow color. They both also have a metallic luster, and neither mineral has cleavage.

Pyrite is known as fool's gold. Based on color, luster, and cleavage alone, you might easily mistake pyrite for gold. A smart gold miner would also compare the minerals' hardness and streak. Pyrite has a hardness of about 6 and gold has a hardness of about 3. Pyrite leaves a greenish-black streak; gold's streak is golden-yellow. Gold has a greater value than pyrite, so it pays to be able to tell them apart. ■

▲ Pyrite, shown here, has some properties similar to those of gold.

▲ Gold, shown here, is softer than pyrite and has a different streak.

UNIT PROJECT LINK

Start a collection of minerals. There are many ways to get mineral samples. You could join a mineral club. There may be some adults in your community who are collectors and would be happy to help you. You could write to students in schools in other parts of the country and trade minerals through the mail. Or you could go out and collect local mineral samples from road cuts and streambeds. To determine the name of any unknown minerals in your collection, see the activity on page E11.

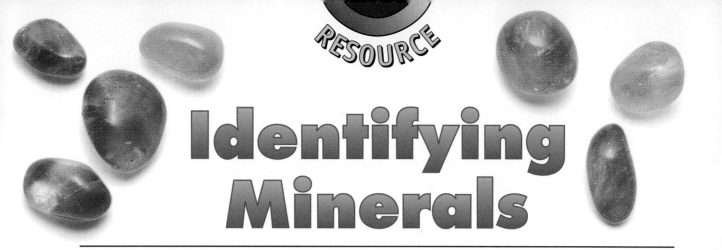

Identifying Minerals

A key is an organizer designed to help you identify things. The table on page E19, "Properties of Minerals," is a key designed to help you identify minerals. To identify an unknown mineral, match the properties you observe in your sample with the properties listed in the table.

Let's try an example. Say you are given the unknown mineral shown below. What is it?

Using the Table: Nonmetallic Minerals
Step 1. Luster
Is it metallic or nonmetallic?

What kind of luster does your mineral have? It doesn't look like polished metal, so it's nonmetallic. Find in the table the column labeled *Luster*, and locate all the nonmetallic minerals.

Step 2. Hardness
What scratches it?

If you had your mineral sample in front of you, you would use the materials from the activity on page E8 to test for hardness. The sample can be scratched with a fingernail. Locate this under the column labeled *Hardness*. Notice that there are only six minerals in the table that are both nonmetallic and softer than a fingernail. Your sample must be one of those six.

Step 3. Cleavage
Is there any? In how many directions?

You can see that your sample does have cleavage in one direction. You can

STEP 1

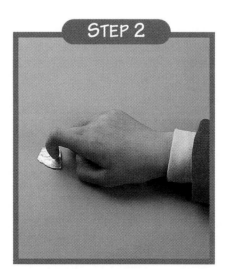

STEP 2

STEP 3

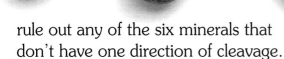

rule out any of the six minerals that don't have one direction of cleavage.

Step 4. Color

What is it?

Observe that your sample is colorless. Look under the column labeled *Color* and notice that two minerals fit the bill: mica and gypsum. Which is it?

Step 5. Special Properties

Are there any?

Find the *Special* column. Since your sample peels easily in thin sheets, as is listed for mica, it must be mica. How might the procedure vary for a metallic mineral? Let's try it for the sample shown.

Using the Table: Metallic Minerals

Step 1. Luster

Is it metallic or nonmetallic?

Notice that the sample looks like polished metal. You can rule out all nonmetallic minerals, so cover the part of the table that shows nonmetallic minerals.

Step 2. Hardness

What scratches it?

If you could test it, you'd find that your sample can scratch glass. Look in the table to see which metallic minerals are harder than glass. Notice that there are only two minerals with this property: magnetite and pyrite.

Step 3. Color

What is it?

Observe that your sample is black. Look under the column labeled *Color* and notice that pyrite is brassy yellow. Your mineral must be magnetite. But to make sure, check its other properties.

Step 4. Streak

What is it?

If you could scratch your sample along a streak plate, you would see that its streak is black. This agrees with the data in the table under the column labeled *Streak*.

Step 5. Special Properties:

Are there any?

If you had a magnet, you would see that your sample is attracted to it. You can use this property and others in the table to confirm that your unknown sample is indeed magnetite. ■

STEP 1

STEP 4

STEP 5

E18

PROPERTIES OF MINERALS

Luster	Hardness	Color	Streak	Special	Name
Metallic	H > G	black	black	magnetic	MAGNETITE
Metallic	H > G	brassy yellow	black	fool's gold	PYRITE
Metallic	S < H < G	steel gray	red or reddish brown	may have reddish patches	HEMATITE
Metallic	C < H < S	brassy to gold yellow	black	often has blue, red, and purple tarnish	CHALCO-PYRITE
Metallic	F < H < C	silver gray	gray to black	heavy, shows cleavage (3)	GALENA

Luster	Hardness	Cleavage	Color	Special	Name
Non-metallic	H > G	yes (2)	white, pink, gray	hardness is very close to glass	FELDSPAR
Non-metallic	H > G	yes (2)	black, green, white	cleavage planes make a diamond shape	AMPHIBOLE
Non-metallic	H > G	yes (2)	black, green	cleavage planes make a square shape	PYROXENE
Non-metallic	H > G	no	colorless, white, pink, smoky, purple	looks glassy, chips or breaks like glass	QUARTZ
Non-metallic	C < H < S	yes (6)	yellow to brown or black	yellowish white streak	SPHALERITE
Non-metallic	C < H < S	yes (4)	purple, green, yellow	crystals are cubes, transparent	FLUORITE
Non-metallic	C < H < S	yes (3)	white, pink	crystal faces are usually curved	DOLOMITE
Non-metallic	F < H < C	yes (3)	colorless, white, yellow	cleavage planes make parallelograms	CALCITE
Non-metallic	H < F	yes (3)	colorless, white	tastes salty, breaks in cubes	HALITE
Non-metallic	H < F	yes (1)	colorless, white	sometimes transparent	GYPSUM
Non-metallic	H < F	yes (1)	colorless, silvery, black	peels in thin sheets, can be green	MICA
Non-metallic	H < F	yes (1)	light green to white	usually flaky	TALC
Non-metallic	H < F	no	yellow to brown	looks like rust	LIMONITE
Non-metallic	H < F	no	red	earthy	HEMATITE

*Numbers in parentheses give number of cleavage planes.

Key: H—hardness; G—glass; S—steel; C—copper; F—fingernail; <—less than; >—greater than.

Diamonds

Have you ever passed a jewelry store window filled with sparkling diamond rings? Just what are diamonds and how do we get them? Diamond is the hardest mineral. It is made of pure carbon. It forms deep underground, where temperature and pressure are very great, in a rock called kimberlite (kim′bər līt). Most kimberlite forms long, tube-shaped rock bodies called pipes. Sometimes these pipes reach Earth's surface.

Mining Diamonds

Diamonds have been discovered in many different parts of the world. The map shows areas that have provided the greatest number of diamonds. A limited number have been found in the United States, in northern California, southern Oregon, Arkansas, and the eastern Appalachian Mountains.

Most diamonds are found in stream deposits called placers. A placer is a deposit of sediment that contains important mineral fragments. Diamond placers form when streams flow over kimberlite pipes and carry kimberlite particles downstream. Because diamonds are heavier than other rock particles, they drop to the bottom of streams and build up on stream beds. Miners remove diamonds in the same way gold is panned.

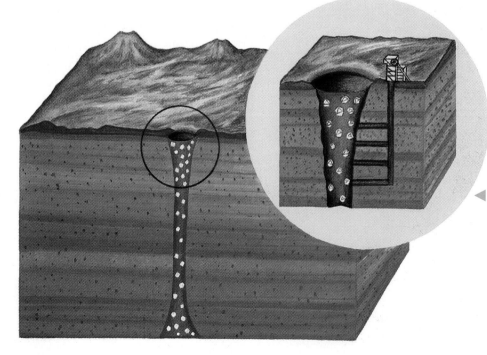

◀ In South Africa, mine shafts are dug into kimberlite pipes and diamonds are removed. Such mines are the world's richest sources of diamonds.

E20

Diamonds are also mined directly from kimberlite. This is done by digging either surface pits or deep underground mine shafts. Once removed from the ground, the kimberlite is crushed and the rock is washed away, leaving behind only the harder diamonds. Any remaining traces of kimberlite are separated and removed by machines.

After mining, diamonds are sorted according to quality. Only two out of every ten diamonds are of good enough quality to be made into jewels. The rest are cut up for other uses, like making abrasives, glass cutters, rock drill bits, and telecommunication products. The better-quality diamonds are then sorted, or graded, according to their color, size, and purity.

A Cut Above

After grading, diamonds are sent to a gem cutter. Gem-quality diamonds are cut because doing so shows off their brilliant nonmetallic luster. Next, the diamond is shaped. Finally, it is polished by holding it at an angle to a spinning disk coated with diamond dust. This step creates the sparkling facets, or faces, highly prized in gemstones. ■

▲ **Raw diamonds are often found in kimberlite.**

▲ **Gem cutters cut and polish selected diamonds.**

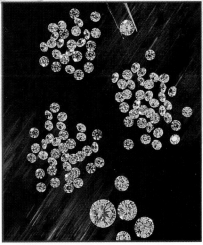

▲ **Finished diamonds are sold around the world.**

INVESTIGATION 1

THINK IT WRITE IT

1. Describe how you would use mineral properties to distinguish quartz from calcite.

2. When trying to identify an unknown mineral, list all the questions you would need to ask and answer about that mineral.

INVESTIGATION 2

WHAT ARE MINERALS USED FOR?

Look around at your classmates. How many are wearing jewelry? You know that minerals are used to make much of that jewelry. Try to name as many minerals (think in terms of gems and metals) used in jewelry as you can. Can you think of other uses for minerals?

Activity
Growing Crystals

Mineral crystals are used in jewelry and in electronics. Some of these crystals are grown in laboratories. In this activity you can grow your own crystals!

Procedure

1. Fill a 500-mL jar with hot water from the tap. Dissolve as much alum as possible in the water (about 100 grams, or 3–4 oz). Cap the jar and let it stand overnight.

2. Pour a small amount of the solution from the jar into the bottom of a bowl and let it stand overnight. The next morning you should find some small crystals in the bowl. Use the spoon to remove one or two good crystals and pour the solution back into the jar.

3. Tie one of the crystals to the end of a piece of thread. Suspend the crystal in the baby-food jar.

4. Nearly fill the baby-food jar with solution from the large jar. Be careful not to pour any crystals into the baby-food jar. Tent a piece of paper over the jar to keep dust out. **Predict** about how much the crystal will grow each day.

5. **Observe** your crystal growing. It may take a few days. Each day, **estimate** the size of the crystal. If the level of solution in the jar goes down, add more. When the crystal stops growing, remove it from the solution and **draw** a picture of it in your *Science Notebook*.

Step 3

Analyze and Conclude

1. About how large was the crystal when you started?

2. How large was the crystal when you stopped growing it?

3. How many days did the crystal grow?

4. Did your crystal grow by the same amount each day? Describe your evidence.

5. Think of ways people use crystals. **Infer** why scientists might want to grow crystals in a laboratory.

INVESTIGATE FURTHER!

EXPERIMENT

You can grow crystals from other substances. Instead of alum, try sugar, Epsom salts, or rock salt. Compare the shape of the crystals and how easy they were to grow.

Quartz
A Versatile Mineral

If you've ever been to a beach or seen pictures of one, you know that beaches are made of sand. The words *sand* and *gravel* really refer to the size of a grain of mineral or rock, sand particles being smaller than gravel. Any rock or mineral can be broken into sand-sized or gravel-sized pieces.

The most common sand in the world is quartz sand. Quartz is also one of the most important minerals. It is made of only two elements, silicon and oxygen. The colors and names of common types of quartz include clear (rock crystal), pink (rose), white (milky), and gray (smoky). Some forms of quartz are semiprecious gemstones such as amethyst, tiger-eye, and citrine.

Native Americans used one form, flint, for tools such as arrowheads.

Building With Quartz

Quartz plays an important role in the building industry. Many building materials are made of rocks and minerals. **Concrete**, for example, is a rock material made of sand and gravel and a binder. The binder, called portland cement, is made by grinding limestone and shale, two kinds of rock, into a powder. This powder is baked at high temperature until it forms balls called clinker. Cooled clinker is crushed to a powder and mixed with gypsum, another mineral. This mixture is then mixed with quartz-rich sand, gravel, and water and allowed to harden to form concrete. How have you seen concrete used in your neighborhood?

From left to right: clear quartz, rose quartz, milky quartz, smoky quartz

▲ Concrete, a building material, is made with quartz and other minerals.

▲ Without quartz, there would not be glass.

Seeing With Quartz

Quartz is also used to make glass. By ancient times, people in the Middle East had a good understanding of quartz and its properties. Glassmaking probably began about 4,000 years ago in Egypt or Mesopotamia. Today the art of glass-making is a worldwide industry.

Glass is easy to make if you have the proper tools. Powdered quartz is mixed with powdered limestone and soda (not the kind you drink, but a solid substance called sodium carbonate). The mixture is heated to about 1,600°C (2,912°F). At this temperature it melts. Then it is cooled quickly so that crystals cannot form. Crystals would make objects seen through the glass look wavy and deformed. Very old glass looks wavy because it has begun to crystallize. Look around you. How many ways can you see glass being used?

The Computer Mineral

Quartz can be separated into its two parts, silicon and oxygen. From the silicon, crystals can be grown (much as you did in the activity on pages E22 and 23) and later cut into thin pieces. These pieces of pure silicon are used in

◀ Quartz, a compound of silicon and oxygen, is one of the most abundant minerals in Earth's crust.

E25

The brain of every desktop computer (*left*) is a silicon chip. Many chips, each the size of a fingernail, are obtained from silicon wafers (*center*). Each chip is etched with the electronic circuits (*right*) that carry out the calculations that make computers such time-savers.

the electronics industry, which is a major part of the world's economy. Computer chips, which are the brains of our computers, and solar cells, which power solar calculators, are made with silicon.

Perhaps the most amazing thing about quartz crystals is that they generate electricity. If the crystals are squeezed, they bend slightly and produce electricity. In addition, when a small electrical current is put through a crystal, it vibrates. The vibrations are very regular, making quartz crystals ideal for keeping time. Tiny quartz crystals are used to keep time in many types of watches.

Maybe you thought quartz was something you walked on as you viewed the ocean. But a world without window glass, portable electronic games, radios, CD players, computers, or concrete would be hard to imagine! ■

◄ You may be carrying a quartz crystal on your wrist. In watches with a quartz crystal, the crystal's vibrations keep time more accurately than those watches that use a spring to keep time.

How Iron Becomes Steel

In Arizona, there is a huge hole in the ground known as the Barringer Meteorite Crater. Scientists hypothesize the crater formed about 25,000 years ago when an 18-m (59-ft) wide chunk of iron from space collided with Earth. The chunk of iron from space shows that iron isn't found only on Earth. It's all over the universe! Maybe it should be called the universal metal!

Iron occurs in minerals. Magnetite and hematite are important iron-containing minerals. Minerals from which metals can be removed are called **ores**. An iron ore is made up of iron and other elements.

The most widespread source of iron is hematite, an ore made up of iron and oxygen. Over 2 billion years ago, hematite layers began to build up in the oceans. Over time the hematite was covered by layers of sediment. Later, parts of the ocean bottom were slowly lifted up to the surface, and the iron deposits eventually became exposed. That was the easy part! For us, the hard part is getting the iron ores out of the ground and the iron out of the ores.

Iron ore is mined all over the planet. In the United States, most of the iron we use comes from hematite mined in Canada and South America. Magnetite

Iron is used to make many different products such as the blades of skates (*left*), the rails of roller coasters (*center*), and the hulls of ships (*right*).

is not as easy to find as hematite, but it's a purer source of iron. The world's largest magnetite mine is in Sweden. Others are located in Wyoming, New York, Utah, South Africa, Austria, Italy, and Russia.

The process of removing metal from ore is called **smelting**. The first smelting of metal may have occurred about 9,000 years ago. Around 3,500 years ago, iron smelting became widespread. Iron was often used in making cooking tools and weapons. Because the intro-duction of iron affected cultures so greatly, that period of time was called the Iron Age. The diagram shows how pig iron is made.

1 To smelt iron, iron ore is mixed with a kind of coal called coke. Crushed limestone is added to the mixture.

2 The mixture is heated in a 10-story-high oven called a blast furnace. Coke burns very hot, so it provides the high temperatures needed to melt the ore. The limestone mixes with unwanted materials to form a waste product called slag.

3 The melted mixture works its way down through the blast furnace, getting hotter as it sinks.

4 Wastes that are less dense separate and float on the molten metal. This slag is drained off.

5 The remaining melted iron, called pig iron, is drained from the bottom of the blast furnace.

▲ **Pig iron is remelted and mixed with a small amount of iron, making steel.**

Because of impurities such as carbon present in pig iron, it is too brittle to be used for purposes requiring great strength. Instead it is remelted and poured into molds. Iron made in this way is called cast iron. Cast iron is used to make bells, wood stoves, bathtubs, railings, and other products.

Pig iron can also be remelted and converted into steel. In a furnace, melted pig iron is brought to a high temperature. Air

is blown over the iron to increase the heat and remove excess carbon. When the metal is free of carbon, a measured amount of carbon is mixed in. It may seem strange that carbon is removed only to be added again, but an exact amount of carbon is needed to make useful steel. Too much carbon makes the steel brittle and too little makes it weak.

▲ **Steel can be produced in a variety of forms, including rolled sheets.**

Steel can be rolled into sheets or made into bars, blocks, and other shapes. It can be made as sharp as a razor or as blunt as a hammer. Other metals can be added to steel to make alloys, or mixtures of metals. For example, chromium is added to make steel resist rusting. Nickel is added to make steel stronger. Titanium makes steel more resistant to heat. Tungsten makes steel strong at high temperatures.

How did you get to school today? If you came by public transportation, car, or bike, steel helped you. What other uses for steel can you think of? ■

▲ **The liquid steel is poured into molds and allowed to cool.**

A World of Minerals

Mineral resources are in the ground all over the world. But they are not distributed evenly. As the map shows, some countries have more mineral resources than do others.

A country can mine its resources and use them to make products. The country can then sell some of its raw resources and products to other countries. The selling countries are called producers. Countries with few mineral resources must buy many resources or products. These buying countries are consumers. Consumers often buy raw resources to make products. If they sell these products to producers, the producers may actually be buying back their raw resources in a new form.

Worldwide Metal Resources

◇ TIN
○ BAUXITE
✕ LEAD & ZINC
◗ GOLD
△ SILVER
★ COPPER
■ IRON

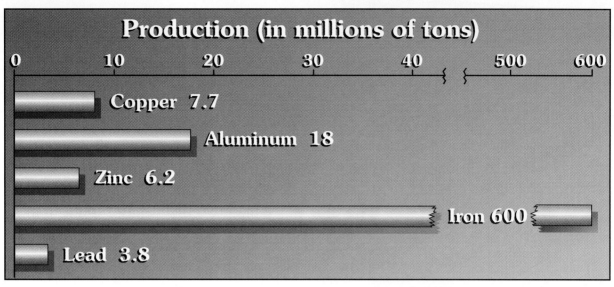

Production (in millions of tons)

| 0 | 10 | 20 | 30 | 40 | | 500 | 600 |

Copper 7.7

Aluminum 18

Zinc 6.2

Iron 600

Lead 3.8

▲ **Worldwide yearly production of selected metals**

For example, raw iron ore may be shipped from the United States to Japan. A Japanese company turns the ore into iron, the iron into steel, and the steel into bike frames. Some frames are sold in Japan and some are sold in other parts of the world, including the United States.

Minerals and mineral products are an important part of the world trading market. There are few places on Earth where iron or steel isn't used in some way. Aluminum is important to canning and cooking industries. Silver is valued for jewelry. What other ways are mineral resources used in the world?

Why Waste?

The uses of mineral resources are unlimited. The amount of mineral resources is not. Although most mineral resources are fairly abundant, finding new sources is getting more difficult. And mineral resources are being used up fast. Your old tricycle may be buried in the middle of a landfill right now. Cars sit rusting in junkyards and on roadsides. Aluminum cans float on ocean waves where they were thrown. Usable mercury gets thrown away inside dead dry-cell batteries. These items are not really gone from our environment. They're still here but they're scattered, making it almost impossible for them to be recovered and reused.

Recycling Mineral Resources

Many communities in the United States have laws stating that certain

▲ **Much of Earth's mineral wealth ends up in places like this.**

▲ **The recycling of minerals helps keep their cost down.**

items must be recycled. In addition to nonmineral products like paper and plastic, metals such as copper, steel, brass, and aluminum are being recycled. Recycling doesn't totally solve the problem of using up a mineral resource, but it does extend our use of such resources.

Many people on the planet still don't recycle, so we slowly but surely lose valuable mineral resources. As a resource becomes scarce, its price rises. Eventually a new resource must be used in its place. Could the same cycle be repeated with the new resource?

World Issues

The way that mineral resources are handled in one country can affect many other countries. Look at the map on page E30 and the bar graph on page E31 and discuss answers to the following questions with your classmates.

Which two metals are produced in the largest quantity? Do you think the U.S. has to import such resources? What happens when a nation doesn't have enough raw resources or money to trade evenly? What happens when countries are in competition for a product in limited supply? What happens if a country holds back on selling raw resources or products needed by other countries of the world? ■

INVESTIGATE FURTHER!

·······························

TAKE ACTION

Write to a local recycling center to find out which minerals can be recycled in your community. Then organize a recycling drive of those materials.

━━━━━━━ **INVESTIGATION 2** ━━━━━━━

1. Name six products made from minerals and at least one mineral used to make each product.

2. If you were building a house, list the materials made from minerals that you would use and explain why you would use them.

WORD POWER

cleavage
concrete
hardness
luster
mineral
ores
smelting
streak

 On Your Own
Review the terms in the list. Then use as many terms as you can to write a brief summary of the chapter.

 With a Partner
Make up a quiz using all the terms in the list. Challenge your partner to complete the quiz.

PORTFOLIO

Make an illustrated chart that shows minerals and products made from those minerals.

Analyze Information

Observe the properties of the mineral sample shown. This mineral's streak is gray to black. The mineral cannot be scratched with a fingernail but can be scratched by glass. Use the "Properties of Minerals" table on page E19 to identify this mineral.

Assess Performance

Obtain one or more samples of minerals from your teacher. Perform the tests needed to identify your samples. Refer to the "Properties of Minerals" table as you collect your data.

Problem Solving

1. You are about to take a mineral-collecting field trip. You plan to identify all the minerals you collect. List the materials you will need to take with you and explain what mineral property each material will be used to identify.

2. Compare the importance of quartz and iron to modern civilizations.

3. What might happen if, from now on, all mineral resources found and used were recycled?

CHAPTER 2

ROCKS

Rocks are made of minerals, and you find rocks of all kinds and sizes everywhere! They range from the sandstone pebble in a city park to the gigantic granite face of a cliff. Most rocks appear sturdy and unchanging. Actually, however, natural processes are constantly changing rocks. People too can transform rocks.

On the Cutting Edge

Edward Torres of Seaside Heights, New Jersey, is a stonecutter. He skillfully turns sheets of white, black, beige, red, or green marble into custom-made items. He crafts such things as fireplace mantels and counter tops.

A typical job for Torres begins when his material is delivered. A 5-ft by 8-ft sheet of 3/4 in.-thick marble, weighing 600 lb, is gently deposited onto his worktable by a forklift! Torres then uses a circular, diamond-toothed, wet saw to precisely cut the hard stone to the proper measurements. (Water cools the saw blade.) The fully processed piece, completed and polished, is a beautiful and useful item.

What *natural* processes change some materials into marble, or into other kinds of rocks, in the first place? What properties distinguish one kind of rock from another? In this chapter you'll explore these and other questions.

Coming Up

◄ Edward Torres, Stonecutter

HOW ARE ROCKS CLASSIFIED?

Rocks are the "stuff" that makes up Earth. About 4 billion years ago, Earth was a molten ball of rock. Although some of Earth's rock is still molten, the rock in the outer layer is solid. You live on this rocky ball. In this investigation you'll find out how rocks are identified and classified.

Activity
Sort of Rocky

Rocks are made of minerals. Some rocks are made of only one mineral, but most rocks are made of more than one. In this activity you'll observe some properties of rocks and use those properties to classify the rocks.

Procedure

1. Number paper punchouts from 1 to 12. With white glue, glue one punchout on each rock specimen.

2. Put all the rocks together on your desktop. **Compare** the rocks to one another and separate them into a dark-colored set and a light-colored set. In your *Science Notebook*, **record** the numbers for each set.

3. Mineral crystals in rocks are usually very small. They are shiny and have flat faces that look like tiny mirrors. Place all the rocks together, **observe** the

rocks with a hand lens, and separate the rocks into a set with crystals and a set without crystals. **Record** the numbers for each set.

4. Use the hand lens to study the rocks again, separating the rocks into two new sets: one set in which the rocks appear to be made of more than one mineral and the other in which the rocks appear to contain only one mineral. **Record** the numbers for each set.

5. Separate the rocks with one mineral into two sets: rocks with crystals and rocks without crystals. Do the same for rocks with more than one mineral. **Record** your results.

6. Now **classify** each of the four sets from steps 4 and 5 into sets that contain dark-colored rocks and light-colored rocks. Then use the egg carton to store your rock specimens.

Analyze and Conclude

1. How many sets now contain only one rock?

2. List the properties that you used in this activity to classify rocks. **Infer** how these properties are used to classify rocks.

UNIT PROJECT LINK

Begin a rock collection. Rocks are easier to find than minerals. Get good clean rocks that are freshly broken so that you can see what the insides look like. Keep a numbered list of your rocks to tell where they came from. Try sorting them according to their properties.

Activity
The Rock Key

A key is used in science to help identify something. The Rock Key will help you use the properties of rocks to find out their names.

Procedure

1. Choose a rock specimen. Look at the descriptions at the left side of the Rock Key. Which description matches your rock? Does it have crystals? If it does, follow the line from "Rock has crystals" to the next level in the key. If it does not have crystals, follow the other line.

2. At most levels in the key, two choices are given. Match a choice to your rock and follow the line to your next observation and choice. Eventually, you will arrive at the name of your rock on the right side of the key. Be sure to follow the lines in the key; don't skip around.

3. If you need to find out whether the rock is hard or soft, test the hardness against glass, the same as you did with minerals. Hard rocks scratch glass; soft ones do not.

4. If you need to find out if a rock with crystals is coarse-grained, medium-grained, or fine-grained, look at the size of crystals. In a coarse-grained rock, most of the rock is made of crystals larger than a grain of rice. In a fine-grained rock, you need a hand lens to see crystals. In a medium-grained rock, you can see the crystals without a hand lens, but they are smaller than rice grains.

Steps 3 & 4

Analyze and Conclude

1. Use the Rock Key to identify each of your rocks. For each rock, **record** in your *Science Notebook* the rock's number, its properties, and its name.

2. Which rocks did you find hard to identify? **Make an inference** about what additional data would have helped you identify them more easily.

THE ROCK KEY

*Rock has crystals

- Has layers
  - Layers are like ribbons
    - Rock is often hard ———— Gneiss — M
  - Layers are not like ribbons
    - Layers are flaky (like wet leaves) or do not make long ribbons; rock is often soft ———— Schist — M
- Has no layers
  - Light-colored rock
    - Soft; usually white, pink, or tan ———— Marble — M
    - Hard
      - Fine-grained ———— Rhyolite — I
      - Coarse-grained ———— Granite — I
  - Dark-colored rock
    - Fine-grained; usually black or dark gray ———— Basalt — I
    - Medium-grained; usually black, dark gray, or greenish ———— Diabase — I
    - Coarse-grained; usually black, dark gray, or greenish ———— Gabbro — I

*Rock has no crystals

- Has layers
  - Feels like sandpaper; can scrape sand off it ———— Sandstone — S
  - Does not feel like sandpaper
    - Thin, flat layers; usually gray, greenish, or red; smooth ———— Slate — M
    - Uneven, wavy layers; smells like mud when wet ———— Shale — S
- Has no layers
  - Looks spongelike
    - Light-colored
      - Like a glass sponge; may float in water ———— Pumice — I
    - Dark-colored
      - Glassy; like a cinder; heavy ———— Scoria — I
      - Not glassy; heavy; black or gray ———— Basalt — I
  - Not spongelike
    - Glass; may be black or black with white or red ———— Obsidian — I
    - Not glass
      - Can scrape sand off it
        - Contains pebbles ———— Conglomerate — S
        - Contains no pebbles ———— Sandstone — S
      - Cannot scrape sand off it
        - Hard
          - White, yellowish, tan, or reddish ———— Quartzite — M
          - Black or dark gray ———— Basalt — I
        - Soft
          - Usually gray, tan, or white ———— Limestone — S

Directions

1. Begin at the * descriptions above at the left.
2. Choose the description that seems to fit your rock specimen.
3. Follow the line to the next choice.
4. Continue until you reach the name of your rock.

Igneous Rocks:
A Hot Item

Rocks are made of minerals. In the activities, you grouped rocks based on how they were similar and different. Scientists, too, place rocks into groups. But they group them as to how they formed. This classification system includes three types of rocks. Let's take a close look at one of those types, called igneous (ig'nē əs) rocks.

Igneous rocks are probably the most common rocks found on Earth. The word *igneous* comes from the Latin word for "fire." Knowing this, can you guess how igneous rocks form? **Igneous rocks** form when hot, melted rock material cools and hardens. Rock that is melted to a liquid form is called molten rock. Where on Earth do you think molten rock is found?

Igneous Rocks From Magma

Deep within Earth, the temperature is much hotter than it is near the surface. Rocks melt, or change from solids to liquids. This molten rock material that forms deep within Earth is called **magma**. Because it is less dense than the material around it, magma tends to slowly rise toward the surface. As magma rises, it sometimes cools and hardens before reaching the surface.

Because it is below the surface, magma cools very slowly. As it cools, mineral grains, or crystals, have a long time to form. So the mineral grains are large in rocks formed from magma. Which rocks in your collection do you think formed from magma?

One of the most common rocks

volcano · lava

Igneous rocks form from both magma and lava. ▼

magma

formed from magma is granite, which is shown below. Notice that it consists of different minerals. The pink-colored and gray-colored mineral is feldspar, the white mineral is quartz, and the black mineral is mica. Notice the size of the mineral grains that make up granite. Have you seen granite in use around your community? If so, how was this rock used?

Stone Mountain, which towers high above the surrounding land in the state of Georgia, is a mountain of granite. Where did this rock harden? How do you think this rock became exposed at Earth's surface?

Not all the igneous rocks that harden from magma are the same. They vary in the kinds of mineral grains that form. The kinds of minerals that form depend on the composition of the magma.

Gabbro is another kind of igneous rock. Like all rocks that cool from magma, it has large mineral grains. But notice that gabbro is mostly made of dark-colored minerals, in this case pyroxene (pī räks'ēn) and olivine. It has few light-colored minerals, such as quartz.

▲ **Stone Mountain in Georgia**

Igneous Rocks From Lava

You know that magma rises toward Earth's surface. What do you think might happen when it breaks through to the surface? Magma that reaches Earth's surface is called **lava**. Look back at the diagram showing lava and magma on page E40. An opening in Earth's surface through which lava flows is called a volcano. When lava cools and hardens at Earth's surface, it also forms igneous rock.

Three kinds of rocks that formed from lava are shown on page E42. Compare them with the photograph of granite. How do the sizes of the mineral grains compare? Use what you have learned about igneous rocks to explain why the grains differ in size.

▼ **Granite**

Gabbro ▶

▲ Basalt   ▲ Obsidian   Rhyolite ▶

Basalt is an igneous rock that forms when lava rich in dark-colored minerals cools and hardens. Find *basalt* on the chart below and note that its composition is similar to that of gabbro. Because it flows out onto Earth's surface, lava cools faster than magma. So rocks cooled from lava, such as basalt, have smaller grains than rocks cooled from magma, such as gabbro. Large areas of the states of Washington and Oregon are covered by basalt, because of past volcanic activity.

Obsidian (əb sid′ē ən) is another igneous rock, often called natural glass. Lava that forms obsidian cools and hardens so quickly that mineral grains have very little time to grow. This rapid cooling gives the rock its glassy look.

Native Americans once used obsidian to make cutting tools such as blades, because obsidian forms sharp edges when broken.

Look at the photograph of the igneous rock rhyolite (rī′ə līt). Find it on the chart. How do you think rhyolite forms? ■

	Contains more light-colored minerals ◀ COMPOSITION ▶ Contains more dark-colored minerals	
LARGE mineral grains: forms from MAGMA	**Granite**	**Gabbro**
SMALL mineral grains: forms from LAVA	**Rhyolite**	**Basalt**
NO mineral grains: forms from LAVA	**Obsidian**	

INVESTIGATE FURTHER!

EXPERIMENT

Work with a partner to make a model that shows how igneous rocks form. Make "magma" by dissolving as much salt or sugar as possible in very little hot water. Cool half the magma very slowly at room temperature. Cool the other half quickly in a refrigerator. Which magma produced larger "minerals"? Why?

Sedimentary Rocks:
Rocks From Pieces

Sedimentary (sed ə men'tər ē) **rocks** are rocks that form at Earth's surface when sediments harden into rock. **Sediments** include bits of existing rocks, minerals, and organic materials. (Remember that things that are called organic were once living.)

There are many different kinds of sedimentary rocks. In fact, you probably use one sedimentary rock every day in school. Can you guess which sedimentary rock is used by students and teachers in the classroom? You also may have used it to draw on the sidewalk. Chalk is a sedimentary rock.

Animal, Vegetable, or Mineral?

Just like igneous rocks, sedimentary rocks can be grouped according to how they form. There are three types of sedimentary rocks: clastic, chemical, and organic. Clastic sedimentary rocks are those in which pieces of rocks, minerals, and organic materials are cemented together. The bits of sediment that make up clastic rocks can be as small as single grains of mud or as large as boulders! As you might expect, sedimentary rocks are common on Earth's surface.

Clastic rocks are grouped according to the size of the sediments they contain. Conglomerate (kən gläm'ər it), shale, and sandstone are examples of clastic rocks. Study the photos of these rocks. How do their sediment pieces compare?

Most clastic rocks form when wind, water, or ice carry and then drop sediments. Over time, these materials

◀ Conglomerate

Sandstone ▶

▲ Shale

E43

become compacted, or squeezed together. Minerals dissolved in water seep into spaces between the materials. As the water dries and the minerals grow, the minerals bind the loose sediments into solid rock. This binding of sediments is called **cementation** (sē men tā′shən).

Sandstone, as you might have guessed, is made of small, sand-sized rock bits. Sandstone often feels gritty, like sandpaper. Where on Earth do you think sandstone might be forming? Can you think of any uses for sandstone?

Chemical sedimentary rocks form when water rich in dissolved minerals evaporates, leaving the minerals behind, or when chemical changes form new minerals. Rock gypsum, rock salt, and some kinds of limestone are examples of chemical sedimentary rocks.

The type of limestone shown in the photograph below consists mostly of calcite, which formed when sea or lake waters evaporated. Limestone is ground and mixed with other ingredients to make certain cements.

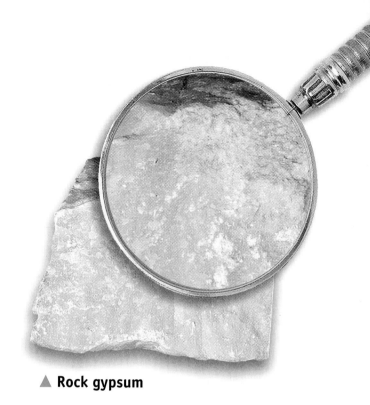

▲ **Rock gypsum**

Rock gypsum forms when water evaporates, leaving behind the mineral gypsum. Gypsum is used in plaster of Paris and plaster walls.

Rock salt, which is almost pure halite, is known to you as table salt. It does, however, have other uses, as you can see in the photo below.

▼ **Limestone**

▲ **Rock salt is commonly used to melt ice and snow.**

E44

The third type of sedimentary rock is called organic rock. Organic rocks form from the remains of plants and animals or from parts, such as shells, of organisms. One type of coal is an organic sedimentary rock that forms when bits of dead plants are compacted over long periods of time. The squeezing removes all the water, leaving behind the carbon that forms coal.

Limestone forms in different ways. Some limestones form when shells of dead sea animals become cemented together. Limestone consists mostly of calcite. Fine-grained limestones, such as chalk, form when calcite comes in contact with acid.

Features of Sedimentary Rocks

Scientists, including budding scientists like you, can learn about how a sedimentary rock was formed by observing the features preserved in the rock. When sediments are dropped by water, wind, or ice, the sediments build up in layers. A layer can be as thin as a sheet of paper or as thick as a few meters! The layers harden over time. And as more sediments are dropped, more layers are formed. So most sedimentary rocks are layered. This layering is often called bedding. Wind, water, and the shape of the land can all affect the formation of beds of sedimentary rock. Use the chart on page E46 to compare how sediment beds form.

SCIENCE IN LITERATURE

Our World
ROCKS, MINERALS AND FOSSILS
Keith Lye

The sedimentary rocks of the Grand Canyon of the Colorado River are more than amazing scenery. The canyon is also a 3-D lesson on the history of Earth! Find out how to "read the rocks" on pages 32 and 33 of *Rocks, Minerals and Fossils*.

Then turn to pages 34 and 35 to see what creatures lived when each of the rock layers of the Grand Canyon formed. These fossils help scientists to read the history of life on Earth.

ROCKS, MINERALS AND FOSSILS
by Keith Lye
Silver Burdett Press, 1991

Sediment Beds

◀ Notice that the surface of this sediment layer looks wavy. These wavy lines are called ripple marks. They are formed by moving water or wind. You may have seen ripple marks near a stream or on a beach. How might they become sedimentary rock?

◀ Most sediment beds, like these in shale, were deposited horizontally, resulting in the characteristic layering of sedimentary rock.

◀ The beds in this sandstone show cross-bedding. They formed when wind dropped sand on the curved slopes of sand dunes. Eventually, the sand beds hardened to form sandstone. What kinds of places can you think of that have sand dunes?

◀ Mud cracks are another feature sometimes preserved in sedimentary rocks. Mud cracks are evidence of wet periods followed by dry periods during the formation of a rock.

If you've ever gone rock collecting or to a natural history museum, you've probably seen fossils. A **fossil** is any remains or evidence of an organism from the past. Sedimentary rocks sometimes contain fossils. The photograph shows a fossil fern. Based on this fossil, what conclusions might you draw about how this rock formed?

Refer to the Rock Key and the rocks that you identified in the activity on page E38. Which rocks in your collection are sedimentary rocks? (The Rock Key uses a letter S to show them.) Try to classify the sedimentary rocks in your collection as clastic, chemical, or organic, based on their properties. ■

Fossil fern ▶

Metamorphic Rocks:
A Change of Identity

The third major group of rocks is the metamorphic (met ə môr′fik) rocks. The word *metamorphic* is made of two word parts that mean "to change form." In some ways, metamorphic rocks are like sedimentary rocks because both kinds form from existing rocks. In other ways, metamorphic rocks are like igneous rocks because both kinds can form at high temperatures and pressures. So what qualities make metamorphic rocks different from both sedimentary and igneous rocks? Let's find out.

New Rocks

Metamorphic rocks are new rocks that form from existing rocks because of changes caused by heat, pressure, or chemicals. The existing rocks that are changed may be sedimentary, igneous, or other metamorphic rocks. The change from one rock type to another is called metamorphism.

Some changes that occur with metamorphism result in changes in texture. *Texture* refers to the size and shape of mineral grains and the way in which they are arranged in a rock. In other cases, changes in composition, or makeup, take place. The changes that occur during metamorphism can result from three different sets of conditions.

Contact metamorphism occurs when hot magma or lava comes in contact with rock. The rock gets "baked" by the molten

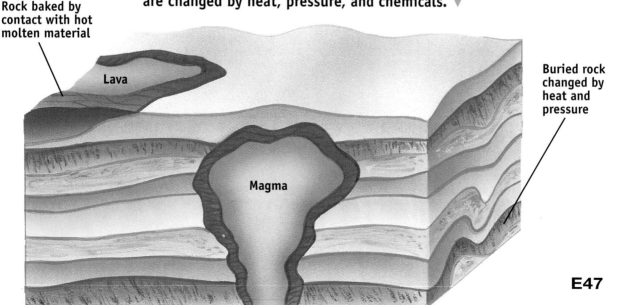

Metamorphic rocks form when existing rocks are changed by heat, pressure, and chemicals. ▼

Rock baked by contact with hot molten material

Lava

Magma

Buried rock changed by heat and pressure

material. So temperature alone, not pressure, causes the rock to change. Changes can occur in the kinds of minerals present and in the sizes of the grains. Liquids and gases escaping from the magma can also chemically change minerals in the surrounding rocks.

A second type of metamorphism is called regional metamorphism. It occurs in rocks that are buried deep below the surface, where temperature and pressure are high. The texture of the rocks changes, particularly in the way the minerals are arranged. Mineral grains tend to become lined up in the same direction because of high pressures. Also, high temperatures cause changes in the original mineral composition of the rocks.

Burial metamorphism causes the least amount of change in a rock. Burial metamorphism occurs when the weight of rocks and sediments burying a rock puts pressure on that rock. During burial metamorphism, the temperatures and pressures involved are low compared with those of other kinds of metamorphism. Low temperatures and pressures, for example, can cause new minerals to grow and textures to change slightly. Such changes cause

shale, a sedimentary rock, to become the metamorphic rock called slate.

Banded Metamorphic Rocks

Metamorphic rocks are grouped according to their textures as banded or nonbanded. As you would expect, rocks with a banded texture look as if they contain bands, or thin layers, which may look wavy or straight. You are probably familiar with some banded metamorphic rocks. Gneiss (nīs) is a banded metamorphic rock that contains quartz, mica, and feldspar. Which igneous rock is made of these same three minerals? Look at the photograph of gneiss. Note the bands of mineral grains. In which direction do you think the pressure was applied during metamorphism?

Another banded metamorphic rock is slate. Recall that slate forms when shale, a sedimentary rock, is exposed to changes in temperature and pressure. Slate is used as a roofing material. Some chalkboards are even made of slate. When exposed to more heat and pressure, slate can become another banded metamorphic rock, called phyllite (fil′īt).

▼ Gneiss

Phyllite ▶

Slate ▶

▲ Marble

▲ Quartzite

Nonbanded Metamorphic Rocks

In nonbanded metamorphic rocks the mineral grains have not been lined up by pressure. The texture of these rocks is described as massive. Look at the photographs of the nonbanded rocks above. Contrast them with the photographs of banded rocks. Can you infer the meaning of the term *massive* as used to describe metamorphic rocks?

Marble is a nonbanded metamorphic rock. Marble forms when limestone is changed by metamorphism. Marble can be white, black, pink, gray, or green with streaks of other colors.

Another nonbanded metamorphic rock is quartzite (kwôrts′īt). Quartzite forms when quartz-rich sandstone is exposed to high pressures and temperatures. ■

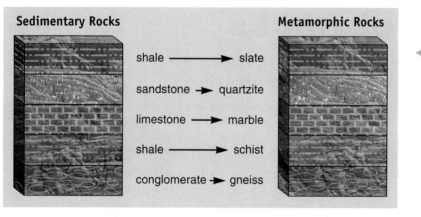

Sedimentary Rocks **Metamorphic Rocks**

shale ⟶ slate

sandstone ➤ quartzite

limestone ⟶ marble

shale ➤ schist

conglomerate ➤ gneiss

◀ **The drawing shows the different parent rocks of metamorphic rocks. Try to match metamorphic rocks in your collection with their parent rocks.**

INVESTIGATION 1

1. Name the three basic types of rocks and describe how each formed.

2. Fossils are found almost exclusively in sedimentary rocks. Suggest a hypothesis to explain this observation.

How Do the Properties of Rocks Make Them Useful?

Make a rock! Punch small holes in the bottom of a paper cup. Pour a handful of sand into the cup. Dilute some white glue with a little water. Pour it into the sand. Let the water drain out. After it has dried, tear off the paper and behold your "rock." What are its properties? Find a use for it!

Activity

Comparing Properties of Rocks

Different kinds of rocks have different properties, which make the rocks useful in different ways.

MATERIALS
• rock set
• hand lens
• *Science Notebook*

Procedure

1. Look at the Rock Key on page E39. The column at the far right lists the letters *I, S,* and *M.* These stand for igneous, sedimentary, and metamorphic.

2. Separate your rocks into three sets so that the first set has all the rocks labeled *I* on the Rock Key, the second set contains those labeled *S,* and the third, those labeled *M.*

3. Predict which sets will have layered rocks. Look for layered rocks and **record** your observations in your *Science Notebook.*

4. **Predict** which sets will have crystalline rocks (rocks with crystals). Look for crystalline rocks and **record** your observations.

5. **Predict** which rocks will be made of particles or fragments. Look for rocks that are made of particles or fragments. **Record** your observations.

6. **Compare and contrast** the rocks in your collection. **Record** as many properties as you can for each rock.

Analyze and Conclude

1. In which group(s) of rocks do you find layers, and in which do you not find layers?

2. In which group(s) of rocks do you find crystals, and in which do you not find crystals?

3. In which group(s) do you find particles or fragments, and in which do you not find particles or fragments?

4. Consider the properties of the rocks in your collection. Then make **inferences** about some uses for the rocks.

INVESTIGATE FURTHER!

RESEARCH

How's your rock collection coming? Do some research to find out how the types of rocks in your collection are used by people.

Rock Quarries

Have you ever seen a fireplace built of rocks? How about a rock wall or a path lined with stones? Chances are, the rocks that make up these things came from a quarry (kwôr′ē). A rock **quarry** is a mine, usually close to or at Earth's surface, from which certain rocks are removed. Billions of tons of granite, sandstone, limestone, slate, marble, and other types of rocks are removed each year from quarries all over the world.

Rock is removed from quarries in two forms. Dimension stones are slabs of rock that are removed from quarries in specific shapes and sizes. Most dimension stones are used to build things that will both last and look decorative, such as buildings. So the slabs must be solid and have an attractive texture, pattern, or color.

Most of the rock removed from quarries is in another form, called crushed stone. Crushed stone consists of bits and pieces of rocks that are primarily used in concrete, cements, and other construction materials.

You've probably tried to break or move a few big rocks at times. It isn't easy. So how do you suppose rocks are mined in quarries? How rocks are mined depends on how they'll be used. Most crushed stone gets blasted from solid rock with the use of explosives. First, holes are drilled into the rock. Then explosives are placed in the holes

Marble being cut at a quarry ▼

Marble slab being lifted by crane ▼

Transporting marble slabs ▼

and set off, causing the rock to break up. Of course, this wouldn't be a great way to quarry dimension stones, unless you are planning to cement the pieces back together!

In most quarries, dimension stones are cut from solid rock by using either a drill or a torch. Air moving through the drill makes the drill bit, or tip, spin rapidly. As it spins, the bit cuts away at the rock. A torch, on the other hand, cuts the rock by melting it. When cut with a torch, the edges of the slabs are smooth.

Once the dimension stones are cut, a huge crane is used to move them. The blocks of rock, which can weigh several tons each, are secured with hooks and chains. Then the crane is used to slowly lift and carry the stones.

From the quarry, loose slabs are transported to a processing mill. Many quarries that mine dimension stones have their own processing mills. At these mills, the rock slabs are cut to certain sizes by using steel wires and rock saws. The saw blades are often made with diamonds. As you learned in Chapter 1, diamonds are the hardest known minerals. They can cut through even the hardest rocks with the greatest of ease.

Once the rocks are cut and sized, they may be polished. Polishing gradually smooths out any wire or saw marks left from the cutting stage. When the dimension stones are highly polished, they are ready to be shipped around the corner, around the country, or around the world. The chart shows some common dimension stones, where they come from, and what they are used for. Do any quarried rocks come from your state? What states might produce the marble for a counter top? Which stones might be used in monuments? ■

Rock	Where From	Uses
Granite	Vermont, Massachusetts, Maine, New Hampshire, Rhode Island, Minnesota, Wisconsin	monuments, buildings, grave markers
Sandstone	New York, Ohio, Pennsylvania, Kentucky, Connecticut	buildings, trim
Marble	Vermont, Georgia	monuments, buildings, flooring, counter tops, kitchen items
Limestone	Texas, Utah, Indiana, Missouri, Florida, Minnesota	decorative trims, buildings, monuments, park benches

A Ton of Bricks!

Is your home or school made of bricks? Do you think bricks are rocks? Although they are hard like most rocks and are made from minerals, bricks aren't actually rocks. "Well, why not?" you may be asking yourself. Rocks are made of one or more minerals, and they form naturally. Since rocks are formed by nature, bricks cannot be rocks because bricks are made by people!

Brick Making Today

What, then, *are* bricks? Bricks are small, rectangular blocks made from a mixture of clays and other sediments. To make bricks, different kinds and amounts of clays are dug from river bottoms or other places on Earth's surface.

To make bricks, clays and sediments are removed from Earth, ground into powder, mixed with water to form a paste, poured into molds, and hardened by baking in kilns. ▼

These minerals are taken to a factory where they are crushed into a fine powder. Sometimes the powder is sifted to remove any large pieces. Water is added to the powder to make a thick, gooey paste. The paste is pressed into molds that are coated with sand or water. The coating helps to prevent the mixture from sticking to the molds, much as butter helps to keep cake batter from sticking to a pan.

Next, molds are placed in a kiln, or drying oven. When the clay mixture is completely dry, the molds are fired in another kiln. Firing chemically changes the clay blocks by heating them for up to 12 hours at temperatures above 800°C (1,500°F). Once fired, the bricks are cooled and taken to other parts of the factory to be packed and shipped.

Brick Making in the Past

Scientists who study ancient cultures discovered that bricks have been used by people for at least 60 centuries! The first bricks were probably simple mud blocks dried in the sun. Adobe (ə dō′bē), or sun-dried brick, is thought to have first been made in dry areas of the world, including parts of Africa, Spain, Peru, and the southwestern part of the United States. Adobe bricks are made with a mixture of clay, sand, and sometimes, straw. The materials are mixed by hand, with bare feet, or with a simple tool. The mixture is then put into molds and allowed to dry for at least two weeks. When dry, the bricks are removed from the molds and used.

About 3,500 years ago, people began to fire bricks. They discovered that firing the clay blocks made them harder and longer-lasting.

Bricks are not rocks. But like sedimentary rocks, bricks are made of sediments. Also, with firing, clay is changed chemically to a different material. How is this similar to the way some metamorphic rocks form? ■

▲ **This structure is made from adobe brick.**

INVESTIGATION 2

1. Identify some ways in which rocks differ.

2. Suppose you were asked to recommend a type of rock that could be used to make a strong but attractive building. Use the Rock Key for help in making your suggestion. Give reasons to support your choice.

HOW DO ROCKS CHANGE OVER TIME?

It may seem that rocks last forever, but they don't. They change, just like everything else. Unwrap some broken crayons and set them on wax paper in the hot sun. What happens? What rock-forming change have you just modeled?

Activity

'Round and 'Round She Goes

It may take hundreds of thousands of years, even millions of years, but Earth materials go through changes called the rock cycle. In this activity you'll investigate this cycle.

MATERIALS
- rock cycle diagram
- rock set
- vial of sand
- vial of clay
- seashell
- *Science Notebook*

Procedure

1. Place the rock cycle diagram on your desktop.

2. Granite, sandstone, sand, and quartzite form part of a loop in the rock cycle. Use those samples from your rock set and **make a model** of the rock cycle by placing the sand and rocks in their correct places on the rock cycle. Then, in your *Science Notebook*, **draw** the part of the loop they make. Label your drawing to show the kinds of materials or rocks and the processes these go through in changing from one to another.

3. Gneiss, sandstone, and sand make a complete loop in the rock cycle. Use those samples and put them in order on the rock cycle. **Draw** and label this loop.

4. Basalt, slate, shale, and clay make another part of a loop. Use your samples and put these in order on the rock cycle. **Draw** and label this loop.

5. Another part of a loop in the rock cycle is made by seashells, marble, and limestone. Get samples of these materials and include them on your rock cycle. **Draw** and label this loop.

Step 2

Analyze and Conclude

1. Explain why the loop in step 3 is a complete cycle that could happen over and over again.

2. In step 2, why don't the materials listed form a complete loop? What is missing to make this loop a complete cycle of the rock cycle?

3. **Suggest a definition** of the rock cycle, based on how you think it works.

INVESTIGATE FURTHER!

EXPERIMENT

Think of another complete loop in the rock cycle, a loop formed by materials you already have or can obtain. Place samples on your copy of the rock cycle; then draw and label your loop.

Coal:
A Fossil Fuel

How might you describe coal to someone who has never seen it or who knows nothing about it? You might explain that one kind of coal is a sedimentary rock and one kind is a metamorphic rock. You might also say that coal can be burned to heat your home. Would you describe coal as a fossil fuel?

As you might suspect from its name, a fossil fuel is a material formed from plant or animal remains that can be burned for energy. Over millions of years, pressures and temperatures have squeezed and changed the remains. Left behind are elements, such as carbon, hydrogen, and oxygen, that once made up the organisms. Coal is one kind of fossil fuel.

Millions of years ago

PEAT
60% Carbon
Coal begins to form when swamp plants die and are quickly buried beneath sediments and other plants. Tiny organisms called bacteria cause organic material to decay and change. Over time, a dark, watery organic material called peat forms.

Peat Layer

LIGNITE
70% Carbon
With time, the peat gets buried by more sediments. The weight of these sediments compacts the peat and squeezes water out. Eventually, the percent of carbon present increases and a sedimentary rock called lignite, a type of coal, forms.

Lignite Layer

All forms of coal are used as fuel. Coal is burned to provide energy to heat homes, offices, and other buildings. Some coal is used to fuel furnaces in factories. In fact, coal provides about 20 percent of the energy needs in the United States.

Bituminous (bi too'mə nəs) coal lights very easily and provides the most energy of all the types of coal. But burning this kind of coal produces a sooty residue and yellow smoke. Anthracite (an'thrə sīt) coal burns much cleaner and longer than bituminous coal, but does not provide as much energy. The diagram below shows the changes coal can go through. ■

▼ Peat

▼ Lignite

▲ Bituminous Coal

▲ Anthracite

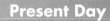

Present Day

BITUMINOUS COAL
80% Carbon
As the rock becomes buried deeper, temperature and pressure increase. Nearly all of the water that was once in the plant parts gets forced out and bituminous coal forms. Recall that bituminous coal, or soft coal, is a sedimentary rock that is mostly carbon.

Bituminous Layer

ANTHRACITE
95% Carbon
With deep burying and great temperature and pressure, bituminous coal becomes metamorphosed to form anthracite. Anthracite is a metamorphic rock. It has the highest percent of carbon of all the forms of coal.

Anthracite Layer

E59

Rocks in Circles

You learned that high temperatures and great pressures can change any rock into a metamorphic rock. But did you realize that any kind of rock—igneous, sedimentary, or metamorphic—can be changed into another kind of rock, not just by metamorphism?

Melting and cooling are just two of Earth's agents of change. They act to change Earth's rock materials. The series of changes that rocks undergo is called the **rock cycle**.

Notice the ovals in the diagram of the rock cycle. They represent five kinds of rock materials: igneous rock, sedimentary rock, metamorphic rock, sediments, and molten rock (magma and lava). Between the ovals are things that cause rock materials to change—factors such as melting and pressure. When you play most board games, you can move in only one direction around the board. But with the rock cycle, rocks may "move," or change, in many ways. To use the diagram to see how one type of rock changes into another, start at any oval. Then move in the direction of any arrow coming out of the oval. Follow the arrows, and you can't go wrong.

Sedimentary to Metamorphic

As you can see from the diagram, there are many factors in the rock cycle that cause change. Find the words *Sedimentary Rock* on the diagram. What's one way in which sedimentary rock can change? You know that sedimentary rocks form at or near Earth's surface. What do you think happens when these rocks become buried? High temperatures and pressures deep below the surface change sedimentary rocks into metamorphic rocks. Follow this change on the diagram.

Metamorphic to Igneous

Now what do you suppose happens when the pressures and temperatures deep below the surface become very high? Melting, or the changing of a solid to a liquid, occurs to change metamorphic rock into molten rock. Find *Melting* on the diagram.

As magma or lava cools, minerals form. When minerals form, they grow into different-sized crystals, so this step is sometimes called crystallizing. Notice in the rock cycle diagram that magma and lava cool and crystallize to form igneous rock. On the diagram, follow the change from metamorphic rock to igneous rock.

THE ROCK CYCLE

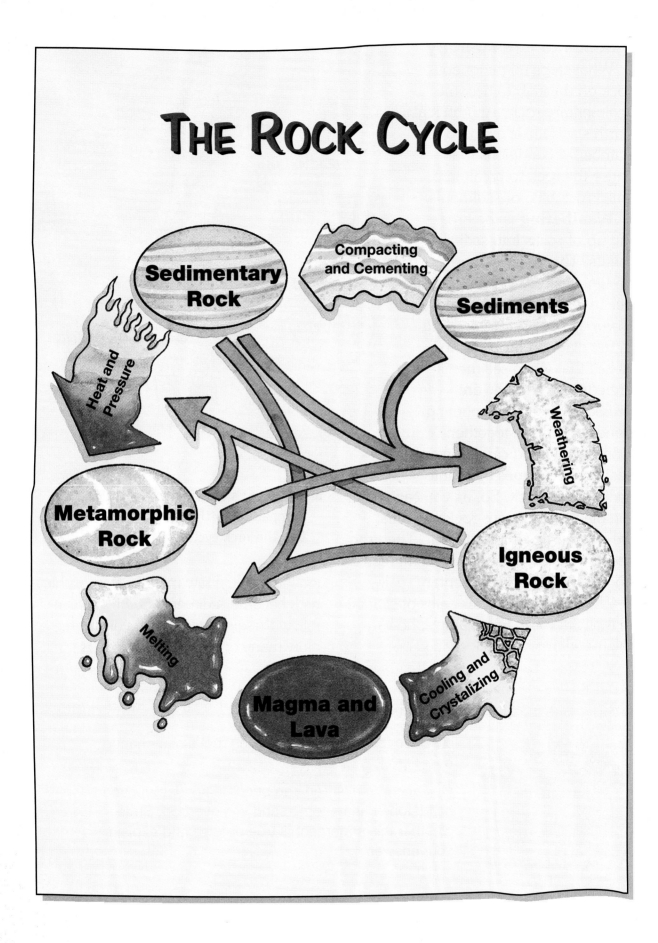

Igneous to Sedimentary

What steps might igneous rock go through to become sedimentary rock? Any rock at Earth's surface is exposed to a number of conditions that cause the rock to break into small rock bits, or sediments.

Weathering is the breaking up of rocks into sediments. Through weathering, an igneous rock can eventually become sediment bits. Find *Compacting* and *Cementing* in the diagram on page E61. Recall that when sediments are compacted, they are pressed together. Cementing bonds sediments together. Compacting and cementing of sediments changes them into sedimentary rock. So, as you can see in the diagram, igneous rock must first weather to become sediment. Then the sediment is compacted and cemented and changed into sedimentary rock.

There are many other paths of change in the rock cycle. For example, how might sedimentary rock change into

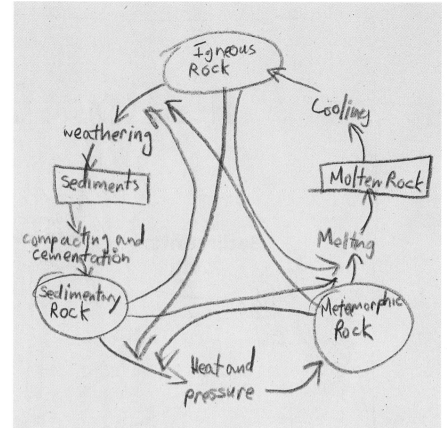

▲ A student's drawing of the rock cycle. Compare it to the diagram on page E61. Can the rock cycle start at any point?

igneous rock? How might metamorphic rock become sediment? See if you can follow these changes on the diagram. How many others can you find? ■

INVESTIGATION 3

1. Describe four ways by which rocks can change over time.

2. Sand in a riverbed can become sandstone, and sandstone can become sand in a riverbed. State whether this statement is true or false and explain your answer.

REFLECT & EVALUATE

WORD POWER

cementation   quarry
fossil   rock cycle
lava   rocks
magma   sediments
igneous rocks
metamorphic rocks
sedimentary rocks

 On Your Own
Review the terms in the list. Then use as many terms as you can in a paragraph about how rocks are related.

With a Partner
Write a slogan for one of the terms. Do not use the term. (You may use other terms in the slogan.) Share the slogan with a group and have them guess the term.

BUILD YOUR PORTFOLIO

Write a story about the trip a rock material makes in one complete cycle through the rock cycle. Be sure to name all rock materials. Be creative, but base your fiction on scientific fact.

Analyze Information

Explain how the cycle shown could be never ending. Then describe an event that could break the cycle.

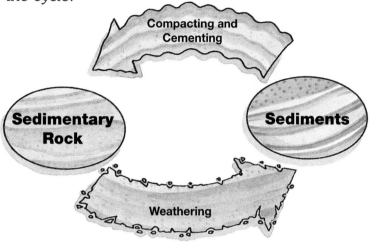

Compacting and Cementing

Sediments

Sedimentary Rock

Weathering

Assess Performance

Obtain several samples of unknown rock. Using a hand lens and the Rock Key on page E39, identify each sample and classify each as igneous, sedimentary, or metamorphic.

Problem Solving

1. You observe that a rock has large crystals and is unlayered. What type of rock would you infer it to be? Explain your inference.

2. How are the rock cycle and the yearly cycle of changing seasons alike and not alike?

3. Make a sketch that illustrates the rock cycle. Use examples of rocks from this chapter in your sketch.

CHAPTER 3

EARTH'S STRUCTURES

Did you know that you can float with both feet on the ground? In fact, you're always floating—even when you think you're standing still. Here's why. The ground under your feet is drifting on a layer of hot, gooey rock. This rock is only one of the remarkable materials that make up Earth. Sometimes the drifting movement leads to earthquakes.

A Deep, Deep Quake

On June 8, 1994, an unusual earthquake struck the country of Bolivia, in South America. The quake was severe, but it caused relatively little damage and no loss of life because the quake was located very deep beneath Earth's surface. Such rare, deep earthquakes usually cause little damage. And they come with a bonus for seismologists (sīz mäl′ə jists), the scientists who study earthquakes. The vibrations caused by a deep quake provide much information about Earth's interior. By measuring the activity from the Bolivia quake at different locations around the world, scientists learned a great deal about the materials that make up the inner Earth. You might say that the scientists received a picture of the interior structure of our planet.

What is inside Earth? What causes earthquakes? The investigations in this chapter will help you find out.

Coming Up

◀ A seismograph recording of the deep earthquake in Bolivia

WHAT IS EARTH'S STRUCTURE?

How do rocks make up the sphere you call Earth? What's at the center of that sphere? This investigation will help you answer such questions about Earth's structure by looking at what's inside as well as outside Earth.

Activity

A Model Earth

An apple makes a good model of Earth's structure. In science, a model is used to help us understand something else. Sometimes a model helps us to ask better questions. Let's look carefully at an apple.

Procedure

1. Place a piece of wax paper on your desktop. Put an apple on the wax paper.

2. Use the apple to **model** the interior of Earth. Cut the apple in half. Carefully **observe** the cut surface from the skin to the center of the apple. In your *Science Notebook*, **sketch** and **describe** what you see.

MATERIALS

- apple
- plastic knife
- wax paper
- *Science Notebook*

Step 2

3. Cut both halves in half again. The skin represents Earth's **crust,** or surface layer. The skin on three of the pieces is a model for the amount of Earth's crust that is covered by oceans.

4. Examine one of the pieces of apple carefully. **Compare** the thickness of the skin to the thickness of the rest of the piece.

Analyze and Conclude

1. Based on your model, how much of Earth's crust is covered by oceans? How much of the crust is land?

2. Earth has a layer below its crust called the **mantle**. The mantle covers a ball, called the **core**, in the middle of Earth. **Infer** which parts of the apple are models for the mantle and the core.

3. **Compare** the thicknesses of the crust, mantle, and core in your model. Based on your model, what conclusions can you draw about the depths, or thicknesses, of the layers of Earth?

Step 3

INVESTIGATE FURTHER!

RESEARCH

Earth's land includes mountains, plains, plateaus, and other types of landforms. Find out how much of Earth's surface is land on which people can plant crops. How much of the land is largely uninhabitable?

The Sphere We Live On

When you hear the word *model*, what do you think of? You may picture a model airplane or a fashion model. In science, a **model** is something used to represent an object or an idea. In the activity on pages E66 and E67, you used an apple as a model of Earth.

What would happen if you took a huge knife and sliced right through Earth instead of through an apple? You'd see four layers instead of three—so your model was a bit too simple. Now take a look at another Earth model, the diagram shown here.

The Crust

Earth's outer layer is called the **crust**. It is the thinnest of all the layers, but it varies in thickness around Earth. It can be as thin as 10 km (6 mi) under the oceans and as thick as 65 km (40 mi) below the continents.

The crust is made up of solid rock. It is mostly granite, gabbro, and basalt, but it also includes all the igneous, sedimentary, and metamorphic rocks you have learned about. Much of the crust is covered by oceans, lakes, rivers, sediments, plants, and soil.

Earth has four layers. ▼

Mantle

Outer core

Inner core

2900 km

2250 km

1206 km

Crust
10-65 km

The crust is broken into many large and small pieces called plates. These plates float like rafts on the layer below the crust. So they can move very slowly around Earth's surface, carrying the continents and oceans with them.

Earth's crust is thicker beneath continents than beneath oceans. ▼

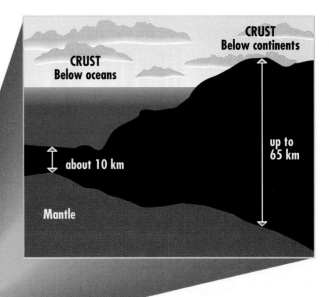

CRUST
Below oceans

CRUST
Below continents

about 10 km

up to 65 km

Mantle

Crust
Mantle
Outer core
Inner core

When you learned about metamorphic rocks, you found out that temperature and pressure increase as you go deeper below Earth's surface. Temperature and pressure are much greater in the mantle than in the crust. As a result, some rock in the mantle melts. This molten rock sometimes makes its way to the surface as lava.

The Mantle

Below the crust is the **mantle**. It is the thickest layer, taking up about 84 percent of Earth's volume. The part of this layer that is closest to the crust is made of solid rock that has the same properties as other solids. However, much of the mantle is solid rock that has some properties of liquids. It can flow like maple syrup or be stretched out like putty.

Much of the mantle is composed of an igneous rock called peridotite. This rock is dark in color and rich in the elements iron, magnesium, and silicon.

The Inner and Outer Core

Below the mantle is Earth's core. The **core** consists of heavy material that sank to Earth's center billions of years ago. The core consists of a solid inner layer and a molten outer layer.

The outer core is made of molten iron and nickel. Scientists think the boundary between the outer core and the mantle is wavy. They think the hills and valleys in this boundary are caused by the movement of molten rock between the outer core and the mantle.

At Earth's center is the inner core, which is made of solid iron and nickel. Temperatures here may exceed 5,000°C (9,000°F)—almost as hot as the surface of the Sun! The extreme pressure here prevents the iron and nickel from melting, in spite of the high temperature.

How do you think the different layers of Earth developed? One hypothesis is that billions of years ago, energy released by the breakdown of elements inside Earth caused the planet to grow hotter and hotter. Much of the iron and nickel found in Earth's rocks melted. Because these are very heavy materials, the molten iron and nickel sank to the center of the planet. Extreme pressure turned these materials back to a solid. Lighter materials also melted, but they rose to the surface. As a result, a crust of light rock and a core of heavy metals formed, with the mantle layer in between.

Journeying to Earth's Center

You may have wondered how scientists know so much about Earth's deep layers. They certainly haven't been able to travel there! However, some rocks that have formed from magma make it possible for us to "see" the mantle. Rocks such as kimberlite that were once magma in the mantle give us clues about the composition of the mantle. But how do scientists know where the layers begin and end?

Think about the last time you tried to figure out what was inside a wrapped present. You couldn't see inside, but you could try to infer what was in the box. Scientists make inferences about Earth's layers by studying earthquake waves.

When you drop a stone in a pond, waves of energy move across the water's surface. In a similar way, when an earthquake occurs, waves of energy travel through Earth in all directions. Earthquake waves travel through some materials faster than others. By measuring the time it takes for the waves to arrive at different places around the world, scientists infer what kind of material the waves traveled through.

In 1909 the boundary between the crust and mantle was discovered by a scientist named Andrija Mohorovičic' (mō hō rō'və chich). He noticed that earthquake waves started to travel faster once they reached a certain depth below Earth's surface. Mohorovičic' inferred that there must be a different kind of rock at this depth. This boundary between the crust and the mantle, named after the man who discovered it, is called the Moho.

Two kinds of earthquake waves, called P waves and S waves, have also been used to make inferences about the properties of the core and its depth below the surface. Look at the figure on the next page to find out what scientists have learned from earthquake waves.

HOW EARTHQUAKE WAVES TRAVEL

An earthquake occurs at this location.

S waves travel through the solid crust and through the mantle but not through the outer core. As a result, scientists concluded that the outer core is liquid.

As P waves move from the mantle to the outer core, they bend and travel more slowly.

As P waves move into the inner core, they speed up again, indicating that the inner core is solid.

Since S waves cannot pass through the core, only P waves are detected on Earth's surface on the side opposite the earthquake. Shadow zones are areas where neither S waves nor P waves are detected.

INVESTIGATION 1

1. Use materials of your choice to make a three-dimensional model showing Earth's layers. Make labels to identify the layers.

2. Scientists know the mass and the volume of Earth. How could this information help them make inferences about the kind of matter that makes up Earth's interior?

HOW CAN FOSSILS HELP TELL US HOW OLD A ROCK IS?

Think of Earth as a book, with layers of rock stacked on top of one another like pages. How can you use the fossils in rocks to number the pages and read the book?

Activity
Layering Fossils

Scientists study rock layers and the fossils in them to learn about ancient forms of life. Find out what scientists can learn by doing this activity.

Procedure

1. Flatten three pieces of clay, each a different color.

2. **Make a model** of a fossil imprint by making an impression of a shell in one piece of clay. Make an impression of a leaf in the second piece of clay and a twig in the third piece of clay. Set aside the shell, leaf, and twig.

Step 2

E72

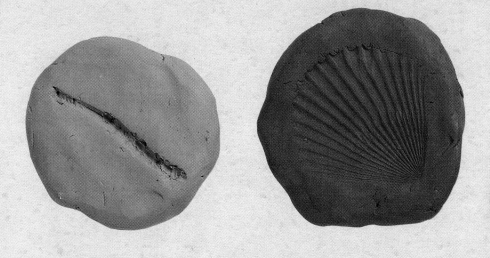

3. Each piece of clay represents a layer of sedimentary rock. Stack your rock layers one on top of the other. In your *Science Notebook*, **record** the order from top to bottom.

Analyze and Conclude

1. Based on what you have learned about how sedimentary rock forms, **infer** which of your "fossils" would be the oldest and which would be the youngest. Explain your reasoning.

2. If the twig is from a bush that lived after the shellfish died but before the tree from which the leaf was taken lived, which fossil would be on the top of the stack? Which fossil would be on the bottom?

3. **Compare** your stack of fossils with the stacks made by other students. Are the fossils in the same order? If not, **infer** the relative ages of the fossils in each of the other stacks.

UNIT PROJECT LINK

Find out about fossils that have been collected in your community or that were discovered in your state. If possible, obtain examples of such fossils for your collection. Be sure to note the exact location where each fossil was found. If you can't get examples, make drawings of the fossils.

Activity

Finding the Order

Geologists often try to find out the order in which rock layers formed. It isn't always easy. In this activity you'll make a model of rock layers and infer the order in which they were made.

MATERIALS

- paper cups
- plastic spoons
- white glue
- food coloring, 4 colors
- sand
- wooden stick
- milk carton (1 pt)
- *Science Notebook*

Procedure

1. In a paper cup, mix a spoonful of white glue with 4 drops of red food coloring. Mix the colored glue with half a cup of sand. In the same way, make blue sand in a second cup, green sand in a third cup, and yellow sand in a fourth cup.

2. Place a small wooden stick against the inside of a milk carton. Then pack one color of sand in the bottom of the carton. Pack a second color on top of the first, and a third on top of the second.

3. Carefully pull the stick out of the carton and fill the hole with the fourth color of sand. Set the carton aside until the next day. **Predict** what the sand layers will look like when you take them out of the milk carton. In your *Science Notebook*, **draw a diagram** of your prediction.

Step 1

WHITE GLUE

4. Carefully tear the milk carton away from the layers. If the glue has not dried, let it set a while longer.

5. **Compare** your layers to the drawing that you made.

6. On your drawing, number the "rock" layers from 1 to 4, with 1 representing the oldest layer, or the layer that you made first.

Analyze and Conclude

1. Which "rock" layer was laid down first? Which one "formed" last?

2. For rock layers that are horizontal, what general statement can you make about where the oldest and youngest layers are located in the stack of layers?

3. What **inference** can you make about the age of a rock layer that cuts through other layers?

INVESTIGATE FURTHER!

EXPERIMENT

Trade rock layers with another student. Infer the order in which the layers were deposited.

Sorting Through Time

People have been digging up fossils for centuries. But not until the 1700s did the idea that fossils were the remains of creatures from the past begin to be accepted. You can bet that William Smith, an English geologist, never realized that his hobby of fossil collecting would show a way of matching rock layers by age! While surveying the land in western England, Smith had a chance to observe many rock layers and collect fossils. First, he noticed that rock layers lie "like slices of bread and butter," stacked in a set order. Next, he saw that each layer of sedimentary rock contained different types of fossils. He soon realized that fossils could be used to recognize rock layers of the same age in different places around the world. And scientists today use fossils to do just that! ■

Mary Ann Mantell discovers the first fossil of a dinosaur, a tooth belonging to a large plant-eater. By 1825 more fossil bones are found, and scientists name the creature *Iguanodon*.

1822

1824

William Buckland, a geology professor, publishes a paper on the fossil bones of *Megalosaurus*, the first dinosaur to be named.

1799

William Smith uses fossils to identify rock layers of the same age.

1780

The bones of a giant sea lizard, called a mosasaur, are discovered in the Netherlands.

Fossils Tell Tales!

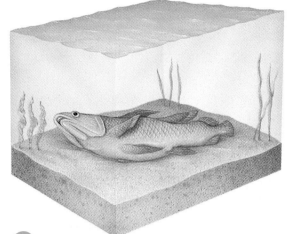

1 An organism dies.

2 The remains get buried quickly by sediment. The soft parts decay.

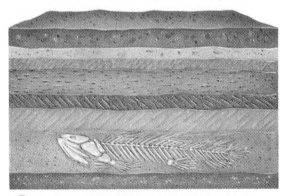

3 With time, the hard parts get replaced with minerals. The sediment layer gets buried deeper and is compacted and cemented to form sedimentary rock.

There aren't many things more exciting than coming face to face with a dinosaur—a dinosaur skeleton, that is. Our knowledge of dinosaurs has come from studying **fossils**, which are the remains and traces of living things preserved in rock. What clues do you think a fossil might provide about Earth's past? A fossil can give clues about where an organism once lived, how it may have moved, what it ate, and what it looked like, not to mention how old the rock it was found in might be.

You Old Fossil!

How does a fossil form? Many fossils form when plants and animals die and are quickly buried by clay, sand, and other sediments. Look at the drawings to see how a fossil might form.

In some cases, bone and other hard material is replaced by minerals. Other

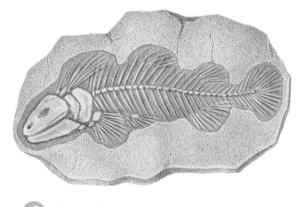

4 A fossil is later exposed due to erosion.

A cast ▶

A mold ▼

fossils form when plants and animals leave imprints in soft sediment. Over time, the organic material dissolves and the imprint gets filled with minerals or sediments. The imprint, or hollow part of the fossil, is called a mold. The material that fills in the imprint is called a cast. Remember when you pressed a shell, a leaf, and a twig into clay in the activity on pages E72 and E73? Did you make molds, or casts?

Relative Age

Scientists began studying fossils partly in the hope that fossils would help them estimate the age of Earth's rocks. There are many clues, including fossils, that you can use to learn about the ages of the rocks you see.

One clue to look for is the position of the rock layers. Recall that most sedimentary rocks begin as horizontal sediment layers. Think about books you might stack before putting them away. The first book you put down is on the

bottom of the stack. It's the same with rock layers. The oldest rock layer was laid down first and is on the bottom. The youngest rock layer was laid down last and is on the top.

When you can say that one rock is older than another, you have found its relative age. A rock's **relative age** is how old it is compared to other rocks.

In addition to a rock's position, scientists also use certain kinds of fossils, called **index fossils**, to help them tell the relative ages of rock. Plant and animal species that lived for only a short time (perhaps only a few million years) but that could be found in large numbers over much of Earth make very helpful index fossils.

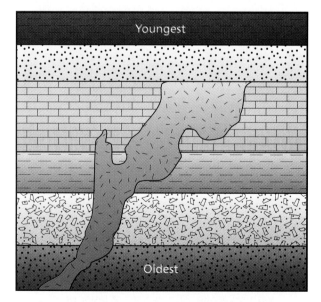

▲ **The sequence of rock layers can be used to determine the relative ages of rocks.**

The fossil shown below is a trilobite. Many kinds of trilobites lived in oceans all over the world. Since certain kinds lived only at certain times in the past, they make good index fossils. When scientists find two rocks in two different places that both contain the same kind of trilobite fossils, they know that both rocks are about the same age.

Absolute Age

When someone asks how old you are, you probably don't answer with your relative age. You probably say, "I'm 11 years old," rather than "I'm older than my sister." At times, scientists need to know more than a rock's relative age. They need to know its **absolute age**, or how old the rock really is.

Some elements found on Earth are not stable. These elements decay, or break down, into other elements at a known rate. Scientists measure how much of a decaying element is present in a rock layer and how much of the new element into which it decays is present. The amount of time required for this level of decay provides the rock's absolute age.

Potassium is an element found in rocks. Some of the potassium found in igneous and metamorphic rocks is not stable. It breaks down to form a certain kind of argon, another element. Scientists have used the amount of potassium and argon in rocks to find the absolute age of those rocks. Some were as old as a few billion years! ■

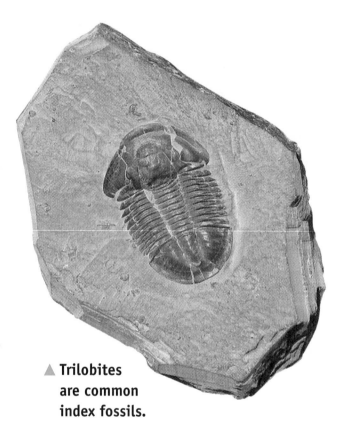

▲ Trilobites are common index fossils.

INVESTIGATION 2

THINK IT WRITE IT

1. How are index fossils used to tell the ages of rocks?

2. Suppose you and a friend each found fossils in different layers of sedimentary rock. How could you tell which fossil is older?

HOW DO ROCKS BEND?

Tonight, before you climb into bed, put your hands flat on top of your covers and push them 10 or 20 cm (8 in.) across the bed. Make them push up into folds. How are these folds, or bends, like mountains?

Activity
Big Wrinkles

The Appalachian Mountains in the eastern United States are folded and eroded mountains. Geologists read them like a book. Here's how.

Procedure

1. Flatten three pieces of clay, each a different color, into slabs about 1 cm thick. Each slab represents a layer of rock. Stack the layers. In your *Science Notebook*, **make a sketch** to show the order of the colors from top to bottom.

2. Gently press the sides of the stack together, folding the layers upward into a mountain. Continue pressing until the sides come together.

Step 2

3. You are going to cut off the top your mountain but before you do, **predict** what the cut surface will look like. **Make a sketch** of your prediction.

4. **Model** erosion by cutting the top off your mountain with a plastic knife so you can see all three layers in the cut surface. Does it look like your prediction? **Sketch** the eroded top. Label the layers by color and title your drawing "Upward Fold."

5. Separate the three colors of clay, flatten each lump again, and make another stack. Keep the order of the colors the same as in step 1.

6. Fold the left and right sides of the stack upward until they meet, forming a mountain.

7. **Model** erosion by cutting the top off your mountain. **Make a sketch** of the eroded top. Label the layers and title your drawing "Downward Fold."

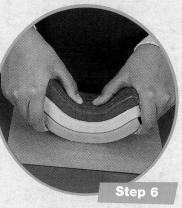

Step 6

Analyze and Conclude

1. Where was the oldest layer of rock in the stack in step 1? in the upward fold (step 4)? in the downward fold (step 7)?

2. If you know the relative ages of rock layers on an eroded surface, explain how you can tell if an upward folding of rocks or a downward folding of rocks has occurred.

UNIT PROJECT LINK

Walk around your community to observe natural landforms. Make a list of the landforms you observe. Try to identify the types of rocks that make up the different landforms. Can you tell which rock layers are oldest?

E81

Activity
Dome Questions

Some rocks get pushed up to form a geologic structure called a dome. Investigate how bending rocks can form this structure.

MATERIALS
- 3 different colors of clay
- small ball (table tennis or golf ball)
- plastic knife
- *Science Notebook*

Procedure

1. Flatten and stack three layers of clay, each a different color. Then press the stack down over a small ball to make a dome.

Step 1

2. **Predict** what the pattern of layers will be when you cut the top off the dome. In your *Science Notebook*, **make a sketch** of your prediction.

3. **Model** erosion by cutting the top off the dome, but do not cut so deep that you can see the ball. Does the pattern of layers match your prediction? **Make a sketch** of the actual pattern and title it "Dome." Be sure to label the order of the layers.

Analyze and Conclude

1. What does the pattern of layers in a dome look like?

2. **Infer** what forces could cause a dome to form. Explain your inference.

INVESTIGATE FURTHER!

EXPERIMENT

Get an ice-cream cone of fudge-ripple ice cream. Observe the pattern of chocolate and vanilla layers. Now erode the ice cream from the top down. How does the pattern change? What kinds of "geologic structures" are you observing?

All Bent Out of Shape

No matter how hard you try, you will probably never be able to bend a rock. But mountains all over the eastern United States formed because rocks can and do bend. Let's explore how this comes about.

Forces Bend Rocks

Every time you push open a door or pull a window shut, you apply a force. A force is a push or a pull. In the activity on pages E80 and E81, you applied forces to layers of clay. You did this with your hands by pushing the clay in different directions.

Sometimes forces in nature push on rocks in the same way. If the forces are strong enough and applied long enough, they can cause the rock layers to bend. A bend in a rock layer is called a **fold**.

Most forces that bend rock layers are caused by Earth's moving plates. As you know, Earth's crust consists of huge plates that move slowly around the surface. When two plates come together, the edges of the plates may become folded. Over millions of years the folds become higher and the folded rock forms mountains.

Folded mountains form as rock layers bend and are pushed upward. ▼

E83

The Appalachian Mountains

The Appalachian Mountains in eastern North America are mountains that formed from folded rock. This mountain range is 3,200 km (1,920 mi) long, stretching from Newfoundland in Canada to Alabama in the southeastern United States. The Appalachian Mountains formed sometime between 600 million and 200 million years ago as the plate carrying Africa collided with the plate carrying North America. With time, the folded rock formed high hills and deep valleys.

When rock layers bend, some layers fold up and some fold down. An **anticline** is an upward fold of rock layers. A **syncline** is a downward fold of rock layers.

Recall that the process of weathering wears all rocks at Earth's surface into sediments. The wearing away and removing of rock materials is called **erosion**. Gravity, moving water, wind, and ice all erode rocks. When the top of an anticline is eroded, new rock layers are revealed at the surface. Notice in the diagram on page E85 that the oldest rock layers of an anticline are found near the center of the fold. The layers get younger and younger as you move away from the center of the anticline. Now compare this to an eroded syncline. When a syncline is eroded, where is the youngest rock located? How do the anticline and syncline compare to the folded layers you created on pages E80 and E81?

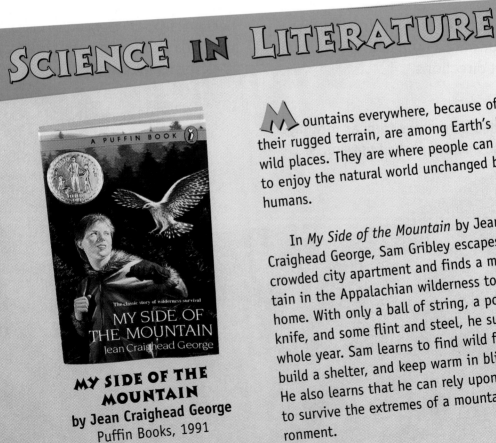

SCIENCE IN LITERATURE

MY SIDE OF THE MOUNTAIN
by Jean Craighead George
Puffin Books, 1991

Mountains everywhere, because of their rugged terrain, are among Earth's last wild places. They are where people can go to enjoy the natural world unchanged by humans.

In *My Side of the Mountain* by Jean Craighead George, Sam Gribley escapes his crowded city apartment and finds a mountain in the Appalachian wilderness to call home. With only a ball of string, a pocket knife, and some flint and steel, he survives a whole year. Sam learns to find wild foods, build a shelter, and keep warm in blizzards. He also learns that he can rely upon himself to survive the extremes of a mountain environment.

The Appalachian Mountains are made up of many anticlines and synclines. All areas do not erode at the same rate. Some rocks are tougher than others and don't wear away easily. Rocks like sandstone and conglomerate resist erosion. Where they are exposed at the surface, these rocks form ridges. Rocks like limestone and shale wear away easily, forming valleys. The combination of folding and erosion has made the Appalachian Mountains a varied terrain. ■

▲ The oldest rock layers of an eroded anticline are near the center.

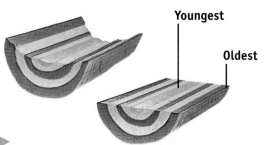

The oldest rock layers of an eroded syncline are farthest from the center. ▶

▲ The Appalachian Mountains, which extend from the southern United States to Canada, have a varied terrain due to folding and erosion.

The Black Hills

Forces pressing on rock from opposite sides can cause rock layers to fold. Over time, the folds may form mountains such as the Appalachians. A mountain called a dome mountain can also form from folded rock layers. The Black Hills of western South Dakota and eastern Wyoming are an example of dome mountains.

A dome mountain forms when forces deep within Earth push rock layers upward. Recall that magma can flow into existing rock. Sometimes the magma pushes the rock layers above it upward, creating a dome.

When erosion wears down the top of a dome, new rock layers are exposed. If more erosion takes place, the rock formed from magma may be exposed.

In the Black Hills, the magma that created the domes is now granite and is exposed at the surface. The center of the dome is granite surrounded by schist. How do you think the schist formed? Around the center are rings of sedimentary rock, including limestone and sandstone. The sandstone is very hard and resists erosion, forming steep ridges sometimes called hogbacks. People have also shaped the Black Hills—by carving the faces of four presidents into Mount Rushmore! ■

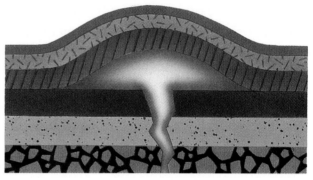

1 A dome forms when a vertical force, such as rising magma, pushes up.

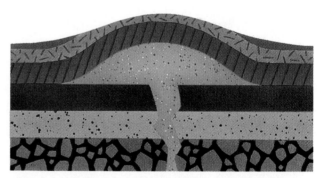

2 In a dome, the youngest rock is the igneous rock formed from the magma.

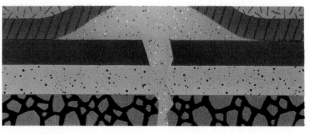

3 Erosion of a dome may expose the igneous rock formed from the magma.

Mr. President...

How many of the likenesses of former presidents carved into this mountain's granite wall can you identify? The national memorial on Mount Rushmore's northeastern side is just over 1800m high. Each head is about 30m tall.

A Real Jewel...

Jewel Cave National Monument is a 100-km long maze of underground rooms and passageways. Its caves formed long ago when water seeped underground and eroded the limestone rock layers.

INVESTIGATION 3

1. How are folded mountains different from dome mountains?

2. Imagine that you come across some folded rock layers that have been exposed by erosion. How would knowing the ages of the layers help you determine if the folding was an anticline or a syncline?

INVESTIGATION 4

WHAT IS A FAULT AND HOW CAN IT MAKE MOUNTAINS?

Mountains are big blocks of rock. You already know rock can be bent to make mountains. In this investigation you'll find out about another way that mountains are made.

Activity

It's Your Fault

Cracks and breaks in sidewalks are common. Sometimes a section of sidewalk is actually thrust up above nearby sections. Sections of rock are also thrust up to make mountains at times!

MATERIALS
- goggles
- wooden meterstick
- 2 pairs of identical books
- *Science Notebook*

SAFETY
Wear goggles.

Procedure

1. A place where rock has moved on one or both sides of a crack is called a **fault**. To **model** how a fault starts to form, have a partner hold one end of a meterstick down on a table, with most of the stick extending off the table.

2. Apply a gentle downward force to the free end of the meterstick. In your *Science Notebook*, **describe** what you **observe**. **Predict** what would happen if you applied a stronger force.

Step 2

E88

3. Make two identical stacks of books, each consisting of two books of different sizes. The book stacks are models of rock layers.

4. Hold one stack on your right hand and the other stack on your left hand. Hold the books so that the top surfaces are level. The open sides of the books should face each other.

Step 4

5. Move the books so that the edges of the covers in your left hand are just under the edges of the covers in your right hand.

6. The separation between the two stacks of books represents a fault. To **model** the motion along a fault, slowly raise your left hand a distance equal to the thickness of one book. **Observe** what happens, especially to the covers. **Record** your observations.

Analyze and Conclude

1. The stick in step 2 represents rock in Earth's crust. What happens to rock if a force strong enough to bend it is applied?

2. After you raised the books in step 6, which books were beside each other on opposite sides of the fault? What do you think happens as layers of rock move vertically along a fault?

3. In step 6, did the covers of the books catch on each other? How might this be like the rocks along a fault?

INVESTIGATE FURTHER!

RESEARCH

The mountain ranges in the Great Basin of the western United States were created by faults in blocks of rock. In which states are these mountains located? What mountain ranges are part of the Great Basin?

It's So Grand

What natural wonder is 446 km (268 mi) long, up to 29 km (17 mi) wide, and more than 1.6 km (1 mi) deep? If you guessed the Grand Canyon, you're right! The Grand Canyon is cut into thousands of meters of rock! What kinds of forces could have created this amazing place? Read on to find out.

If you could peer over the edge of the canyon rim, you would see layer upon layer of rock. Long before the canyon existed, all these rock layers were formed. Recall that when rock layers are stacked one on top of the other, the oldest layer is on the bottom. The oldest rocks exposed at the very bottom of the Grand Canyon are metamorphic and igneous rocks that were formed as many as 1.5 billion years ago. The youngest rocks at the top of the rim are limestone that formed on an ocean floor 225 million years ago.

The Grand Canyon ▼

◀ A normal fault

◀ A reverse fault

A strike-slip fault ▼

The Rocks' Fault

After the rock layers in the Grand Canyon formed, a variety of events caused them to change. One such event involved forces being applied to rock, causing it to break. A break in rock along which movement has occurred is called a **fault**. As with folded rock, the forces that form faults usually are caused by Earth's moving plates.

Forces that come from different directions cause different kinds of faults to form in rock. In a game of tug of war, you pull on a rope in one direction and your friend pulls in the opposite direction. When forces on rock pull in opposite directions, a break called a normal fault can form. Notice in the diagram that rock layers on one side of the break move down in relation to those on the other side.

When moving plates caused rock in the Grand Canyon area to be stretched, many normal faults formed. Some of these faults have been given magical names, like the Crystal, Dragon, and Phantom faults. Tipoff Fault is one that cuts right across the canyon.

Recall that forces can fold rock layers into anticlines and synclines. When such pushing forces cause rock to break, a reverse fault forms. In this type of fault, rock layers on one side of the fault are pushed up in relation to those

on the other side. Use the diagram above to compare movement along a reverse fault with the movement along a normal fault.

You modeled movement along a fault in the activity on pages E88 and E89. When you moved one stack of books, books that had been next to each other weren't that way any longer. The books changed position relative to each other along the break. The same thing happens along normal and reverse faults. Older rock layers can get moved next to or even above younger rock layers. For example, just west of Las Vegas, Nevada, there is a reverse fault called the Keystone Thrust. Along this fault,

▲ Butte Fault is one of many faults that cut through the Grand Canyon.

limestone layers were pushed up so that they sit above sandstone layers. But the sandstone is about 300 million years younger than the limestone above it!

When blocks of rock move along normal and reverse faults, special kinds of mountains called fault-block mountains can form. Ranges of fault-block mountains occur throughout the states surrounding the Grand Canyon.

Not all movement along faults is up and down. Plate movements sometimes cause rock layers to break and slide sideways. With a strike-slip fault, rock on either side of the fault moves horizontally in opposite directions. One example of this type of fault is well known: the San Andreas Fault in California.

Carving a Canyon

Have you ever stood at the edge of the Grand Canyon? People who have are always amazed by how *big* the canyon is—photographs just can't capture its size. How do you think the canyon got carved so deep and wide?

Millions of years ago, the Colorado River flowed through northwestern Arizona just as it does today. Because it was a powerful river with a lot of fast-flowing water, it cut down into the rock over which it flowed and carried away billions of tons of sediment. Even today the Colorado River continues to erode away thousands of tons of rock material each day!

Although erosion accounts for how the Grand Canyon became so deep, the process of weathering accounts for how it became so wide. Recall that weathering is the breaking up of rock. Over time, bits of rock weathered off the sides of the canyon and fell to the bottom. There they were carried away by the river. The more rock that weathered from the canyon walls, the wider the canyon became. ■

The power of the Colorado River carved the Grand Canyon and today propels these white-water rafters. ▼

Earthquake!

▲ **Bridge damaged by the 1994 Los Angeles earthquake**

Can you imagine how scary it must be to wake up with the room shaking around you? That's what happened to millions of people around Los Angeles in 1994. The ground was shaking because an earthquake had begun along a fault in California.

Why did this happen? As you have learned, forces within Earth can cause rock to break and move. When this occurs, energy is released. As a result, the ground shakes. This shaking of the ground is called an earthquake. Movement along a fault is not the only thing that causes an earthquake, although it is the most common cause.

The place where movement first occurs along a fault is below Earth's surface and is called the focus. The place on Earth's surface above the focus is called the epicenter.

Have you ever struck a bell to make it ring? If so, you know it starts to vibrate. In the same way, waves of energy move out from the focus and start the ground shaking. These waves damage land and buildings. In general, as the depth of the focus increases, so does the size of the area that will be damaged by the earthquake waves.

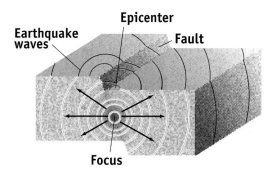

▲ **Earthquakes occur when there is movement along a fault.**

Why do you think earthquakes don't occur all the time along the system of faults under California? Faults are jagged and rough. So as plates move, sections of rock on either side catch on each other and lock together. Eventually enough force builds up so that the rocks unlock and slip past each other. This sudden movement causes an earthquake.

Most earthquakes occur at shallow depths, above 650 km (400 mi). Below this depth, temperature and pressure are so high that all rock bends and flows rather than breaks. Along the famous San Andreas Fault, most earthquakes occur at depths less than 30 km (18 mi).

There have been major earthquakes along the San Andreas Fault. In 1857, a section of the fault 120 km (74 mi) from Los Angeles moved 9 m (30 ft). In 1906 the fault shifted 6 m (20 ft) and the earthquake that resulted destroyed San Francisco. Since scientists believe the San Andreas Fault is about 20 million years old, you can bet there were many more major earthquakes along this fault before such occurrences were recorded.

Slow movement occurs along the San Andreas Fault all the time. Each year, crust along the fault moves several centimeters. Scientists believe that in about 10 million years, Los Angeles will have moved so far north that it will sit just across the fault from San Francisco! In about 60 million years, it will be completely separated from the rest of California. As long as the crust along the San Andreas Fault continues to move, earthquakes will keep happening, and the residents of California must keep expecting them. ■

▲ **Signs of movement along the San Andreas Fault**

INVESTIGATION 4

1. How do faults result in the formation of mountains?

2. Along what type of fault is a mountain not likely to occur? Explain your answer.

REFLECT & EVALUATE

WORD POWER

fault
anticline
core
crust
erosion
fold
absolute age

fossil
index fossil
mantle
model
relative age
syncline

 On Your Own
Review the terms in the list. Then use as many terms as you can in a paragraph about Earth's structure.

 With a Partner
Write a definition for each term in the list. Have your partner match each definition to the correct term.

BUILD YOUR PORTFOLIO

Collect pictures from magazines that show rock formations of various kinds. Try to identify faults, folds, and other features in the pictures.

Analyze Information

Study the drawing. Then identify the layers of Earth shown.

Assess Performance

Using materials of your choice, model movement along the three types of faults. Describe the forces acting in each case.

Problem Solving

1. Compare and contrast folding and faulting.

2. A sandstone layer is found atop a shale layer. A thick section of gabbro, which hardened from magma, cuts upward through both layers. A fault cuts through all three rocks. What are the relative ages of the fault and the three rock layers? Explain your reasoning.

3. Make a sketch of a syncline and an anticline. Then make a sketch showing the eroded top of each formation. Label the rock layers from oldest to youngest in each sketch.

Throughout this unit, you've investigated questions related to Earth and its structures. How will you use what you've learned and share that information with others? Here are some ideas.

Hold a Big Event
to Share Your Unit Project

Set up a rock, mineral, and fossil exhibit using the collections your group and the other groups assembled. Prepare identification cards for each sample. Also publish a guide to rocks, minerals, and fossils for your area. Distribute copies to parents and friends who attend the exhibit and invite them to use the guide to learn about the types of rocks, minerals, and fossils present in your community.

Experiment

With the help of a mineral guide and a hand lens, classify your minerals based on crystal structure. You might also grow crystal gardens, using different materials—alum, salt, sugar, and so on. Try adding a few drops of food coloring to each solution. What happens to the crystals? When the crystals are grown, examine them with a microscope or hand lens. Which crystals look like the cubes? Which have six faces? What other shapes of crystals did you grow? Draw and label the characteristcs of the crystals in your *Science Notebook*.

Research

Which topic in this unit would you like to investigate further? Try finding out more about rock layers or erosion. (You might wish to ask a partner to work with you.) To do so, locate a rock face or any rock formation where you can observe layers of rocks. Study the rock formation as closely as you can. Sketch or photograph the layers. Take rock samples. If possible, ask a geologist to help you interpret what you see. Then assemble your research into an informative display.

LIGHT AND SOUND

Theme: Models

GET READY TO

OBSERVE & QUESTION

How is sound transmitted and recorded?

Today, sounds—and images—are transmitted in an instant to all parts of the world. Find out how this instantaneous transmission of music, voices, and images affects you.

EXPERIMENT & HYPOTHESIZE

How are lenses used in telescopes and microscopes?

Telescopes were first invented in the early 1600's. Build your own telescope much like the ones built hundreds of years ago.

INVESTIGATE!

RESEARCH & ANALYZE

As you investigate, find out more from these books.

- ***Tuning In: The Sounds of the Radio*** by Eve and Albert Stwertka, Illustrated by Mena Dolobrowsky (Julian Messner, 1992). How can music and information travel invisibly from a radio station to your house? Find out what radio waves are and how radios work.

- ***Extremely Weird Micro Monsters*** by Sarah Lovett (John Muir Publications, 1993). Discover how powerful microscopes can take pictures that make incredibly small creatures look gigantic!

- ***That's a Wrap: How Movies Are Made*** by Ned Dowd, Photography by Henry Horenstein (Silver Burdett Press, 1993). How are stunts and special effects recorded? How does sound make a film exciting? Find out how movies are made by reading this book.

WORK TOGETHER & SHARE IDEAS

How can you put together a sound and light show?

Working together, you'll have a chance to apply what you have learned. You and your class will stage a puppet show. You'll write, rehearse, and perform your own narration. Then you'll mix lights of different colors to achieve special effects. Finally you'll build models of musical instruments from around the world and provide the music for your show.

1

PROPERTIES OF LIGHT

Black lamps don't seem to give off much light. But shine them on surfaces covered with a certain kind of paint and see what happens! What is light, anyway? How can light be black?

• •

Lighten Up

Richard Green is founder of Wildfire Incorporated, a company in Los Angeles that creates lighting effects for music videos, television commercials, theme parks, and movies. Richard is a lighting specialist, someone who designs and produces just the right lighting for shows and other events.

One popular lighting technique involves making objects fluoresce, or glow. Richard covers objects with fluorescent paint and then shines a black light on them. The objects seem to glow! He says that people experience fluorescent objects in different ways. For some it is like stepping into an animated cartoon world of bright, crazy colors. For others the color and light seem to appear from nowhere.

Coming Up

◀ These people seem to glow because of fluorescent paint and black lights.

WHAT IS LIGHT AND WHERE DOES IT COME FROM?

Have you ever been home when the electric power went out? A power failure can make you stop and think about something you take for granted—light! In this investigation you'll find out about light you can see and its relatives you can't see.

Activity

Seeing the Light

There are lights all around you. Try a "scavenger hunt" to find some of them.

MATERIALS
- *Science Notebook*

Procedure

Work with a group of other students to investigate light sources in various places. Look for all possible light sources. List the locations and the light sources in your *Science Notebook*. **Record** the kind of energy you think is being used to produce the light.

Rank the light sources from brightest to dimmest, using 1 for the brightest. Note whether any heat was given off from each light source.

Analyze and Conclude

1. What were the light sources your group found?

2. For each source, what kind of energy change produces the light? What can you **infer** about the connection between light and heat?

Activity

All Aglow

MATERIALS
- light bulb A
- 3 batteries (size D)
- insulated copper wire
- light bulb holder
- light bulb B
- tape
- *Science Notebook*

A simple electric circuit contains one battery, a light bulb, and a couple of connecting wires. What changes can you see in the light as you experiment with the different parts of the circuit?

Procedure

1. Insert light bulb A into a light bulb holder. Connect one battery to light bulb A, using copper wire. Use tape to hold the wire in place.

2. **Observe** what happens when you complete the electric circuit. Carefully note if the bulbs are warm. **Record** your observations in your *Science Notebook*.

3. **Predict** what will happen if you add a second battery to the circuit. **Record** your prediction. Then add the second battery and **record** the results.

4. Add a third battery to the circuit and again **record** your observations.

5. Replace light bulb A with light bulb B. Repeat steps 1–4. **Record** the results.

Step 1

Analyze and Conclude

1. In step 3, how did your prediction match what happened?

2. What happened when you added more batteries to the circuit? **Suggest a hypothesis** to explain what you observed.

3. What change occurred when you replaced bulb A with bulb B? Why did this change occur?

4. What do you think is flowing from the battery to the bulb through the copper wire?

5. What causes the bulbs to glow? Were the bulbs warm?

6. What evidence do you have that light is energy?

Lighting the Way

Imagine that it is summertime and you are lying on a sandy beach. Through your sunglasses you can see the light of the Sun. You can feel the heat of the Sun on your bare skin. The Sun's rays provide Earth with light and heat,  which are both forms of energy. You may recall that **energy** is the ability to do work or cause a change in matter.

The Sun, a star, supplies nearly all of Earth's natural light energy. From Earth you can see other stars during the night, but the amount of light from those stars is very small compared to the amount received from the Sun. Moonlight, the light Earth receives from the Moon, is really sunlight that has bounced off the Moon's surface.

Energy From the Sun

The Sun gives off huge amounts of energy that travel to Earth through the vacuum of space. The energy given off by the Sun is called **electromagnetic radiation** (ē lek trō mag net'ik rā dē ā'shən). There are many kinds of electromagnetic (E-M) radiation; some kinds you can see, and others you can't see. **Visible light** is the type of E-M radiation that you can see.

Most types of E-M radiation are invisible. For example, infrared radiation and ultraviolet radiation are two types of invisible E-M radiation. Infrared radiation from the Sun is what causes you to feel warm when you

X-rays

gamma rays

Electromagnetic radiation from the Sun includes visible and invisible radiation. ▶

stand in sunlight. Heat lamps also produce infrared radiation.

Ultraviolet radiation, or UV light, is sometimes called black light because an ultraviolet lamp looks dark to us when it is on. But some materials glow, or give off visible light, when UV light shines on them. That painful sunburn you get from lying too long on the beach is caused by ultraviolet radiation.

Electromagnetic radiation can cause changes in matter. For example, sunlight heats water in the oceans. Light can also be used to heat water in solar collectors. Have you ever seen a solar calculator? When light shines on the calculator's solar cells, electricity to run the calculator is produced. In each case, light is changed to other forms of energy.

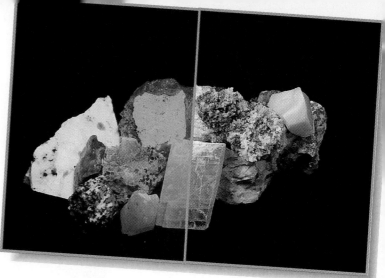

▲ Certain minerals glow under ultraviolet (UV) light (*left*). The same minerals are shown under normal light (*right*).

Light starts many chemical reactions. One of the most important reactions started by light is photosynthesis, the food-making process of plants. During photosynthesis, plant cells convert carbon dioxide and water to oxygen and sugar. In this reaction, light energy is stored as chemical energy.

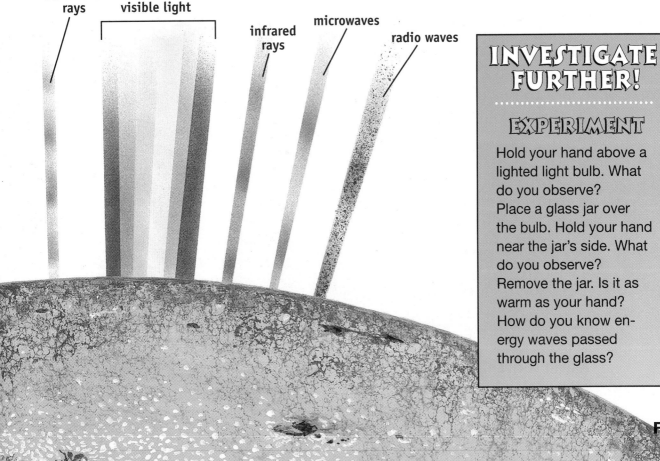

ultraviolet rays   visible light   infrared rays   microwaves   radio waves

INVESTIGATE FURTHER!

EXPERIMENT

Hold your hand above a lighted light bulb. What do you observe? Place a glass jar over the bulb. Hold your hand near the jar's side. What do you observe? Remove the jar. Is it as warm as your hand? How do you know energy waves passed through the glass?

Making Light

How many light sources can you think of other than the Sun? Light bulbs are the most common sources of artificial light. But fire was the first source of light that humans were able to control.

A campfire is a chemical reaction that gives off light. When a substance burns, the energy stored in it is given off as heat and light. The matter being burned is not used up. Instead, it is changed to other substances.

▲ A campfire is a chemical reaction in which light and heat are given off.

Most of the chemical reactions that give off light also produce heat. With a campfire, you may be more interested in the heat than in the light. If you light a candle, on the other hand, you're interested in the light that is released. If you burn a candle, less than 1 percent of the stored energy in the candle is changed to light. The rest is changed to heat.

Have you ever carried a "light stick"? People often take these along on camp-

ing trips for emergency lights. The plastic tubes contain two sets of chemicals. When you bend the light stick, you break a small tube inside it. When the inner tube breaks, chemicals mix. A reaction occurs that gives off light. This reaction does not make much heat, so the tube does not get hot.

In an incandescent light bulb, there is a very thin wire, called a filament, that carries electricity. The wire gets very

A light stick before its chemical reaction (*left*); breaking the tube releases chemicals that mix, causing a chemical reaction (*center*); the glowing light stick (*right*)

Sources of light: fluorescent light bulbs (*left*); lightning bolt (*center*); sparks given off during welding (*right*)

hot when the electricity goes through it. This makes the wire glow. But only about 2 percent of the electrical energy is changed into light.

Your classroom probably is lighted by fluorescent (floo res'ənt) lamps. These electric lights don't contain a filament. Instead, they contain a gas that gives off ultraviolet light when electricity flows through it. Remember that you can't see ultraviolet light. To make visible light, the fluorescent tube is lined with chemicals that glow when ultraviolet light strikes them. Ultraviolet lights do a much better job of changing electrical energy into light energy than do incandescent lights. About 30 percent of the electrical energy is changed into light. As a result fluorescent bulbs don't get as hot as incandescent bulbs do.

One familiar source of light doesn't last very long, but it can be very bright. What is it? Lightning! Lightning is a very bright electrical spark. Perhaps you've seen a lightning flash light up the night sky so that it's as bright as day. What are other examples of light coming from sparks? ■

▲ **Incandescent light bulb with glowing filament**

Light
Through the Ages

For thousands of years the only sources of light humans had were the Sun and fire. Progress in producing artificial light occurred very slowly over long periods of time. Finally, in the mid-1700s, real strides were made. In recent years the advances in light technology have been fantastic! Follow the time line to see the changes that have occurred in light through the ages.

Kerosene replaces whale oil in house lamps.

1850

Whale blubber oil is used in oil lamps

1800-1900

Sumerians used oil-burning lamps. Candles and oil lamps are used to light homes for many centuries.

3000-2500 B.C.

EARLY 1800s

Gaslights are used in cities. The gas was carried to buildings by a series of pipes. As cities grew, gas lighting became common in homes and apartments. At twilight, lamplighters went around the city, lighting gas-fueled street lamps.

A.D. 1786

First attempts to provide inside gas lighting in Germany and England

18,000 B.C.

People learn to make torches out of pieces of wood tipped with flammable tree resin.

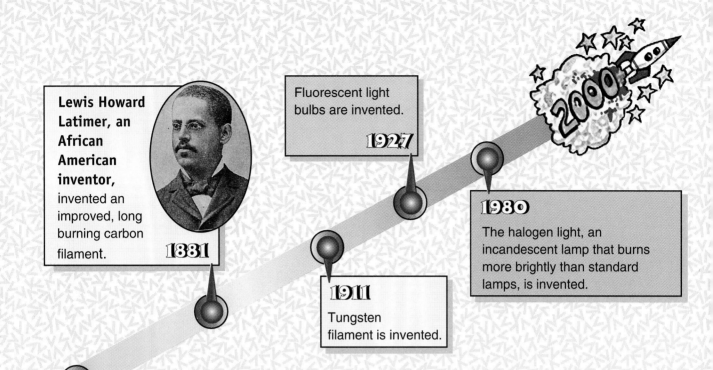

Lewis Howard Latimer, an African American inventor, invented an improved, long burning carbon filament. **1881**

Fluorescent light bulbs are invented. **1927**

1911
Tungsten filament is invented.

1980
The halogen light, an incandescent lamp that burns more brightly than standard lamps, is invented.

2000

1879
Thomas Edison (American) and Joseph Swan (British) invent an improved light bulb. Both Edison and Swan had been experimenting with light bulbs. At the same time, both came up with the same idea. On October 21, 1879, using a carbon filament made from a burned thread, Edison made a light bulb that lasted for 13.5 hours before the filament burned out.

Building a Better Light Bulb

Since 1980, advances in lighting technology have taken place. Most recently, scientists have invented different kinds of lighting that are brighter or use less energy.

One of these energy-efficient light sources is the compact fluorescent bulb. It uses 75 percent less energy than an incandescent light bulb and can last for about 10,000 hours! In the years ahead, engineers will be working to create lighting that is brighter, lasts longer, and saves more energy. ■

INVESTIGATION 1

THINK IT WRITE IT

1. Describe two different ways that you can produce light energy.

2. Imagine that you are an engineer who is designing an improved light bulb. Describe the characteristics that your improved light bulb would have.

HOW DOES LIGHT TRAVEL?

Have you ever been in a sports stadium when one section starts a "wave"? Think about how the motion travels from one part of the stadium to another. The traveling of light is a little like this human wave.

Activity
Light Waves

Light is a form of energy that travels in waves. Can you imagine what a light wave looks like? This activity will show you a model of the way a light wave travels.

MATERIALS
- goggles
- large plastic coil spring
- *Science Notebook*

SAFETY
Wear goggles.

Procedure

1. Work with a partner. Stretch a plastic coil spring between yourself and your partner. Be careful that you don't overstretch and damage the coils.

2. While your partner holds one end of the coil spring still, make one quick motion to the side and back to the center position. **Observe** the wave you created. **Record** your observations in your *Science Notebook*.

3. Repeat step 2 several times and **record** your observations.

Step 1

4. **Predict** what will happen if you move the coil spring up and down. **Record** your prediction. Then try moving the coil spring up and down. **Record** how the wave moves this time. **Make a sketch** of the wave.

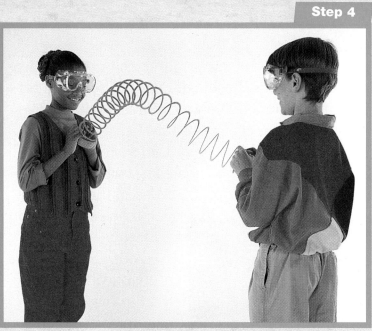

Step 4

Analyze and Conclude

1. Write a statement describing two ways the coil spring moves.

2. What evidence is there that the wave carries energy as it travels along the coil?

UNIT PROJECT LINK

You can use your investigations of light and sound to help you plan a puppet show. Start by making a catalog of the different shadows you can create with common objects. Choose objects with interesting shapes. Look around your classroom or your home for the objects.

Darken the room. Shine a flashlight at the objects from different angles to produce different shapes. Try moving the flashlight far away from the objects and then near them to see what happens. Choose one object. On a sheet of white paper, trace the different shadows you can make from that object. Remove all the objects. Then see if anyone can guess the object that made the shadows.

Lasers

What do supermarket checkouts, CD players, and rock concerts have in common? Lasers! Laser beams are used in the scanners that make barcode readers and CD players work. Laser beams are also used in concert light displays. How does a laser work? What makes laser light different from ordinary light?

All light beams travel in a straight line, but ordinary light beams spread out as they travel. Ordinary light beams aren't as bright after they spread out. Laser beams, however, don't spread out, allowing them to travel a long distance without getting dim.

▲ **Laser lights at rock concert**

One use for lasers is in communications. Lasers are used to send signals along telephone and television cables. The cables are made of optical fibers, which are long, thin strands of glass. Even if the fibers are bent, the light bounces off the sides of the fiber wall and follows the bending pathway.

Today, laser beams and optical fibers are used in medicine. For example, laser light can help repair a detached retina in the eye. It can cut and seal blood vessels or destroy skin cancers. Optical fibers and lasers make microsurgery possible. Doctors can use optical fibers to work through a small incision in the body. ■

PARTS OF A LASER This laser contains a ruby crystal surrounded by a coil of light. As the light flashes, energy builds up in the crystal. When enough energy has built up, an intense beam of laser light is released.

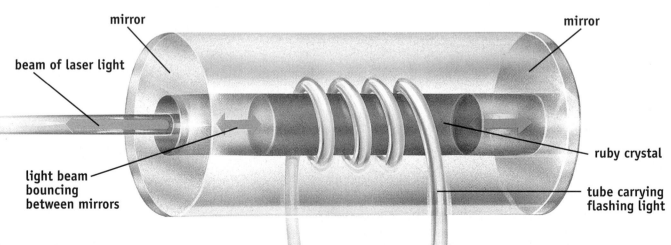

mirror

beam of laser light

light beam bouncing between mirrors

mirror

ruby crystal

tube carrying flashing light

Light as a Wave

A **wave** is a disturbance that moves away from its starting point. As a wave moves, it transfers energy. Think about what happens if you drop a stone into a pond. As the stone hits the water, it creates waves that travel out across the pond from that spot. As they reach the shore, the waves may move sand and pebbles.

Light also travels as a wave. Light waves are different from water waves in an important way. Without water, there would be no water waves. But light waves don't need water or air or any kind of matter to carry them. Light waves can travel through a vacuum. A **vacuum** is a space that is empty of any matter. Light

▲ **Waves travel outward from a pebble tossed into water.**

waves from the Sun travel through space without being carried by matter.

The Shape of a Wave

You can see light, but you can't see light waves. Still, scientists know that light waves do many of the same things that other kinds of waves do. So scientists use the wave model to explain how light behaves. To use and understand the wave model of light, you need to know the parts of a wave. Refer to the drawing below as you read the following description.

Measuring Light Waves

The lengths of light waves can be

▼ **Parts of a wave**

WAVELENGTH The distance between two consecutive high points, or low points, in a wave

CREST The high point of a wave

AMPLITUDE The height of the wave from its resting position to its highest point

TROUGH The low point of a wave

F17

measured. **Wavelength** is the distance from one crest of the wave to the next crest. Of course, you can't place a ruler next to a light wave because you can't see it. But the wavelength of light has been measured in the laboratory. Scientists have found that each color of light has a different range of wavelengths. The wavelengths of visible light are shown in the table. Because light wavelengths are so short, they are measured in a tiny unit called a nanometer (nm). One nanometer equals one billionth of a meter.

Wave Frequency

The number of waves produced each second is the **frequency** of a wave. Wave frequency is measured in a unit called the **hertz** (Hz). If ten waves are produced each second, the frequency of the wave is 10 Hz. The frequency of light waves is measured in a unit called a megahertz (MHz). One megahertz is equal to 1 million hertz.

Speed of Light

Although each color of light has a different range of wavelengths and frequencies, all light waves travel at the same speed. The speed of light is 300,000 km/s (186,000 mi/s).

The electromagnetic spectrum ▼

Wavelengths of Light

Color of Light	Wavelength (nm)
Violet	350–400
Indigo	400–450
Blue	450–500
Green	500–550
Yellow	550–600
Orange	600–650
Red	650–700

Imagine light traveling through an optical fiber wrapped around the equator. Light travels so quickly that it could travel around the world 7.5 times in one second! Light traveling from the Sun, which is 150 million km (about 93

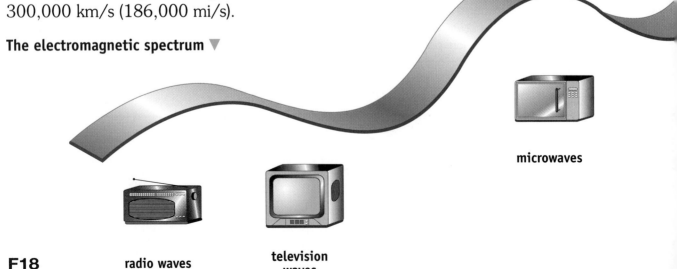

microwaves

radio waves

television waves

million mi) away, takes 500 seconds, or 8.3 minutes, to reach Earth.

The speed of light depends on the material through which it moves. The value 300,000 km/s is the speed of light traveling in a vacuum.

The Electromagnetic Spectrum

As you know, light is only one kind of electromagnetic radiation. E-M radiation also includes gamma rays, microwaves, infrared waves, X-rays, radio waves, and other kinds of waves.

From the drawing below, you can see that radio waves have the longest wavelengths and gamma rays have the shortest wavelengths. How do the wavelengths of visible light compare to those of radio waves? to microwaves?

The energy of electromagnetic radiation is related to wavelength—the shorter the wavelength, the more energy carried by the wave. How does UV light compare with visible light in terms of energy?

Although the wavelengths, frequencies, and energy levels of electromagnetic waves vary, E-M waves have two things in common: (1) When traveling through space, they all travel at the same speed, and (2) they all can travel through a vacuum. ■

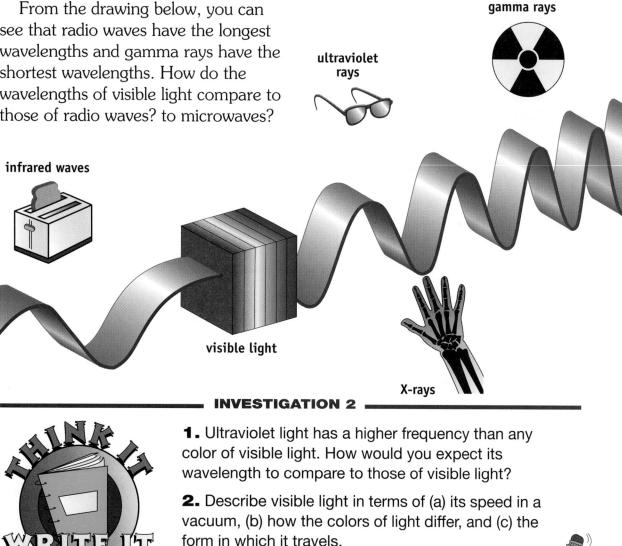

gamma rays

ultraviolet rays

infrared waves

visible light

X-rays

INVESTIGATION 2

THINK IT WRITE IT

1. Ultraviolet light has a higher frequency than any color of visible light. How would you expect its wavelength to compare to those of visible light?

2. Describe visible light in terms of (a) its speed in a vacuum, (b) how the colors of light differ, and (c) the form in which it travels.

INVESTIGATION 3

HOW DOES LIGHT BEHAVE?

Have you ever used mirrors to look around a corner or over a wall? If so, you know that some kinds of matter can change the direction that light travels. In this investigation you'll find out under what conditions light bounces and bends.

Activity

How Mirrors Affect Light

In this activity you'll see how three different kinds of mirrors change the direction that light travels.

MATERIALS

- flashlight
- plane mirror (flat)
- large piece of cardboard
- concave mirror (curves inward)
- convex mirror (curves outward)
- *Science Notebook*

Procedure

Darken the room. Turn a flashlight on and point it at an angle toward a plane mirror. Hold a large piece of cardboard at the edge of the mirror, as shown. **Record** your observations in your *Science Notebook*.

Repeat the above procedure, but this time use the concave mirror. **Observe** and **record** your results. **Predict** what will happen with the convex mirror. Try it. **Observe** what happens and **record** your results.

Analyze and Conclude

Describe the effect of each mirror on the light beam. What uses can you think of for each mirror?

Activity
The Bending Pencil

Sometimes things aren't quite what they appear to be. That's the idea behind many of the tricks that magicians perform. With some water and oil, you can "break" a pencil in two. To do the trick, you have to learn how to bend light.

MATERIALS

- 1 pencil
- 1 tall narrow plastic jar
- water
- paper towel
- vegetable oil
- *Science Notebook*

Procedure

1. Place a pencil in a plastic jar. **Observe** the jar and pencil from the side. In your *Science Notebook*, **draw** the jar and pencil. Label the drawing *Step 1*.

2. Keep the pencil in the jar. Then fill the jar almost to the top with water. **Observe** the jar and pencil from the side and from above. In your *Science Notebook* **draw** pictures of what you observe from the side and from above. Use a dotted line to show where you think the pencil in the water *actually* is. Label the drawings *Step 2*.

3. Remove the pencil from the jar. Pour out the water. Use a paper towel to dry the inside of the jar. Now, fill the jar almost to the top with vegetable oil. **Predict** how the pencil will look from the side and from the top. **Record** your prediction. Then place the pencil back in the jar. **Observe** and **draw** as you did in step 2. **Label** the drawings *Step 3*.

Step 2

Analyze and Conclude

1. What is the difference between the way the pencil looked in step 1 and step 2? What evidence is there that light changes direction as it leaves the water?

2. Describe the difference between the appearance of the pencil in water and its appearance in vegetable oil. Give a reason for any difference.

INVESTIGATE FURTHER!

EXPERIMENT

Predict what would happen if you used other liquids in this activity. Try several liquids and compare the results.

Bouncing Light

▲ **Image in a fun-house mirror**

You see objects because light coming from them enters your eyes. The Sun, lamps, and candles give off light, but most objects don't. You can see such objects because of reflected light.

Reflection (ri flek′shən) is the bouncing back of light (or sound, or water) from a surface. Think of a lamp as it gives off light. Some of the light hits a chair. Part of the light that hits the chair is absorbed by the chair, but most of the light is reflected off the chair. Light that reflects off the chair to your eyes lets you see the chair.

Plane Mirrors

Any object with a very smooth surface, including still water and highly polished metals, can act as a mirror. The type of mirror you are most familiar with is called a plane mirror. A **plane mirror** is a mirror with a flat surface.

Light reflects from a plane mirror in the same pattern and at the same angle

▼ **Reflection in a plane mirror**

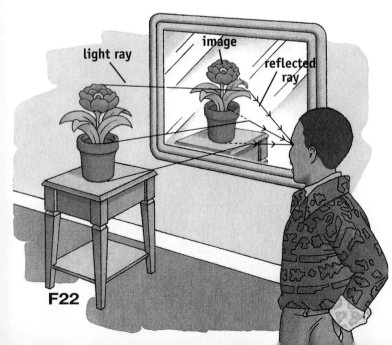

light ray

image

reflected ray

▼ **Image in a plane mirror**

at which it strikes the mirror's surface. However, the light changes direction as it is reflected. If you stand in front of a mirror, light bouncing off your body strikes the mirror's surface. Some of this light is reflected off the mirror and back to your eyes. Because the light reflects off the mirror with the same pattern as the light that struck the mirror, you see an image.

The image you see in a plane mirror is right-side-up and the same size as the object being reflected. The image is not distorted, or out of shape. But it is reversed from left to right, so you don't see yourself exactly as others do.

Use the drawing on page F22 to follow the path that light takes to form an image in a plane mirror. Some light rays from the object travel toward the mirror. As these light rays strike the mirror, they are reflected. These rays enter your eye and form an image. Your brain forms a mental picture of where the light seems to come from. Because light travels in straight lines, the image seems to be behind the mirror.

Concave Mirrors

The images you see in curved mirrors often are distorted and are usually not the same size as the object. There are two kinds of curved mirrors. A **concave mirror** curves inward at the middle. A **convex mirror** curves outward at the middle.

Shaving and makeup mirrors are often concave. When an object is close to a concave mirror, the image formed in the mirror is larger than the object. Concave mirrors are also used as reflectors to concentrate light. The reflected light rays come together and are focused at one point. A concave mirror can be used to focus solar rays and cook food in a solar oven.

Convex Mirrors

A convex mirror produces an image that is smaller than the object. It also allows you to see much more of an area than other kinds of mirrors do. Because convex mirrors reflect light from such a wide area, they are useful as side-view mirrors on cars and trucks. ■

▲ **Concave mirror and the image it produces**

▲ **Convex mirror and the image it produces**

Bending Light

A Change in Direction

In the activity on page F21, you saw that light passing through different materials can produce a strange image —like a broken pencil. The illusion occurs because light rays bend, or change direction, as they travel from one material into another. This bending of light as it passes from one material into another is called **refraction** (ri-frak'shən). In the activity, light was refracted as it passed from water into air.

The speed of light changes as it passes from one material into another. For example, light travels at close to 300,000 km/s (186,000 mi/s) in air and at 225,000 km/(140,000 mi/s) in water.

A Change in Speed

When light waves pass from air into water, they slow down. This change in speed of the light waves is what causes the light to refract, or change direction. You can see in the drawing on page F25 how light waves change direction as their speed increases when they pass from water into air.

Look at how a glass prism affects a beam of white light passing through it in the photograph below. The light slows down as it enters the prism, causing the beam of light to refract. But the different colors of light are bent at different angles. So a rainbow, or spectrum, is produced as the light leaves the prism.

▲ Refraction of light as it passes from air through a glass prism

Tricks With Refracted Light

Have you ever tried to catch a fish in a fish tank? If you looked at the fish from above, you probably had trouble. The fish looks closer to the surface than it is. Look at the diagram of the fish tank. Light reflecting from the fish is refracted as it leaves the water. The light enters your eye, and your brain "assumes" that the light has traveled in a straight line. So your brain forms an image of where the fish seems to be. But that isn't where the fish really is! Refraction of light fools you.

If you have watched someone in a pet store try to net a fish, you probably noticed that the person looked at the fish through the side of the tank. By

▲ **Refraction of light in water can fool you. Where is the fish?**

looking straight into the water, that person had a better chance of catching the fish. When light rays move from one material to another along a line that is perpendicular to the surface, there is no refraction. Since the light rays don't bend, you don't get fooled.

SCIENCE IN LITERATURE

■ AT HOME WITH SCIENCE ■

TUNING IN
THE SOUNDS OF THE RADIO

EVE AND ALBERT STWERTKA
ILLUSTRATED BY MENA DOLOBOWSKY

TUNING IN
THE SOUNDS OF THE RADIO
by Eve and Albert Stwertka
Illustrated by Mena Dolobowsky
Julian Messner, 1993

Bending light, bouncing light. Not only does light "bend" and "bounce," so do other forms of electromagnetic radiation. Radio waves are a familiar and useful form of electromagnetic radiation. These waves travel at the speed of light. Like light waves, radio waves can be bounced and bent.

Find out how radio waves behave and how they are put to use by reading *TUNING IN: The Sounds of the Radio* by Eve and Albert Stwertka. Do the "Try this . . . " activity on page 6 of *Tuning In*. Compare your results with those of your classmates.

Air Bends Light

Have you ever ridden in a car on a hot, dry day and thought you saw a pool of water in the road? Was your mind playing tricks on you? Actually, the mirage you see is a result of light traveling at different speeds in cool air and warm air. Light from the Sun was refracted toward your eyes by the heated air near the road's surface. The pool you saw was really refracted sunlight. In effect, you were seeing an image of the sky on the road surface ahead of you. Your brain interprets the light as coming to you in a straight line from the road. ■

Mirages are most common during summer months, when air near the ground is much warmer than air higher in the atmosphere. ▷

As light waves from above pass into the layer of warm air near the surface, the light bends, or refracts. If these light waves enter your eyes, you see an image of the sky, but you see it on the road surface. ▷

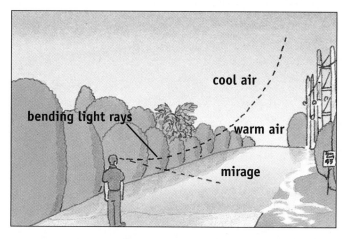

cool air

bending light rays

warm air

mirage

INVESTIGATION 3

1. You are in water up to your waist in a local swimming pool. As you look down into the water, your legs and feet look short and stubby. You're really tall and thin. What happened?

2. Compare and contrast the reflection of light with the refraction of light.

REFLECT & EVALUATE

CHAPTER 1 REVIEW

WORD POWER

energy
hertz
vacuum
visible light
wavelength
concave mirror
convex mirror
electromagnetic radiation

frequency
plane mirror
reflection
refraction
wave

 On Your Own
Review the terms in the list. Then write one new thing you learned about each term.

With a Partner
Write a definition for each term in the list. Have your partner match each definition to the correct term.

PORTFOLIO

Make several drawings of devices that use different kinds of electromagnetic radiation. If you prefer, make a collage of pictures of these devices cut from magazines.

Analyze Information

If you were the person on the pier in the drawing, where would the snorkeler appear to be?

Assess Performance

Examine a flashlight and locate the mirror near the bulb. What is the shape of the mirror? Turn on the flashlight and notice the path of the light. If possible, unscrew the front cover of the flashlight and get a better look at the mirror. Make a drawing to show how the mirror affects the light produced by the bulb.

Problem Solving

1. Describe and sketch the energy path that leads to light in a flashlight.

2. Make a sketch that shows a wave of red light and a wave of violet light. Label the sketch and explain how the waves differ.

3. Use a diagram to show that light travels in straight lines, even when it bends, or refracts, and when it reflects off a surface.

CHAPTER 2

LIGHT, LENSES, AND COLOR

Scientists seek to understand our planet, our solar system, and even the universe. This often involves getting the best possible view of things. Telescopes extend our vision to the galaxies. Microscopes help us see the tiny, complex world that is invisible to our unaided eyes. How is it possible for us to see so far and so much?

A Young Astronomer

Marian Toro, 17, is a Native American of the Tohono O'odham Nation. She lives on a reservation about 96 km (60 mi) west of Tucson, Arizona, near Kitt Peak. According to Marian, long ago her people looked at the Moon and stars to tell if the harvest would be a good one. Now she studies those stars with the aid of a telescope.

Marian hopes to become an astronomer. She became an amateur astronomer at the astronomy camp of the University of Arizona. Using the Mount Lemmon telescope, Marian tracked satellites and observed planets. She watched scientists at the university make some of the world's largest telescope mirrors. Marian also built a small telescope.

Why is it important for an astronomer to know about light and lenses?

Coming Up

◄ A student observes the stars through the Mount Lemmon telescope.

HOW DO LENSES HELP CONTROL LIGHT?

Do you know someone who wears contact lenses? A contact lens changes the direction of light passing through it. This investigation should help you understand how lenses help a person see more clearly.

Activity
Becoming Focused

You've seen that as light passes from one material to another it can change direction. When a material such as glass is shaped into a lens, it directs—or redirects—the path of light. Explore how lens shape affects the way light passes into and out of the lens.

MATERIALS
- lens paper
- convex lens
- manila folder
- flashlight
- metric ruler
- newspaper
- concave lens
- *Science Notebook*

SAFETY
Be careful when handling glass lenses.

Procedure

1. In your *Science Notebook* **make a chart** titled "Comparing Convex and Concave Lenses." **Record** all observations during this activity in the chart.

2. Take a piece of lens paper and feel the shape of the convex lens through it. **Make a sketch** of the lens.

3. Darken the room. Using a manila folder as a screen, place a flashlight about 30 cm from the screen. Point the flashlight toward the screen.

4. Place the convex lens between the flashlight and the screen so that the light passes through the lens and shines onto the screen.

Step 4

5. **Observe** what happens on the screen as you move the lens back and forth between the light and the screen. **Infer** how the lens is affecting the light. **Record** your inference.

6. Stand with your back toward a window. Hold the lens in one hand and extend your arm so that the light from the window passes through the lens.

7. Have a classmate hold the screen so that the light passing through the lens shines on the screen. Move the screen and lens as needed until a clear image appears on the screen. Look at the image carefully and **record** your observations.

8. Place the convex lens on the print on a piece of newspaper. Raise the lens slowly and **observe** the print. **Record** your observations.

9. Repeat steps 2–8, using a concave lens. In the chart, **record** your observations about the concave lens.

Analyze and Conclude

1. In step 5, how did the appearance of the beam of light on the screen change for each lens?

2. Describe the image you saw on the screen as you moved each lens back and forth in step 7. What was unusual about the image?

3. How does a convex lens affect light when it focuses light to a point? How do convex and concave lenses differ in the way they affect light?

UNIT PROJECT LINK

Your group is going to put on a puppet show, using different colored lights to produce special visual effects. Cover a flashlight with cellophane of different colors. Experiment with blue, red, and green, in turn. Create situations to act out, using your puppets. Decide which colors of light to use to create the right emotion for each situation. Then give your show.

Light and Lenses

How Lenses Bend Light

You've probably had fun playing with a hand lens. Held close to an object, a hand lens lets you see details you didn't know were there. Held at arm's length, it shows a world turned upside down! What "magic" is at work here?

Actually, you already know something about this "magic." When light passes from one transparent material into another, the light bends, or changes direction. A **lens** is a transparent object with at least one curved surface. Lenses come in a variety of shapes, but all types refract light that passes through them.

Lens Shape

A lens that is thicker in the center than it is at the edges is called a **convex lens**. Such a lens brings parallel light rays together at a point known as the **focal point**. The thicker the lens, the more it bends light. So the thicker the lens, the closer the focal point is to the lens.

As you saw in the activity on lenses on pages F30 and F31, when you hold an object near a convex lens and look through the lens, you'll see a right-side-up image that is larger than the object. This is how hand lenses work. It's refraction, not magic, that produces a larger image. If a convex lens isn't very close to an object, the image that forms is small; it's also upside down!

A lens that is thicker at the edges than at its middle is called a **concave lens**. A concave lens causes parallel light rays to spread apart. The image of an object viewed through a concave lens is smaller than the object but the image formed is always right side up.

The Eye and a Camera

Both the human eye and a camera contain convex lenses. An important difference between your eyes and a camera is that a camera takes only one picture at a time. But your eyes are constantly "taking pictures." The lens of your eye focuses an image on the **retina** (ret'n ə). The retina is the light-sensitive layer at the back of the eye.

A convex lens brings light rays together at a focal point (*left*); a concave lens causes light rays to spread apart (*right*).

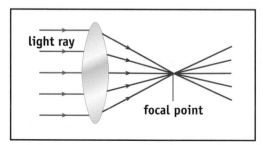
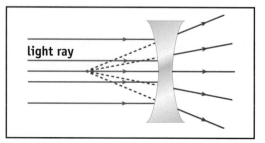

Comparing the Human Eye to a Camera

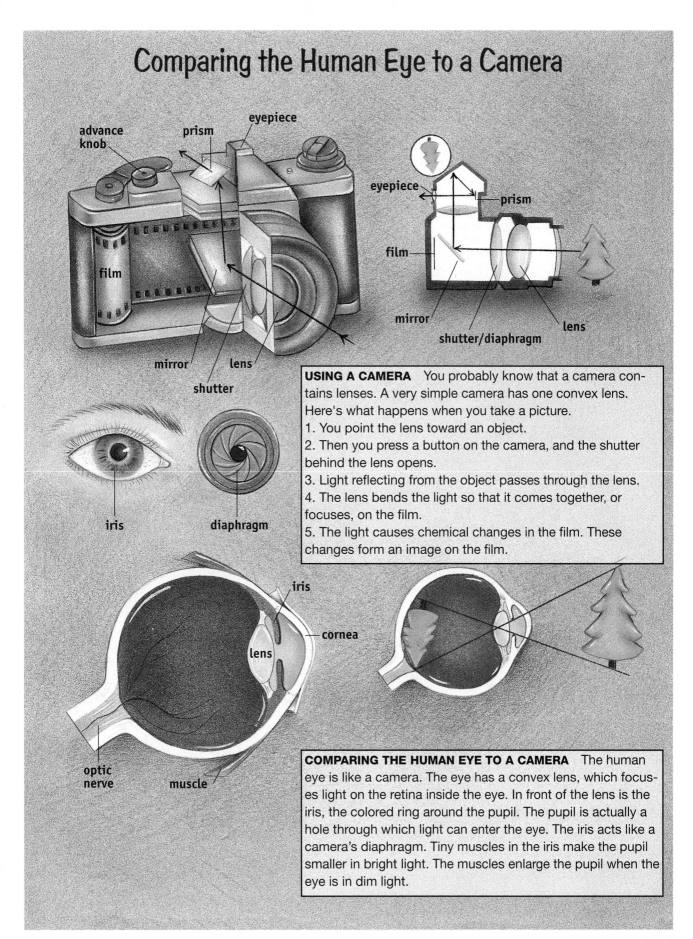

advance knob

prism

eyepiece

eyepiece

prism

film

film

mirror

mirror

shutter/diaphragm

lens

lens

shutter

iris

diaphragm

iris

cornea

lens

optic nerve

muscle

USING A CAMERA You probably know that a camera contains lenses. A very simple camera has one convex lens. Here's what happens when you take a picture.
1. You point the lens toward an object.
2. Then you press a button on the camera, and the shutter behind the lens opens.
3. Light reflecting from the object passes through the lens.
4. The lens bends the light so that it comes together, or focuses, on the film.
5. The light causes chemical changes in the film. These changes form an image on the film.

COMPARING THE HUMAN EYE TO A CAMERA The human eye is like a camera. The eye has a convex lens, which focuses light on the retina inside the eye. In front of the lens is the iris, the colored ring around the pupil. The pupil is actually a hole through which light can enter the eye. The iris acts like a camera's diaphragm. Tiny muscles in the iris make the pupil smaller in bright light. The muscles enlarge the pupil when the eye is in dim light.

F33

It sends nerve impulses to the brain along the optic nerve. The brain then interprets the pictures and figures out what you're seeing.

Another difference between your eyes and a camera is in how the eyes focus. You can focus on objects that are close to you and on objects that are far away, but the eye's lens can't move in and out the way a camera lens does. Instead, the lens of the eye changes shape. When you look at something nearby, muscles in the eye pull on the edges of the lens and make it thinner. When you look at something far away, the muscles relax, and the lens gets thicker again.

Correcting Vision

Many people wear glasses. Nearsighted people see nearby things clearly, but cannot see distant objects clearly. As the drawings below show, the eyes of a nearsighted person focus images in front of the retina. Glasses with concave lenses correct such a condition by spreading out the light rays before they enter the eye. The eye's lens then focuses the light rays on the retina.

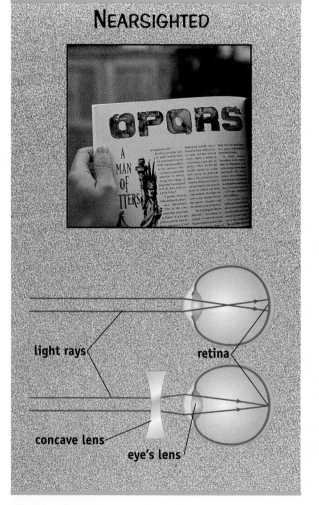

▲ **Correcting nearsightedness**

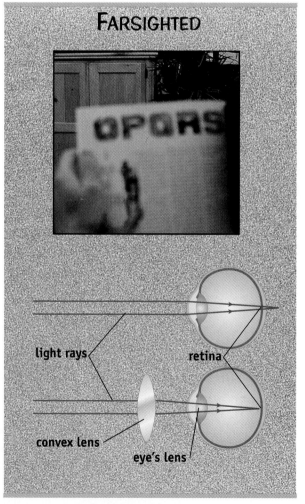

▲ **Correcting farsightedness**

People who are farsighted see far-away objects clearly, but they have trouble seeing nearby things. This condition is corrected with convex lenses, which bring the light rays closer together before they enter the eye. The lens of the eye then properly focuses the light rays on the retina.

Contact Lenses

Many people wear contact lenses instead of eyeglasses. **Contact lenses** are clear, thin lenses that are placed on the eye in front of the cornea. Contact lenses don't contact, or touch, the eye. They stick to a thin layer of tears that covers the cornea.

Like eyeglasses, contact lenses change the path of light. But with contact lenses, concave lenses are used for both nearsighted and farsighted people. Because contact lenses are so close to the eye, they don't need to be thick to bend the light enough to correct a person's vision.

The earliest contact lenses were made of rigid plastic and were often uncomfortable. In 1965, soft contact lenses were invented. These lenses are flexible and more comfortable than the older lenses. Most soft contact lenses must be

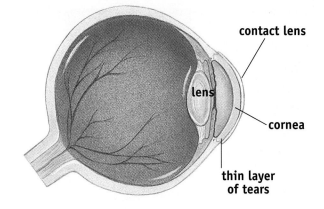

▲ **A contact lens floating on a layer of tears**

removed and cleaned each day. The removal also allows oxygen to reach the living tissue of the cornea. Some soft contact lenses let oxygen pass through, so they can be worn for many days at a time. When they are taken out, they also must be carefully cleaned. ■

INVESTIGATE FURTHER!

EXPERIMENT

To see how the iris responds to the brightness of light, work with a partner. Take turns observing each other's eyes in dim light. Then turn on bright lights or move toward a sunny window. Observe the pupils of your partner's eyes. How did the pupils look in dim light? How did they change in bright light?

INVESTIGATION 1

1. A convex lens projects an image that is upside down. If the image on your retina is upside down, why doesn't the world look upside down to you?

2. Compare and contrast the way light is changed as it moves through convex and concave lenses.

HOW ARE LENSES USED IN TELESCOPES AND MICROSCOPES?

Lenses can be used to show us things too small or too far away to be seen with our unaided eyes. Much of what we know about life on Earth and objects in space is a result of combining lenses and mirrors.

Activity
Telescopic View

Back in the early 1600s, lens makers in Europe began experimenting with lenses. Before long, several lens makers had placed two lenses of different sizes in a tube, forming a telescope. You can build a telescope very much like the ones built hundreds of years ago.

MATERIALS
- scissors
- cardboard tubes
- metric ruler
- tape
- convex lens A, 15 cm focal length
- convex lens B, 5 cm focal length
- modeling clay
- *Science Notebook*

SAFETY
NEVER LOOK DIRECTLY AT THE SUN! Be careful when handling glass lenses.

Procedure

1. Use scissors to cut a cardboard tube into two pieces: one piece 12 cm long, the other piece 15 cm long.

2. In the shorter tube, make a lengthwise cut as shown. Turn the cut edges inward, forming a slightly tapered tube. Tape the cut edges as shown in the drawing on page F37.

lens B   lens A

Step 2

12 cm   15 cm

3. Use modeling clay and tape to attach lens A to one end of the longer tube. Use more clay to attach lens B to one end of the shorter tube.

4. Place the open end of the shorter tube into the open end of the longer tube. You have just made a simple telescope!

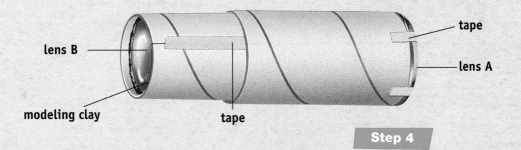

lens B

modeling clay

tape

tape

lens A

Step 4

5. Hold the telescope up to your eye and look through the lens that is in the shorter tube.

6. Use the telescope to **observe** various objects outdoors.

7. Move the shorter tube back and forth inside the longer tube until the image of the object you are observing is clear.

Analyze and Conclude

1. Describe in your *Science Notebook* how the objects you observed looked when viewed through your telescope.

2. Make sketches of how several objects look when viewed directly and when viewed through a telescope.

INVESTIGATE FURTHER!

....

EXPERIMENT

Look in your daily newspaper to find out which planets are visible at this time. Then use your telescope to observe the Moon and these planets.

The Telescope—
From Galileo to Hubble

No one knows for certain who made the first telescope. Evidence suggests that it was probably constructed in Holland in the early 1600s.

Galileo (gal ə lē′ō) Galilei was the first person to use a telescope to study the sky. An Italian scientist who lived from 1554 to 1642, Galileo built his first telescope in 1609. He had been studying the stars and planets for many years and was eager to get a better look. Galileo's telescope magnified by 32

times what he saw. But with the telescope he was able to see mountains and craters on the Moon. When he studied the planet Jupiter through his telescope, he discovered four of its moons.

Galileo's telescope was a **refracting telescope**. As the name suggests, this telescope used lenses that refracted light to make an image. The drawing on the next page shows a refracting telescope that uses two lenses. Light from a faraway object first passes through the objective lens, or lens

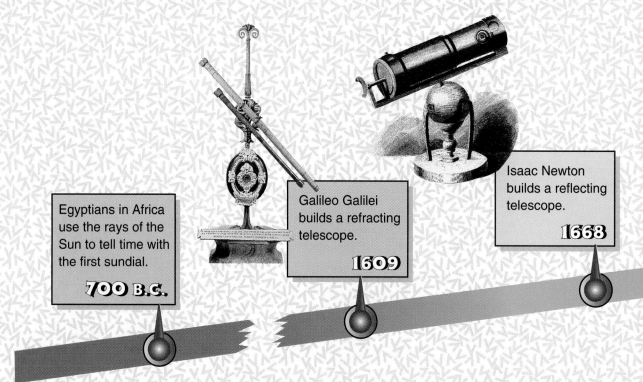

Egyptians in Africa use the rays of the Sun to tell time with the first sundial.

700 B.C.

Galileo Galilei builds a refracting telescope.

1609

Isaac Newton builds a reflecting telescope.

1668

objective lens

eyepiece lens

concave mirror

plane mirror

eyepiece lens

▲ **A simple refracting telescope**

▲ **A simple reflecting telescope**

closer to the object, forming a very small image. Then the eyepiece, or lens nearest the eye, magnifies the first image.

In 1668, Isaac Newton made a reflecting telescope, using a concave mirror. In a **reflecting telescope**, light strikes a mirror and is reflected to a focal point, where an image forms. A small flat mirror is used to reflect this image to a lens that magnifies the image.

The mirror in Newton's telescope had a diameter of only about 3 cm

(1.2 in.). A larger mirror can focus on smaller or more distant objects. The reflecting telescopes used by modern astronomers are much larger than Newton's.

The Hubble Space Telescope, also a reflecting telescope, is in orbit above Earth's atmosphere. The advantage of having a telescope in orbit is that the light from distant objects is not changed by passing through air. The Hubble Space Telescope was named in honor of Edwin P. Hubble. ■

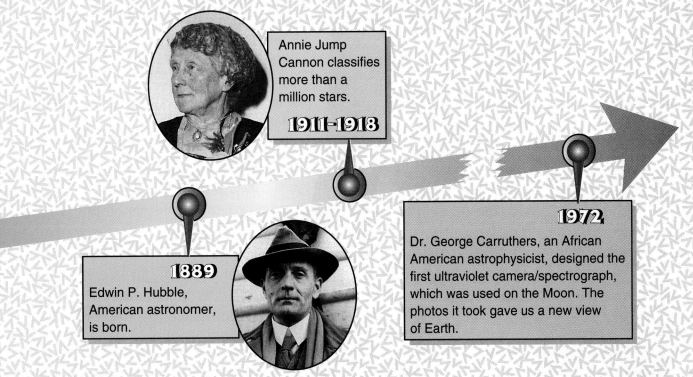

Annie Jump Cannon classifies more than a million stars.
1911-1918

1889
Edwin P. Hubble, American astronomer, is born.

1972
Dr. George Carruthers, an African American astrophysicist, designed the first ultraviolet camera/spectrograph, which was used on the Moon. The photos it took gave us a new view of Earth.

F39

Lyman Spitzer
and His Magnificent Dream

SCIENCE TECHNOLOGY & SOCIETY

In 1946, Lyman Spitzer wrote that a telescope in space could provide the information needed to answer some very difficult questions: How big is the universe? What is the structure of galaxies? What is the nature of the planets?

In 1957 the Soviet Union launched the *Sputnik* satellite. The American space agency, the National Aeronautics and Space Administration (NASA), was started the following year. In the 1960s and 1970s, two observatories carrying telescopes were placed in orbit by NASA. The success of these telescopes in space showed that Spitzer's idea for a large space telescope could work.

▲ **Lyman Spitzer**

In 1977, NASA's space telescope project was approved. In 1990 the telescope, known to the world as the Hubble Space Telescope, was finally placed in orbit.

While it did give scientists some good information, the telescope had problems. The mirror had not been shaped correctly. During a space shuttle mission in December 1993, astronauts successfully repaired the telescope. Since that time, the telescope has taken photographs of Pluto and its moon. It has also found a black hole at the core of a galaxy.

Spitzer's dream has become a reality. The information needed to answer his questions is now being gathered. ■

▼ **The Hubble Space Telescope**

The Microscope

During the 1600s, grinding lenses was a popular hobby. Anton van Leeuwenhoek (än'tôn vän lā'vən-ho͞ok) was a Dutch cloth merchant and lens grinder. From one of the many lenses he ground, he made a **simple microscope**. The photo at right shows a model of this microscope, which had only one lens that was held between two metal plates. The object to be examined was stuck on the end of a pin placed beside the lens. A person using the microscope had to bring it up close to the eye. The lens could magnify objects more than 200 times their normal size.

With his microscope, Leeuwenhoek looked at insect parts, hair, ivory, and droplets of pond water. In the water, he found tiny organisms that could not be seen with only the human eye. He called these organisms *tierken*, which in Dutch means "little animals."

After Leeuwenhoek reported that he had found parasites on fleas, the English poet Jonathan Swift wrote:

So naturalists observe, a flea
Has smaller fleas that on him prey;
And these have smaller still
   to bite em;
And so proceed *ad infinitum*.

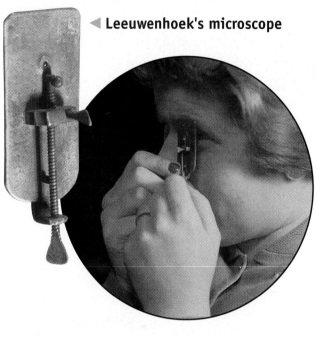

◀ **Leeuwenhoek's microscope**

What do you think he meant by these four lines of poetry?

A few years prior to Leeuwenhoek, Zacharias Janssen had invented a compound microscope. The **compound microscope** uses two convex lenses. A mirror reflects light toward an object that is on a clear glass slide. Light reflecting from the object enters the microscope tube containing the lenses. Light passing through the objective lens forms the first image. Light rays from this image pass through the eyepiece lens, which enlarges the image.

Robert Hooke, an English scientist, studied many objects through a compound microscope that he built. In

1665, Hooke published a book, *Micrographia*, that contained his drawings of the things he had seen. One of the objects he had looked at was cork. Hooke noticed that the cork was made of tiny boxes. He called the boxes *cells*. The cells Hooke saw weren't living. What he saw were the outer parts of the cells that had once been alive.

The compound microscope made it possible for people to see the structures of living things. People saw tiny living things that they had never known about. Scientists have also used microscopes to study organisms that cause diseases. In fact, microscopes have had a far greater impact on human life than most people realize.

Drawings of microscopic organisms from Robert Hooke's book, *Micrographia*. ▼

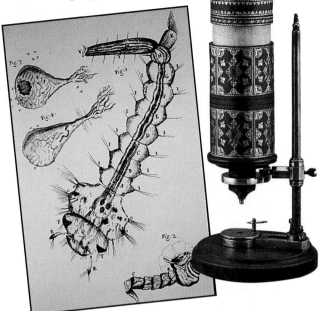

Hooke's compound microscope ▲

SCIENCE IN LITERATURE

EXTREMELY WEIRD MICRO MONSTERS
by Sarah Lovett
John Muir Publications, 1993

Are you ready for the microscopic world? It can be pretty scary! Powerful light microscopes—and even more powerful electron microscopes—can take pictures that make incredibly small creatures look downright monstrous! You can take a look at 22 colorful microscopic portraits in *Extremely Weird Micro Monsters* by Sarah Lovett.

Choose your favorite creatures and then read all about them. Do you get the feeling that microscopes make the world seem much more crowded?

Flu virus seen with this microscope ▼

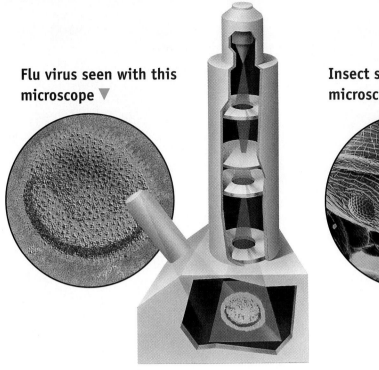

Insect seen with this microscope ▼

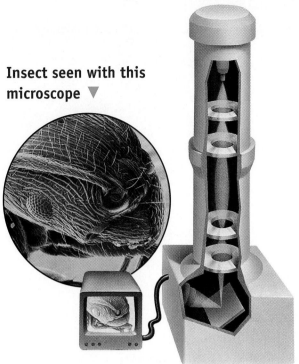

▲ Transmission electron microscope   ▲ Scanning electron microscope

Modern compound light microscopes can magnify as much as 2,000 times. An **electron microscope** can make things appear hundreds of thousands of times bigger than they actually are. The electron microscope uses a beam of electrons instead of a beam of light. In 1935 the first commercial model of an electron microscope became available. Since that time this powerful microscope has been much improved and refined.

There are two kinds of electron microscopes. A transmission electron microscope passes electrons from an electron gun through the object and onto a fluorescent screen. The microscope often displays the object in white against a black background. The flu virus shown here had color added to it.

A scanning electron microscope moves electrons across the object being viewed. Then the electrons enter a collector and produce an enlarged image on what looks like a television screen. This kind of microscope is excellent for showing objects in three dimensions. ■

INVESTIGATION 2

1. One way to study a leaf is to look at very thin slices of the leaf under a compound microscope. Why is it important to view a thin slice and not the whole leaf?

2. How are microscopes and refracting telescopes similar? How are they different?

F43

INVESTIGATION 3

HOW ARE LIGHT AND COLOR RELATED?

Have you ever been at a school show where red or blue lights were shone on the stage? A stage crew probably used filters of different colors. Did the performers and scenery change color, too? How do you think filters cause color changes?

Activity

Circles of Light

You have probably mixed paints of different colors together. Think back to what happened. Do you think the same colors will result when you mix different colors of light? Try this activity and find out.

MATERIALS

- 3 flashlights
- 3 rubber bands
- red, blue, and green cellophane
- *Science Notebook*

Procedure

1. Cover the lens of a flashlight with red cellophane. Fasten the cellophane tightly over the lens with a rubber band.

2. Repeat step 1 with the remaining two flashlights. Cover one flashlight with blue cellophane and cover the other flashlight with green cellophane.

Step 2

F44

3. Darken the room. Direct the light from the flashlight covered with red cellophane onto a white wall or screen. Repeat with each of the other two flashlights.

4. **Observe** the wall and **record** your findings in your *Science Notebook*.

5. **Predict** what will happen when you direct red and green light from the flashlights onto the wall or screen so that the circles of light overlap. Try it. **Record** your observations.

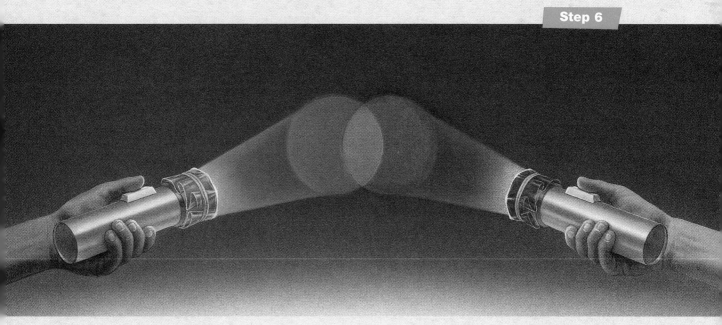

Step 6

6. Repeat step 5, using all the possible combinations of two colors of light. **Record** your results.

7. **Predict** what will happen if you make all three circles of color overlap. Then overlap the circles of color. **Observe** what happens and **record** your results.

Analyze and Conclude

1. Did your predictions of what would happen match what actually happened? If they did not, explain why.

2. What color light results from mixing red and blue light? red and green light? blue and green?

3. What color light results from mixing all three lights?

4. What conclusion can you draw about white light?

INVESTIGATE FURTHER!
....
RESEARCH
Find out about the color filters photographers use on their camera lenses to achieve various effects. What are these filters made of? What are some of the effects of using filters?

Activity
Filtered Light

Why is a red apple red and a green apple green? Can the eye be fooled into seeing another color when an object is red or green?

MATERIALS
- assorted small objects of different colors, including a black object and a white object
- red, green, and blue cellophane for filters
- *Science Notebook*

Procedure

1. Place an assortment of small colored objects on a piece of white paper. In your *Science Notebook*, **record** the name and color of each object.

2. **Predict** how the objects will look if they are seen through filters of different colors. **Discuss** your predictions with other students. Then look through the blue filter at the objects. **Record** your observations of the appearance of the objects.

3. Repeat step 2, using the green filter.

4. Repeat step 2, using the red filter.

5. **Predict** how the objects will look if they are seen through several filters at one time. **Discuss** your predictions. Then repeat step 2, using combinations of the filters. **Record** your observations.

Step 2

Analyze and Conclude

1. How does each filter affect the appearance of objects that are the same color as the filter?

2. How does each filter affect the appearance of objects that are of different colors from the filter?

3. The white light shining on objects contains many colors. Knowing this, **suggest a hypothesis** to explain why most objects seem to have only one color.

4. Use your hypothesis to explain why some objects are black and some are white.

Seeing Color

"Look, a rainbow!" That brilliant, multicolored band arching across the sky usually causes people to stop and stare. You probably know that a rainbow comes from white light. White light is made up of all the colors of the visible spectrum. Sunlight passing through water droplets in the air is refracted by these "natural" prisms, or lenses. The different colors are refracted in different amounts, so the colors spread out and are then reflected off the droplets to your eyes—treating you to a rainbow.

white light

prism

You can make a rainbow by shining light through a prism. When you do this, you separate white light into red, orange, yellow, green, blue, indigo, and violet.

As you saw earlier, the color of visible light is related to its wavelength. Violet light has the shortest wavelength. Red light has the longest wavelength. So your eyes and your brain are really responding to differences in wavelengths of light and interpreting these differences as colors.

The Colors of Objects

When you look at a red apple, what color of light is reaching your eye? You may need to think about this question for a moment. The answer involves knowing what happens to the light that strikes an object.

Most objects are **opaque** (ō pāk′), which means that they do not let light pass through them. Wood, books, and apples are opaque. When light strikes an opaque object, some of the light is absorbed, or taken in, by the object. This light changes to heat in the object, warming it. Some of the light is reflected. If the object is a red apple, red light is reflected and the other colors are absorbed. What color of light is reflected by a green apple? Some objects, including lenses, are **transparent**.

A prism separates white light into a rainbow. ▶

F47

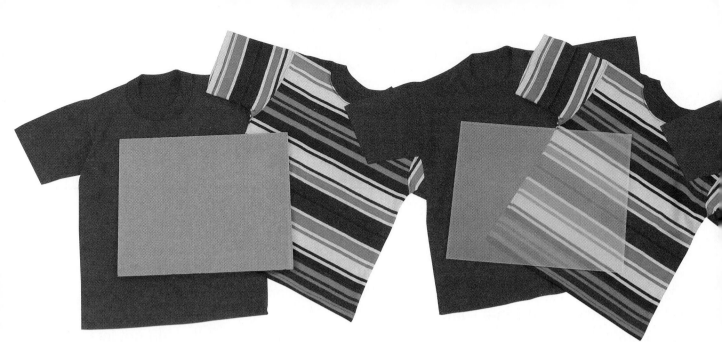

▲ An opaque screen   ▲ A translucent screen

Light passes through them. Transparent matter is said to transmit light. Clear glass and shallow water are transparent. They absorb very little light. They do reflect some light, but most light passes through. In the photos above, which object lets the most light pass through?

Colored glass is partially transparent. It allows only certain colors of light to pass through. Red glass absorbs all colors of light except red. Some red light is reflected, but most passes through the glass. Remember, an object's color is the color that reflects off or passes through the object. It's the color that reaches your eye.

Translucent objects, such as frosted glass and wax paper, let light pass through them. However, the light does not follow straight-line paths through the material. It is scattered in many directions. This makes it impossible for you to see clearly through translucent materials, even though the colors of objects behind the translucent material can be seen.

Making Colors by Adding Light

During a live stage show, colored lights are often used to create special effects. Stage lights have a colored transparent material in front of the bulb. These colored materials, or **filters**, absorb some colors of light and let others pass through. Each kind of filter transmits a different color. The

▲ Examples of color addition, the mixing of light

▲ **A transparent glass**

makes magenta light. Combining blue light and green light makes a blue-green color called cyan (sī´ən). Mixing colored light in this way is called color addition because colored lights are combined, or added together. The "Circles of Light" activity included experiments on color addition.

As the photograph on page F50 shows, shining red, green, and blue light onto the same area of a screen produces white light. These three colors are called primary colors because you can mix them to make other colors.

most common filters used are red, blue, and green. By shining several of these different-colored lights on the same spot, the stage crew can make other colors, or even white light.

Look at the overlapping circles of light on these pages. Mixing red light and green light produces yellow light. Combining red light and blue light

Subtracting Light

Recall how filters absorb some colors of light. Instead of adding light, a filter takes some light away. So filters make light by color subtraction. Opaque materials, including paints and dyes, are color subtractors.

A white object appears white because it reflects all colors of light. A black object, on the other hand, appears black because it absorbs all colors and reflects no light. If you paint a white object red, the object will reflect red light but will absorb other colors.

Suppose you're wearing your favorite red sweater. You know it looks red in a well-lighted room, but what happens under colored light? If you look at your red sweater under red light, the sweater still appears red. But in blue light or green light, the sweater will look black! Remember that the sweater reflects only red light. The sweater cannot reflect blue or green light. Since no red light is reflected, the sweater looks black.

F49

Rose under normal light ▼   **Rose under blue light** ▼

Color subtraction also occurs when filters are combined. A cyan, or blue-green filter, lets blue light and green light pass through while it absorbs red light. Now suppose you put a yellow filter on top of the cyan filter. Which light can pass through both filters?

Only green light can pass through both cyan and yellow filters. A cyan filter lets blue light and green light pass through. A yellow filter lets red light and green light pass through. The only color that can pass through both filters is green. So you would see green light. ■

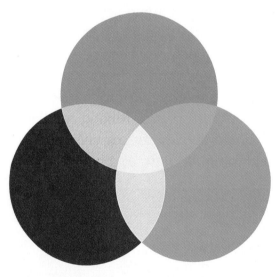

▲ **The effect of overlapping light**

INVESTIGATION 3

1. Sodium-vapor street lamps are used in some cities. The light that comes from the bulbs in these lamps does not contain any red light. How would a red-and-yellow striped shirt look under such light? How would a magenta-and-blue striped shirt look?

2. What colors of light are reflected and absorbed by the different areas of the American flag?

REFLECT & EVALUATE

WORD POWER

filter   lens
compound microscope
concave lens
contact lenses
convex lens
electron microscope
focal point
opaque
reflecting telescope
refracting telescope
retina
simple microscope
translucent
transparent

On Your Own
Write a definition for each term in the list.

With a Partner
Mix up the letters of each term in the list. Provide a clue for each term and challenge your partner to unscramble the terms.

BUILD YOUR PORTFOLIO

Write a story about what things around you would look like if sunlight contained only yellow light.

Analyze Information

Study the drawing. Then use the drawing to describe, in your own words, how light is absorbed, reflected, or transmitted by the objects. Tell if each object is transparent, translucent, or opaque.

Assess Performance

Design and carry out an experiment to see how a convex lens projects an image from a night-light bulb. Vary the distance of the lens from the bulb and note the changes in the image. Compare your results with those of others. What do the results tell you about convex lenses?

Problem Solving

1. The eye is able to focus an image of both nearby and distant objects, but not at the same time. Make sketches showing the lens shape when focused on a nearby object and when focused on a distant object.

2. Microscopes have become more and more powerful. How do you think this has affected the kinds of things scientists study with microscopes?

3. Color film contains three different light-sensitive chemicals. Each one is sensitive to a different color. Which three colors, do you think, does film record? Explain your answer.

CHAPTER 3

PROPERTIES OF SOUND

The community where you live has landmarks that make it special and give it character. Your community also has soundmarks. A soundmark is a unique sound that people recognize and remember. It might be a sound made by a clock, bell, whistle, or horn. What are some soundmarks in your community?

Big Eyes/Big Ears

Bill and Mary Buchen are sonic architects. They design and build interactive sound sculptures, games, and playgrounds. One of their playgrounds is at Public School 23 in the South Bronx area of New York City. Another is at Candlestick Point Recreation Area in San Francisco.

At each playground or playspace, children can explore a variety of instruments, including the wind gamelan, an instrument played by the wind. Another is the sound observatory, a series of stainless steel drums played with the feet.

These playgrounds have equipment that allows children to explore the sounds of their neighborhoods. Big Eyes/Big Ears is an echo chamber 3 m (10 ft) above the children's heads that amplifies and transmits captured sounds to the children on the ground. If the chamber were in your neighborhood, what captured sounds would you hear?

Coming Up

◀ A student explores the sounds
that can be made on steel drums.

WHAT IS SOUND?

Have you ever sat perfectly still and listened to the sound around you? Try it sometime and you may be amazed at what you hear. In this investigation you'll see how sound is produced and how it travels. In the process, you may hear some sweet—and sour— sounds!

Activity

Rubber-Band Banjo

How are sounds produced? Construct a simple banjo and use it to find out.

Procedure

Stretch a rubber band lengthwise over a ruler. Then insert a pencil under the rubber band at each end of the ruler so that the rubber band is lifted away from the surface of the ruler. Pluck the rubber band at any point between the two pencils. **Observe** what happens. **Record** what you see and hear in your *Science Notebook*. Press your finger at different points along the rubber band, plucking it each time. **Describe** the sounds produced.

Analyze and Conclude

1. **Hypothesize** how the rubber band produces sound.

2. How did the sound change when you pressed the rubber band at different points on the ruler?

Activity
Waves and Sound

Sound is a form of energy that travels through different objects and materials. In this activity you'll build a model of the way a sound wave moves.

Procedure

1. Use a piece of string to tie one end of a coil spring to a table leg. Stretch the coil spring and use another piece of string to tie the other end to another table leg. Make sure that the spring is stretched tightly enough so that it doesn't touch the floor.

2. Fold pieces of yarn in half. Starting at one end of the spring, hang a piece of yarn on every tenth coil.

3. **Predict** what will happen to the yarn if you pinch five end coils together and then release them. **Discuss** your prediction with your group. **Record** your prediction in your *Science Notebook*.

4. Pinch together five coils at one end of the spring and quickly release them. **Record** your observations of the coil spring and the yarn.

5. Repeat step 4 several times. **Record** your observations each time.

Step 1

Analyze and Conclude

1. Write a general statement about the way the spring coil behaved when you pinched and then released the five end coils.

2. What evidence did you observe that energy was transferred along the coil?

The Nature of Sound

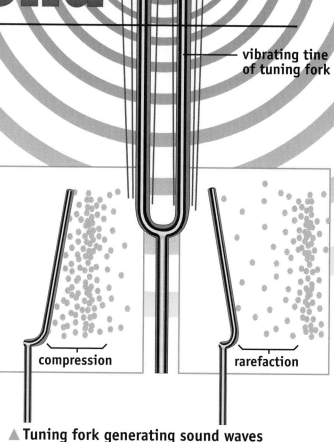

vibrating tine of tuning fork

The melody of a popular song, the roar of the crowd at a basketball game, and the clatter of a jackhammer cutting a hole in a sidewalk all have something in common. They all are produced by vibrations. **Vibrations** (vī brā'shənz) are back-and-forth movements of matter.

If you pluck a stretched rubber band, as suggested in the activity "Rubber-Band Banjo," or if you pluck a guitar string, you can see the rubber band or string vibrate as you hear the sound the vibrations cause. Air carries the vibrations to your eardrums and causes them to vibrate. The vibrations in your ears produce nerve impulses that are carried to your brain. There the impulses are interpreted as sounds.

compression   rarefaction

▲ **Tuning fork generating sound waves**

Sound Waves

Sound is a form of energy that travels through matter as waves. Anything that is in motion has energy, and sound is certainly in motion. If you tap a tuning fork with a rubber hammer, you transfer energy from the moving hammer to the tines of the tuning fork.

Parts of a sound wave ▼

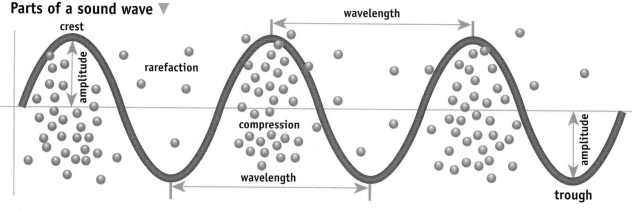

crest
amplitude
rarefaction
wavelength
compression
wavelength
amplitude
trough

The back-and-forth motion of the tines pushing against air particles around them creates sound waves that travel outward from the tuning fork. The region where the particles have been pushed closer together is called a **compression** (kəm presh'ən). Air pressure is greater than usual in this region. The region where there are fewer particles than normal is called a **rarefaction** (rer ə fak'shən). Air pressure is lower than usual in this region. A sound wave is a series of compressions and rarefactions moving outward from the source of a vibration.

A sound wave can be represented as a more familiar up-and-down wave, as shown at the bottom of page F56. In the drawing, the **crests** represent the compressions of a sound wave, or regions of greater air pressure. The **troughs** (trôfs) represent the rarefactions, or regions of lower air pressure.

When a sound wave travels from its source to your ear, the particles that carry the wave do not travel along with the wave. Like the coils of the spring in the activity "Waves and Sound," the particles in air move back and forth. But after the wave passes, they are still in the same general location, much as the coils remained where they were. (Think back to the pieces of yarn in the activity.)

Measuring Sound Waves

The distance from one compression to the next is the **wavelength** of a sound wave. Wavelength depends on the frequency of vibration of the source of the sound. **Frequency** is the number of complete waves produced in a unit of time, such as a second. A high sound is one that has a high frequency. A great many waves are produced each second. A low sound is one that has a low frequency. Fewer waves are produced each second.

The **amplitude** (am'plə tood) of the wave in the drawing represents the difference in air pressure between the

Sound wave of a loud sound, such as a moving freight train ▼

Sound wave of a soft sound, such as a whisper ▼

compressions and the rarefactions. It is a measure of the amount of energy in a sound wave. A loud sound is represented by a sound wave with a large amplitude. A soft sound is represented by a sound wave with a small amplitude.

Quality of Sound—Timbre

The drawing on page F56 of the up-and-down sound wave is simple. It represents a pure sound made by a tuning fork. A tuning fork may produce a note, or tone, with a single frequency and a simple wave pattern. But most of the sounds you hear, such as music on the radio and TV, are very complex. They are made up of several waves, which combine to form complex sounds.

Whether produced by a vibrating string or a vibrating air column, every musical tone is mixed with other, fainter tones known as **overtones**. The blending of these tones produces a unique quality that makes the sounds of different instruments, or the voices of different people, unique. Even if two instruments are producing the same note, you can tell that one sound comes from a flute, for example, and one comes from a trumpet. The quality of a musical tone is called its **timbre** (tim′bər). Musicians often use words such as *mellow, bright,* or *tinny* to describe differences in the timbre of sounds.

Noise

You may disagree with your family and friends about what is "good" music. But you'll probably agree that the tones and overtones of music combine in very

SCIENCE IN LITERATURE

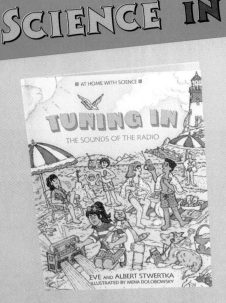

TUNING IN:
THE SOUNDS OF THE RADIO
by Eve and Albert Stwertka
Julian Messner, 1993

Suppose you want to hear the sounds made by musicians who are far away. Since sound waves can't be heard over very long distances, you'll need a little technical help. Radios can help you hear a concert that you can't attend in person.

Find out how sound waves are changed to radio waves by reading pages 18–25 in *Tuning In: The Sounds of the Radio* by Eve and Albert Stwertka. Then make a chart that summarizes the steps taken in broadcasting a radio show.

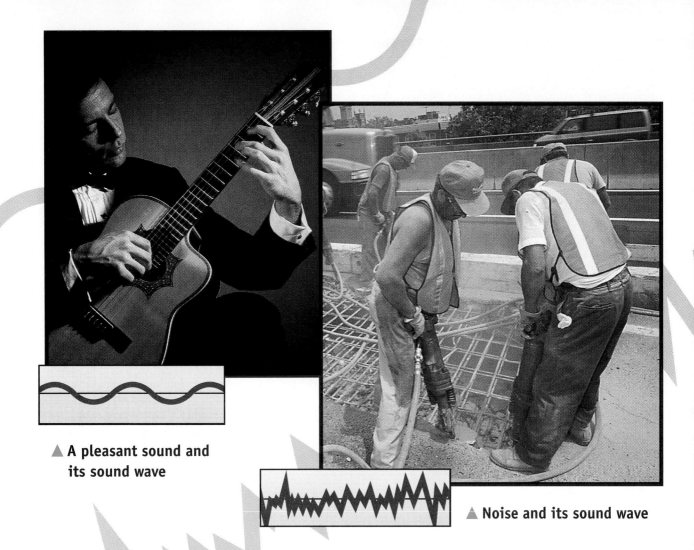

▲ A pleasant sound and its sound wave

▲ Noise and its sound wave

pleasant ways. Many sources of sound produce combinations of waves that are unpleasant. You would probably agree that the sounds of jackhammers, squealing brakes, or a tray of dishes being dropped are unpleasant. Unpleasant sounds, or noises, have irregular sound waves. From the drawings below the photographs, you can see that the wave pattern of music is smooth and forms a repeating pattern. The wave pattern of noise is irregular. ■

INVESTIGATION 1

1. Describe three main characteristics of a sound.

2. Make sketches of sound waves to represent
(a) a shout and a whisper,
(b) a bird's chirp and a lion's roar, and
(c) music and noise.

HOW DOES MATTER AFFECT HOW SOUND TRAVELS?

INVESTIGATION 2

Have you ever gone swimming and noticed that sounds are different under water? As you experiment with sound, you'll find out how the material through which sound passes affects the properties of sound.

Activity
Ear to the Wall

Press your ear to a wall. What can you hear?
Does sound travel better through some materials
than through others?

Procedure

Tap your fingernails on your desk. Then place your ear on your desktop. Again, tap your fingernails. **Compare** the two tapping sounds. **Record** your observations in your *Science Notebook*. Next, place an empty plastic cup upside down on the desk. Press your ear against the bottom of the cup. Tap lightly on the cup. Repeat, using an empty aluminum can. **Discuss** your observations with your group. **Record** your findings.

Analyze and Conclude

1. What can you **infer** about how well sound travels through wood, plastic, and metal?

2. Why can you often hear a conversation in another room when you press your ear to the wall?

Activity

A String Phone

You might have made string telephones when you were younger. In this activity you'll figure out how they work.

MATERIALS
- 2 paper cups
- sharpened pencil
- 6 m of strong string
- 2 paper clips
- *Science Notebook*

Procedure

1. Use a pencil to punch a hole in the center of the bottom of two paper cups.

2. Put one end of a piece of string through the hole in one cup and tie the string around a paper clip on the inside of the cup.

3. Repeat step 2 with the other end of the string and the other cup.

4. Find a quiet area where you and a partner can stand far enough apart so that the string is stretched tightly.

5. Have your partner say something quietly. **Observe** how well you can hear what your partner says.

6. Now hold the cup up to your ear. Have your partner quietly say something into the other cup. **Record** your observations in your *Science Notebook*.

7. While your partner is speaking into the cup, pinch the string about 30 cm from your end. Listen carefully to the sound produced. **Record** your observations.

8. Reverse roles with your partner and repeat steps 5 through 7.

Step 2

Analyze and Conclude

1. **Compare** how well you could hear your partner with and without the string phone.

2. Through what did the sound travel to reach your ear each time? What happened when you pinched the string?

3. **Hypothesize** how you could improve this telephone. **Test your hypothesis**.

INVESTIGATE FURTHER!

RESEARCH

Naval vessels often used air tubes to communicate from one part of a ship to another part. What are the advantages of an air-tube system? How do modern intercom systems work?

RESOURCE

When Sound Travels and
When It Doesn't

The pitcher winds up and then releases the ball. The batter swings, and the bat connects with the ball right over home plate. But you don't hear the bat hit the ball until about a second later. Why does this happen?

Sound waves travel much more slowly than light waves do. The speed of sound in air is about 346 m/s (1,125 ft/s). The speed of light is about 300 million m/s (985 million ft/s)—almost 900,000 times greater than the speed of sound!

The speed of sound varies with the material through which it moves. The

table on page F63 compares the speed of sound in several different materials. Recall in the activity "Ear to the Wall" that the sound of your fingers tapping on the desk was much louder when you placed your ear directly on the desktop. Sound travels faster through wood than it does through air. The closely packed particles in the wooden desk are springy and transmit the sound more quickly than do the particles in air. Less sound energy is changed to other forms of energy in the wood. So the sound of your fingers tapping is louder.

The speed of sound also varies with the temperature of the material through which the sound moves. From the table, compare the speed of sound in air at 0°C and at 25°C. Particles of matter move faster at higher temperatures than at lower temperatures. Why does this difference affect the rate at which

◀ **Why don't you *hear* the bat hit the ball at the same time that you *see* it?**

THE SPEED OF SOUND IN DIFFERENT MATERIALS	
Material	**Speed (m/s)**
Air at 0°C	331
Air at 20°C	343
Air at 25°C	346
Water at 25°C	1,498
Sea water at 25°C	1,531
Copper	3,100
Brick	3,650
Glass	4,540
Steel	5,200

The drawings below show that sound waves cannot travel through a vacuum. If you put a ringing alarm clock inside a jar filled with air, you'll hear the alarm going off. Then if you slowly pump air from the jar, you'll find that the sound gets fainter and fainter until you can no longer hear it. So the girl in the drawing does not hear the ringing clock. ■

▲ Sound waves travel through air.

sound travels? As the temperature rises, particles take less time to collide with one another. As a result, they pass along the wave energy more quickly.

Unlike light waves, sound waves can travel only when there is matter to carry them. You can see the light from the Sun because it travels through the vacuum of space. But you don't hear the roaring nuclear explosions that are the source of the Sun's energy. You can't hear them because sound waves require matter for their transmission.

▲ Sound cannot travel through a vacuum.

INVESTIGATION 2

1. Explain how the matter through which sound travels affects the sound. Give a specific example to support your explanation.

2. After lunch you put your head down on your desk to rest. You hear very loud footsteps that you hadn't noticed before. Why are the footsteps so loud now?

HOW DO HIGH SOUNDS DIFFER FROM LOW SOUNDS?

When your best friend calls you on the telephone, you know his or her voice right away. You can also tell the difference between a guitar and a trumpet. What makes sounds different? How can you tell one sound from another?

Activity

Highs and Lows

The pitch of a sound is its highness or lowness. What are some ways you can vary pitch?

MATERIALS

- 3 identical small-necked plastic bottles
- water
- *Science Notebook*

SAFETY

Clean up any spills immediately.

Procedure

Get three identical bottles. Leave one bottle empty, fill a second halfway with water, and fill the third almost to the top with water. **Predict** what will happen if you blow across the top of each bottle. **Discuss** your prediction with your group. Then blow across the top of each bottle until you hear a clear tone from it. **Infer** why there were differences between the tones. **Record** your observations in your *Science Notebook*.

Analyze and Conclude

1. How did the sounds in the three bottles compare? How did the quantity of water affect the pitch?

2. **Infer** what was vibrating—the water, the air, or the bottle. Explain your inference.

3. **Hypothesize** about what causes the pitch of a sound to vary.

Activity
Changing Pitch

In this activity you'll explore ways to change the pitch of a vibrating rubber band. What do you think some of the ways might be?

MATERIALS
- goggles
- 3 rubber bands (1 thin, 1 medium, 1 thick)
- cardboard box
- small wooden dowel, 10 cm long
- *Science Notebook*

SAFETY //////
Wear goggles when working with rubber bands.

Procedure

1. Stretch three rubber bands lengthwise over a box as shown in the picture.

2. **Predict** how the pitch of each of the three rubber bands, when plucked, will differ. **Discuss** your predictions with your group.

3. Pluck each rubber band and listen to the pitch. **Record** your observations in your *Science Notebook*.

4. Select one of the rubber bands and twist a dowel near one end of the rubber band to tighten it. Pluck the rubber band and **record** your observations.

5. Repeat step 4 three times, each time turning the dowel a little bit more. **Record** your observations.

6. Repeat steps 4 and 5 with each of the other rubber bands. **Record** your observations.

Step 1

Analyze and Conclude

1. How is the thickness of a rubber band related to the pitch of the sound it produces when plucked?

2. **Compare** the sounds produced by the rubber bands in steps 3 and 4. What can you conclude about any differences?

3. What did you do to the rubber band when you twisted the dowel? How did this affect the pitch of the sound produced when it was plucked?

4. Imagine that the rubber bands are strings on a guitar. What general statements can you make about the pitches of sounds produced by guitar strings?

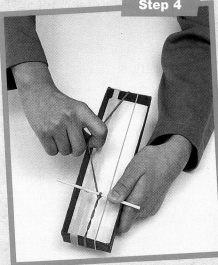

Step 4

Wind Instruments
Around the World

In Japan, it's called a *fuye* (foo'yä); in South Africa it's known as the *naka ya lethlake* (nä'kä yä le-lä'kä); in China, the *ti-tzu* (di dzoo). What is it? All of these words describe the same thing—the musical instrument you know as the flute. Wind instruments in different parts of the world vary in shape and sound. But they are all alike in one way—they depend on a vibrating column of air to produce sound.

The pitch made by the vibrating air depends on the length of the air column, as you observed in the activity on page F64. A shorter column produces a sound with a higher pitch; a longer column produces a lower pitch.

Reed Instruments

The orchestral clarinet uses a reed to produce sounds. A reed is a short, thin piece of wood attached to the mouthpiece. When you blow into the mouthpiece, the reed vibrates, and this vibration causes the column of air inside the clarinet to vibrate. The mouthpiece is attached to a cylindrical tube with holes in it. Covering and uncovering the holes changes the length of the column of air, thereby changing the note that is played. The sound comes out the

bell at the base of the tube.

Compare the orchestral clarinet with the zummara (zoo mä'rə), shown below. The zummara, an instrument played with a reed, has two joined pipes. Made of cane, the zummara has twelve holes, six in each pipe. It is played in Tunisia, a country in northern Africa.

Brass Instruments

You have seen that a wind instrument such as the clarinet uses a reed to make the air vibrate. Brass instruments such as the trumpet and the trombone have no reeds. The player's lips vibrate against the mouthpiece, causing the air in the instrument to vibrate.

Orchestral clarinet ▶

Zummara, a double-pipe reed instrument from Tunisia

The orchestral trumpet uses valves to control the length of the air column and to control the pitch of the sound. The trombone has a slide that changes the length of the air column. In some parts of the world, musicians play trumpets that do not use valves. Instead, the trumpeters use only the vibration of the their lips to change the pitch. Such an instrument is the neku, shown below.

Kinds of Flutes

Flutes also lack reeds. A narrow opening cut in the tube produces sound when air passes over it or through it. In an orchestral flute, this opening is on the side of a long, thin tube. The multiple flute has more than one pipe. This *dvojnice* (dvoi'nē tsə) has a twin pipe carved from a block of wood. Like the orchestral flute, this flute has a mouthpiece and finger holes. However, it does not have keys, and the air is blown in from the top rather than from the side.

Wind instruments from around the world look and sound different. A flutist living in the United States might not be familiar with an African flute. However, people from any country can enjoy the music from these instruments. ■

UNIT PROJECT LINK

Instruments and other devices are used to create music and sound effects in shows. Work with your team to plan a show based on a folk tale, using the puppets from the puppet show in Chapter 2. After you decide which folk tale you'll use, try telling the tale from a different point of view. Plan the sound effects that you will need. You may even want to build your own instruments and sound-effects devices. Add lighting, using the cellophane-covered flashlights. When your plans are complete, begin your rehearsals.

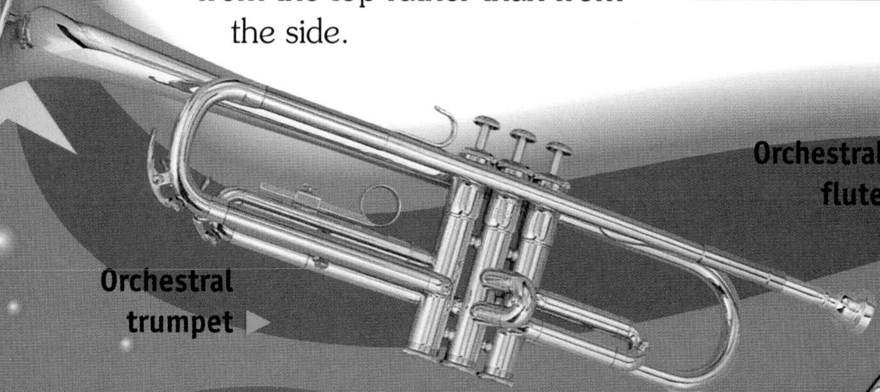

Orchestral flute ▶

Orchestral trumpet ▶

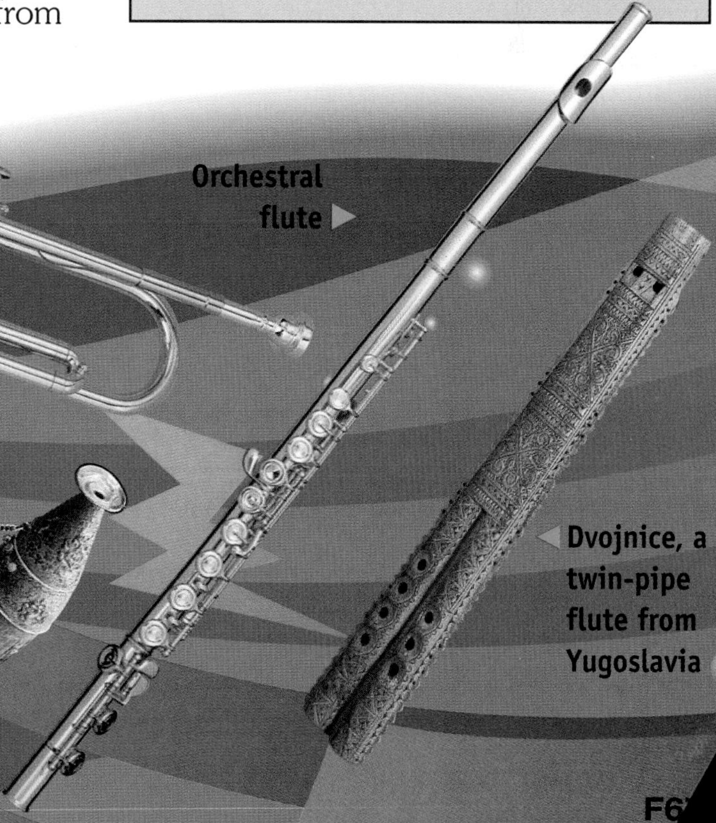

▶ Dvojnice, a twin-pipe flute from Yugoslavia

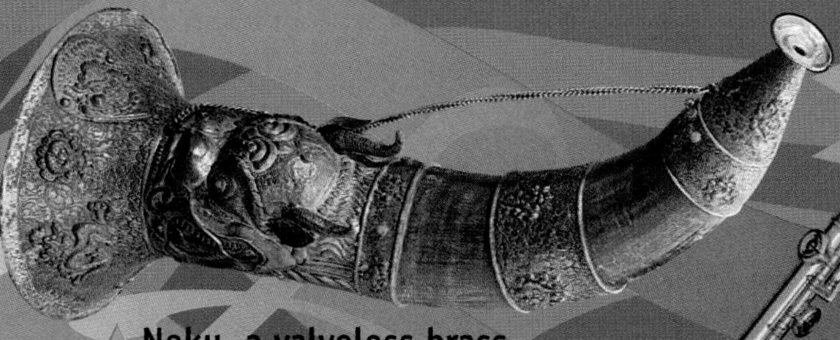

△ Neku, a valveless brass instrument from Nepal

Pitch

Singing the national anthem is not easy for many people, especially when it comes to hitting the high notes. But a good singer can sing the notes having the highest and lowest pitches. **Pitch** is the highness or lowness of sound. It is related to the frequency of the sound waves produced. The frequency of a sound wave is the number of waves passing a location, such as your eardrum, each second. High-pitched sounds produce many sound waves per second and so have a high frequency. Low-pitched sounds produce fewer sound waves per second and so have a lower frequency.

The frequency of a sound wave is measured in a unit called the **hertz** (Hz), or cycles per second. Humans have a certain range of frequencies that they can hear and a range that they can produce, as shown in the graph below. Also shown is what certain other animals can hear and produce. People can hear sounds as low as 20 Hz and as high as 20,000 Hz. How does this compare with what bats can hear and produce?

Ranges of frequencies heard and produced by certain animals and humans ▼

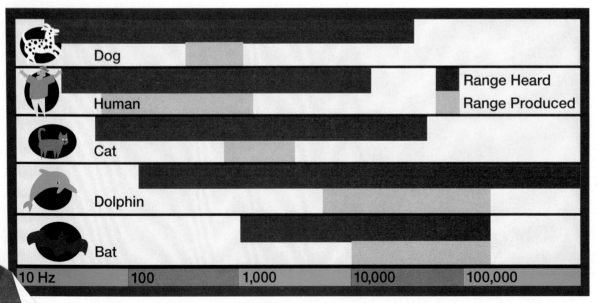

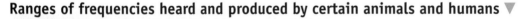

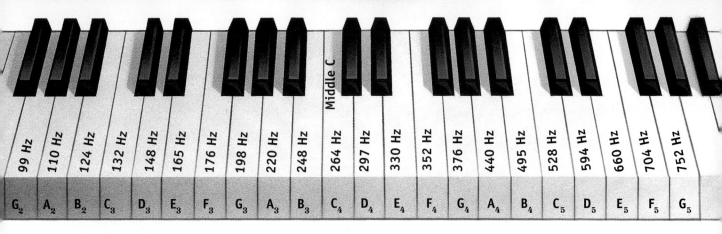

| G₂ | A₂ | B₂ | C₃ | D₃ | E₃ | F₃ | G₃ | A₃ | B₃ | C₄ | D₄ | E₄ | F₄ | G₄ | A₄ | B₄ | C₅ | D₅ | E₅ | F₅ | G₅ |

The frequencies (top to bottom): 99 Hz, 110 Hz, 124 Hz, 132 Hz, 148 Hz, 165 Hz, 176 Hz, 198 Hz, 220 Hz, 248 Hz, 264 Hz (Middle C), 297 Hz, 330 Hz, 352 Hz, 376 Hz, 440 Hz, 495 Hz, 528 Hz, 594 Hz, 660 Hz, 704 Hz, 752 Hz

▲ The frequency of notes on a piano keyboard. Middle C, which has a frequency of 264 Hz, is in the center of the keyboard.

Pitch and Music

Do you play the piano, organ, or electric keyboard? If you do, you know that the keyboard is divided into octaves. Each series of eight notes makes up an **octave** (äk′tiv). The keyboard above shows the frequencies of notes of several octaves. Notice that middle C, which has a frequency of 264 Hz, is written as C_4. The note that is one octave below middle C is another C, written C_3. The note C that is one octave above middle C is written C_5. A similar method is used to show octaves for other notes.

Look at the frequencies of C_3, C_4, and C_5. Note how the frequencies are related. Each time you go up an octave, the frequency of the note doubles. How might this explain why we hear all these notes as C? Is this pattern also true of other notes that are one or two octaves apart, such as E_3 and E_4 or G_3 and G_4? Check the frequencies of the notes on the keyboard to find out.

The graph below shows the frequency range for a number of musical instruments and for human voices. In general, men have longer, thicker vocal cords than women. As a result, men find it

Range of frequencies produced by various instruments and the human voice ▼

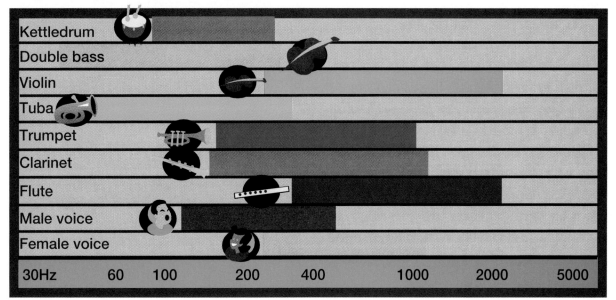

| | Kettledrum | Double bass | Violin | Tuba | Trumpet | Clarinet | Flute | Male voice | Female voice |

Scale: 30Hz, 60, 100, 200, 400, 1000, 2000, 5000

1 When the guitarist strums the full length of a string, she produces a low note.

2 When she presses her finger on a string, she shortens it, and produces a higher note.

easier to sing notes with lower pitches. Women can more easily sing notes of higher pitches. Because the vocal cords of children are shorter than those of adults, children tend to speak and sing at higher pitches than adults.

Musical Highs and Lows

If you've ever played a guitar, you know that the thicker strings produce the lower notes, and the thinner strings produce the higher notes. The guitar player changes the length of a string by holding the string down against the frets, the bars on the guitar neck. When a string is held against a fret, the part of the string that vibrates is shorter, so the pitch is higher. At the top of the guitar are the pegs that change the tension on the strings. If a string is tightened, the pitch gets higher. If the string is loosened, the pitch gets lower. How does this compare with what you observed in the activity on page F65?

The pitch of the sounds produced by wind instruments depends on the length of the vibrating column of air. The shorter the column, the greater the frequency of vibration and the higher the pitch. As the graph on page F69 shows, the frequency ranges of instruments differ.

Controlling Loudness

The amplitude of the sound waves produced by musical instruments is heard as loudness. For stringed instruments, the loudness depends on how a string is plucked or bowed. The harder you pluck or bow the string, the louder the sound. For wind instruments, the harder the musician blows, the louder the sound. For percussion instruments, such as drums and cymbals, the loudness depends on how forcefully the instruments are struck. ■

INVESTIGATE FURTHER!

EXPERIMENT

Place a plastic ruler on a table, with about half the ruler extending beyond the edge of the table. Hold the ruler firmly on the table top. Use your free hand to "pluck" the free end of the ruler. Note the rate of vibration and the pitch of the sound you hear. Think of a way to change the pitch of the sound produced by plucking the ruler. Discuss this idea with other students and then try it out.

Synthesizing Sound

HOW IT Works

A **sound synthesizer** is an electronic device that can produce a wide variety of sounds. The first electronic sound synthesizer was developed by Harry Olson and Herbert Belar at Radio Corporation of America (RCA) in 1955. Olson and Belar built the synthesizer to carry out research on the properties of sound. But a number of composers recognized the great potential for sound synthesizers to produce real music.

Music Synthesizers

Today synthesized music is produced using a keyboard or a sound bank that creates specific groups of sound waves. Synthesizers can produce sounds that resemble many traditional instruments, such as pianos and flutes, and they can also combine tones to form new sounds. Some synthesizers can also produce special effects, including echoes and reverberations.

A synthesizer can produce the sounds of every known musical instrument fairly well. So it can sometimes be used to replace an orchestra, and it has become a popular means of providing music for radio, television, and movies.

Music synthesizer ▶

Speech Synthesizers

Did you ever call directory assistance for a telephone number and hear a robot-like voice? That was synthesized speech! Synthesized speech has many uses. It can provide instructions to children on how to use a computer. It can alert pilots, astronauts, and drivers about conditions that may need their attention. A speech synthesizer can be used by people with various kinds of disabilities.

How does a speech synthesizer work? It stores sounds that are later combined to produce words and sentences that sound like those spoken by a human voice. Most speech synthesizers use the basic sounds of a language such as English. Each of the sounds, when spoken into a microphone,

▲ **Simulated speech at the supermarket**

produces a distinct electric current that can be stored in a computer as part of a magnetic pattern. A set of rules, also stored, is used to put the sounds back together. Following these rules, the computer can produce syllables, words, and sentences. The speech synthesizer can then produce the sounds of a human voice.

When you hear a speech synthesizer, you can usually tell that it is not a real person speaking. But the computer programs of synthesizers are improving, and the voices are becoming more humanlike in quality.

Recognizing Voices

The sound waves that form when people speak can be changed to electrical pulses by a microphone. Some computers have been successfully programmed to respond to the electrical signals produced by voice commands. Instead of typing commands, a person can ask the computer to bring up a certain file. For example, with some telephone systems, you can just say someone's name into the phone, and the system finds that person's number in your directory. You don't even have to dial! ■

The boy is learning to use a speech synthesizer. ▼

━━━━━━━━━━━ **INVESTIGATION 3** ━━━━━━━━━━━

THINK IT WRITE IT

1. Explain what causes a high sound to differ from a low sound. Give examples to support your answer.

2. A piccolo is an instrument that looks like a short flute. Would you expect a piccolo to produce higher or lower sounds than a flute? Explain your answer.

F72

REFLECT & EVALUATE

WORD POWER

amplitude
compression
crest
frequency
hertz (Hz)
octave
overtone
wavelength

pitch
rarefaction
sound
sound
synthesizer
timbre
trough
vibration

On Your Own
Review the terms in the list. Then use as many terms as you can in a paragraph about sound.

With a Partner
Mix up the letters of each term in the list. Provide a clue for each term and challenge your partner to unscramble the terms.

Make a graph of the frequencies of the notes of one octave of a musical scale. Make a second graph showing a different octave. How do the patterns of the two octaves compare?

Analyze Information
Study the photograph of the recorder, a simple wind instrument. Then use the photograph to explain how the recorder produces the highest pitch and the lowest pitch.

Assess Performance
Can you make a glass xylophone? Get several drinking glasses of the same size. Put different amounts of water in the glasses. Adjust the amounts until you can play a song by tapping the glasses with a pencil. How does the amount of water in a glass affect the pitch of the sound?

Problem Solving

1. Why would a motorboat sound closer when you're underwater than it actually is when you come to the surface?

2. The keys of a piano are attached to strings. Imagine that you are looking inside a grand piano. Compare the appearance of the strings that produce low notes with that of the strings that produce high notes.

3. In many science-fiction movies, a *whooshing* sound is heard as a spacecraft moves by. The spacecraft and the sound are the products of special effects. Imagine you are in a spacecraft and another flies by. Explain whether you would—or would not—hear a sound.

F73

CHAPTER 4

HEARING AND RECORDING SOUND

Some of the things that people enjoy most in life are sounds. We hear a special person's voice, the laughter of a child, our favorite music. All these are possible because of the existence of sound.

In Your Ear

There are about 28 million Americans who have some type of hearing impairment that could be helped by the use of a hearing aid. But only one in four of these people actually gets one. Many people simply don't like the looks of the traditional hearing aid that rests in the cup of the outer ear. Now scientists, led by electrical engineer Henri Garcia, have developed the first "invisible" hearing aid. It consists of a tiny cylinder about .64 cm (.25 in) wide and 1.3 cm (.5 in) long.

This hearing aid is so small that it can be planted inside the ear canal, almost touching the eardrum, where no one can see it. It is crafted from spongy, flexible material. This design allows it to fit comfortably inside the ear while protecting the delicate electronic parts of the device itself.

A hearing aid makes sound louder. In what other ways can sound be changed or controlled?

Coming Up

◀ Henri Garcia holds the technology award he received for inventing the "invisible" hearing aid. The tiny device fits into the ear canal, as shown.

HOW CAN YOU CONTROL SOUND?

Have you ever been to a rock concert? If you have, you know how loud sounds can be made. People are often controlling sound—making it louder, softer, higher, or lower. In this investigation you will explore some of the ways sound can be controlled.

Activity
Directing Sound

Outdoors, bands sometimes play in front of a curved band shell. How does a band shell control sound?

Procedure

With your class, go to an open area outdoors. Have one student stand about 50 m away, face the class, and make an announcement, such as "The football team will practice at 3 P.M." **Record** how well you heard him or her. Next have the student cup both hands around his or her mouth and repeat the announcement at the same volume. **Record** how well you heard the announcement.

Finally, have the student roll a piece of construction paper into a megaphone, or cone shape. Have the student place the megaphone up to his or her mouth and again make the announcement. **Record** how the sound of the student's voice compares to the two other times he or she spoke.

Analyze and Conclude

1. When could you best hear the student speak? Why?

2. Where are megaphones used? What is their purpose?

3. How are a megaphone and a band shell alike?

Activity
Muffling Sound

Have you ever been kept awake by the sound of a ticking clock or a dripping faucet? Can you control how far a sound carries?

MATERIALS

- small empty cardboard box with top removed
- wind-up alarm clock with loud ticking sound
- meterstick
- sound-absorbing materials (cloth, cotton, bubble packing, shredded newspaper, plastic-foam "peanuts")
- *Science Notebook*

Procedure

1. Place a small cardboard box on its side with the opening toward you. Place a ticking clock inside the box.

2. Walk away from the box in a straight line until you can no longer hear the clock ticking. **Measure** this distance with a meterstick. **Record** the distance in your *Science Notebook*.

3. With the alarm clock still in place, fill the box with one of the sound-absorbing materials. **Predict** how far you will be from the box when you will no longer be able to hear the clock ticking. Repeat step 2.

Step 3

4. Repeat step 3, using a different material. **Predict** the sound-absorbing quality of each material. Continue until all the materials are used.

5. Make a list of all the materials, rating them from best to worst. (*Best* means "best at muffling sound.") **Compare** your results with those of other groups in your class.

Analyze and Conclude

1. Do some materials muffle sound better than others? **Give evidence** to support your answer.

2. Which of the materials muffled sound best? What did the best mufflers have in common?

3. Would the addition of more of the same material muffle sound better? **Design an experiment** to find out.

4. Did all the students in your class have the same results with the materials they tested? Account for any differences in the results.

Turn Up the Sound

TURN DOWN THAT RADIO!

"Turn down that radio!" "Could you please turn up the TV a little?" What are you changing when you turn the radio "down" or the TV "up"? You are changing the volume, or loudness of the sound. **Volume** describes how loud—or soft—a sound is. It is related to the **intensity** of the sound, which is a measure of the energy of a sound wave. Recall from Chapter 3 that if you make a drawing of a sound wave, a loud sound would have a large amplitude. A soft sound would have a small amplitude.

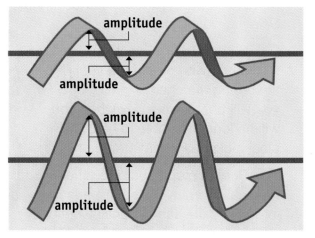

Sound wave of a soft sound (*top*); sound wave of a loud sound (*bottom*)

Sounds vary in intensity, or volume. The intensity of sound is expressed in decibels (dB). ▼

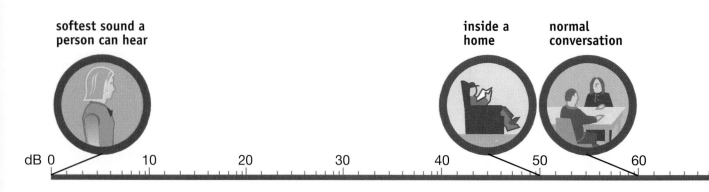

softest sound a person can hear

inside a home

normal conversation

dB 0   10   20   30   40   50   60

Measuring Volume

The unit used to measure sound intensity, or volume, is the **decibel** (des′ə bəl). A sound that most people can just barely hear has an intensity of 0 decibels, or 0 dB.

The table on this page lists various common sounds and their intensity, or volume, in decibels. The sound of normal breathing or rustling leaves, which has an intensity of 10 dB, is 10 times as loud as a sound that a person can just barely hear—0 dB. A 20-dB sound is 100 times as loud as a 0-dB sound and 10 times as loud as a 10-dB sound. Every increase of 10 decibels means the intensity of the sound has increased by a factor of 10.

Of course, whether a sound is loud enough to disturb you depends on other factors. The sound of a rustling newspaper is 10 times as loud as the sound of a whisper, but a whisper may disturb you if you're trying to study. The sound of street traffic is 1,000 times as loud as a rustling newspaper, but you may ignore it if you're playing ball on the playground. Also, devices such as megaphones, which direct sound toward you, can make sounds seem louder than they actually are.

A sound of 120 dB is loud enough to cause pain in the ears. Such sound is 1 billion times as loud as the 30-dB sound of a rustling newspaper. Where might you hear a sound this loud?

Source Sounds	Intensity (dB)
Barely audible	0
Breathing	10
Whispers	20
Rustling newspaper	30
Quiet conversation	40
Normal conversation	60
Street traffic	70
Rush hour traffic	90
Subway (near)	100
Thunder (near)	110
Loud rock music	120
Jet airplane (near)	140
Rocket engine (near)	180

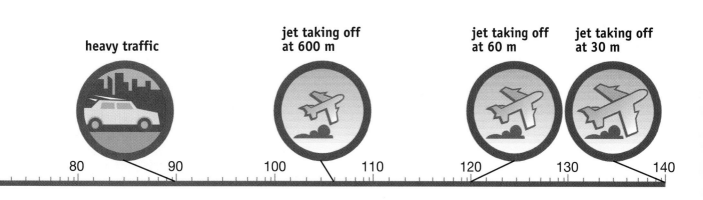

heavy traffic • jet taking off at 600 m • jet taking off at 60 m • jet taking off at 30 m

80 90 100 110 120 130 140

Noise Pollution

The growth of cities and technology has led to sounds and sound volumes that were unknown until recent centuries. Studies have shown that exposure to loud noise or loud music can damage a person's hearing. Besides causing damage to the ear itself, noise can cause stress-related disorders such as hives, ulcers, or high blood pressure. The occurrence of damaging sound in the environment even has a name— **noise pollution**!

An understanding of the properties of sound can help you reduce noise pollution. Like light, sound is absorbed by some materials and reflected by others. Materials that are hard, such as concrete or brick, reflect most of the sound that reaches them. Highway engineers

▲ **In a recording studio a complex control panel allows the sound engineers to control sounds produced by the recording artists.**

SCIENCE IN LITERATURE

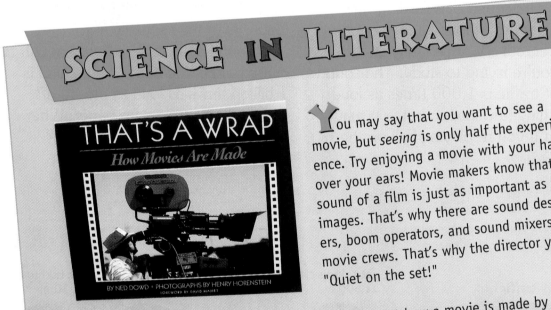

THAT'S A WRAP
How Movies Are Made

BY NED DOWD • PHOTOGRAPHS BY HENRY HORENSTEIN
FOREWORD BY DAVID MAMET

**THAT'S A WRAP:
HOW MOVIES ARE MADE**
by Ned Dowd
Books for Young Readers,
Simon & Schuster, 1991

You may say that you want to see a movie, but *seeing* is only half the experience. Try enjoying a movie with your hands over your ears! Movie makers know that the sound of a film is just as important as its images. That's why there are sound designers, boom operators, and sound mixers on movie crews. That's why the director yells, "Quiet on the set!"

Find out how a movie is made by reading *That's a Wrap: How Movies Are Made* by Ned Dowd. You'll learn how the stunts and special effects are recorded. From a whispered secret to an explosion, sounds make movies thrilling.

F80

take advantage of this property by building wooden or concrete barriers between highways and surrounding homes. These barriers help reduce noise by reflecting it.

Materials that are soft, such as cloth, plastic foam, and acoustical plaster, absorb much of the sound that reaches them. These materials are useful in reducing noise within buildings. In many buildings, ceilings and walls are built of such sound-absorbing materials. The hanging banners in school gymnasiums help absorb sound so that you can hear the gym teacher speaking. ■

A large cafeteria can be a very noisy place if it has no materials to absorb sound (*left*). A restaurant is often a quiet place because its chairs, floors, and walls have sound-absorbing materials (*right*).

INVESTIGATION 1

1. Describe at least two specific ways that people can control sound.

2. What is a decibel? Draw and explain a scale that shows sounds around you expressed in decibels.

INVESTIGATION 2

How Do People Hear?

Every day you are bombarded by sound. You may wake up to the jarring noise of an alarm clock. On the street, recyclers may be collecting your used glass. How can you tell one sound from another? This investigation explores hearing—and not hearing.

Activity

Identifying Sounds

How distinctive are sounds? Are there any two voices—or sounds—that are exactly alike? In this activity you'll test how well you can tell one sound from another.

MATERIALS
- blindfold
- assorted sound makers (bells, whistles, rattles)
- *Science Notebook*

Procedure

1. Blindfold one member of your group. Then have each student in your group, one by one, say a word or phrase. Have the blindfolded student identify each person who speaks. **Record** in your *Science Notebook* whether the blindfolded student could identify each person.

2. Repeat step 1. This time, have each student *whisper* the same word or phrase. **Record** whether each person was identified. **Discuss** your findings with your group.

3. Blindfold a different group member. Have each student, one by one, make a sound with a different sound maker.

4. **Record** whether the blindfolded student identified each sound maker. **Discuss** your findings as a group.

Step 3

Analyze and Conclude

1. In step 1, could the student correctly identify each person who spoke? What do you think allowed the blindfolded student to identify the speakers? If the student couldn't identify each person, give a reason why not.

2. In step 2, could the blindfolded student identify each student who spoke? Why might it have been difficult to identify the speakers?

3. Could the blindfolded student identify each sound maker? Which ones couldn't be easily identified?

4. In general, what properties of a sound can be used to identify it?

UNIT PROJECT LINK

Plan a soundtrack for the folk tale you have begun rehearsing. Include the instruments and other devices needed for the sound effects. Choose a narrator to tell the story. Decide how long the show will last. Then make an audiotape of the soundtrack, including the narration. Make sure the puppets' movements are synchronized with the soundtrack.

American Sign Language

"I even got to ride on an elephant!" Sara was excited as she told her parents about the trip to the zoo that day. She described the antics of the monkeys and the sheep, but she didn't say a word. How did Sara tell her story? She used American Sign Language—a method of communication that uses the hands, face, and body to express ideas.

People who can hear acquire language by listening to people around them and imitating what they hear. Deaf people need another way to learn language. They often use one of the many sign languages from around the world.

One form of sign language, American Manual Sign Language, uses hand gestures to spell out the letters of words. When using this sign language, a person must "sign" each letter of the word he or she wishes to express. The letters are put together to form words.

By contrast, American Sign Language, or ASL, uses signs to express single words or groups of words often used together. But ASL is not just a direct translation of English into signs. It is a language all its own, with unique expressions and ideas. Many of these expressions cannot be directly translated into the spoken word.

Many members of the deaf community prefer ASL over American Manual Sign Language because it offers more freedom of expression. ■

A girl signing "I sign in American Sign Language." ▼

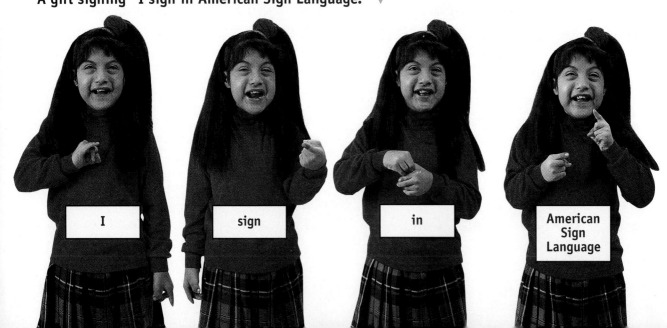

| I | sign | in | American Sign Language |

How the Ear Works

The Structure of the Ear

How do you hear sound? Sound waves are collected by the parts of the outer ear. Then the sound waves move to the middle ear, where they cause the eardrum to vibrate. The eardrum is connected to three tiny bones that transmit the force of sound vibrations from the eardrum. The last of the three bones pushes against a membrane that separates the middle ear from the inner ear.

In the inner ear, vibrations are transmitted to the cochlea. The cochlea contains fluid, which also vibrates. A membrane that runs along the entire length of the cochlea has about 30,000 tiny hair cells (not the same as the hairs on your head). When the fluid in the cochlea vibrates, some of these hairs move. Their movement causes nerve impulses to travel along the **auditory nerve** to the brain. The brain interprets the nerve impulses as sounds.

A Tunnel and Balance

The **eustachian tube** (yoo stā′kē ən toob) is a tunnel that connects the middle ear to the throat. It allows air to pass between the middle ear and the throat, which helps keep air pressure within the ear the same as the outside air pressure. Have your ears ever hurt while you were flying in an airplane? The pain is caused when the air pressure inside your ear is different from the air pressure around you.

Your inner ear, especially the **semicircular canals**, helps you keep your balance. These canals are filled with fluid and contain hair cells that respond to movement. Nerve impulses from these cells give the brain the information needed to keep the body balanced. ∎

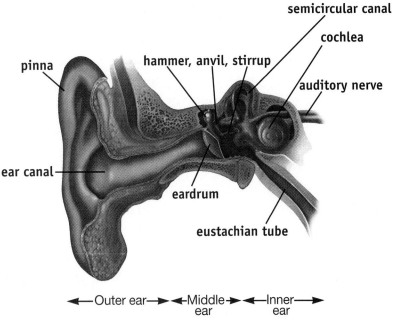

semicircular canal

cochlea

hammer, anvil, stirrup

auditory nerve

pinna

ear canal

eardrum

eustachian tube

←—Outer ear—→ ←Middle→ ←—Inner—→
ear   ear

F85

Help for Hearing Loss

About 10 percent of the population has some form of hearing loss, or deafness. There are several kinds of loss. Some people can't hear certain frequencies of sound; others hear all sounds but hear them more faintly than they are heard by people with normal hearing.

Hearing loss has many causes. A damaged eardrum can cause hearing loss, as can injury to the auditory nerve—the nerve leading from the ear to the brain. Damage to the auditory nerve cannot be corrected. But most deafness, including that due to nerve damage, can be helped through hearing aids and sometimes with surgery.

If your great-grandparents had hearing problems, they may have used an ear trumpet. This device, similar to a reverse megaphone, was used to funnel more sound into the ear.

Today, most hearing loss can be at least partially helped with a battery-powered hearing aid. A **hearing aid** receives sound waves and converts them into electrical impulses. The electrical signals are amplified, converted back to sound waves, and channeled to the eardrum through a plastic piece molded to fit inside the outer ear. The hearing aids are so tiny that it's difficult to tell if someone is wearing one.

Before hearing aids were invented, ear trumpets were used to funnel sound to the ear. ▶

Two kinds of electronic hearing aids are shown on this page. Both are comfortable and help with certain kinds of hearing loss. As you read on the opening page of this chapter, a new, tiny hearing aid is now available. This hearing aid is implanted deep in the ear canal. Because the device is placed very close to the eardrum, it prevents many of the problems of standard hearing aids. People who use this device find that they can understand normal conversation much more easily. The aid allows people to hear high-frequency sounds that are often distorted by other hearing aids.

Not all people with hearing loss can use this hearing aid. For example, some may have ear canals that are not the right shape to hold the hearing aid. Fortunately, engineers are always working on new ways to help hearing-impaired people. ■

▲ **Two kinds of hearing aids—worn mainly behind the ear (*top*) and worn inside the ear (*bottom*)**

◀ **Girl wearing the hearing aid with a battery that fits behind the ear**

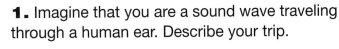

INVESTIGATION 2

1. Imagine that you are a sound wave traveling through a human ear. Describe your trip.

2. How is a hearing aid somewhat like a compact microphone and stereo set?

How Is Sound Transmitted and Recorded?

Within the last century, inventors achieved a long-time goal: to record great artists' performances so they could be heard by future generations. This investigation explores how sound is transmitted and recorded. It also explores some ideas for the future.

Activity
Magnetic Sounds

You've probably purchased audiocassettes of your favorite recording artists. Perhaps you've taped your own voice. Do you have any idea how sounds are recorded? This activity will give you a hint about how it happens.

Procedure

Carefully **examine** the tape inside a blank audiocassette. In your *Science Notebook*, **record** your ideas on how sound is recorded on the tape. **Discuss** these ideas with your group. Then place a bar magnet close to the exposed part of the tape. **Observe** what happens and **record** your observations.

Analyze and Conclude

1. What happened when you brought the bar magnet close to the tape?

2. Based on your observations, what can you **infer** about the nature of the tape?

MATERIALS
- blank audiocassette
- bar magnet
- *Science Notebook*

F88

Activity

Tape-Recording

You should keep your audiocassettes away from magnets. In this activity you will deliberately place a bar magnet near an audiocassette that contains a recording. What do you think will happen?

Step 1

Procedure

1. Tape-record the voices of the members of your group. Have each student say at least one sentence.

2. Rewind the tape and then play back the taped sentences.

3. In your *Science Notebook*, **record** how each student sounds. For example, **record** whether the taped students' voices sound the same as in normal conversation.

4. Remove the audiocassette from the tape recorder. While holding a bar magnet near the surface of the exposed tape, use a pencil to rewind the tape completely. **Predict** what you think will happen. **Discuss** your predictions with other members of your group.

5. Now play the tape. In your *Science Notebook*, **record** what you hear on the tape. Note whether there are any changes in the students' voices.

Analyze and Conclude

1. Compare how the students' voices sounded in step 2 and step 5. Account for any differences you heard.

2. If you heard any differences in the voices, **suggest a hypothesis** to explain what happened.

3. Write a statement about the effect of a bar magnet on tape-recorded sound. Why should you keep magnets away from audiocassette tapes?

Recorded Sound

cylinder ————

▲ An early phonograph

Early Recordings

Thomas A. Edison had a knack for inventing devices that fascinated the public. In 1877 he invented a sound-recording device—the **phonograph** (fō′nə graf). To record sound, he used a thin metal disc that vibrated when sound waves struck it. A metal penlike device called a stylus was attached to the disc. The tip of the stylus touched a sheet of metal foil that was wrapped around a rotating cylinder.

When sounds made the disc vibrate, those vibrations were transferred to the stylus. As the stylus vibrated, the sound

was recorded as a pattern of tiny hills and valleys in a spiral track on the cylinder.

By reversing the recording process, it was possible to hear the sounds on the

Thomas A. Edison and the phonograph he invented ▼

cylinder. As the cylinder was turned, a stylus rose and fell over the hills and valleys in the recorded soundtrack. The vibrations produced sounds that traveled out through a megaphone attached to the stylus.

Edison's phonograph was a wonderful invention, but it did have some problems. The sound reproduction was poor, and the cylinders wore out after being played only a few times. Only one cylinder could be recorded at a time. A singer had to sing each time a recording was made on a cylinder.

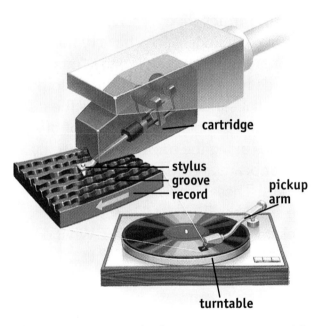
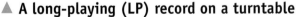

▲ A long-playing (LP) record on a turntable

Invention of the Record

In 1888, Emile Berliner dramatically improved sound recording by inventing the disc record. Berliner produced a "master" copper plate that contained all the patterns of the recording. This copper plate could then be used to stamp out large numbers of copies on shellac resin discs. From then on, a singer had to sing a song only once—for the master disc—and then many copies could be made. The great opera singer Enrico Caruso made a recording that sold more than a million copies by 1900!

Inventions Improve Recordings

When plastics were developed, they were used to replace the shellac resin records. Plastic records were lighter and were less likely to break. But the greatest advantage of plastic records was that they could be made with narrower and more closely packed soundtracks. Only one song could fit on the old shellac resin records, but several songs could be recorded on one plastic record. Plastics led the way to long-playing (LP) records, which first appeared in 1948.

Sound in Stereo

Ten years later, stereophonic (stereo) records were introduced. Two separate microphones were used during the recording, and two separate soundtracks were cut in the recording disc. When a stereo record was played, each soundtrack was connected to a separate loudspeaker. The two speakers produced sound that was like a live performance. People quickly replaced their old one-speaker record players with new "stereos."

Sound on Tape

But then a new method for recording sound was developed—coating plastic tapes with a magnetic material such as iron oxide. Today, many people use

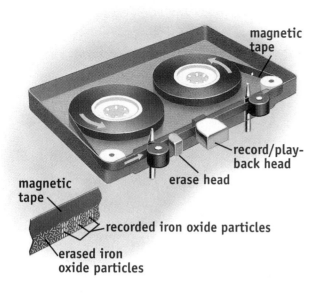

magnetic tape

record/play-back head

erase head

magnetic tape

recorded iron oxide particles

erased iron oxide particles

◀ An audiocassette, showing the magnetic tape on small reels

audiocassettes—miniature versions of the older reel-to-reel tapes. When you record sound on tape, as you did on page F89, electric currents produced by sound waves entering a microphone are sent through the coil of an electromagnet (the recording head). The changing electric current in the coil causes changes in the magnetic field of the recording head. As the tape moves through the changing magnetic field of the head, a magnetic pattern is formed in the tiny crystals of iron oxide on the surface of the tape. The tape can then be passed through another head, called the playback head. This causes it to produce weak electrical signals that are then amplified. When these amplified electrical signals are fed to a loudspeaker, they reproduce the sounds that first entered the microphone.

By the mid-1980s audiocassettes were outselling records. This was due mainly to their convenience. Tapes could be played anywhere—even in a moving car.

Compact Discs (CDs)

Tapes store a magnetic "image" of sounds. Today, digital signals can also be used to store sound. In a digital recording, the electrical signal from the microphone is changed to a series of on-or-off electrical pulses that are recorded as strong or weak magnetic fields.

A **compact disc**, or CD, contains a digital recording. Along the very thin recording track of the disc, the "offs" are recorded as pits. The "ons" are recorded as the flat surface of the disc. As the disc spins on a CD player, the codes of offs and ons along the track are scanned by a laser beam and changed to electrical signals. These signals are then sent to the speakers. Today, CDs are fast replacing audiocassette tapes. What do you think might replace CDs? ■

A compact disc (CD), showing an enlargement of "pits" (holes) and "flats" (flat surfaces) ▶

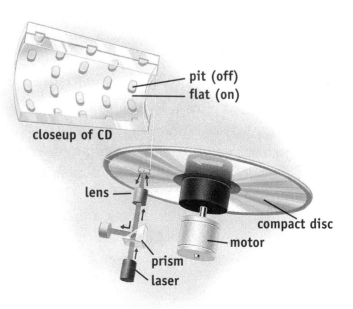

pit (off)

flat (on)

closeup of CD

lens

compact disc

motor

prism

laser

Delivering
Information

**SCIENCE
TECHNOLOGY
& SOCIETY**

Television provides the world with an amazing variety of entertainment. You can enjoy comedy, drama, music, and sports all on the same day in the comfort of your home. Satellites in orbit above Earth make it possible for people in nearly all parts of the world to view an Olympic event as it happens.

Through TV, you can see world leaders in action and observe the effects of wars and natural disasters. You can also see that even though people have different backgrounds and cultures, people all over the world have many of the same needs and interests.

The Information Superhighway

Your television will soon be part of the communication system of the future— the **information superhighway**. The telephone,

computer, and television will be combined to link people together in a way that was not possible before. Imagine being part of a worldwide network joining communication, entertainment, and information. Your telephone line will be your link to the information superhighway.

Small but powerful computers linked by telephone lines and television cable systems will take you to any stop you choose along the information superhighway. Even now, many personal-computer users browse through libraries and databases and communicate with

Fiber-optic bundles ▶

other users on Internet. **Internet** is a data highway made up of more than 10,000 computer networks.

In the future the information superhighway will let you access over 500 TV channels and watch almost any movie ever made. You will also be able to make airline and hotel reservations, as well as shop at your favorite stores, while sitting in your living room. You'll be able to buy whatever you wish by inserting a credit card into a slot beside your TV screen.

Your doctor will be able to provide you with better care because he or she will be able to reach the medical special-

▲ **The information superhighway**

ist you need through the information superhighway. The specialist will be able to view, examine, and talk with you and your family doctor.

What lies beyond the information superhighway? In another two or three decades you'll know! ■

==================== INVESTIGATION 3 ====================

1. Choose a sound-recording system, either old or new, and describe how sound is recorded on this device.

2. Describe how you think your life may be changed if your home or school is linked to the information superhighway.

REFLECT & EVALUATE

WORD POWER

audiocassette
auditory nerve
compact disc
decibel
eustachian tube
information superhighway
noise pollution
phonograph
semicircular canal

intensity
Internet
hearing aid
volume

 On Your Own
Review the terms in the list. Write one new thing you learned about each term.

 With a Partner
Write each term in the list on one side of an index card and the definition on the other side. Use the cards to quiz your partner.

PORTFOLIO

Design a poster to make people aware of the danger of loud noises. Show why loud noises are dangerous and suggest ways people can protect themselves.

Analyze Information

Look at the graph below. How does the sound shown at 50 dB compare with the sound at 60 dB? Suggest a sound that could be placed at 0 dB.

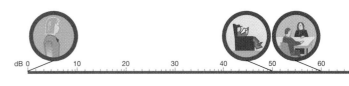

Assess Performance

Some rooms in your home or school might be very noisy because they have few sound-proofing materials in them. Choose such a room and plan a way to reduce the noise level of the room.

Problem Solving

1. One thing actors must learn is to speak loudly enough to be heard by the audience. This skill is called "projecting the voice." Why do actors have to project more when an audience is present than at rehearsals?

2. One type of frequently used hearing aid was not worn in the ear. Instead, it was hooked over the ear and rested against the bone behind the ear. How, do you think, did this hearing aid help a person hear?

3. Devices such as LPs, cassette tapes, and CDs do not actually "store" sound itself. Explain what is meant by this statement.

Throughout this unit, you've investigated questions related to light and sound. How will you use what you've learned and share that information with others? Here are some ideas.

Hold a Big Event
to Share Your Unit Project

You and your class have been putting together a sound and light show using puppets as the characters. You've written and rehearsed the narration and worked on the special lighting effects. You've made models of musical instruments from different parts of the world and have rehearsed the songs played on the instruments. Now is the time to put the finishing touches on your show. Go over all the details until everything is perfect—the narration, the lighting, and the music. Then put on the show for another class or the entire school. You may even wish to invite your family and friends to enjoy the show!

Experiment

In this unit, you investigated the effects of mixing different colors of light. Create an experiment to discover if mixing different colors of paint pigments yields the same results as mixing different colors of light. Make a poster showing the results of your experiment.

Research

Choose a topic in this unit to investigate further at the library. You might want to learn more about musical instruments of different cultures. You might want to explore how the colors and sounds in fireworks are created. Or, you might want to find out what sound pollution is and why it can be dangerous. Find an interesting way to share what you learn.

MOVEMENT AND CONTROL

Theme: Systems

GET READY TO

OBSERVE & QUESTION

How can you respond to things around you?

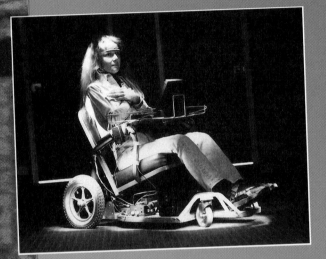

What if there was a wheelchair that could be completely controlled by a disabled person's brain waves? Learn how scientists are making connections between mind and body by using new technologies.

EXPERIMENT & HYPOTHESIZE

What are the parts of the skeletal system?

Make a bone model and discover how bones move at a joint. Can you predict where each type of joint is found in your body? Check out your predictions with a model of the human skeleton.

INVESTIGATE!

RESEARCH & ANALYZE

As you investigate, find out more from these books.

- **Peak Performance** by Emily Isberg (Simon & Schuster Books for Young Readers, 1989). Discover how up-to-the-minute scientific technology helps athletes all over the world. Read about the workings of the U.S. Olympic Training Centers.

- **Native American Doctor: The Story of Susan LaFlesche Picotte** by Jeri Ferris (Carolrhoda Books, 1991). This biography takes you to the Great Plains in the 1860's. Learn how alcohol abuse was fought by the first Native American woman to earn a medical degree.

WORK TOGETHER & SHARE IDEAS

What's your plan for a sports event that involves three systems of your body?

You'll design a series of activities to show how your skeletal, muscular, and nervous systems all work together. Have fun planning and competing in your Bone, Muscle, Brain Triathlon!

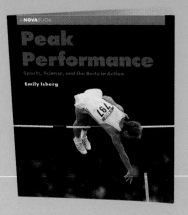

Triathlon

CHAPTER 1

BONES AND MUSCLES

Watch the ways athletes move. They use their legs to run and jump in the air. They use their hands to catch balls of different shapes. It's a blur of motion. What systems of the body allow for these amazing movements? How do these systems work together?

Will I Walk Again?

In 1992, New York Jets defensive lineman 270-lb Dennis Byrd collided with a 275-lb teammate on the field. Byrd shattered a vertebra, one of the 33 bones of the spine. This caused injury to the nerve tissue of the spinal cord. The muscles in his arms and legs didn't work, and Dennis Byrd couldn't move.

"Am I going to be paralyzed?" Byrd kept asking. The Jets team doctor feared that the answer would be "Yes." But Dennis Byrd was determined not to give up. Two weeks after extensive surgery on his spine, he began physical therapy. At first, therapists had to move Byrd's limbs for him. But after several weeks of intensive exercises, he was not only moving his limbs on his own but was racing around in a wheelchair. Gradually, Dennis Byrd learned to walk again.

In this chapter you'll learn how the bones and muscles of the body make walking and other movements possible.

Coming Up

◀ Dennis Byrd prepares for his physical therapy.

INVESTIGATION 1

WHAT ARE THE PARTS OF THE SKELETAL SYSTEM?

How many bones do you think make up the human skeleton? Would you say 50? 100? You might be surprised to learn that the human skeleton has 206 bones! These range from the long bone in your thigh to the tiny bones in your ears. Find out more about your skeletal system in Investigation 1.

Activity

A Closer Look at Bones

Although you have a full set of bones, you really can't study them. But in this activity you'll get a chance to look closely at a bone.

MATERIALS

- goggles
- gloves
- paper towels
- hand lens
- bone specimen
- *Science Notebook*

SAFETY

Wear goggles and gloves when handling the bone specimen.

Procedure

Observe the outside covering and features of the bone. **Describe** the bone in your *Science Notebook*. Next, **observe** the inside of the bone. Notice how the inside structure differs from the outside structure. **Describe** the inside of the bone. **Make a drawing** of the bone. **Talk** with your group. What can you **infer** about the material that makes up the bone?

Analyze and Conclude

1. **Compare** and **contrast** the inside structure of the bone with the outside structure of the bone.

2. Do you think that bones are living material? What evidence supports your conclusion?

Activity
Where Bones Meet

What would happen if all of your bones were fixed in place? How would you move? Find out what structures allow movement of your skeleton.

Procedure

1. Work with a partner. Cut out the bone diagrams and tape them together to form two long bones. Paste the bones on posterboard and cut them out.

2. Use a fastener to attach an end of one bone to an end of the other bone. **Observe** the ways in which the bones of your model move. **Describe** in your *Science Notebook* how the bones move.

3. **Predict** where in the human skeleton bones move in a similar way to your model. **Record** your predictions.

4. **Examine** your own body or a model of a human skeleton to find places where bones move in a similar way to your model. **Record** these places.

Step 2

Analyze and Conclude

1. **Compare** your observations of your skeleton or the human skeleton model with your predictions. How are they alike? How do they differ?

2. The place where two bones meet is called a joint. What can you **infer** about the functions of joints?

3. Did you find additional bones in your body or in the skeleton model moving like your long-bone model? Where were they located?

4. How did bones in your body move differently from your model?

Bone Basics

◀ **What's missing that could turn this blob into a human being?**

Think of yourself as a blob, squirming around beneath your desk. Your eyes, ears, nose, and mouth sit generally atop your body, which looks something like a balloon filled with jelly. Your stomach, lungs, liver, and heart are floating in there somewhere, though in no particular place. Forget about arms and legs—you're just a lumpy mass of guts plopped on the floor.

Now that's a scary thought! What could be added to this blob that would transform it into the stunning person you are? Bones, of course! And those bones wouldn't just be thrown in there anywhere. They would have to be organized into an appropriate system that would give your body protection, shape, and the ability to move.

The Skeletal System

A **bone** is a kind of body tissue made of both living cells and nonliving material. Each human body contains 206 different bones. All the bones in the body, together with tissues that bind and protect the bones, form the **skeletal system**, or the skeleton.

Have you ever done a jigsaw puzzle?

The pieces fit together so perfectly that no glue is needed and no gaps are seen in the completed picture. Most bones of the skeleton don't fit together in such a perfect fashion. And unlike a jigsaw puzzle, a skeleton has to stay together when you run or jump or move.

The place at which two bones meet is called a **joint**. Some joints, such as those in the skull, are almost like the pieces of a jigsaw puzzle. But at many joints—the elbows, knees, wrists, and others—movement occurs. At these joints the bones are held in place by strong bands of fiber called **ligaments**. Ligaments allow some movement while keeping the bones generally in place.

Bones are protected at joints by **cartilage**, a tissue much like bone but softer and more flexible. Cartilage is also found in the nose, the ears, and the tip of the breastbone. It forms part of the skeletal system.

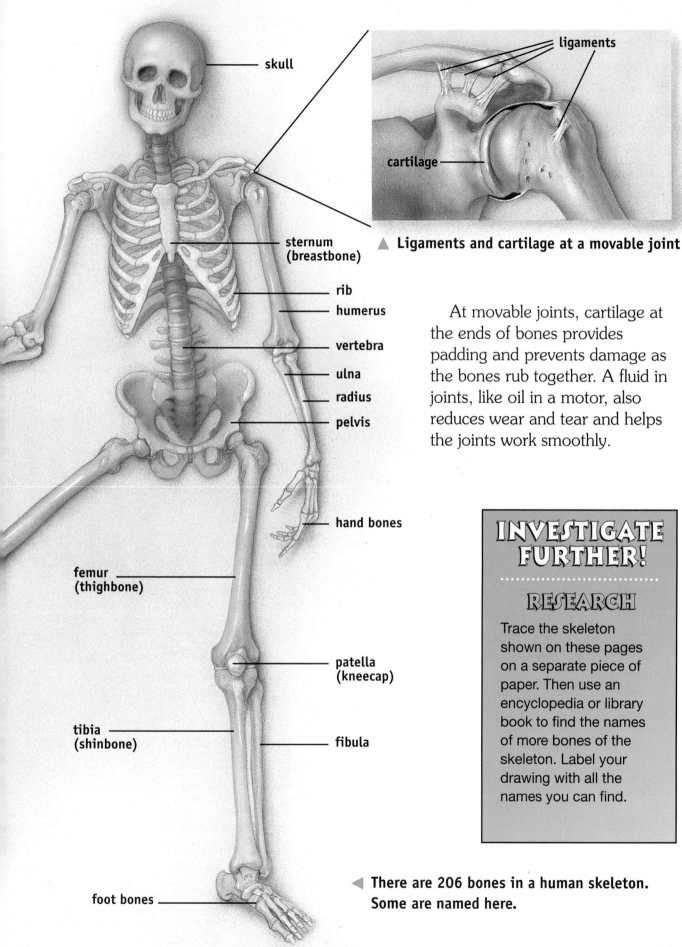

skull

ligaments

cartilage

▲ Ligaments and cartilage at a movable joint

sternum
(breastbone)

rib

humerus

vertebra

ulna

radius

pelvis

hand bones

femur
(thighbone)

patella
(kneecap)

tibia
(shinbone)

fibula

foot bones

At movable joints, cartilage at the ends of bones provides padding and prevents damage as the bones rub together. A fluid in joints, like oil in a motor, also reduces wear and tear and helps the joints work smoothly.

INVESTIGATE FURTHER!

RESEARCH

Trace the skeleton shown on these pages on a separate piece of paper. Then use an encyclopedia or library book to find the names of more bones of the skeleton. Label your drawing with all the names you can find.

◄ There are 206 bones in a human skeleton. Some are named here.

Inside a Bone

A bone has a complex structure, as you discovered in the activity on page G6. Bone isn't just a nonliving building material. A typical long bone, such as the one pictured at right, is enlarged at both ends with a shaft in between. A membrane called the periosteum (per ē-äs'tē əm) covers the bone. Under the periosteum is a layer of very hard material called compact bone. This layer gives the bone its strength.

Beneath the layer of compact bone is a material called spongy bone. Spongy bone is softer than compact bone and contains many hollow spaces. Those spaces help prevent the bone from breaking, because they act as shock absorbers when the bone is hit or banged. Spongy bone makes up most of the material at the ends of long bones.

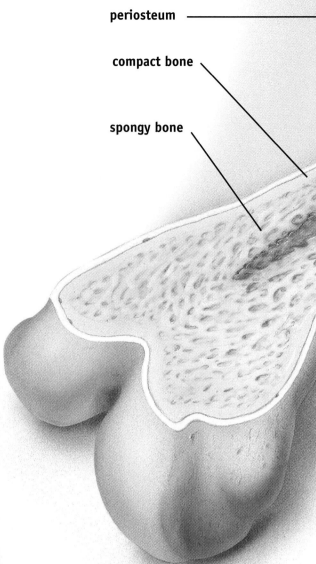

periosteum

compact bone

spongy bone

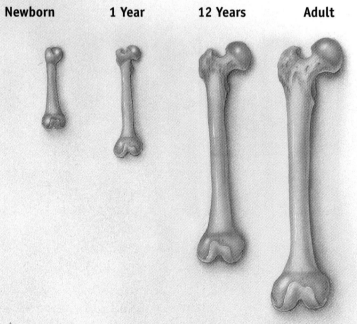

Newborn   **1 Year**   **12 Years**   **Adult**

▲ **THE GROWTH OF BONE** A baby's skeleton is composed of cartilage. As a baby grows into a child and then an adult, most of the cartilage is gradually replaced by bone.

Inside the shaft of long bones is a soft tissue called marrow. This is where the body's blood cells are produced. The blood cells leave the bone through blood vessels that weave their way throughout the bone. Like other living tissues in your body, your bones must be supplied with blood or they will die.

G10

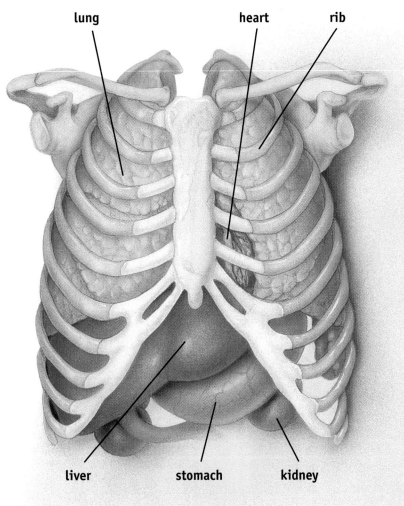

shaft

blood vessels

marrow

A bone is living tissue with a complex structure.

A System That Supports and Protects

Without a skeletal system, you would be just a blob, like the one described on page G8. Your skeleton gives you your shape. It supports your other body parts and allows you to stand erect. With your bones and their joints, you can move around and do many amazing things.

Your skeleton also serves you in another important way. It protects the soft organs within your body. Could you live long without a barrier around your lungs, heart, and liver? The ribs provide that barrier, giving protection against the hard knocks that you experience every day. Can you think of other bones that protect soft organs? ■

Part of the skeleton, the ribs protect vital organs and soft tissues. ▼

lung
heart
rib

liver
stomach
kidney

What Kind of Joint Is This?

In the activity on page G7, you identified places in the skeletal system where bones fit together—the joints. In fact, you identified movable joints, those that allow for the movement of bones. The body also contains immovable joints, places where bones come together but there is no movement. The best examples of immovable joints are the ones in the skull. There is no reason for these joints to move, since the purpose of the skull is to protect the brain.

As you learned when you read about the human skeletal system on page G8, movable joints are held together by ligaments. The ligaments allow some movement, but not enough so that a joint slips apart. Joints give you the freedom to move your body. A skeleton without joints would be like a statue.

You may have noticed that different joints allow different kinds of movement. Think of how the elbow moves. Compare that with how the shoulder moves. The elbow's movements are limited, while the shoulder has a much wider range of motion. The difference in how these two joints function is the result of their different structures. That is, they are different kinds of joints.

What joints does the soccer player on page G13 use to kick the ball? Without these different kinds of joints, the actions would be impossible!

UNIT PROJECT LINK

As you continue learning about bones and muscles, plan an athletic event that you feel demonstrates how your bones and muscles work together to cause movement. Make a poster to show the main bones, muscles, and joints that are involved in the activity. On your poster, show which muscles contract and relax to cause movements during the activity.

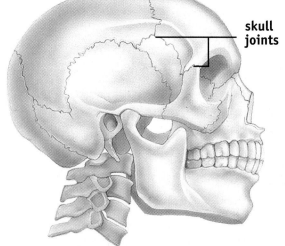

skull joints

▲ **The bones of the skull come together at immovable joints.**

PIVOT JOINT
A pivot joint in the neck lets the player turn his head to follow the path of the ball after he kicks it.

BALL-AND-SOCKET JOINT
This joint allows a great range of motion. In the hip it allows the player to make a full swing of his leg to kick the ball. The same kind of joint is used in a car's gearshift and for the joystick of some games.

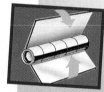

HINGE JOINT
This joint works like a door's hinge. In the knee, it lets the lower leg move back and forth like a door opening and closing. This hinge joint allows the player to pull back his lower leg to kick the ball.

GLIDING JOINT
This joint also allows a great range of motion. In a gliding joint, one bone slides over another. This gliding joint in the ankle allows the player to snap his foot into the ball.

INVESTIGATION 1

THINK IT WRITE IT

1. Describe the structure of bones and explain how they are held together to form the skeletal system.

2. You've learned about four different types of movable joints and have an example of each. Now classify other joints in your body by type.

G13

HOW DO BONES AND MUSCLES CAUSE MOVEMENT?

Smack! You hit the ball far out into center field. You run as fast as you can—past first, past second, past third. Home run! Your skeletal system made it around the bases, but not without help from another system. Can you name it? It's your system of muscles!

Activity

MATERIALS
- tape measure
- *Science Notebook*

Push or Pull?

To make something move, you can either push it or pull it. Do your muscles push your bones to make them move, or pull them?

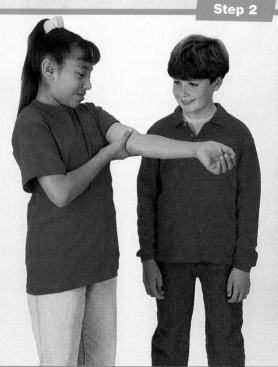

Step 2

Procedure

1. The biceps is the muscle on the front of the upper arm. The triceps is the muscle on the back of the upper arm. Locate your biceps and triceps.

2. Wrap the fingers of your right hand around your left upper arm so you can feel both the top and bottom of your arm at the same time. Bend and straighten your forearm slowly several times. **Describe** in your *Science Notebook* how your biceps and triceps changed as you moved your arm.

3. Have a group member **measure** the length of your biceps and triceps when your arm is straight and when it is bent. **Make a chart** and **record** the measurements.

4. Have a group member **measure** the thickness around your arm when it is straight and when it is bent. Measure halfway between your elbow and shoulder. **Record** these measurements in your chart.

Analyze and Conclude

1. How did your biceps and triceps change as you bent and straightened your arm?

2. Based on your data, **hypothesize** how your muscles cause your bones to move. **Make a drawing** to show your hypothesis.

3. How do the biceps and triceps work together to cause your arm to move?

INVESTIGATE FURTHER!

....

EXPERIMENT

Add two rubber bands to the model you made for the activity on page G7. One rubber band should act like a biceps and one should act like a triceps. Compare your model with other students' models.

Step 3

Step 4

Activity
Tired Muscles

MATERIALS
• spring clip
• timer
• *Science Notebook*

Work can tire you out. What does feeling tired have to do with your muscles?

Procedure

1. While a group member watches the timer, count how many times you can open the spring clip with your right hand in 60 seconds. **Record** this number in your *Science Notebook* in a chart such as the one shown below.

2. Rest for one minute. Then repeat step 1.

3. Now repeat steps 1 and 2, using your left hand.

4. **Compare** your data with those of others.

Step 3

	Right Hand		Left Hand	
Name	Trial 1	Trial 2	Trial 1	Trial 2

Analyze and Conclude

1. Was there a difference in the number of times you opened the spring clip with your right hand between the first and second trial? Was there a difference with your left hand? Was there a difference in your performance between your right hand and your left hand?

2. **Infer** why any differences occurred.

3. Which muscles are stronger, those in your right hand and arm or those in your left hand and arm? Explain. Why do you think this must be so?

How Do Muscles Work?

When you think of muscles, you probably think of the fleshy bulges on your arms and legs. These muscles that are attached to bones are called **skeletal muscles**. The body also has two other kinds of muscles. The muscles of your digestive system—the ones that push food through the digestive organs—are called **smooth muscles**. The muscles of your heart that cause it to beat are called **cardiac muscles**.

Skeletal muscles are the kind that move your bones. Although they vary in size and shape, these muscles all have one thing in common: they are attached to bones by **tendons**, which are strong, ropelike fibers.

When you did the activity on pages G14 and G15, you discovered that the thickness of your biceps and triceps changed depending on whether you bent or straightened your arm. With

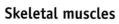

▲ Skeletal muscles

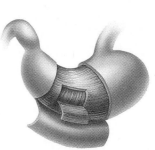

▲ Smooth muscles

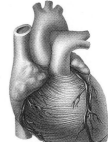

▲ Cardiac muscles

that data, you hypothesized about how your muscles cause your bones to move. Now check your hypothesis against an illustration of how the process works.

The drawings show how the two muscles work together. When the biceps contracts, the triceps stretches and relaxes, and the arm bends at the elbow. When the triceps contracts, the biceps stretches and relaxes, and the arm straightens. Movement of any part of your skeleton occurs when a pair of muscles alternately contract and relax. ∎

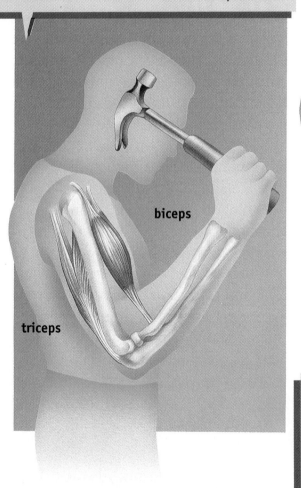

BICEPS CONTRACTED This person is ready to hit a nail with the hammer. The biceps is contracted, or shortened. It pulls on the bones of the forearm, and the arm bends at the elbow joint. The triceps on the opposite side of the upper arm is relaxed, or stretched. This allows the forearm to move with the contraction of the biceps.

biceps

triceps

TRICEPS CONTRACTED The person has hammered the nail hard. Notice the difference in the biceps and triceps. Now, the triceps is contracted, pulling the forearm down. The biceps is relaxed and stretched, which allows the triceps to move the forearm.

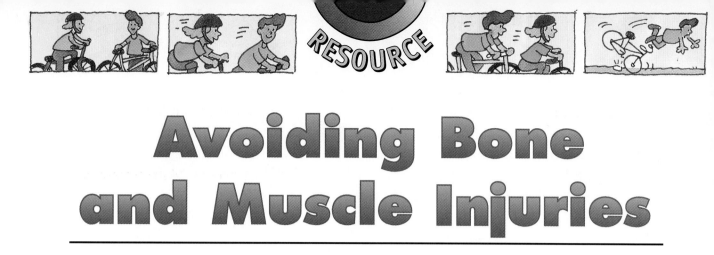
Avoiding Bone and Muscle Injuries

You're dribbling down the court on a fast break. There's no one between you and the basket, and you can already see yourself making the winning points on an easy layup. This will be sweet. But then tragedy strikes. A terrible pain shoots through the back of your leg, and you stumble to the floor. As you grip your leg, you watch the ball—and your glory—roll out of bounds.

Of all the times to strain a muscle, this is the worst. Could you have prevented this injury? Maybe, if you had warmed up properly before the game.

Not all injuries to bones and muscles can be prevented. But if you use the proper equipment, exercise regularly, eat well, and get enough rest, you just may be able to make that winning basket or do something that would be equally as special to you.

Sprains, Strains, Tears, and Cramps

How are muscles and bones injured? One of the most common injuries to dancers and other athletes is the sprain. A **sprain** involves the tearing of a ligament at a joint. The ligament itself might tear, or the ligament might tear away from the bone. This usually happens when the joint is unnaturally

Torn ligaments at a joint cause a sprain. ▼

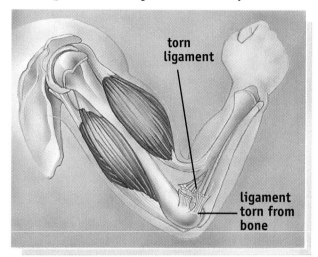

torn ligament

ligament torn from bone

A strain results when a muscle or tendon is stretched too far or incurs a minor tear. A muscle tear is a major tear of a muscle. ▼

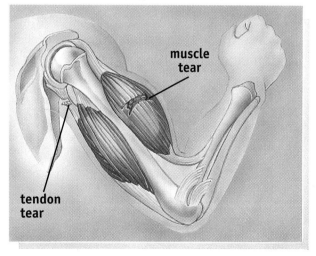

muscle tear

tendon tear

twisted because of a misstep or a blow. A sprain can be a slight injury or a serious injury that takes surgery to repair.

G19

A **strain**, in contrast, involves an overstretching or slight tearing of a muscle or a tendon that holds the muscle to the bone. A strain is sometimes called a "pulled muscle." If the muscle is stretched even farther, a muscle tear can result. A muscle tear takes weeks or months to heal.

Have you ever had a "charley horse"? A muscle contracts sharply and simply will not relax. This is called a muscle cramp. The cause of this is often muscle tiredness. Though painful for a moment, a muscle cramp usually does not result in serious injury.

Fractures and Torn Cartilage

Bones are hard, but not so hard that they can't break. Luckily, since bones are living tissue, they almost always heal to become as good as new again.

Any break or crack of a bone is called a **fracture**. This term is used whether a bone is just slightly cracked or broken clear through. Unless the bone pierces the skin—which happens only in extreme cases—a fracture must be detected through an X-ray.

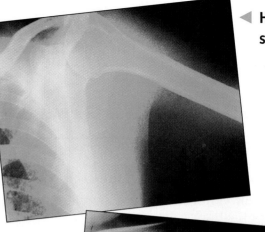

◀ Healthy shoulder

▲ **In a dislocation, bones pull apart at a joint.**

Torn cartilage, a tear in the padding at joints, often cannot be detected by X-rays. However, a technique called MRI does allow images of the cartilage to be filmed. The cartilage at joints does not heal as well as bones. For this reason, torn cartilage can be a lasting and troublesome injury.

How to Avoid Injuries

Accidents can happen to you, and sometimes you can't do anything to avoid them. But if you take precautions, you can usually avoid injury and disappointment.

First, wear the proper equipment when doing physical activities. You

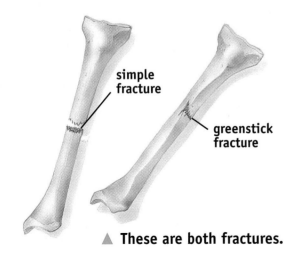

simple fracture

greenstick fracture

▲ **These are both fractures.**

don't have to wear knee pads when playing soccer, but you'll avoid injuries if you do. And when you ride your bike or skate, wear a helmet. Can you think of other safety equipment that can help prevent injuries?

Second, do warm-up exercises before a physical activity and cool-down exercises when you're through. Your muscles need to stretch out a little before working hard. And they also need to stretch out after being used in a difficult dance or sport. Such stretching can help avoid strains and tears.

Avoid injuries by wearing a helmet, wrist guards, and elbow and knee pads while in-line skating. ▶

SCIENCE IN LITERATURE

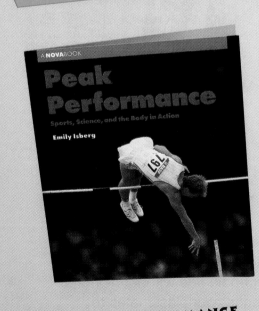

PEAK PERFORMANCE
by Emily Isberg
Simon & Schuster, 1989

Kids are involved in competitive sports at younger and younger ages. But competition can lead to injuries to bones and muscles. By the age of 11, Siri Larsen had already been training as a gymnast for five years. Now she was representing Norway at international meets. But during one meet she misses the parallel bar and falls. X-rays show a fracture, a torn ligament, and a dislocation at the elbow.

In *Peak Performance* by Emily Isberg, you can read how sports medicine helped Siri make a remarkable comeback. You can also find out how football and basketball knee injuries occur—and what can be done to repair, and even prevent, them.

Third, treat your body with respect. Eat the right foods—fruits and vegetables are the best. Also get enough sleep. A tired body is much more likely to be injured than a well-rested one. Stay away from alcohol and drugs. They can cause you to lose control.

What you do while you are young will affect you for the rest of your life. Now is the time for you to build the healthy body that will serve you well in the years ahead. ■

Here are some warm-up exercises to do before an activity and some cool-down exercises to do after the activity is completed. ▼

INVESTIGATION 2

1. Think about kicking a ball. Describe how the muscles and bones in your leg work together to cause this motion.

2. All studies show that wearing a helmet when riding a bicycle helps to prevent serious injuries and death. Still, many people ride without helmets. Think of a way to influence your classmates to always wear a helmet when they ride a bike.

REFLECT & EVALUATE

WORD POWER

bone
cartilage
fracture
joint
strain
sprain

cardiac muscles
skeletal muscles
skeletal system
smooth muscles
ligaments
tendons

 ### On Your Own

Review the terms in the list. Then make two lists to show those terms that relate to bones and those that relate to muscles.

With a Partner

Write each term in the list on one side of an index card and the definition on the other side. Use the cards to quiz your partner.

PORTFOLIO

Draw a diagram of the skeletal muscles, such as the one on page G17. Use an encyclopedia or library book to label some of the major muscles.

Analyze Information

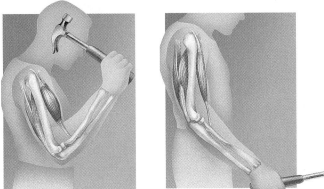

Study the drawings. Then use them to describe, in your own words, how the biceps and triceps work together to cause the forearm to move.

Assess Performance

Design a test to determine whether the muscles in your right upper leg or your left upper leg are stronger. After your teacher has reviewed your design, work with a partner to carry out the test. Compare your results with those of others.

Problem Solving

1. Compare your skeleton, which is on the inside of the body, to the skeleton of an insect, which is on the outside of the body. What are some advantages and disadvantages of each?

2. For a moment, pretend that the gliding joints in your ankles are replaced with hinge joints. What changes would this cause in how you are able to move?

3. Imagine that you're the trainer for a famous ballet dancer. What things would you suggest to avoid bone and muscle injuries?

CHAPTER 2

THE NERVOUS SYSTEM

Have you ever been nervous? Your hands tremble, your stomach muscles tighten, and your mouth gets dry. Your nervous system senses things about your surroundings and causes your body to respond. How does the nervous system control and coordinate what your body does?

Snails on the Scent

What can you smell? Burning leaves? Sour milk? Chocolate cake? You may think you have a keen sense of smell. But among the creatures of the animal kingdom, humans have a rather dull sense of smell.

Ronald Chase is a neurobiologist (nŏŏ′rō bī äl′ə jist), a scientist who studies the nervous system. At McGill University in Montreal, Canada, he has investigated the land snail's sense of smell. Land snails have been around for about 350 million years. Half of the brain of a land snail deals mainly with smells and tastes.

Dr. Chase has spent years training snails to follow different smells by rewarding them with food. He has even taught snails to follow smells they don't like! Chase claims to have set a record by training snails to remember particular scents for as long as 120 days.

Do you think humans' sense of smell would improve if it were the only way to find food?

G24

▶ Dr. Ronald Chase tests the land snail's sense of smell.

INVESTIGATION 1

WHAT ROLE DO THE BRAIN AND NERVES PLAY?

Think about the operation of a clothing-store chain. Workers in each store call Headquarters with reports on what's selling. Headquarters makes decisions and calls back, saying, "Put slacks on sale; order more shirts!" Now investigate what goes on in your body's "headquarters" and how messages get there and back.

Activity

Walk Straight and Tall

How do muscles and bones work together with the brain and nerves? This activity will help you understand how.

MATERIALS
- book
- *Science Notebook*

Procedure

Try to balance a book on your head and walk across the room without dropping it. Before you do this, **predict** what you think will happen. **Record** your prediction in your *Science Notebook*. Have a partner **observe** you as you walk while balancing the book. Each of you **record** your own observations. Next, **observe** as your partner walks across the room. Again, each **record** your own observations.

Analyze and Conclude

1. How did your observations compare to your prediction?

2. How did muscles and bones enable you to balance a book on your head and to walk across the room? **Infer** what role your nervous system played in this activity.

Activity

Measuring Reaction Time

How are your brain and nerves needed for you to react to a falling object? How long does it take them to "get the message"?

MATERIALS
- meterstick
- *Science Notebook*

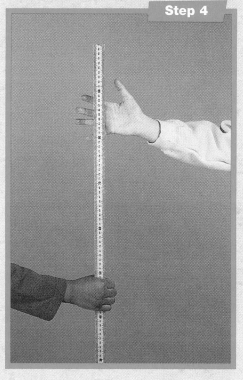

Step 2

Procedure

1. Hold out your arm and spread your thumb and forefinger slightly apart.

2. Have your partner hold a meterstick above your hand so that the 0-cm end of the stick is between your thumb and finger.

3. Without warning, your partner will let go of the meterstick. **Predict** at which centimeter mark you will catch the falling meterstick. **Record** your prediction in your *Science Notebook*.

4. Catch the meterstick as it falls. Look at the centimeter mark where you caught it. **Record** that number in a chart.

5. Repeat steps 1 through 4 nine more times. **Compare** your data with that of other groups.

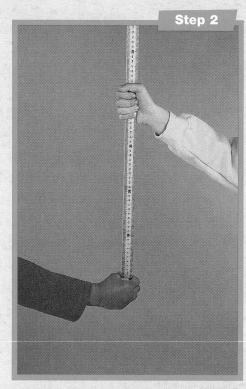

Step 4

Analyze and Conclude

1. The time it takes the body to recognize and react to something is called reaction time. How did your reaction time change as you did this activity? Why do you think it changed?

2. What do you think happens between your eyes, brain, and hand from the time the meterstick starts to fall until you catch it?

3. Infer why there was a reaction time between when you saw the meterstick fall and when you caught it.

The Path of a
Nerve Impulse

Do you think you responded quickly to the falling meterstick in the activity on page G27? No matter how fast you grabbed the meterstick, there was still a little time that passed after you saw it fall. This time—your reaction time—was the time it took for a nerve impulse to make its way through your nervous system.

A **nerve impulse** is a message carried through your body by nerve cells, or **neurons** (nōo'ränz). Neurons are found throughout your body.

Certain neurons, the **sensory neurons**, pick up signals from the environment. These signals, or **stimuli** (stim'yōo lī), start a nerve impulse. Your muscles move in reaction to the messages carried to them by another type of neuron, the **motor neurons.** Bundles of neurons are called nerves.

What happens between a stimulus and your response? To answer this question, follow the path of the nerve impulse in the illustration on page G29.

Now you know the path of a nerve impulse. These impulses are similar to electrical signals and are caused by changes in chemicals in the neurons. A nerve impulse can travel through your nervous system at speeds from 10 to 120 m/s. That's why you can respond so quickly to a stimulus. ■

In a neuron, impulses travel along extensions to other neurons. ▼

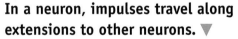

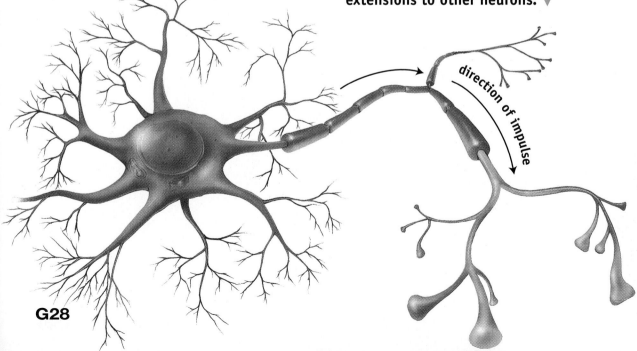

FOLLOWING THE NERVE IMPULSE

The nerve impulse begins with a stimulus. The impulse travels through sensory neurons either directly to the brain, or to the spinal column and then to the brain. The brain analyzes the message and decides what action to take. Then the brain sends an impulse back down the spinal column and out through motor neurons to the muscles. As the muscles contract, the body makes the proper response.

The stimulus is the sight of the falling meterstick.

The stimulus activates a nerve impulse in sensory neurons in the student's eyes. The impulse travels through the neurons to the brain.

The brain, which contains millions of neurons, analyzes the message. It then sends a message about what to do back through the nervous system by way of the spinal cord.

The spinal cord, a mass of neurons, serves as a path to and from the brain. The spinal cord sends the message to the motor neurons.

The motor neurons pass the message to the muscles of the hand, which provide the response needed to catch the falling meterstick.

A Tour of the Brain

"All aboard for a tour of the brain! Check all sharp objects at the gate. Once we get past the skull, we must ensure that the soft tissue of the brain remains uninjured by our journey. Take your seats, please. Here we go!"

Off to a Bony Start

What if you could take a tour of the brain? You'd have to shrink yourself down to board a miniature inner-space ship that will make its way through the complex structure of this control center of the nervous system.

Your first obstacle will be getting through the brain's protective covering, the skull. The brain is composed of very soft tissue. Without the skull the brain could be seriously injured by the slightest bump. In addition to the bony covering, the brain is protected by three layers of membranes, one of which is tough and leathery. Finally, a watery fluid surrounds the brain, cushioning it from any impact.

Once inside, you'll find an extremely complex organ containing about 15 billion neurons—not surprising, considering the important role the brain plays in the body! You'll see that the brain has three main parts: the cerebrum, the cerebellum, and the medulla.

The three main parts of the brain together weigh about 1.5 kg (3 lb). ▼

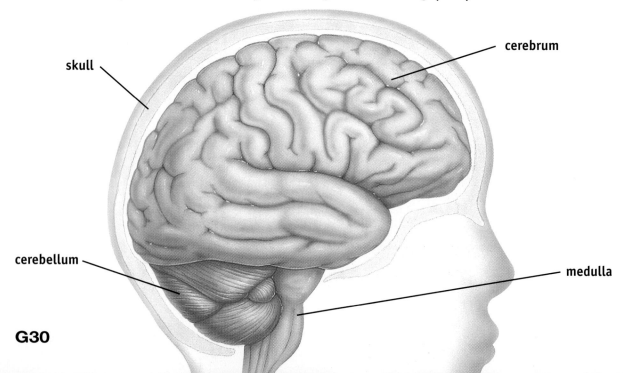

skull

cerebrum

cerebellum

medulla

G30

Rolling Gray Hills and Valleys

Once inside the skull, you'll find yourself in the **cerebrum** (sə rē′ brəm), the largest part of the brain. You can easily get lost in the cerebrum, since its outer layer—the cortex—contains many folds and grooves. These folds give the brain an increased surface area—more thinking space. Your first impression will be one of total grayness. The outer part of the cerebrum contains the gray matter of the brain.

The cerebrum is divided into two halves, or hemispheres. A band of neurons connects the halves, carrying nerve impulses from one to the other.

Thinking takes place in your cerebrum. It is where you store memories and make decisions. The cerebrum is also the place where your emotions and

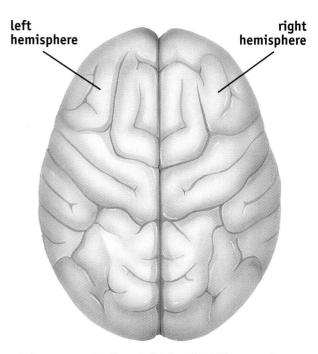

▲ **In general, the right half of the cerebrum controls the left side of the body, and the left half controls the right side.**

attitudes originate. Notice on the map the cerebral areas controlling different parts of the body.

Body parts and functions controlled by areas of the cerebrum ▼

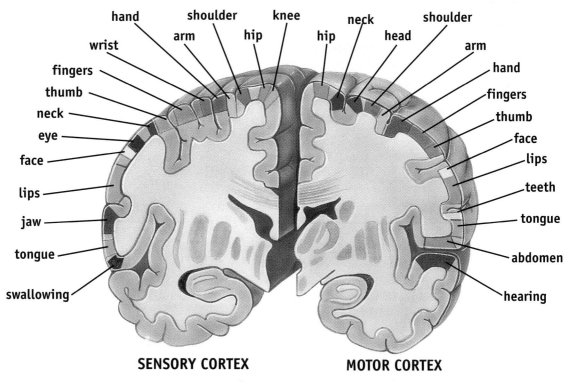

SENSORY CORTEX   MOTOR CORTEX

South of the Cerebrum

After exploring the gray matter, you'll go to the cerebellum, below and to the rear of the cerebrum. The **cerebellum** (ser ə bel'əm), the second largest part of the brain, coordinates the body's muscles. Your sense of balance comes from the cerebellum.

When you first learn a physical activity—a dance routine or swim stroke—you are really training the cerebellum. The nerve impulses that direct your muscles start in the cerebrum but pass through the cerebellum on their way to your muscles. The cerebellum makes sure your movements are smooth and coordinated.

Last Stop

No trip to the brain would be complete without a stop at the medulla. The **medulla** (mi dul'ə) connects the brain to the spinal column. You'll probably notice that, in addition to some gray neuron groups, the medulla contains white matter.

The medulla controls the involuntary actions of the body—the actions that you don't think about. These include heart rate, blood pressure, breathing, blinking, and coughing. Imagine if you had to think about all those actions all the time! The medulla directs such basic functions, leaving your cerebrum free to take care of other things.

SCIENCE IN LITERATURE

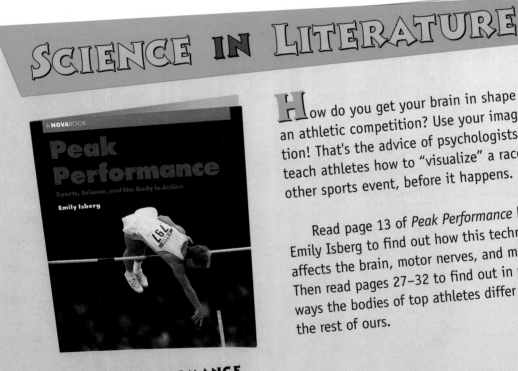

PEAK PERFORMANCE
by Emily Isberg
Simon & Schuster, 1989

How do you get your brain in shape for an athletic competition? Use your imagination! That's the advice of psychologists who teach athletes how to "visualize" a race, or other sports event, before it happens.

Read page 13 of *Peak Performance* by Emily Isberg to find out how this technique affects the brain, motor nerves, and muscles. Then read pages 27–32 to find out in what ways the bodies of top athletes differ from the rest of ours.

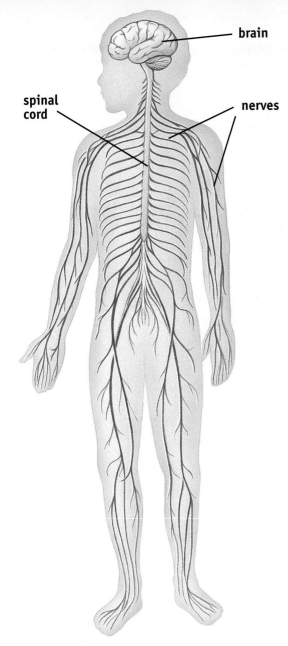

brain

spinal cord

nerves

▲ The brain is the control center for the nervous system. Nerves connect the brain to all parts of the body.

Side Trips Optional

You could end your tour here, since you've visited the three main parts of the brain. Or you could keep on going, following the path of a nerve impulse out of the brain. First, you would travel through the spinal cord. From there, you could choose any number of nerves that lead to all of the other parts of the body.

"Next stop, spinal column. After that, we head down to the toes." Good luck. You've got a long, exciting journey ahead of you! ■

INVESTIGATE FURTHER!

TAKE ACTION

The brain can become injured, just as other parts of the body can. But when the brain is injured, the effects can also show up in other parts of the body. Interview a doctor or nurse to find out about the consequences of head injuries. What are some of the best ways for you to avoid head injuries?

INVESTIGATION 1

1. Compare the functions of the three main parts of the brain.

2. A skier had a severe injury to her lower back, damaging the spinal cord. As a result, her legs and feet are paralyzed. Explain her condition, based on what you've learned about the nervous system.

INVESTIGATION 2

How Can You Respond to Things Around You?

It's time for lunch! You smell food and hear laughter from the lunchroom. Hungry kids bump into you as they join the line. You eye the choices and decide on a bowl of soup. Find out how the senses work with your nerves and brain to respond to all the choices in your environment.

Activity
Test Your Mind

How does the brain get the information it needs to learn and remember? Try this activity to find out how memory is related to how quickly you respond.

Procedure

1. With a marker, write a large letter *A* on one side of an index card. Do the same for the letters *B* through *F*. Then make another set of cards to match the first. You will have six pairs of cards when finished.

2. Have a partner mix up the cards and lay them on a table, letter-side down, in three neat rows of four cards each. Don't watch!

3. Your partner will tell you when to begin and will time you. You should select two cards to turn over, trying to match similar letters. If the cards don't match, place them face down in position again. When you make a match, leave the cards face up in their places.

Step 1

4. Continue until you have matched all the pairs of cards. **Record** in a chart in your *Science Notebook* the time it took you to do this.

5. **Predict** what will happen when you do this test again with the cards in the same places. **Record** your prediction.

6. Repeat steps 3 and 4. **Compare** your times.

7. Now your partner will mix the cards around, keeping three rows. **Predict** what will happen when you do the test this time.

8. Repeat steps 3 and 4. **Compare** your times. **Compare** your data with the data of other groups.

Analyze and Conclude

1. In which case did you match all the letters in the shortest amount of time?

2. How did your time for the third test compare with your times for the other tests?

3. What role do you think learning and memory played in this activity? **Tell what evidence** you can cite to support your answer.

INVESTIGATE FURTHER!

EXPERIMENT

Make pairs of cards for six more letters and repeat the activity with six rows of four cards in each row. How do your times compare to those with twelve cards? Explain why this happened.

Activity
Reflex Action

Have you ever touched something hot and pulled your hand away before you felt any pain? This is another way your nervous system can respond to your environment.

MATERIALS
- chair
- *Science Notebook*

Procedure

1. Sit in a chair and cross your legs so that the top leg can swing freely.

2. **Predict** what will happen if your top leg is gently tapped just below the kneecap. **Record** your prediction in your *Science Notebook*.

3. Have a partner use the side of his or her hand to gently tap your top leg just below the kneecap. **Record** the results.

4. Repeat step 3, but this time try to keep your top leg from moving.

Step 3

Analyze and Conclude

1. What happened to your leg when your partner tapped it? How did this compare to your prediction?

2. What happened when you concentrated on controlling your leg? Why did this happen?

3. A reflex is an automatic response that you can't control. In what ways do voluntary actions, which you can control, differ from reflex actions?

The Senses

Can you name your five senses? Reread the description on page G34 of standing in the lunch line and try to identify the senses. Your senses let you collect information from your environment. When your brain receives this information, it analyzes it and decides on the proper actions by your body.

Your senses work because of sense **receptors,** which are special sensory neurons that can receive stimuli from the environment. These receptors are found in your five sense organs—the skin, tongue, nose, eyes, and ears.

Touch

The skin is the body's largest organ. Your skin protects you, but it also provides you with your sense of touch. Under the skin's surface are receptors that can sense the texture of objects. Other receptors deeper in the skin sense pressure. Still other receptors sense heat, cold, and pain.

These receptors collect this information and pass it along to sensory neurons. The information reaches the brain through nerve impulses, as you saw in the diagram on page G29.

Receptors in the skin provide you with your sense of touch. ▼

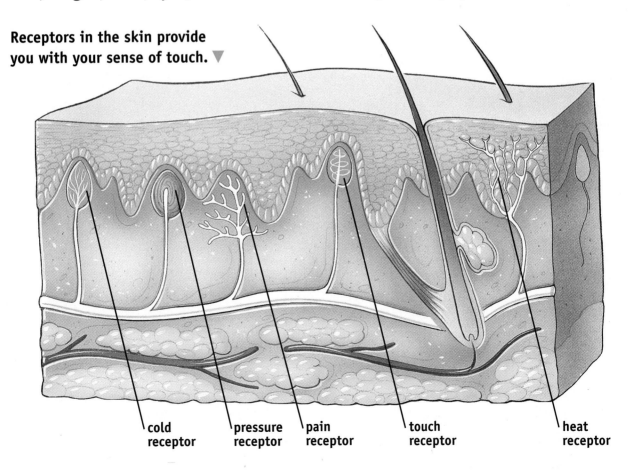

cold receptor | pressure receptor | pain receptor | touch receptor | heat receptor

Taste

Your sense of taste is centered in your tongue, which has taste receptors on its surface. These receptors are bunched together in small round bumps called **taste buds.** Most taste buds lie on the tip and back of the tongue.

Your taste buds only respond to four basic tastes: bitter, sour, sweet, and salty. The many combinations of these four tastes produce the wide variety of tastes you experience.

Smell

Your sense of smell results from receptors in your nose that sense chemical particles floating in the air. These receptors have tiny hairs that extend into the air passages in your nose.

When they sense chemicals, the receptors send nerve impulses to a smell center in the brain. The brain uses its memory bank and interprets these nerve impulses from the nose as odors, or smells.

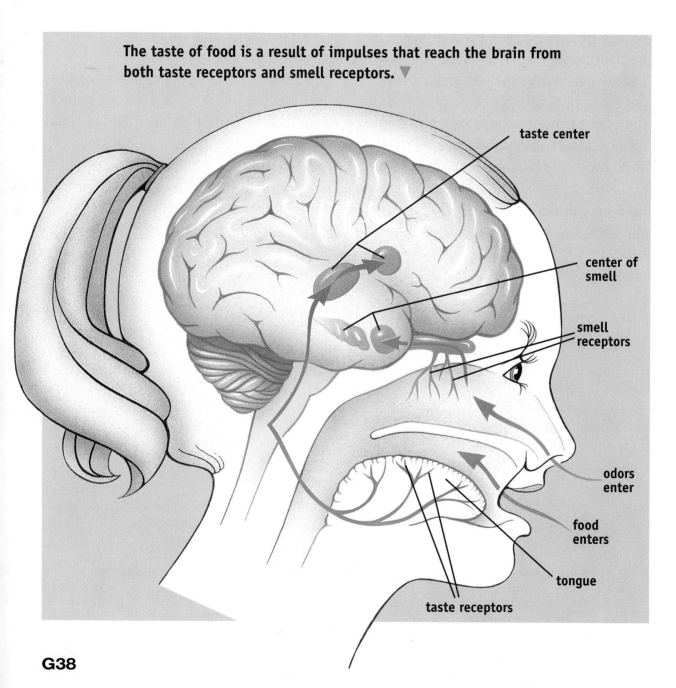

The taste of food is a result of impulses that reach the brain from both taste receptors and smell receptors. ▼

taste center

center of smell

smell receptors

odors enter

food enters

tongue

taste receptors

Sight

Your sense of sight—your vision—is a result of sense receptors within your eyes. These receptors gather information from light rays.

Light enters the eye through the lens, which focuses an image on the surface of the retina (ret′′n ə), at the back of the eye. The light affects receptors on the retina, producing nerve impulses. These nerve impulses travel to the brain along a bundle of neurons called the **optic nerve**. So you actually "see" with your brain.

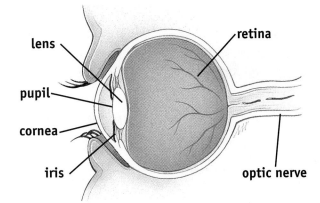

▲ **Light rays are focused by the lens onto the retina. Receptors sense the light and send impulses to the brain through the optic nerve.**

Hearing

Your sense of hearing is a result of receptors in your ears. These receptors sense vibrations in the air.

Sounds are really vibrations that move through the air in waves. Your outer ear collects these sound waves and funnels them in through your ear canal. At the end of the ear canal is a membrane called the eardrum, which vibrates with the sound waves. These vibrations are passed into the inner ear, where receptors turn them into nerve impulses. The impulses travel to the brain through the **auditory nerve.** Your brain interprets these impulses as sound. ■

Your ears are organs that can translate sound waves into nerve impulses. ▼

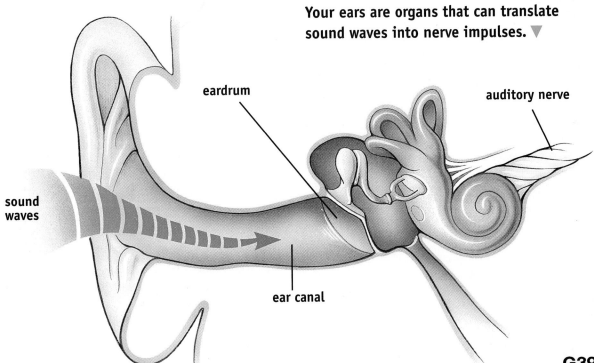

Stages of Mental Development

 TIME Capsule

You've grown quite a bit in the last few years. You're probably much stronger now than you were in the second grade, and you can do things today that you couldn't do before.

Your brain has been growing along with the rest of your body. As you experience more of life and as your brain grows, you gain the ability to think in more complex ways. This process has been going on since you were born.

Everyone is different, and each person's mental abilities develop in different ways. But in some ways we're all alike. We all gain certain mental abilities at about the same stage of life, as you can see in this time line.

Remember, every person develops differently in both physical and mental abilities. Because you're still growing, you can be sure that some things you can't do or understand now will become easier as you grow older. Isn't it nice to know you have things to look forward to!

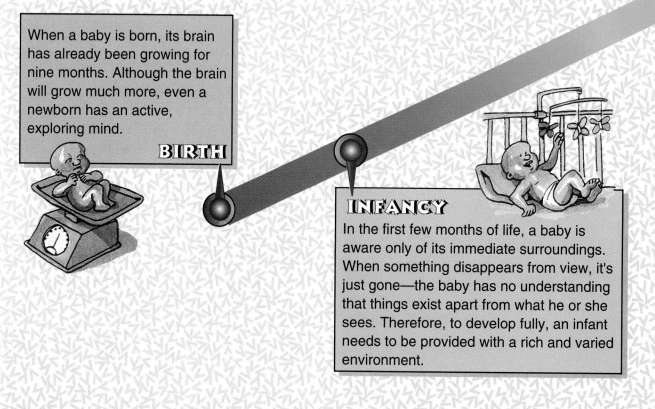

When a baby is born, its brain has already been growing for nine months. Although the brain will grow much more, even a newborn has an active, exploring mind.

BIRTH

INFANCY

In the first few months of life, a baby is aware only of its immediate surroundings. When something disappears from view, it's just gone—the baby has no understanding that things exist apart from what he or she sees. Therefore, to develop fully, an infant needs to be provided with a rich and varied environment.

Children become much more logical at this stage of mental development. They begin to better understand concepts such as time and geography. They not only can find their way around but also can draw a map for others to use. They can now predict how others might think or feel in a situation.

MIDDLE CHILDHOOD

LATE CHILDHOOD

When a young person reaches this stage, he or she can think in terms of symbols and can solve complex mental problems. A person at this stage can approach a problem by forming hypotheses—and testing those hypotheses in a logical way. This is also when a person can begin to reflect upon his or her own life and thoughts.

EARLY CHILDHOOD

As children pass into this stage of life, they master language ability. Using language, they can talk and think about the past—and anticipate the future. This is the time when a child seems always to be asking, "Why?" Children are discovering the world, though at this stage they think the world revolves around them.

UNIT PROJECT LINK

Just as there are stages of mental development, your body too develops over time. And all physical activities are controlled by the nervous system. With your group, think of a physical activity that demonstrates the coordination of the skeletal and muscular systems by the nervous system. The activity should be challenging but not impossible. Make a flowchart to show the pathways of nerve impulses during the activity.

The Path of a Reflex

In Investigation 1 you learned about the path a nerve impulse takes—from a sensory neuron to the spinal cord, to the brain, and then back to a motor neuron. But sometimes there isn't time to think about the action. In those cases, the body responds with a **reflex,** or an automatic reaction to a stimulus.

You investigated your own reflexes in the activity on page G36. Now compare the path of a reflex, pictured below, with the path of a nerve impulse, shown on page G29. The boy's brain is informed that he has taken this reflex action, because another nerve impulse goes up the spinal cord to his brain. But in this instance the brain isn't involved in pulling the hand away.

Can you see why reflexes are important for our survival? Reflexes protect our bodies from harm by allowing us to quickly react to pain or danger. ■

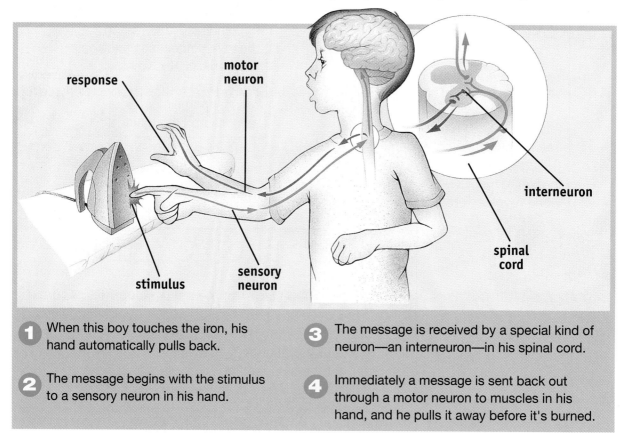

1 When this boy touches the iron, his hand automatically pulls back.

2 The message begins with the stimulus to a sensory neuron in his hand.

3 The message is received by a special kind of neuron—an interneuron—in his spinal cord.

4 Immediately a message is sent back out through a motor neuron to muscles in his hand, and he pulls it away before it's burned.

Brain Power

STS
SCIENCE
TECHNOLOGY
& SOCIETY

As you've already read, nerve impulses are electrical in nature. Neurons have a chemical makeup that gives them the ability to send nerve impulses. The brain contains billions of neurons, and they all produce nerve impulses. In fact, the nerve impulses from your brain—called brain waves—can be measured and recorded by machines. Doctors often record brain waves if they think a patient may have an illness that has affected the brain.

▲ **Doctors measure brain waves to discover the source of some illnesses.**

Using Brain Waves

Some scientists are now working to develop ways to use brain waves in performing simple tasks. This notion may not be so far-fetched. This task involves using a machine to detect brain waves and having a computer respond by signaling electricity to flow.

The first difficulty faced by these scientists has been to figure out how to identify just the brain waves for a specific action. The brain produces so many impulses—so many things are going on at once in a person's head—that it's not clear which brain wave is connected to which mental activity.

Recording Brain Waves

To record brain waves, scientists attach a number of electrodes to a person's head. Electrodes are small metal disks that can pick up electric currents. Wires connect the electrodes to a piece of machinery.

With practice, some people have actually been able to direct a piece of machinery to do certain tasks, such as making a line on a computer screen. The scientists are not sure exactly which impulses from the brain are actually causing the computer to respond and the task to be done. But one thing is clear: Sometimes a thought can be used to direct the action of a machine.

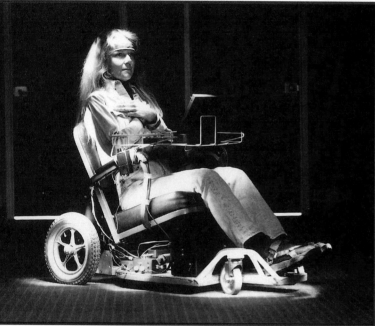

▼ "Look, Mom, no hands!" Could this be you in the not-too-distant future?

Brain-Actuated Technology

What these scientists have been developing is called brain-actuated technology, meaning the machines used are directed by brain waves. The first application of this technology may be in devices for people who have lost the use of parts of their bodies. If a wheelchair could be steered by brain waves, then a person without the use of arms and legs could live a much fuller life.

If this technology is perfected, the future might see all kinds of fantastic technologies. Imagine flying a plane just by thinking about what the plane should do! ■

▲ A brain-actuated wheelchair would be a tremendous help to someone who has lost control of the arms and legs.

INVESTIGATION 2

1. Describe how your nervous system allows you to sense your environment and respond to it. What are the major organs involved?

2. In a physical examination a doctor usually uses a small rubber mallet to test a patient's reflexes. Explain why you think this procedure is important in assessing a person's health.

REFLECT & EVALUATE

WORD POWER

auditory nerve   neurons
cerebellum   receptors
cerebrum   reflex
medulla   stimuli
motor neurons
nerve impulse
optic nerve
sensory neurons
taste buds

 On Your Own
Review the terms in the list. Then use as many terms as you can to make a labeled diagram of the nervous system.

 With a Partner
Write a clue for each term in the list. Then design a crossword puzzle, using the terms. Trade puzzles with your partner.

PORTFOLIO

Draw a diagram of the brain. Label each part and tell what it does.

Analyze Information

Study the drawing. Then describe the path of a nerve impulse during a reflex. Compare this path with the normal path of a nerve impulse.

Assess Performance

Design an experiment to measure reaction time when there are distracting noises. Work with a partner to carry out the experiment. Compare your results to the results from the activity on page G27.

Problem Solving

1. The brain is one of the best-protected organs in the body. Why is this protection important?

2. Dogs have a very keen sense of smell, and bats have highly developed hearing. Which senses are most developed in humans? How are these an advantage? Which senses are not so highly developed? How are these a disadvantage?

3. Reflexes are a means for your body to protect itself. Imagine that you don't have reflexes. What are some things that could happen to you?

CHAPTER 3

STAYING IN CONTROL

Drug abuse. What images come to your mind when you read this phrase? Perhaps you see a person who is out of control, ranting wildly. Or maybe you imagine a dazed person staring blankly into the distance. Now think about an ordinary drugstore and its over-the-counter and prescription medicines. Can even these legal drugs be abused?

Getting the Point

Sally Dan practices acupuncture (ak′yo͞o puŋk chər), an ancient Chinese technique. She uses thin needles to probe points on her patients' bodies. These points seem to be linked with certain functions, such as breathing, or with certain organs, such as the liver. Only a mild tingling or sometimes a stinging sensation is felt.

Acupuncture has long been used to treat pain. But today it also helps addicts break the habit of using heroin, cocaine, nicotine, or alcohol. Recent studies show that those addicts who use acupuncture along with regular rehabilitation techniques stay drug-free longer than those who do not.

Why would people put into their bodies substances that can block awareness and lead to life-threatening disease? What decisions will you make about your own use of drugs?

Coming Up

◀ Acupuncture points are found throughout the body.

INVESTIGATION 1

HOW DO DRUGS AFFECT THE BODY?

Many diseases that commonly killed people in the past are now easily treated with modern drugs. Drugs can be very helpful when they are properly used. What happens to the systems of the body when drugs are misused?

Activity
Ad Power

Both helpful drugs and harmful drugs are common in today's society. How do magazine advertisements influence people about drugs? Find out!

MATERIALS
- posterboard
- marker
- magazines
- scissors
- paste or tape
- *Science Notebook*

Procedure

1. Work in groups of three or four. In your *Science Notebook*, write survey questions to find out people's attitudes about taking medicines and about using tobacco and alcohol. Do people think medicines, alcohol, and tobacco are safe? Do people think these products are safe all the time?

2. With your group, survey ten students and tally the results. Then **create a chart** on posterboard. Show the result of each survey question.

Step 2

3. Look through magazines to find ten advertisements for medicines, alcohol, and tobacco products. Cut out the ads and display them on another piece of posterboard.

4. Show the ads to the same students you surveyed in step 2. Then ask them the survey questions again.

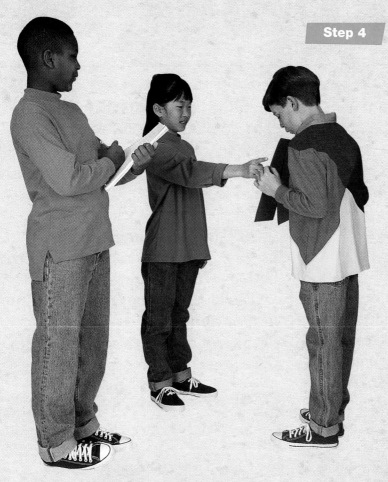

Step 4

5. Tally the results from the second survey and add them to the chart. **Compare** your data from the two surveys. **Discuss** your results with your group and other groups.

Analyze and Conclude

1. Describe the results of your first survey in your *Science Notebook*.

2. Did the results of your second survey differ from those of your first survey? If so, how?

3. Consider the methods the magazine advertisements used to influence readers. What can you conclude about how the ads influenced the students you surveyed?

INVESTIGATE FURTHER!

TAKE ACTION

Survey at least ten adults, using the same survey questions. Create charts to display your results. Then compare the adults' responses with the students' responses. How do the results compare? What can you conclude?

The Misuse of Drugs

Drugs are a common part of our lives. When you are sick, you hope that taking a drug will provide a cure—or at least give some relief. But drugs can also be misused. And when they are misused, they can be very dangerous—even life threatening.

Drugs and Drug Abuse

A **drug** is a substance that can affect the function of body cells and tissues. The kinds of drugs that people can buy in stores are called over-the-counter medicines. To obtain certain types of medical drugs, you need permission from a doctor. Those drugs are called prescription medicines.

Of course, it is very important that you be extremely careful with all drugs. You should not take *any* type of drug—either over-the-counter or prescribed—unless it is given to you by a doctor or by another adult whom you trust. Don't *ever* take even a small amount of a drug on your own.

Certain drugs are found in products that some people use every day. **Caffeine** (ka fēn′) is a drug found in coffee, some teas, chocolate, and some soft drinks. **Alcohol** is a drug found in beer, wine, and other, similar beverages.

Nicotine (nik′ə tēn) is a drug found in tobacco products, such as cigarettes, chewing tobacco, and snuff. Alcohol and nicotine are legal for adults, although their use is regulated.

Finally, there is a whole group of drugs classified as **illegal drugs**. The use of any of these drugs by a person of any age is against the law at all times.

The misuse of any drug is called **substance abuse**. Because drugs affect the function of the body's cells and tissues, the abuse of *any* drug is dangerous.

▲ **Caffeine is found in many familiar food products.**

Alcohol and Tobacco

In our society, adults can legally drink alcoholic beverages and use tobacco products. It is *not* legal for young people to *ever* use these substances. Drinking alcohol in moderate amounts is generally considered to be "socially acceptable" by some people. But when drinking is done to excess, alcohol can cause tremendous problems. You will look closely at alcohol abuse later in this chapter.

Using tobacco is also considered "socially acceptable," but it has become less so in recent years. To many people, smoking cigarettes, cigars, or pipes seems dirty and annoying. Smoking is also extremely unhealthy.

Smoking is a factor in the deaths of over 400,000 Americans every year. It is the major cause of lung cancer and contributes to heart disease. Even when tobacco is chewed rather than smoked, it can cause disease. Cancers of the mouth and throat are related to the use of chewing tobacco and snuff.

If tobacco is so bad, why do so many people use it? Nicotine, the drug found in tobacco, causes an addiction. An **addiction** is a condition in which a person has extreme difficulty in stop-

ping the use of a drug. The addicted person feels powerless to stop because of the physical or mental problems that would result. Many drugs besides nicotine are addictive.

Most adults who smoke began smoking at a young age, usually as teenagers. In most places it is now illegal to sell tobacco products to children and young teenagers. Although many smokers have been able to quit smoking, many more have been unsuccessful, even with help. Don't let yourself be fooled into starting smoking.

UNIT PROJECT LINK

You've read that the use of drugs affects the function of body cells and tissues. The misuse of drugs can impair the body's coordination. With your group, think of an activity, such as a three-legged race, that demonstrates such impaired coordination. The activity should be safe and easy to do. Make up an advertising slogan about your activity. Warn others of the effect of losing physical control due to the misuse of drugs.

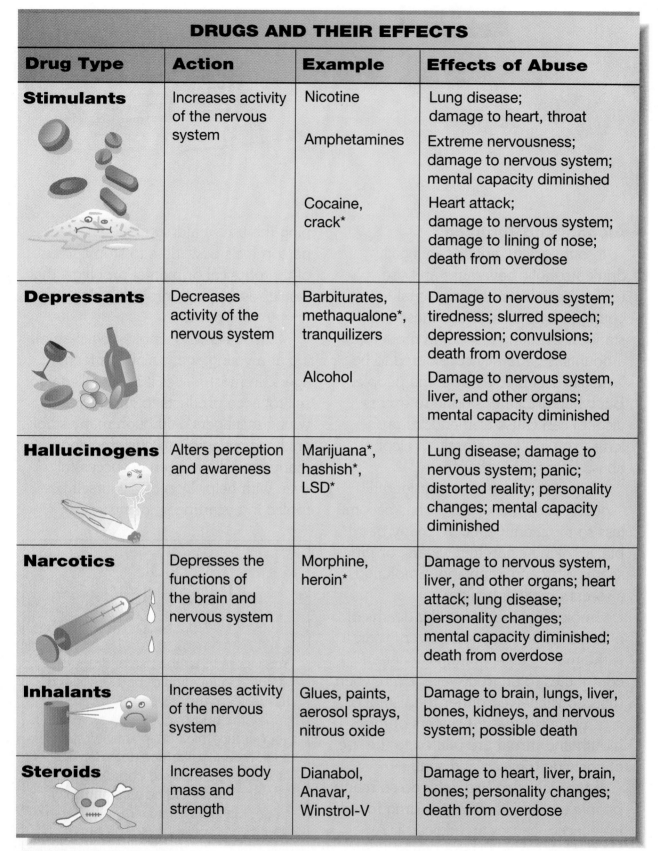

DRUGS AND THEIR EFFECTS

Drug Type	Action	Example	Effects of Abuse
Stimulants	Increases activity of the nervous system	Nicotine	Lung disease; damage to heart, throat
		Amphetamines	Extreme nervousness; damage to nervous system; mental capacity diminished
		Cocaine, crack*	Heart attack; damage to nervous system; damage to lining of nose; death from overdose
Depressants	Decreases activity of the nervous system	Barbiturates, methaqualone*, tranquilizers	Damage to nervous system; tiredness; slurred speech; depression; convulsions; death from overdose
		Alcohol	Damage to nervous system, liver, and other organs; mental capacity diminished
Hallucinogens	Alters perception and awareness	Marijuana*, hashish*, LSD*	Lung disease; damage to nervous system; panic; distorted reality; personality changes; mental capacity diminished
Narcotics	Depresses the functions of the brain and nervous system	Morphine, heroin*	Damage to nervous system, liver, and other organs; heart attack; lung disease; personality changes; mental capacity diminished; death from overdose
Inhalants	Increases activity of the nervous system	Glues, paints, aerosol sprays, nitrous oxide	Damage to brain, lungs, liver, bones, kidneys, and nervous system; possible death
Steroids	Increases body mass and strength	Dianabol, Anavar, Winstrol-V	Damage to heart, liver, brain, bones; personality changes; death from overdose

*an illegal drug

Illegal Drugs

As you know, drugs affect the body's cells and tissues. The short-term effects of many drugs might seem good to the user. Drugs can relax, excite, or give energy. People take illegal drugs to experience these effects.

But illegal drugs have been made illegal because they also have bad effects. Many drugs are extremely addictive. And most, when used for even a short time, can damage vital body organs, such as the liver, brain, and heart. People who abuse illegal drugs are ignoring the long-term harm simply to get short-term pleasure.

Some illegal drugs are taken by using a needle to inject the drug into the bloodstream. There are many risks associated with injections involving unclean needles. AIDS—a fatal disease of the body's immune system—can be spread by improper use of needles.

Taking illegal drugs involves more than just a health risk. People are arrested and jailed for using illegal drugs. If you think about all that you could lose by using illegal drugs, you won't even be tempted for a minute.

Avoiding Drug Abuse

At some point you may be offered some kind of drug to use. First, you should know exactly what is being offered. Study the table of Drugs and Their Effects on page G52 to gain an understanding of the different kinds of drugs that people use and abuse.

Second, think about the reasons *not* to use drugs. Consider both the health risks and the legal risks.

Third, decide now what you would say if someone offered you an illegal drug or suggested you misuse a legal product. You could simply say, "That's trouble, and I don't want any part of it!" ■

▲ **People can learn to overcome their addiction to drugs at treatment centers such as this.**

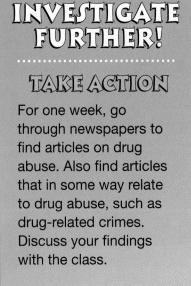

INVESTIGATE FURTHER!

TAKE ACTION

For one week, go through newspapers to find articles on drug abuse. Also find articles that in some way relate to drug abuse, such as drug-related crimes. Discuss your findings with the class.

Drugs and Sports

At the sound of the gun, the runners exploded from the starting blocks. This was the 100-meter dash at the 1988 Summer Olympics in Seoul, South Korea. The winner of the race would be called the fastest human alive.

No one who saw the event will ever forget the scene. The sprinters ran in a pack for about half the distance. Then Canada's Ben Johnson seemed to take off like a jet. He crossed the finish line in a burst of speed as the excited crowd cheered its new hero.

But within a few days, Johnson's prized gold medal had been taken back, and his name had been erased forever from the record books. Medical tests showed that Johnson had taken certain drugs to build up his muscles and make himself run faster.

Why Athletes Use Drugs

Athletes feel great pressure to perform. They want to make the first team or win the big race. They know the coach is counting on them. They want to impress their families and friends. Also, winning often means big money.

For those reasons, some athletes try to improve their performances by using drugs. These drugs might help in building muscles, or they might take away the pain of an injury. They might even help the athlete run faster or run longer.

The pressure to use steroids is greatest in sports where strength makes a big difference, such as weight lifting and football. ▼

Kinds of Drugs Used

Athletes who abuse drugs mainly use three kinds of drugs—stimulants, narcotics, and steroids. **Steroids** (stir′-oidz) are drugs that act like certain natural chemicals found in the body called hormones. Steroids can help an athlete build up muscles and gain strength. This is the kind of drug that Ben Johnson took. He did get short-term benefits, but he also put himself at risk for long-term damage. The use of steroids can harm the heart and other organs as well as cause personality changes and possible death.

Athletes also use **stimulants**, which speed up the nervous system. A stimulant may make an athlete more active and alert. But abuse over a long period can damage the nervous system.

Finally, athletes with injuries may be tempted to use **narcotics**—heroin, for example. Narcotics can lessen pain, but they're also very addictive. And they can damage many body systems.

Banned From Sports

Athletic organizations forbid the use of steroids, stimulants, and narcotics for two reasons. First, the drugs can be

▲ Although Ben Johnson was the greatest sprinter in Canadian history, his use of steroids cost him an Olympic gold medal.

very harmful to those who take them. And second, they give an unfair advantage to those who use the drugs over those who don't. Ben Johnson cheated, and for that reason he lost his medal.

Sports organizations test athletes for drugs, usually just after a performance or event. A person caught using drugs may be banned from the sport.

Most athletes don't use drugs. With hard work, a good diet, and proper rest, they are able to win fairly and without risking their health. ■

INVESTIGATION 1

1. A friend has just asked you to help her convince young people not to smoke. How would you try to encourage your classmates to avoid tobacco?

2. Explain the difference between the short-term and the long-term effects of drugs. Why should you consider the long-term effects over the short-term effects if you're ever tempted to try drugs?

INVESTIGATION 2

HOW DOES ALCOHOL AFFECT THE BODY?

When a person takes a drink of alcohol, it goes into the bloodstream almost immediately. Within a few minutes, the alcohol causes changes in the way the person feels and acts. Find out more about the effects of alcohol in Investigation 2.

Activity

Alcohol Advertising: Pro and Con

Billboards, magazines, and newspapers all show ads for alcohol, even though it is a drug. What's your stand on whether these ads should be allowed?

Procedure

1. Your teacher will divide your class into teams for a debate. Your team will be either for or against alcohol advertising.

2. **Discuss** your side of the debate with your team members. Divide research responsibilities among members.

3. Use reference materials to find information to support your side of the debate. Also **talk** to people who might give you helpful information. **Record** your information in your *Science Notebook*.

4. **Talk** with your team members and share information. Decide on your strongest points. **Predict** what points the other side will make. Plan your arguments.

5. Debate the other team. Your teacher will act as a moderator.

Analyze and Conclude

1. What were the strongest points your team made? What arguments against these points did the other team use?

2. What were the strongest points made by the other team? What arguments against these points did your team members use?

3. Which team do you think won the debate? Explain.

Step 5

INVESTIGATE FURTHER!

TAKE ACTION

Use the best points from your debate to write a letter to an editor of a newspaper or magazine. Explain how you feel about the issue of alcohol advertising.

Alcohol in the Body

Have you ever seen adults who have been drinking beer or wine? They can seem pretty silly, with a little too much laughter and loud talking.

Actually, people may drink alcoholic beverages just to get those kinds of effects. Sometimes, alcohol can seem to lift a person's spirits. Shyness falls away, and it seems easier to relax.

The problem is that alcohol can be very dangerous to the body, especially when abused. You may decide you want to drink when you become an adult. But before you do, you should learn what alcohol does to the body.

What Happens to the Body

Alcohol is a part of every alcoholic beverage, including beer, wine, and the various liquors. When a person drinks one of these beverages, the alcohol in the drink is absorbed directly into the bloodstream through the walls of the stomach. Unlike food, alcohol does not need to be digested, and so it quickly moves throughout the body.

In the body, alcohol increases both the heart rate and the blood pressure. The blood vessels in the skin expand. That effect often results in a reddishness of the drinker's nose and cheeks. Sometimes people think the drinker

looks warm, and maybe the face is. But alcohol actually causes a loss of heat from the body. No one should ever drink alcohol to keep warm.

Another misunderstanding is that drinking alcohol adds fluids to the body. Actually, alcohol causes the tissues of the body to lose water. So despite drinking even a large amount of alcohol, a person could end up with less fluid than his or her body needs.

Alcohol is a depressant drug. It depresses the workings of the nervous system. It affects how well the brain functions and how well the neurons throughout the body carry messages.

This effect on the nervous system is what causes people to become less shy, for example. But the effect also accounts for many of the dangers of drinking alcohol. Physically, people become slow and clumsy. All kinds of accidents can result. Also, thinking is affected. Bad judgment can lead to accidents as well as to lost friendships and missed opportunities.

A Drinker's Fate

Bad things can happen to a person in just a few hours of drinking. A person who has been drinking is more likely than others to cause accidents.

G58

WHAT ALCOHOL DOES TO THE BODY

Alcohol affects every part of the body because it is carried throughout the body by the bloodstream.

BRAIN Alcohol kills brain cells and affects the functioning of neurons. The result is slurred speech, clumsy movements, slow thinking, and bad judgment. Over the long term, alcohol can cause mental illness.

BLOOD VESSELS Alcohol causes blood vessels to expand in the skin, resulting in a reddishness and heat loss.

LIVER Alcohol damages the liver.

HEART Alcohol raises the heart rate and increases the blood pressure. Over the long term, it can cause heart disease.

KIDNEYS Alcohol reduces the amount of fluid reabsorbed by the kidneys.

STOMACH Alcohol upsets the stomach in the short term and damages the digestive system over time.

Violent behavior often accompanies drinking too much alcohol. A person who abuses alcohol over many years causes serious damage to the body.

Some people can become addicted to alcohol just as they can become addicted to other drugs. The disease that results is called **alcoholism**. The alcohol addict, or alcoholic, may suffer from many illnesses or disorders.

Alcohol destroys brain cells. The alcoholic gradually loses brain function and may become mentally ill. Alcohol severely damages the liver, and many alcoholics die from liver disease. Over a period of time, alcohol also causes digestive problems and heart disease. There is no question that alcohol has destroyed many lives.

Perhaps more tragic is that alcohol can also affect an unborn child. When a pregnant woman drinks alcohol, the alcohol also enters her baby's system. This can then result in fetal alcohol syndrome, a condition in which the baby is born deformed or with a damaged nervous system.

Avoiding Alcohol Use

Sometimes it might seem like most adults drink alcohol. Actually, only about half do. Many adults have decided that the long-term risks to health are not worth any short-term pleasure.

Certainly it is more risky for young people to drink, because their bodies are still growing. It is also illegal for a person your age to drink alcohol. ∎

SCIENCE IN LITERATURE

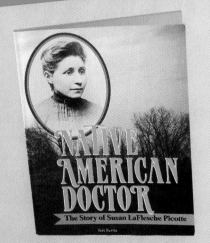

NATIVE AMERICAN DOCTOR: THE STORY OF SUSAN LAFLESCHE PICOTTE
by Jeri Ferris
Carolrhoda Books, 1991

By the 1860s the Native Americans of the Great Plains had lost their best hunting and farming lands to white settlers. White traders had slaughtered the buffalo. Many Native American traditions seemed meaningless. But then a new hero emerged. Susan LaFlesche Picotte—an Omaha Indian, the first Native American woman to receive a medical diploma—worked to build bridges between her people and the white world.

Native American Doctor by Jeri Ferris is the story of this remarkable woman. She was a doctor, advisor, and translator to the Omaha of Nebraska. In all her roles, she fought against alcohol abuse, which she saw as the greatest medical problem of her people.

Alcohol and Driving

A leading cause of death among teenagers is drunk driving. ▶

SCIENCE TECHNOLOGY & SOCIETY

The leading cause of death among American teenagers is accidents. Alcohol is a factor in about half of all accidents that are auto-related. It contributes to the deaths of as many as 20,000 people every year.

The high number of auto deaths involving alcohol has caused Americans to take a harsh view of anyone who drinks and then drives. Penalties for such lawbreaking are severe.

Highway Safety

Every state has laws against driving under the influence of alcohol. When an accident occurs, the police check whether a driver has been drinking by testing the person's **blood alcohol concentration (BAC)**. A BAC test shows how much alcohol is in the person's blood, and that tells how many drinks the person has had.

The table on page G62 shows how a certain number of drinks changes the BAC and affects the drinker. In most states a person is considered legally intoxicated, usually known as being drunk, when the BAC is 0.1 percent or more. But no one should drive after having even one drink, because judgment will have been impaired.

Young People and Drunk Driving

Teenagers who are old enough to drive are just gaining experience at that skill. Imagine adding the effects of illegal alcohol consumption to their inexperience! The result of this combination is that a large number of alcohol-related traffic accidents involve teenagers.

What does this mean for you? Don't *ever* get into a car with anyone who has been drinking. And when you're on a bike or crossing a street, watch carefully for reckless drivers. Stay alert so that you won't become involved in an alcohol-related accident. ■

▲ **Police may use a BAC-testing device if they suspect a driver has been drinking.**

Drinks in 1 hr	BAC (%)	Effects on a Driver (weight, 120 lb)
1	0.03	Increase in heart rate; decrease in coordination
2	0.05	Reduced ability to make good decisions; reduced coordination
3	0.08	Decrease in attention and alertness; slurred speech; slowness in reactions; further decrease in ability to make good decisions
4	0.10	Legally intoxicated; very slow reaction time; terrible coordination; loss of balance; further decrease in ability to make good decisions
5	0.13	Visibly intoxicated; vomiting; poor body control and decision making
6	0.16	Limited awareness; almost no control of body or decision making

INVESTIGATION 2

1. Describe some of the short-term and long-term effects of alcohol on the body. How are some of the short-term effects dangerous not only to drinkers but also to others around them?

2. Why is a warning to avoid drinking alcohol often shown on medicines that depress the activity of the nervous system?

WORD POWER

addiction
alcohol
alcoholism
blood alcohol concentration
caffeine
drug
illegal drugs
narcotics
nicotine
steroids
stimulants
substance abuse

On Your Own
Write a definition for each term in the list.

With a Partner
Make up a quiz, using all the terms in the list. Challenge your partner to complete the quiz.

BUILD YOUR PORTFOLIO

Make a concept map, starting with the word *drug*. On your concept map, include both legal and illegal drugs and some of their effects.

Analyze Information

Study the drawing. Then identify the organs that are affected by alcohol and explain how alcohol reaches those organs.

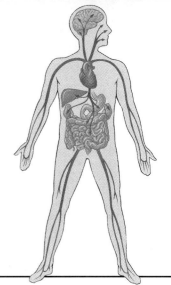

Assess Performance

Design a test to find out how advertisements for drugs influence people. You might want to have people answer questions about various ads or challenge them to match slogans to the correct products, or you may have a different idea. Discuss your findings with your classmates.

Problem Solving

1. Imagine there's a debate over whether to allow members to smoke at your youth center. What arguments could you use to convince others that it's not a good idea to allow smoking?

2. Why might it be harmful for you to take some of another family member's leftover prescription medicine when you have similar symptoms?

3. How could you discourage a friend on your team from using steroids when he or she feels a lot of pressure to succeed in a sport?

4. You've arranged to ride home from a party with a friend. Your friend's sister picks you up, and you haven't gone far before you realize that she's been drinking. What should you do?

Throughout this unit you've investigated questions related to movement and control. How will you use what you've learned and share that information with others? Here are some ideas.

Hold a Big Event
to Share Your Unit Project

Work with your classmates to plan The Bone, Muscle, Brain Triathlon. This competitive athletic meet will have three categories: Movement Events, Coordination Events, and Impaired Coordination Events. Use the physical activities that your group planned for the Unit Project Links. Gather any props and equipment you may need. Then invite families and friends to come enjoy the Triathlon...and have fun!

Experiment

Explore this test of muscular control. Tape your thumb to the side of your hand. Then use that hand to pick up a pencil. Can you control your fingers well? What adjustments do you have to make? What can you conclude about the importance of having an opposable thumb?

Research

Choose a sport that you enjoy or would like to learn. Find out which muscles must be developed to excel in this sport. Does a baseball player, for example, need to stretch, build upper or lower body strength, or need aerobic exercise? Write and share a report about your sport.

Take Action

Think of a way to educate others about the dangers of tobacco, alcohol, and other drugs. You might write a story or poem, produce radio announcements, design posters, or do something else that will discourage people from using drugs. Carry out your plan yourself or with some classmates.

SCIENCE Handbook

THINK LIKE A SCIENTIST

You don't have to be a professional scientist to act and think like one. Thinking like a scientist mostly means using common sense. It also means learning how to test your ideas in a careful way.

In other words, *you* can think like a scientist.

Make a Hypothesis

Plan and Do a Test

Make Observations

To think like a scientist, you should learn as much as you can by observing things around you. Everything you hear and see is a clue about how the natural world works.

Ask a Question

Look for patterns. You'll get ideas and ask questions like these:

- Do all birds eat the same seeds?

- How does the time that the Sun sets change from day to day?

Make a Guess Called a Hypothesis

If you have an idea about why or how something happens, make an educated guess, or *hypothesis*, that you can test. For example, let's suppose that your hypothesis about the sunset time is that it changes by one minute each day.

Plan and Do a Test

Plan how to test your hypothesis. Your plan would need to consider some of these problems:

- How will you measure the time that the Sun sets?

- Will you measure the time every day?

- For how many days or weeks do you need to measure?

Record and Analyze What Happens

When you test your idea, you need to observe carefully and write down, or record, everything that happens. When you finish collecting data, you may need to do some calculations with it. For example, you might want to calculate how much the sunset time changes in a week or a month.

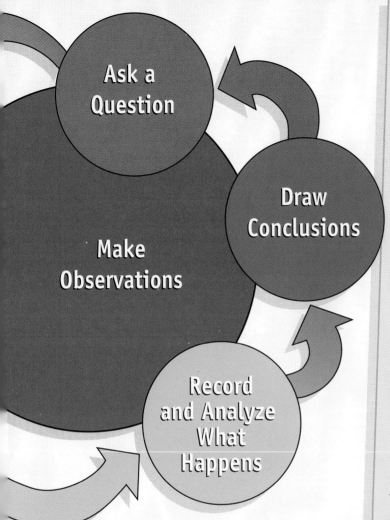

Ask a Question

Make Observations

Draw Conclusions

Record and Analyze What Happens

Draw Conclusions

Whatever happens in a test, think about all the reasons for your results. For example, you might wonder what causes the time of sunset to change. You might also ask when the earliest and latest sunsets occur during the year. Sometimes this thinking leads to a new hypothesis.

If the time of the sunset changes by one minute each day, think about what else the data shows you. Can you predict the time that the Sun will set one month from now?

PRACTICE SCIENTIFIC REASONING SKILLS

To think like a scientist, you need to practice certain ways of thinking.

Always check for yourself.
Always ask, "How do I really know it's true?" Be willing to find out for yourself.

Be honest and careful about what you observe.
It's easy to only look for the results you expect. It's harder to see the unexpected. But unexpected results lead scientists to ask more questions. They also provide information on how things work.

Don't be afraid to be wrong.
Based on their observations, scientists make many hypotheses. Not all of these hypotheses turn out to be correct. But scientists can learn from wrong "guesses," because even wrong guesses result in information that leads to knowledge.

Keep an open mind about possible explanations.
Make sure to think about all the reasons why something might have happened. Consider all the explanations that you can think of.

WHAT CAUSES THE ROCK IN STATUES TO WEAR AWAY?

Donelle and Ramon were walking through downtown when Ramon pointed to a statue, laughed, and said, "Look, that poor guy's nose has fallen off." Donelle laughed and as they both took a closer look at the statue, they could see that most of the statue's face was missing. Even the statue's body was pitted.

Donelle thought she knew why. She suspected that rain, snow, and ice were destroying the statue. "But it's stone," Ramon argued. "Stone doesn't dissolve in water. Does it?" "But don't we get acid rain here?" Donelle replied. "Maybe acid rain destroys stone."

The next day in school, Donelle described the "melting" statue to the

Make Observations

Ask a Question

class. Mr. Reynolds, their teacher, suggested that the class set up an experiment to find out what might be causing the damage to the statue. To begin, they came up with some questions that they wanted to answer.

What is destroying this statue?

Is rain destroying this statue?

Are cold winter temperatures destroying this statue?

The class decided that the first question was not specific enough. They

Here's an example of an everyday problem and how thinking like a scientist can help you explore it.

Make a Hypothesis

Before the class could begin setting up an experiment, there were some things they had to find out about the problem. First, they had to find out what the statue was made of. Ramon contacted City Hall and found out that the statue was made out of a stone called limestone.

Donelle told her classmates that she thought that the rain that fell on their town was sometimes acid. So Donelle and her classmates took samples of rainwater. They tested the rainwater with litmus paper and discovered that the rain was acidic.

The class thought about the new information they now had. It was time to use this information to formulate a hypothesis that they could test. Their hypothesis was "Acid rain eats away limestone."

decided to test whether rain could be destroying the statue. Students were curious about whether pollution in the air, and thus in the rain, might be affecting the statue.

Scientific investigations usually begin with something that you have noticed or read about. As you think about what you already know, you'll discover some ideas that you're not sure about. This will help you to ask the question that you really want to answer.

When you use what you have observed to suggest a possible answer to your question, you are making a *hypothesis*. Be sure that your hypothesis is an idea that you can test somehow. If you can't think of an experiment or a model to test your hypothesis, try changing it. Sometimes it's better to make a simpler, clearer hypothesis that answers only part of your question.

Plan and Do a Test

Make Observations

Ramon, Donelle, and their classmates designed a way to test their hypothesis. First, Mr. Reynolds got some fairly equal-sized lumps of limestone for the class to use. Donelle set up three flat-bottomed beakers big enough to hold the chunks of limestone. Ramon created a table for recording information.

The students had discussed what kind of solutions they should use in each beaker. They decided to put rainwater they'd collected in one beaker. They decided to put a more acidic solution in the second beaker. Mr. Reynolds provided them with a solution of weak sulfuric acid. The students knew that the third beaker should contain only pure, distilled water.

The third beaker served as the students' control. The control part of an experiment is almost identical to the other parts of the experiment. It is different in just one way: it doesn't have the condition that is being tested. In this case, the class was testing the effects on limestone of water that is acidic. To make sure that their results only reflect the effects of acid, and not something else that might be in water, the students set up a control in which acid was missing.

After the three beakers were each filled with their specific liquid and labeled, the students found the mass of each chunk of limestone and then put one in each beaker.

The students placed the beakers on a lab table at the back of the classroom. A square piece of glass was placed over each beaker to keep out dirt and dust that might affect the results.

One way to try out your hypothesis is to use a test called an experiment. When you plan an experiment, be sure that it helps you to answer your question. But even when you plan, things can happen that make the experiment confusing or make it not work properly. If this happens, you can change the plan or the experiment, and try again.

Record and Analyze What Happened

Make Observations

After seven days, the mass of each limestone chunk was found again. The mass was recorded on the chart on the board. The chunk was replaced in the same beaker. This was repeated every seven days.

The students recorded the mass of the limestone chunks for fourteen weeks. At the end of the experiment, their chart looked like the one on the next page.

The students analyzed the data on their chart. Donelle noted that the more acidic the solution in the beaker, the more mass the limestone "lost." Ramon noted that the mass of the limestone in the beaker containing distilled water remained the same. The limestone in the rainwater beaker "lost" some mass, but not as much as the limestone chunk in the beaker containing sulfuric acid.

Mass of Limestone Each Week (in grams)

| | \multicolumn{14}{c|}{Week} |
	1	2	3	4	5	6	7	8	9	10	11	12	13	14
Rainwater	83	83	82	82	81	80	80	79	79	78	77	77	76	75
Sulfuric acid solution	76	74	71	69	68	65	63	60	59	55	53	50	48	45
Distilled water	79	79	79	79	79	79	79	79	79	79	79	79	79	79

When you do an experiment, you need to write down, or record, your observations. Some of your observations might be numbers of things that you counted or measured. Your recorded observations are called data. When you record your data, you need to organize it in a way that helps you to understand it. Graphs and tables are helpful ways to organize data. Then think about the information you have collected. Analyze what it tells you.

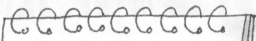

in the same way, or if it destroyed only limestone. Ramon posed his question to Mr. Reynolds and the other students. Then Patrick added, "And I wonder if cold weather makes the effects of acid rain even worse."

It was soon evident that though their experiment had showed that acid rain does affect limestone, a whole new set of questions occurred to them.

After you have analyzed your data, you should use what you have learned to draw a conclusion. A conclusion is a statement that sums up what you learned. The conclusion should be about the question you asked. Think about whether the information you have gathered supports your hypothesis or not. If it does, figure out how to test out your idea more thoroughly. Also think about new questions you can ask.

Make Observations

Draw Conclusions

Both Ramon and Donelle thought that it looked like their hypothesis was supported. Water containing an acid, or acid rain, did eat away limestone. But Ramon was still not completely satisfied. He wondered if acid rain affected all kinds of stone

SAFETY

The best way to be safe in the classroom is to use common sense. Prepare yourself for each activity before you start it. Get help from your teacher when there is a problem. Most important of all, pay attention. Here are some other ways that you can stay safe.

Stay Safe From Stains

- Wear protective clothing or an old shirt when you work with messy materials.
- If anything spills, wipe it up or ask your teacher to help you clean it up.

Stay Safe From Flames

- Keep your clothes away from open flames. If you have long or baggy sleeves, roll them up.
- Don't let your hair get close to a flame. If you have long hair, tie it back.

Stay Safe From Injuries

- Protect your eyes by wearing safety goggles when you are told that you need them.
- Keep your hands dry around electricity. Water is a good conductor of electricity, so you can get a shock more easily if your hands are wet.
- Be careful with sharp objects. If you have to press on them, keep the sharp side away from you.
- Cover any cuts you have that are exposed. If you spill something on a cut, be sure to wash it off immediately.
- Don't eat or drink anything unless your teacher tells you that it's okay.

Stay Safe During Cleanup

- Wash up after you finish working.
- Dispose of things in the way that your teacher tells you to.

MOST IMPORTANTLY

If you ever hurt yourself or one of your group members gets hurt, tell your teacher right away.

DON'T MAKE A MESS If you spill something, clean it up right away. When finished with an activity, clean up your work area. Dispose of things in the way your teacher tells you to.

HAIR Keep it out of the way of a flame.

EYES Wear safety goggles when you are told to.

MOUTH Don't eat or drink ANYTHING unless your teacher tells you it's okay.

HANDS Keep your hands dry around electricity. Cover any cuts. Wear gloves when told to. Wash up after you finish.

CLOTHES Keep long sleeves rolled up. Protect yourself from stains. Stay away from open flames.

Using a Microscope

A microscope makes it possible to see very small things by magnifying them. Some microscopes have a set of lenses to magnify objects different amounts.

Examine Some Salt Grains

Handle a microscope carefully; it can break easily. Carry it firmly with both hands and avoid touching the lenses.

1. Turn the mirror toward a source of light. **NEVER** use the Sun as a light source.

2. Place a few grains of salt on the slide. Put the slide on the stage of the microscope.

3. While looking through the eyepiece, turn the adjustment knob on the back of the microscope to bring the salt grains into focus.

4. Raise the eyepiece tube to increase the magnification; lower it to decrease magnification.

Using a Calculator

After you've made measurements, a calculator can help you analyze your data. Some calculators have a memory key that allows you to save the result of one calculation while you do another.

Find an Average

The table shows the amount of rain that was collected using a rain gauge in each month of one year. You can use a calculator to help you find the average monthly rainfall.

1. Add the numbers. When you add a series of numbers, you don't need to press the equal sign until the last number is entered. Just press the plus sign after you enter each number (except the last one).

2. If you make a mistake while you are entering numbers, try to erase your mistake by pushing the clear entry (CE) key or the clear (C) key. Then you can continue entering the rest of the numbers you are adding. If you can't fix your mistake, you can push the (C) key once or twice until the screen shows 0. Then start over.

3. Your total should be 1,131. You can use the total to find the average. Just divide by the number of months in the year.

These keys run the calculator's memory functions.

This key erases the last entry.

Rainfall	
Month	**Rain (mm)**
Jan.	214
Feb.	138
Mar.	98
Apr.	157
May	84
June	41
July	5
Aug.	23
Sept.	48
Oct.	75
Nov.	140
Dec.	108

Using a Balance

A balance is used to measure mass. Mass is the amount of matter in an object. Place the object to be massed in the left pan. Place standard masses in the right pan.

Measure the Mass of an Orange

1. Check that the empty pans are balanced, or level with each other. The pointer at the base should be on the middle mark. If it needs to be adjusted, move the slider on the back of the balance a little to the left or right.

2. Place an orange on the left pan. Notice that the pointer moves and that the pans are no longer level with each other. Then add standard masses, one at a time, to the right pan. When the pointer is at the middle mark again, the pans are balanced. Each pan holds the same amount of mass.

3. Each standard mass is marked to show the number of grams it contains. Add the number of grams marked on the masses in the pan. The total is the mass in grams of the orange.

Using a
Spring Scale

A spring scale is used to measure force.
You can use a spring scale to find the weight
of an object in newtons. You can also use
the scale to measure other forces.

Measure the Weight of an Object

1. Place the object in a net bag, and hang it from the hook on the bottom of the spring scale. Or, if possible, hang the object directly from the hook.

2. Slowly lift the scale by the top hook. Be sure the object to be weighed continues to hang from the bottom hook.

3. Wait until the pointer on the face of the spring scale has stopped moving. Read the number next to the pointer to determine the weight of the object in newtons.

Measure Friction

1. Hook the object to the bottom of the spring scale. Use a rubber band to connect the spring scale and object if needed.

2. Gently pull the top hook of the scale parallel to the floor. When the object starts to move, read the number of newtons next to the pointer on the scale. This number is the force of friction between the floor and the object as you drag the object.

Using a Thermometer

A thermometer is used to measure temperature. When the liquid in the tube of a thermometer gets warmer, it expands and moves farther up the tube. Different units can be used to measure temperature, but scientists usually use the Celsius scale.

Measure the Temperature of a Cold Liquid

1. Half-fill a cup with chilled liquid.

2. Hold the thermometer so that the bulb is in the center of the liquid.

3. Wait until you see the liquid in the tube stop moving. Read the scale line that is closest to the top of the liquid in the tube.

Measuring

Volume

A graduated cylinder, a measuring cup, and a beaker are used to measure volume. Volume is the amount of space something takes up. Most of the containers that scientists use to measure volume have a scale marked in milliliters (mL).

Measure the Volume of Juice

1. Pour the juice into a measuring container.

2. Move your head so that your eyes are level with the top of the juice. Read the scale line that is closest to the surface of the juice. If the surface of the juice is curved up on the sides, look at the lowest point of the curve.

3. You can estimate the value between two lines on the scale to obtain a more accurate measurement.

▲ The bottom of the curve is at 50 mL.

This graduated cylinder has marks for every 1 mL. ▶

This beaker has marks for each 25 mL. ▼

This measuring cup has marks for each 25 mL. ▼

Each container above has 50 mL of juice.

MEASUR

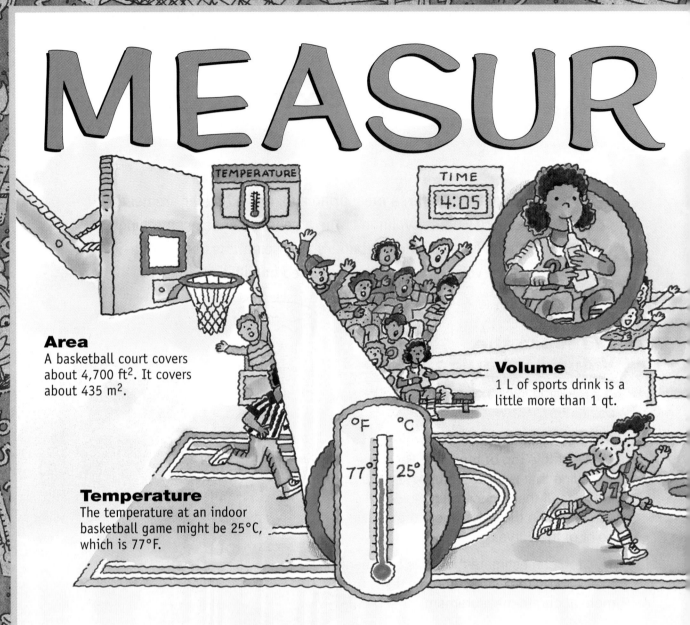

Area
A basketball court covers about 4,700 ft². It covers about 435 m².

Volume
1 L of sports drink is a little more than 1 qt.

Temperature
The temperature at an indoor basketball game might be 25°C, which is 77°F.

SI Measures

Temperature
Ice melts at 0 degrees Celsius (°C)

Water freezes at 0°C

Water boils at 100°C

Length and Distance
1,000 meters (m) = 1 kilometer (km)

100 centimeters (cm) = 1 m

10 millimeters (mm) = 1 cm

Force
1 newton (N) =
1 kilogram x meter/second/second
(kg x m/s²)

Volume
1 cubic meter (m³) = 1 m x 1 m x 1 m

1 cubic centimeter (cm³) =
1 cm x 1 cm x 1 cm

1 liter (L) = 1,000 milliliters (mL)

1 cm³ = 1 mL

Area
1 square kilometer (km²) = 1 km x 1 km

1 hectare = 10,000 m²

Mass
1,000 grams (g) = 1 kilogram (kg)

1,000 milligrams (mg) = 1 g

EMENTS

Mass and Weight
A basketball has a mass of about 650 g.
It weighs about $1\frac{1}{2}$ lb.

Length/Distance
A basketball rim is about
10 ft high, or a little more
than 3 m from the floor.

Rates (SI and English)
km/h = kilometers per hour

m/s = meters per second

mph = miles per hour

English Measures

Volume of Fluids
8 fluid ounces (fl oz) = 1 cup (c)

2 c = 1 pint (pt)

2 pt = 1 quart (qt)

4 qt = 1 gallon (gal)

Temperature
Ice melts at 32 degrees
Fahrenheit (°F)

Water freezes at 32°F

Water boils at 212°F

Length and Distance
12 inches (in.) = 1 foot (ft)

3 ft = 1 yard (yd)

5,280 ft = 1 mile (mi)

Weight
16 ounces (oz) = 1 pound (lb)   2,000 pounds = 1 ton (T)

GLOSSARY

Pronunciation Key

Symbol	Key Words
a	c**a**t
ā	**a**pe
ä	c**o**t, c**a**r
e	t**e**n, b**e**rry
ē	m**e**
i	f**i**t, h**e**re
ī	**i**ce, f**i**re
ō	g**o**
ô	f**a**ll, f**o**r
oi	**oi**l
oo	l**oo**k, p**u**ll
o͞o	t**oo**l, r**u**le
ou	**ou**t, cr**ow**d
u	**u**p
ʉ	f**u**r, sh**i**rt
ə	**a** in **a**go
	e in ag**e**nt
	i in penc**i**l
	o in at**o**m
	u in circ**u**s
b	**b**ed
d	**d**og
f	**f**all

Symbol	Key Words
g	**g**et
h	**h**elp
j	**j**ump
k	**k**iss, call
l	**l**eg
m	**m**eat
n	**n**ose
p	**p**ut
r	**r**ed
s	**s**ee
t	**t**op
v	**v**at
w	**w**ish
y	**y**ard
z	**z**ebra
ch	**ch**in, ar**ch**
ŋ	ri**ng**, dri**n**k
sh	**sh**e, pu**sh**
th	**th**in, tru**th**
th	**th**en, fa**th**er
zh	mea**s**ure

A heavy stress mark ′ is placed after a syllable that gets a heavy, or primary, stress, as in **picture** (pik′chər).

A

absolute age The actual age of an object. (E79) The *absolute age* of this statue is 3,500 years.

absolute magnitude The measure of a star's brightness, based on the amount of light it actually gives off. (B61) The Sun's *absolute magnitude* is less than that of many stars, but its apparent magnitude exceeds that of any other star.

adaptation (ad əp tā'shən) A structure or behavior that enables an organism to survive in its environment. (A70, A86) The thick fur of some animals is an *adaptation* to cold environments.

addiction (ə dik'shən) A condition in which a person has extreme difficulty in stopping the use of a drug. (G51) Sometimes it takes only a short time to develop an *addiction* to a drug.

alcohol (al'kə hôl) A drug that is found in some beverages, such as beer and wine. (G50) If a person drinks *alcohol* to excess, problems can occur.

alcoholism (al'kə hôl iz əm) A disease that results from the continual misuse of alcohol. (G60) Doctors continue to learn more about *alcoholism*.

amplitude (am'plə tood) A measure of the amount of energy in a sound wave. (F57) The *amplitude* of a loud sound is greater than the amplitude of a soft sound.

anticline (an'ti klīn) An upward fold of rock layers. (E84) Bending layers of rock formed an *anticline*.

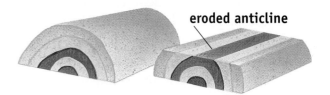

eroded anticline

apparent magnitude The measure of a star's brightness as seen from Earth. (B61) A star's *apparent magnitude* depends on the amount of light it gives off and on its distance from Earth.

asexual reproduction (ā sek'shoo əl rē prə duk'shən) A process in which offspring are produced from one or more cells of a single parent. (A62) In *asexual reproduction*, the offspring is identical to the parent.

audiocassette (ô'dē ō kə set) A small container holding magnetic tape that is used for playing or recording sound. (F92) We inserted an *audiocassette* into the tape recorder.

auditory nerve (ô'də tôr ē nʉrv) A nerve in the ear that carries nerve impulses to the brain. (G39, F85) The *auditory nerve* contains sensory neurons.

axis The imaginary line on which an object rotates. (B13) Earth's *axis* runs between the North and South poles.

Big Bang Theory A hypothesis, supported by data, that describes how the universe began with a huge explosion. (B39) The *Big Bang Theory* holds that everything in the universe was once concentrated at one tiny point.

biodiversity (bī ō də vʉr′sə tē) The variety of organisms that live in Earth's many ecosystems; the variety of plants and animals that live within a particular ecosystem. (D58) The *biodiversity* of an ecosystem quickly changes after a natural disaster.

biome (bī′ōm) A major land ecosystem having a distinct combination of plants and animals. (D48) Some *biomes*, such as the tundra, do not easily support human populations.

biosphere (bī′ō sfir) A self-sustaining natural system of living things and their environment. (B87) For humans to survive in space, they must bring along a version of their *biosphere.*

black dwarf The cool, dark body that is the final stage in the life cycle of a low-mass star. (B66) When the Sun dies, it will become a *black dwarf.*

black hole An extremely dense, invisible object in space whose gravity is so great that not even light can escape it. (B67) Scientists think that the remains of a very massive star can collapse following a supernova explosion to form a *black hole.*

blood alcohol concentration A test that determines the level of alcohol in a person's blood. (G61) A police officer can easily find out if a driver is drunk by giving a *blood alcohol concentration* test.

bone The hard tissue that forms the skeleton. Also, one of the organs that makes up the skeleton. (G8) The human hand contains many small *bones.*

caffeine (ka fēn′) A drug that acts as a stimulant and is present in coffee, many teas, cocoa, and some soft drinks. (G50) Many people prefer to drink herbal teas that do not have *caffeine* in them.

carbon dioxide–oxygen cycle *See* oxygen–carbon dioxide cycle.

cardiac muscle (kär′dē ak mus′əl) Involuntary muscle tissue that makes up the heart. (G17) *Cardiac muscle* contracts rhythmically.

carnivore (kär′nə vôr) A consumer that eats only other animals. (D19, D30) Lions are *carnivores* that prey on zebras and other large plant eaters.

cartilage (kärt′əl ij) Tough, flexible tissue that is part of the skeleton. (G8) *Cartilage* helps protect bones as they move at joints.

cell The basic unit of structure of all living things. (A24) Even though plant *cells* can be different sizes, they still have many of the same structures.

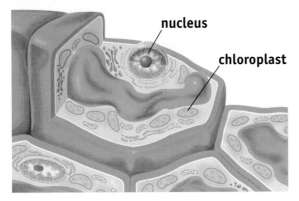

nucleus

chloroplast

cell membrane A thin layer that surrounds all cells and allows water and dissolved materials to pass into and out of the cell. (A24) In plant cells, the *cell membrane* lies inside the cell wall.

cell respiration The process of using oxygen to release energy from food. (A35, A45, D34) Animals and plants release carbon dioxide as a waste product of *cell respiration*.

cell wall The tough outer covering of a plant cell that gives the cell its rigid shape. (A24) A *cell wall* is not found in animal cells.

cementation (sē men tā′shən) A process in which minerals, deposited as water evaporates, bind sediments into solid rock. (E44) Sandstone is a sedimentary rock formed by *cementation*.

cerebellum (ser ə bel′əm) The second largest part of the brain, coordinating the body's muscles. (G32) The *cerebellum* allows smooth movement.

cerebrum (sə rē′brəm) The largest part of the brain in which the processes of thinking, learning, and reasoning take place. (G31) The *cerebrum* is the part of the brain that allows people to understand and remember ideas.

chloroplast (klôr′ə plast) A structure in plant cells that captures light energy that is used in the food-making process. (A24, A33) *Chloroplasts* are located within cells in the leaves of a plant.

cleavage (klēv′ij) The tendency of some minerals to split along flat surfaces. (E15) Salt, or halite, shows *cleavage* in three planes.

clone (klōn) An exact copy of a parent organism produced by asexual reproduction. (A62) One way to *clone* a parent plant is to place a cutting from that plant in water.

coastal ocean A saltwater ecosystem that is relatively shallow and close to the shoreline and that supports an abundance of life. (D54) The *coastal ocean* is an ecosystem that lies beyond the shoreline.

comet (käm′it) A small object in space, made of ice, dust, gas, and rock, that orbits a star and that can form a gaseous tail. (B24) As a *comet* approaches the Sun, it begins to melt.

commensalism (kə men′səl iz əm) A close relationship between two kinds of organisms that benefits one of the organisms while neither benefiting nor hurting the other. (D21) The way that some insects use their resemblance to plants to hide from predators is an example of *commensalism*.

community (kə myo͞o′nə tē) All the organisms living together in a particular ecosystem. (D10) Raccoons, deer, and trees are part of a forest *community*.

compact disc (käm′pakt disk) A small disk on which sounds are digitally recorded and played back when read by a laser beam. (F92) This *compact disc*, or CD, contains one hour of music.

compound machine A machine that is made up of two or more simple machines. (C62) A pair of scissors is a *compound machine* because it contains two kinds of simple machines—a lever and a wedge.

compound microscope A viewing instrument that uses two lenses to magnify objects many times. (F41) The human hair appeared 1,000 times larger than actual size under the *compound microscope*.

compression (kəm presh′ən) A region in a sound wave where particles have been pushed together. (F57) The *compressions* produced by a vibrating tuning fork are areas of greater than normal air pressure.

concave lens (kän′kāv lenz) A lens that is thicker at the edges than it is in the middle and that causes light rays to spread apart. (F32) A *concave lens* is used to correct nearsightedness.

concave mirror A mirror that curves inward at the middle. (F23) A *concave mirror* is used in a reflecting telescope.

concrete (kän′krēt) A mixture of rock material and cement that is used as a building material. (E24) This sidewalk is made of *concrete*.

condensation (kän dən sā′shən) The process by which water vapor is changed to liquid water. (D36) *Condensation* can occur on a glass containing ice cubes.

conduction (kən duk′shən) The transfer of heat energy by direct contact between particles. (C13) Heat travels through a metal by *conduction*.

conifer (kän′ə fər) A tree or shrub that bears its seeds in cones. (A80) The cones of each species of *conifer* are distinct and different from each other.

constellation (kän stə lā′shən) A group of stars that form a fixed pattern in the night sky. (B10) The *constellation* Orion is best seen in the winter.

consumer (kən so͞om′ər) A living thing that obtains energy by eating other living things. (A36, D19) Meat eaters and plant eaters are *consumers*.

contact lens A thin lens worn over the cornea of the eye, usually to correct vision problems. (F35) Some people use *contact lenses* rather than eyeglasses to improve their vision.

convection (kən vek'shən) The transfer of heat energy through liquids and gases by moving particles. (C13) Heat is carried throughout water in a pot on the stove by *convection.*

convex lens (kän'veks lenz) A lens that is thicker in the middle than at the edges and that brings light rays together. (F32) A *convex lens* is used to correct farsightedness.

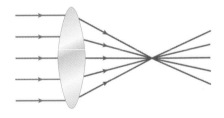

convex mirror A mirror that curves outward at the middle. (F23) The side-view mirror of a car is a *convex mirror.*

core The innermost layer of Earth, which consists of a molten outer part and a solid inner part. (E69) Temperatures inside the *core* of Earth are nearly as hot as those on the Sun's surface.

crest The highest point of a wave. (F57) The top of a water wave is its *crest.*

crust The outer layer of Earth. (E68) Earth's *crust* is a thin layer of rock.

cytoplasm (sīt'ō plaz əm) The jellylike substance that fills much of the cell. (A24) The nucleus, vacuoles, and many other cell structures float in the *cytoplasm.*

decibel (des'ə bəl) A unit used to measure the loudness or intensity of sound. (F79) Sounds that have an intensity greater than 120 *decibels* (db) can hurt your ears.

decomposer (dē kəm pōz'ər) A living thing that breaks down the remains of dead organisms. (A37, D19) *Decomposers,* such as bacteria, get their energy from the dead plants and animals they break down.

deciduous forest (dē sij'oo əs fôr'ist) A biome that contains many trees and in which rainfall is moderate. (D51) *Deciduous forests* support a great variety of animal life.

deforestation (dē fôr is tā'shən) A mass clearing of a forest. (A93) *Deforestation* is a major concern of environmentalists.

desert A biome in which plant life is not abundant and rainfall is low. (D50) Because *deserts* are dry, desert plants have adaptations to conserve water.

dicot (dī'kät) A flowering plant that produces seeds with two seed leaves, or food-storing leaves. (A81) A trait of a *dicot* is that its leaves have netlike veins.

drug A substance, other than food, that can affect the function of body cells and tissues and that produces a change in the body. (G50) A person sometimes takes a pain-killing *drug* after suffering a back injury.

ecosystem (ek′ō sis təm) An area in which living and nonliving things interact. (D10) An oak tree and the organisms that inhabit it can be thought of as a small *ecosystem.*

effort force The force that must be applied to an object to move the object. (C30) The tow truck applied enough *effort force* to pull the car away.

electromagnetic radiation (ē lek trō-mag net′ik rā dē ā′shən) Wave energy given off by the Sun and some other objects. (F8) Visible light is a form of *electromagnetic radiation.*

electron microscope (ē lek′trän mī′krə skōp) A viewing instrument that magnifies objects thousands of times by using a beam of electrons instead of a beam of light. (F43) Doctors studied the virus through an *electron microscope.*

embryo (em′brē ō) An organism in its earliest stages of development; in most plants it is found inside a seed. (A61) When conditions for growth are suitable, the *embryo* inside the seed develops into a young plant.

endangered In danger of becoming extinct. (A92, D61) As the destruction of the Amazon rain forest continues, the number of *endangered* species increases.

energy The ability to do work or cause change. (C9, F8) *Energy* from the Sun warms the air.

erosion (ē rō′zhən) The wearing away and removing of rock and soil caused by such forces as wind and flowing water. (E84) The pounding waves caused *erosion* of the sandy shoreline.

eustachian tube (yōō stā′kē ən tōōb) A tube that connects the throat and the middle ear. (F85) The *eustachian tube* equalizes the air pressure on both sides of the eardrum.

evaporation (ē vap ə rā′shən) The process by which liquid water changes to water vapor. (D36) One phase of the water cycle is the *evaporation* of water from lakes, rivers, and oceans.

extinct (ek stiŋkt′) No longer living as a species. (A92, D61) Traces of some *extinct* species can be found in fossils.

extraterrestrial (eks trə tə res′trē əl) A being from outer space; any object from beyond Earth. (B90) It would be extraordinary for scientists to discover that there is *extraterrestrial* life.

fault A break in rock along which rocks have moved. (E91) Forces within Earth's crust produce *faults*.

fern A nonseed plant that has roots, stems, and leaves and that is found mostly in moist, shady areas. (A79) On *ferns* that grow in tropical places, the fronds grow to a very tall size.

fertilization (fʉrt ′l ə zā′shən) The process by which a male sex cell joins with a female sex cell. In flowering plants, fertilization takes place in the pistil. (A60) *Fertilization* occurs after a pollen tube reaches the ovary.

filter A device that lets certain colors of light pass through while absorbing others. (F48) The stage manager placed a red *filter* over the spotlight.

flower The reproductive structure of a flowering plant. (A16) Petals protect the reproductive parts of a *flower*.

flowering plant Living organisms that reproduce by seeds formed in flowers and that have roots, stems, and leaves. (A81) *Flowering plants* are the most common group of plants on Earth today.

focal point The point at which light rays passing through a lens come together. (F32) Rays of light meet at the *focal point*.

fold A bend in a layer of rock. (E83) Forces within Earth can cause a *fold* to form in rock layers.

food chain The path of energy transfer from one living organism to another in an ecosystem. (A36, D29) Energy moves from producers to consumers in a *food chain*.

food web The overlapping food chains that link producers, consumers, and decomposers in an ecosystem. (A37, D30) Some consumers in a *food web* eat both plants and animals.

force A pull or a push. (C28) When you open a door, you apply a *force*.

fossil (fäs′əl) The remains or traces of a living thing from the past, preserved in rock. (E46, E77) *Fossils* can include imprints of animal skeletons pressed into rock.

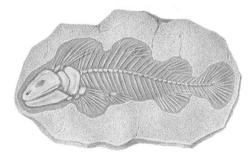

fracture (frak′chər) A break or crack in a bone. (G20) The skier suffered a leg *fracture* when he hit an icy patch.

free fall The motion of a freely falling object, such as a spacecraft in orbit around Earth. (B79) Astronauts experiencing *free fall* in space feel weightless.

frequency (frē'kwən sē) The number of waves (such as light or sound) produced in a unit of time, such as a second. (F18, F57) The *frequency* of light waves varies with the color of the light.

friction (frik'shən) Force produced by the rubbing of one thing against another; a force that acts to oppose motion. (C31) *Friction* prevents sneakers from slipping on a gym floor.

fruit The enlarged ovary of a flower that protects the developing seeds. (A61) Some *fruits*, such as peaches or mangoes, contain only one seed.

fulcrum (ful'krəm) The fixed point around which a lever pivots. (C50) If you use a lever to lift an object, the *fulcrum* is located between you and the object you are lifting.

galaxy (gal'ək sē) A vast group of billions of stars that are held together by gravity. (B70) The Milky Way is a typical spiral *galaxy*.

gas giant A large planet that is made up mostly of gaseous and liquid substances, with little or no solid surface. (B47) Jupiter is a *gas giant*.

geocentric model (jē ō sen'trik mäd''l) A representation of the universe in which stars and planets revolve around Earth. (B37) Ptolemy proposed a *geocentric model* of the universe.

glucose (gloo'kōs) A sugar produced by plants that is the main source of energy for cells. (A33) *Glucose* is produced during photosynthesis.

grassland A biome containing many grasses but few trees and having low to moderate rainfall. (D50) Taller grasses occur in *grasslands* that have more abundant rainfall.

hardness A measure of how easily a mineral can be scratched. (E13) The *hardness* of diamond is greater than that of any other mineral.

hearing aid A small battery-powered electronic device that makes sounds louder. (F86) Most people who wear a *hearing aid* have improved hearing.

heliocentric model (hē lē ō sen'trik mäd''l) A representation of the relationship between the Sun and planets in which the planets revolve around the Sun. (B37) Copernicus hypothesized a *heliocentric model* of the solar system.

herbivore (hur'bə vôr) A consumer that eats only plants or other producers. (D19, D30) Panda bears are *herbivores* that have a very limited diet because they only eat bamboo.

hertz (herts) A unit used to measure wave frequency. (F18, F68) If 100 waves are produced per second, the frequency of the wave is 100 *hertz*.

igneous rock (ig′nē əs räk) A type of rock that forms from melted rock that cools and hardens. (E40) *Igneous rock* forms from both magma and lava.

illegal drug A substance whose use is prohibited by law. (G50) One *illegal drug* in the United States is heroin.

inclined plane A simple machine with a sloping surface. It allows objects to be raised or lowered from one level to another without lifting them. (C43) A ramp is a kind of *inclined plane*.

index fossil (in′deks fäs′əl) A fossil used to determine the relative age of rock. (E78) The remains of a living thing that lived only at a certain time in the past makes a good *index fossil*.

information superhighway The futuristic concept of communications as an electronic highway system in which telephones, computers, and televisions are linked. (F93) The *information superhighway* will let students do library research from their homes.

intensity (in ten′sə tē) A measure of the amount of energy of sound. (F78) A sound that has high *intensity* is loud enough to be heard from a distance.

Internet (in′tər net) A system of interconnected computer networks. (F94) Telephone lines link computer users with the *Internet*.

joint The place where two bones meet. (G8) Your elbow *joint* enables you to bend your arm.

joule (jo͞ol) The basic unit of energy and of work. (C19) Scientists measure amounts of energy in *joules*.

kinetic energy The energy that something has because of its motion. (C20) As a boulder rolls down a steep hill, it gains *kinetic energy*.

lake A freshwater ecosystem characterized by still, or standing water. (D53) *Lakes* support fish, birds, algae, and other forms of life.

lava (lä′və) Melted rock material that reaches Earth's surface before it cools and hardens. (E41) A volcano carries *lava* to Earth's surface.

leaf A plant part in which photosynthesis takes place. (A14) In a plant such as cabbage, it is the *leaf* that people eat.

lens A piece of glass or other transparent material with at least one curved surface that brings together or spreads apart light rays passing through it. (F32) The *lens* in a camera focuses an image on the film.

lever (lev'ər) A simple machine made up of a bar that pivots around a fixed point (a fulcrum). (C50) A *lever* can help lift a heavy object with less effort.

ligament (lig'ə mənt) A band of strong tissue that connects bones and holds them in place. (G8) A *ligament* holds bones together at a joint.

light-year A unit of measurement representing the distance that light travels in one year. (B61) Scientists use the unit called a *light-year* when measuring the distances to stars.

luster (lus'tər) The way that the surface of a mineral looks when it reflects light. (E13) Silver and gold have a shiny, metallic *luster.*

machine A device that makes work easier by reducing the amount of force needed to do a job. (C43) A *machine* can make it easier to move, lift, carry, or cut something.

magma (mag'mə) Melted rock material that forms deep within Earth. (E40) Some igneous rocks, such as granite, form from *magma.*

mantle A thick layer of rock between the crust and the core of Earth. (E69) The top of the *mantle* is solid rock but below that is a section of rock that can flow.

mechanical advantage (mə kan'i-kəl ad vant'ij) The number of times that a machine multiplies the effort force applied to it. (C44) To find the *mechanical advantage* of an inclined plane, divide the length of its sloping surface by its height.

medulla (mi dul'ə) The part of the brain that controls the involuntary functions of the body, such as heart rate and breathing. (G32) The *medulla* is located in the brain stem and controls many things you do without thinking.

metamorphic rock (met ə môr'fik räk) A type of rock that forms from existing rocks because of changes caused by heat, pressure, or chemicals. (E47) Slate is a *metamorphic rock* that forms from the sedimentary rock shale.

meteor (mēt'ē ər) A piece of rock or metal from space that enters Earth's atmosphere. (B25) A *meteor* appears as a streak of light, which is why it is also called a shooting star.

meteorite (mēt'ē ər īt) The remaining material of a meteor that has landed on the ground. (B25) In 1902, scientists were able to examine the largest *meteorite* ever known to land in the United States.

Milky Way Galaxy A gigantic cluster of billions of stars that is home to our solar system. (B70) The Sun is located in one of the arms of the *Milky Way Galaxy*.

mineral A solid element or compound found in nature and having a definite chemical composition and crystal structure. (E12) Quartz is a *mineral*.

model Something used or made to represent an object or an idea. (E68) The plastic *model* was a miniature copy of the actual airplane.

monocot (män'ō kät) A flowering plant that produces seeds with a single seed leaf, or food-storing leaf. (A81) About one third of all flowering plants are *monocots*.

moon A natural object that revolves around a planet. (B44) The planet Mars has two known *moons*.

moss A small nonseed plant that lacks roots, stems, and leaves and grows mostly in moist areas in woods or near stream banks. (A78) The leaflike part of a *moss* only grows a few centimeters above ground.

motor neuron (mōt'ər noo'rän) A nerve cell that carries impulses from the brain and spinal cord to muscles and glands in the body. (G28) When people exercise, *motor neurons* carry impulses from the spinal cord to different muscles in the body.

mutualism (myoo'choo əl iz əm) A close relationship between two or more organisms in which all organisms benefit. (D22) Bees carrying pollen from flower to flower as they obtain nectar is an example of *mutualism*.

narcotic (när kät'ik) A habit-forming drug that depresses the function of the nervous system. (G55) Morphine is a *narcotic* drug that is often given to cancer patients.

nebula (neb'yə lə) A huge cloud of gas and dust found in space. (B64) A *nebula* can form when a supernova explodes.

nerve impulse (nʉrv im'puls) A message carried through the body by neurons. (G28) *Nerve impulses* pass from one neuron to another as they move through the body.

neuron (noo'rän) A nerve cell. (G28) The brain is connected to all parts of the body by *neurons*.

neutron star (n$\overline{oo}$′trän stär) The remains of a massive star that has exploded in a supernova. (B67) A typical *neutron star* is less than 20 km in diameter.

newton A unit used to measure force. (C29) About 300 *newtons* of force was applied in moving the rock.

nicotine (nik′ə tēn) A drug found in the tobacco plant. (G50) People become addicted to cigarettes because of the *nicotine* in the tobacco.

nitrogen cycle The cycle through which nitrogen gas is changed into compounds that can be used by living things and then is returned to the atmosphere. (D42) The *nitrogen cycle* is of great importance to all life forms because nitrogen is needed to make protein.

noise pollution The occurrence of loud or unpleasant sound in the environment. (F80) The sounds of city traffic are a form of *noise pollution*.

nonseed plant A plant that reproduces without forming seeds. (A78) Mosses are *nonseed plants*.

nucleus (n$\overline{oo}$′klē əs) The cell structure that controls all of a cell's activities. (A24) The *nucleus* was clearly visible after it was stained.

octave (äk′tiv) The series of eight notes that makes up a musical scale. (F69) The music student practiced playing *octaves* on the piano.

omnivore (äm′ni vôr) A consumer that eats both plants and animals. (D19, D30) Because they eat both meats and vegetables, many humans are *omnivores*.

opaque (ō pāk′) Not letting light through. (F47) The *opaque* curtains kept out the sunlight.

open ocean A large saltwater ecosystem containing both floating and free-swimming organisms. (D55) The *open ocean* covers much of Earth's surface.

optic nerve A bundle of neurons that carries impulses from the eye to the brain. (G39) If there is damage to the *optic nerve*, messages from the eye cannot be received by the brain.

ore (ôr) A mineral or rock that contains enough of a metal to making mining the metal profitable. (E27) Hematite is an *ore* mined for its iron content.

overtone A fainter, higher tone that harmonizes with the main tone produced by a musical instrument or the human voice. (F58) The blending of *overtones* gives the flute its unique sound.

oxygen–carbon dioxide cycle A natural cycle in which plants and other producers use carbon dioxide and produce oxygen, and living things use oxygen and produce carbon dioxide. (B86, D34) The *oxygen–carbon dioxide cycle* must be duplicated in space if humans wish to make long voyages to other planets.

parasitism (par′ə sīt iz əm) A relationship between two organisms in which one organism lives on or in the other, feeds upon it, and usually harms it. (D21) The way in which fleas live off dogs is an example of *parasitism*.

phloem cell (flō′əm sel) A plant cell that, when linked with other similar cells, forms a system of tubes for carrying nutrients from the leaves down through the stem and root. (A11) The *phloem cells* form a major transport system in plants.

phonograph (fō′nə graf) A device that reproduces sounds recorded on a disk. (F90) We played old records on the *phonograph*.

photosynthesis (fōt ō sin′thə sis) The process by which producers, such as plants, make their own food by using energy from the Sun. (A33) *Photosynthesis* takes place primarily in the leaves of plants.

pistil (pis′til) The female reproductive structure of a flower. (A16) A *pistil* consists of three main parts—the stigma, the style, and the ovary.

pitch The highness or lowness of a sound. (F68) A tuba produces sounds with a low *pitch.*

plane mirror A mirror that has a flat surface. (F22) The mirror over the bathroom sink is a *plane mirror.*

planet A large body in space that orbits a star and does not produce light on its own. (B17) Earth is one of nine known *planets* that revolve around the Sun.

plant kingdom A major group of living things that are multicellular and that carry out photosynthesis. (A78) Living organisms in the *plant kingdom* make their own food.

pollination (päl ə nā′shən) The transfer of pollen from the male part of one flower to the female part of another flower. (A60) Some *pollination* is done by insects.

population (päp yōō lā′shən) A group of the same kind of organisms that live in an area. (D10) There is a huge *population* of frogs in that marsh.

potential energy The energy that an object has because of its position or structure; stored energy. (C18) A coiled spring has *potential energy.*

precipitation (prē sip ə tā'shən) The process by which water from clouds falls back to the Earth. (D36) *Precipitation* falls to the Earth in the form of rain or snow.

producer (prō dō͞os'ər) An organism that makes its own food through photosynthesis. (A36, D18) Plants and algae are examples of *producers.*

protein (prō'tēn) Organic compounds that form the structure and control the processes that take place in living things. (D41) *Proteins* provide the body with materials that help cells grow and repair themselves.

protostar (prōt'ō stär) A concentration of matter found in space that is the beginning of a star. (B64) When the temperature inside a *protostar* becomes high enough, nuclear reactions begin and it turns into a star.

pulley (pō͞ol'ē) A simple machine made up of a wheel around which a rope or chain is passed. (C53) A *pulley* helps lift objects that would be too heavy to lift directly.

quarry (kwôr'ē) A mine, usually near or at Earth's surface, from which rock is removed. (E52) Granite, sandstone, limestone, slate, and marble are some rocks that come from a *quarry.*

radiation (rā dē ā'shən) The transfer of energy by waves. (C11) Energy given off by the Sun travels as *radiation* through space.

radio telescope A gigantic antenna designed to receive radio signals from space. (B92) *Radio telescopes* are important tools for studying distant stars and galaxies.

rarefaction (rer ə fak'shən) A region in a sound wave where there are fewer particles than normal. (F57) The *rarefactions* that a vibrating violin string produces are areas of lower than normal air pressure.

receptor (ri sep'tər) A sensory neuron that receives stimuli from the environment. (G37) Sensory *receptors* in the skin make it possible for people to feel heat, cold, pressure, touch, and pain.

red giant A very large old reddish star that has greatly expanded and cooled as its fuel has begun to run out. (B65) As the Sun reaches old age, it will turn into a *red giant.*

reflecting telescope An instrument for viewing distant objects that uses a curved mirror at the back of its tube to gather light and produce an image. (B22, F39) This observatory uses a *reflecting telescope* to observe faraway galaxies.

reflection (ri flek'shən) The bouncing of light or sound off a surface. (F22) The *reflection* of sunlight off the snow made us squint.

reflex (rē'fleks) A simple behavior pattern involving an automatic response to a stimulus. (G42) The girl's automatic *reflex* quickly got her foot out of the hot water.

refracting telescope An instrument for viewing distant objects that uses two lenses to gather light and produce an image. (B21) The *refracting telescope* gave us a closer look at the Moon.

refraction (ri frak'shən) The bending of light as it passes from one material into another. (F24) Light traveling from air into water will undergo *refraction.*

relative age The age of an object as compared to other objects. (E78) The order of layers of rock shows the *relative ages* of the layers.

resistance force A force that resists, or opposes, motion. (C30) Friction is a *resistance force.*

retina (ret''n ə) The light-sensitive area at the back of the eye on which an image is formed. (F32) The *retina* contains two kinds of cells.

revolution (rev ə loo'shən) The movement of an object around another object or point. (B14) It takes about 365 days for Earth to make one *revolution* around the Sun.

river A freshwater ecosystem characterized by running water. (D52) Salmon are able to swim against the current in a *river.*

rock The solid material composed of minerals that forms Earth's crust. Also, the material, sometimes molten, that forms Earth's inner layers. (E40) *Rocks* are weathered by wind and rain.

rock cycle The continuous series of changes that rocks undergo. (E60) In the *rock cycle*, changes are brought about by factors such as weathering, melting, cooling, or pressure.

root The underground part of a plant that anchors the plant and absorbs water and nutrients. (A10) Carrots and turnips have only one large single *root.*

rotation (rō tā'shən) The spinning motion of an object on its axis. (B14) It takes about 24 hours for Earth to make one complete *rotation.*

sapling (sap'liŋ) A young tree. (A67) The year after a tree seed germinates, the young plant is called a *sapling.*

satellite (sat''l īt) A natural or human-built object that revolves around another object in space. (B44) The Moon is a natural *satellite* of Earth.

sediment (sed'ə mənt) Bits of weathered rocks and minerals and pieces of dead plants or animals. (E43) Over time, *sediments* can form sedimentary rocks, such as sandstone and limestone.

sedimentary rock (sed ə men'tər ē räk) A type of rock that forms when sediments harden. (E43) Most *sedimentary rocks* form in layers.

seed coat A tough, protective covering on a seed, enclosing the embryo and its food supply. (A 61) When the leaves on a young plant start to grow and open up, the *seed coat* falls off.

seed dispersal The scattering of seeds away from the parent plant. (A88) The wind is one way in which *seed dispersal* is carried out.

seed leaf A first leaf found inside a seed, providing food for the tiny developing plant. (A66) A monocot seed contains one *seed leaf*.

seedling (sēd'liŋ) A young growing plant after it first sprouts and develops new leaves. (A66) In spring the forest floor is covered with green *seedlings*.

seed plant A plant that reproduces by forming seeds. (A78) Corn and wheat are *seed plants*.

semicircular canal Any of three curved tubelike structures of the inner ear that help the body to maintain balance. (F85) The *semicircular canals* respond to movements of the head.

sensory neuron (sen'sər ē nōō'rän) A nerve cell that carries impulses from the senses to the brain and spinal cord. (G28) *Sensory neurons* carry impulses from your eyes to your brain.

sexual reproduction The production of offspring that occurs when a male sex cell joins a female sex cell. (A59) The *sexual reproduction* of flowers is greatly aided by insects.

shoreline The ecosystem where land and ocean meet. (D54) The *shoreline* varies in width around the world.

simple microscope A microscope that uses a single lens to magnify objects. (F41) A magnifying glass is a *simple microscope.*

skeletal muscle Voluntary muscle tissue; also, one of the muscles that moves bones. (G17) Tendons attach *skeletal muscles* to bones.

skeletal system The system of bones and tissues that supports and protects the body. (G8) The human *skeletal system* contains 206 bones.

smelting (smelt'iŋ) The process of melting ore to remove the metal from it. (E28) Workers obtain iron by *smelting* iron ore in a blast furnace.

smooth muscle Involuntary muscle tissue that lines the inside of blood vessels, intestines, and other organs. (G17) *Smooth muscles* move food through the digestive system.

solar system The Sun and the planets and other objects that orbit the Sun. Also, any star and the objects that revolve around it. (B34) Our *solar system* consists of the Sun, nine known planets, and many smaller objects.

sound A form of energy that travels through matter as waves. (F56) The *sound* made the floor vibrate.

sound synthesizer (sound sin'thə-sī zər) An electronic device that can produce a wide variety of sounds. (F71) The composer used a *sound synthesizer* to create a new musical composition.

sprain An injury in which the ligament at a joint is torn or twisted. (G19) An ankle *sprain* can take weeks to heal.

stamen (stā'mən) The male reproductive structure of a flower. (A16) Pollen is produced in the *stamens*.

star A huge object in space, made up of hot gases, that shines by its own light. (B17) Many *stars* are believed to have systems of planets.

starch (stärch) A substance found in plants that is a storage form of glucose. (A35) Potatoes contain a lot of *starch*.

stem The part of a plant that supports the leaves and flowers and carries water to these parts of the plant. (A12) The trunk of a tree is a *stem*.

steroid (stir'oid) A drug that helps to build up muscle tissue and strength. (G55) Some athletes have used *steroids*.

stimulant (stim'yoo lənt) A drug that increases the activity of the nervous system. (G55) Many people drink coffee because it acts as a *stimulant*.

stimulus (stim'yoo ləs) An event or environmental condition that triggers a nerve impulse, thus causing an organism to respond. (G28) The *stimulus* of a loud sound can make a person jump.

stoma (stō'mə; *pl.* stō ma'tə) One of many small openings, or pores, usually on the underside of a leaf, through which gases enter and leave a plant. (A46) The *stomata* on a water lily are on the top of the leaf.

strain An injury in which a muscle or tendon is torn slightly or stretched too far. (G20) Lifting the heavy couch gave me a back *strain*.

streak (strēk) The colored powder made by rubbing a mineral against a ceramic surface. (E15) Although pyrite is yellow, it produces a black *streak*.

substance abuse (sub'stəns ə-byoos') The improper use, or abuse, of alcohol or drugs. (G50) *Substance abuse* can damage a person's health.

supernova (soo'pər nō və) An exploding star. (B66) When a red giant star uses up all its fuel, it collapses and explodes in a *supernova*.

syncline (sin'klīn) A downward fold of rock layers. (E84) Forces in Earth pushing on rock formed a *syncline*.

taiga (tī′gə) A biome that contains many coniferous trees and in which rainfall is moderate. (D51) The *taiga* is south of the tundra.

taste bud A receptor on the surface of the tongue that responds to different substances and makes it possible to taste. (G38) There are only four basic types of *taste buds*.

tendon (ten′dən) A strong cord of tissue that joins a muscle to a bone. (G17) *Tendons* pull on bones like strings pull on the limbs of a puppet.

terrestrial planet (tə res′trē əl plan′it) An object in space that resembles Earth in size, in density, and in its mainly rocky composition. (B44) Mars is a *terrestrial planet*.

timbre (tam′bər) The quality of sound that sets one voice or musical instrument apart from another. (F58) The same note played on a violin and on a trumpet differ in *timbre*.

translucent (trans lōō′sənt) Letting light through but scattering it; objects cannot be clearly seen through translucent material. (F48) The *translucent* glass dimmed the room.

transparent (trans per′ənt) Letting light through; objects can be clearly seen through transparent material. (F47) Window glass is usually *transparent* so that people can see through it.

transpiration (tran spə rā′shən) A process in which a plant releases moisture through its stomata. (A46) *Transpiration* adds water to the air.

tropical rain forest A biome distinguished by lush vegetation, abundant rainfall, and plentiful sunlight. (D50) The *tropical rain forest* supports the greatest variety of life of any biome.

tropism (trō′piz əm) A growth response of a plant to conditions in the environment, such as light or water. (A50) Growing toward a light source is an example of a plant *tropism*.

trough (trôf) The long narrow hollow between two waves. (F57) A *trough* occurs between two wave crests.

tundra (tun′drə) A biome characterized by cold temperatures and low precipitation. (D51) The *tundra* blooms in summer.

universe (yōōn′ə vʉrs) The sum of everything that exists. (B70) Our solar system is part of the *universe*.

vacuole (vak′yōō ōl) A cell part that stores water and nutrients. (A24) Some plant cells have large *vacuoles*.

vacuum (vak'yoō əm) A space that is empty of any matter. (F17) Light waves can travel through a *vacuum*.

vibration A back-and-forth movement of matter. (F56) It is the *vibration* of the guitar strings that produces sound.

visible light A form of electromagnetic energy that can be seen. (F8) The eye responds to *visible light*.

volume The loudness or softness of a sound. (F78) Please turn up the *volume* on the radio.

water cycle A continuous process in which water moves between the atmosphere and Earth's surface, including its use by living things. (B87, D36) The *water cycle* is powered by energy from the Sun.

wave A disturbance that carries energy and that travels away from its starting point. (F17) The experiment measured how quickly light *waves* travel.

wavelength The distance between one crest of a wave and the next crest. (F17, F57) Red light has a longer *wavelength* than does blue light.

weathering The breaking up of rocks into sediments by such forces as wind, rain, and sunlight. (E62) Through *weathering*, igneous rock can be broken down into sediments.

wetland Any one of three ecosystems—marsh, swamp, or bog—where land and fresh water meet. (D53) *Wetlands* help purify water.

wheel and axle A simple machine made of two wheels of different sizes that pivot around the same point. (C58) A doorknob, along with its shaft, is an example of a *wheel and axle*.

white dwarf A very small, dying star that gives off very little light. (B65) When the Sun's fuel runs out, it will collapse into a *white dwarf*.

work The movement of a force through a distance. (C28) *Work* is done in lifting an object.

xylem cell (zī'ləm sel) A plant cell that, when joined with other similar cells, forms a transport system throughout a plant. (A11) The wood of a tree is formed mainly of *xylem cells*.

* Activity

CREDITS

Cover: *Design, Art Direction, and Production:* Design Five, NYC; *Photography:* Jade Albert; *Photography Production:* Picture It Corporation; *Illustration:* Deborah Haley Melmon. **TOC:** Dom Doyle, Patrick Gnan, Robert Pasternack, Michael Sloan, Elsa Warnick.

ILLUSTRATORS

UNIT 5A Chapter A1: Steve Buchanan: 12, 13, 15; Susan Johnston Carlson: 25; Fran Milner 24, 27; Patrick O'Brien: 18, 19, 20, 21; Walter Stuart: 10, 11. **Chapter A2:** David Barber: 38; Barbara Cousins: 34; Brad Gaber: 47; Patrick Gnan: 50, 51, 52; Carlyn Iverson: 36, 39; Merri Nelson: 46; Mary Ellen Niatas: 44, 45; Debra Page-Trim: 37. **Chapter A3:** Glory Bechtold: 59, 60, 61; Catherine Deeter: 66, 67; Eldon Doty: 68, 69; Wendy Smith-Griswold: 73. **Chapter A4:** Jennifer Hewitson: 82, 83; Karen Minot: 90, 91; Merri Nelson: 88, 89; Wendy Smith-Griswold: 78, 82, 83, 95; Elsa Warnick: 92, 93.

UNIT 5B Chapter B1: Delores Bego: 9; Michael Carroll: 14; Dale Glasgow & Assoc.: 10, 11; Jeff Hitch: 13; Fred Holz: 22; Tony Novak: 15; Tom Powers: 11, 27; Robert Schuster: 17; Jim Starr: 24, 25; Lane Yerkes: 21. **Chapter B2:** Michael Carroll: 38, 39, 50; Dennis Davidson: 34, 35, 42, 43; Dale Glasgow & Assoc.: 30, 36, 37, 40, 50; Joe LeMonnier: 72; Susan Melrath: 36, 37; Verlin Miller: 36; John O'Connor: 41; Robert Schuster: 44, 45, 47, 48, 49, 50. **Chapter B3:** Michael Carroll: 70; Joe LeMonnier: 72; Lu Matthews: 60, 61; Tom Powers: 57, 67, 71, 73; Joe Spencer: 64, 65. **Chapter B4:** Terry Boles: 79; Richard Courtney: 87; Dale Glasgow & Assoc.: 94; Nina Laden: 84; Andy Myer: 93; Scott Ross: 83; Stephen Wagner: 80, 86, 95.

UNIT 5C Chapter C1: Delores Bego: 35; Kieran Bergin: 18, 19; Ka Botzis: 22; Carolyn Bracken: 12; Sarah Jane English: 22, 23; Ron Fleming: 12; David Uhl: 20, 21; Arden Von Haeger: 32, 33; Richard Waldrep: 28, 29. **Chapter C2:** Andrea Baruffi: 43; Gregg Fitzhugh: 48, 49, 53, 54, 55, 63; Dale Glasgow & Assoc.: 50, 51; Patrick Gnan: 58, 59; Susan Hunt Yule: 44, 45; A. J. Miller: 60; Miles Parnell: 43, 44, 45; Michael Sloan: 61, 62; Leslie Wolf: 53, 54.

UNIT 5D Chapter D1: Lori Anzalone: 20; Patrick Gnan: 8, 9; Robert Hynes Studio: 10, 11; Jim Salvati: 12, 13; Wendy Smith-Griswold: 17. **Chapter D2:** David Barber: 28; Andy Lendway: 30, 31, 43; Jim Starr: 38; Don Stewart: 34, 35, 36, 37, 41, 42. **Chapter D3:** Joe LeMonnier: 56; Paul Mirocha: 52, 53, 54, 55; Carlos Ochagauia: 59; Rodica Prato: 48, 49, 50, 51.

UNIT 5E Chapter E1: Jeanette Adams: 28; Lingta Kung: 12, 13, 14, 15, 16; Bill Morse: 30, 31; Wendy Smith-Griswold: 20, 21. **Chapter E2:** Terry Boles: 61, 63; Brad Gaber: 40, 58, 59; Robert Pasternack: 47; Scot Ritchie: 54; Robert Schuster: 49; Michael Sloan: 60. **Chapter E3:** Absolute Science: 71, 77; Eldon Doty: 76; Dale Glasgow & Assoc.: 68, 69, 95; J.A.K. Graphics: 78; Joe LeMonnier: 85, 93; Susan Melrath: 78, 79; Verlin Miller: 86; Robert Pasternack: 85, 91; Tom Powers: 67; Scot Ritchie: 70; Jim Starr: 87.

UNIT 5F Chapter F1: Jeanette Adams: 16; Bob Brugger: 25, 27; Michael Carroll: 8, 9; Jim Deigan: 22; Eldon Doty: 12; Susan Hunt Yule: 26; Robert Pasternack: 17, 18, 19; Scot Ritchie: 8. **Chapter F2:** Rose Berlin: 51; Bob Bredemeier: 39; Marie Dauenheimer: 33, 35; Jim Fanning: 45; J.A.K. Graphics: 32, 34; George Kelvin: 36, 37; Andy Miller: 43; Len Morgan: 47. **Chapter F3:** Mark Bender: 69; Terry Boles: 62, 63; Roger Chandler: 68, 69; Dale Glasgow & Assoc.: 56, 57, 59; Tom Lochray: 66, 67; Larry Moore: 71, 72; Terry Ravanelli: 72. **Chapter F4:** Tim Blough: 94; Marty Bucella: 78; Dale Glasgow & Assoc.: 93, 94; Dale Gustafson: 91, 92; Ellen Going Jacobs: 85; Ray Vella: 78, 79, 95.

UNIT 5G Chapter G1: May Cheney: 8, 9, 10, 11; Kathleen Dunne: 8, 19, 20, 21, 22; Jackie Heda: 12, 19, 20; Bob Swanson: 13; Kate Sweeney: 17, 18, 23. **Chapter G2:** Scott Barrows: 30, 31; Eldon Doty: 40, 41; Dom Doyle: 28; Marcia Hartsock: 37, 38, 39, 42, 45; Jackie Heda: 31; Jane Hurd: 31, 32; Robert Margulies: 33; Steve McInturff: 44; Briar Lee Mitchell: 29. **Chapter G3:** Medical Art Co.: 59, 63; Bob Novak: 50, 51, 53; Ray Vella: 52, 61.

Glossary: Lori Anzalone, Patrick Gnan, Carlyn Iverson, Fran Milner, Robert Pasternack.

Handbook: Kathleen Dunne, Laurie Hamilton, Catherine Leary, Andy Meyer

PHOTOGRAPHS
All photographs by Silver Burdett Ginn (SBG) unless otherwise noted.

Unit A Opener 1: *border* G. Shih-R. Kessel/Visuals Unlimited. **Chapter 1** 4–5: *bkgd.* Will Houghton/Fairchild Tropical Garden, Miami; *insets* Courtesy, Fairchild Tropical Gardens. 6–9: Ken Karp for SBG. 10: Alfred Pasieka/Peter Arnold. 12: © John Buitenkant/Photo Researchers, Inc. 13: © Cecil Fox/Science Source/Photo Researchers, Inc. 14: *t.* © Jerome Wexler/Photo Researchers, Inc.; *b.* Milton Rand/Tom Stack & Associates. 15: *l.* Milton Rand/Tom Stack & Associates; *r.* © Scott Camamzine/Photo Researchers, Inc. 16: *l.* E. R. Degginger/Color-Pic, Inc.; *r.* © Arthur Beck/Photo Researchers, Inc. 17: *t.* © Anthony Mercieca/Photo Researchers, Inc.; *b.l.* Brokaw Photography/Visuals Unlimited; *b.m.* Rod Planck/Tom Stack & Associates; *b.r.* John Gerlach/Visuals Unlimited. 19: *t.* © Blair Seitz/Photo Researchers, Inc.; *b.* Gary Milburn/Tom Stack & Associates; *inset*

H48